MEDIA U

Media U

HOW THE NEED TO WIN AUDIENCES HAS SHAPED HIGHER EDUCATION

Mark Garrett Cooper and John Marx

Columbia University Press
New York

Columbia University Press
Publishers Since 1893
New York   Chichester, West Sussex
cup.columbia.edu

Library of Congress Cataloging-in-Publication Data
Names: Cooper, Mark Garrett, author. | Marx, John.
Title: Media U : how the need to win audiences has shaped higher education /
Mark Garrett Cooper and John Marx.
Description: New York : Columbia University Press, 2017. | Includes bibliographical
references and index.
Identifiers: LCCN 2017058611 (print) | LCCN 2018013657 (ebook) |
ISBN 9780231546607 (e-book) | ISBN 9780231186360 (cloth : alk. paper) |
ISBN 9780231186377 (pbk. : alk. paper)
Subjects: LCSH: College publicity—United States—History. | Universities and
colleges—Public relations—United States—History. | Education, Higher—Aims and
objectives—United States—History.
Classification: LCC LB2342.82 (ebook) | LCC LB2342.82 .C67 2017 (print) | DDC 378.1/01—dc23
LC record available at https://lccn.loc.gov/2017058611

Columbia University Press books are printed on permanent and durable acid-free paper.
Printed in the United States of America

Cover design: Catherine Casalino

CONTENTS

ACKNOWLEDGMENTS

In writing this book, we each received research support from our home universities. At the University of South Carolina, Mark was supported by a Provost's Humanities Grant and an English Department Research Professorship. John received a residential research fellowship from the University of California Humanities Research Institute. In addition, a Mellon Foundation initiative at television station WGBH Boston funded our research there. We are grateful for all of this assistance.

We also owe a debt of gratitude to those who invited us to give talks drawn from our research in progress as well as those kind enough to attend those talks: the University of California, Davis, English Department; the University of South Carolina English Department; the University of Delaware English Department (thanks to Ed Larkin); the Florida State University English Department (thanks to Barry Faulk and Robin Goodman); the Oklahoma State University English Department and Screen Studies Program (thanks to Jeff Menne); the University of Pittsburgh Film Studies Program (thanks to Mark Lynn Anderson); the University of California Humanities Research Institute (thanks to Kelly Anne Brown and David Theo Goldberg); the University of California, Santa Barbara, Film and Media Studies Department; the University of Toronto Jackman Humanities Institute (thanks to Charlie Keil); and Vanderbilt University (thanks to Paul Young and Jennifer Fay).

We were helped along the way by colleagues and friends who were neither shy about disagreeing with us nor reluctant to tell us what to read. Thanks to Richard Abel, Lindsay Baltus, Ralph Berry, Duncan Buell, Karen Cariani, Jed Esty, Kris Fallon, Jane Gaines, Michael Gavin, Orit Halpern, Julie Hubbert, Tony Jarrells, Alex Kupfer, Aims McGuinness, Justus Nieland, Margaret Ronda, Ellen Rooney, Michael Szalay, Matthew Vernon, Johannes von Moltke, Mark Williams, Charles Wolfe, and Michael Zryd.

Special thanks to Philip Leventhal for an incisive reading of the near-final manuscript and to Heidi Rae Cooley for repeated readings all along the way.

Rachael Kennedy Stoeltje, of Indiana University's Moving Image Archive; Heather Heckman, Benjamin Singleton, and Scott Allen, of the University of South Carolina's Moving Image Research Collections; and Leah Weisse and Allison Pekel at WGBH assisted in the retrieval of archival materials we otherwise would have found difficult to obtain.

Simon Tarr made the banner for our work-in-progress blog, humanities afterhollywood.org.

PA Broheen Elias facilitated the healing of an inopportune broken arm (John's).

Early versions of arguments that ultimately found their way into various parts of the book appeared in *differences: A Journal of Feminist Cultural Studies* (2014) and the WGBH OpenVault Scholarly Exhibit on New Critical Television.

While living on opposite sides of the country, each of us wrote and rewrote every word of this book. Some acknowledgment of the infrastructure that made that possible seems in order. We would not know, however, whom to single out among the software engineers at Google Docs, the telephone and cable technicians who kept the bits flowing, or the air-traffic controllers who ensured that our fights did not go down. A blanket thank you to these workers and more will have to suffice.

Throughout the project of writing this book, finally, Beth Anderson and Heidi Rae Cooley remained remarkably tolerant of digressive brooding and wayward enthusiasm. We are grateful.

MEDIA U

In the United States of America, research universities exist neither to produce nor to curate knowledge but to connect people by means of it. They
are media institutions. For the past century and a half, American universities have built and maintained audiences through football games as much
as through curricula, through film, radio, television, and digital computers as much as through print. Homecoming games and freshman composition, movies and research publications, Twitter feeds and humanities
centers are not in fact the adversaries stereotyped by so many accounts of
US higher education. [A common imperative informs them: through feats
of mediation, universities bind individuals into groups and certify hierarchical distinctions.]

Any university's ability to safeguard culture, produce research breakthroughs, train a workforce, or make ethical citizens depends on the widely
shared conviction that its credentials and findings have value. Like paper
money, undergraduate degrees and peer-reviewed publications have worth
because people agree that they do. Notably, such university documents
are backed not by the government but rather by a congeries of mostly nongovernmental associations. For over a century, the Carnegie Foundation's
unit, or credit hour, has provided the mediating measure of every student's
degree progress. Often taken for granted, the credit hour was historically
necessary to call the current system of American postsecondary education

into being. It did so, first, by abstracting educational attainment from the content of any particular course and, second, by providing far-flung students, parents, teachers, and administrators a shared measure. Critics of higher education have sometimes denounced the first function of the Carnegie unit. Our focus is on the second, an audience-building and -maintaining function that the credit hour shares with other defining features of the US system.

Although the unobtrusive Carnegie unit may seem different in kind from a spectacular football game, the running battle over academic freedom, and all manner of public relations initiatives to promote particular schools, it is a mistake to pry these varieties of mediation apart. When the University of Chicago bootstrapped itself into being in the 1890s by recruiting the football star Amos Alonzo Stagg alongside academic luminaries such as the physicist Albert A. Michelson and the philosopher John Dewey, it addressed itself to parents, students, faculty, and donors who could be expected to recognize these celebrities. By enlisting their talents, President William Rainey Harper expected not only to elevate the quality of football, classroom instruction, and research but also to secure the new university's reputation. Similarly, the University of Wisconsin both promoted itself and propagated a durable rationale for tenure by including a précis of the university's contributions along with the "Wisconsin Magna Carta," which grabbed national headlines in 1894 and proclaimed an intention to free faculty to pursue their research without fear of dismissal for political reasons. Such efforts sometimes fall flat. Legislators, voters, parents, students, donors, employers, and even professors have often looked askance at universities' specific claims to add value. What holds the system together is not the success of any particular pitch but the constellation that makes it possible for pitches to be successful. To approach the university as a media institution is to investigate how phenomena as various as football, physics, tenure, and credit hours participate in binding audiences and making social distinctions.

We take it as given that the American university is propelled by a contradictory directive to flatten social hierarchy and reproduce it at the same time.[1] Perhaps no other nation on earth relies upon its educational institutions to resolve so many fundamental problems while providing so little central coordination of their activities. Americans expect their universities to underwrite social leveling by lending opportunity to individual merit.

They also look to universities to restaff the businesses, courtrooms, hospitals, newsrooms, and government bureaus that preserve, direct, and—one can always hope—improve the republic. Although contradictory, neither proposition is wrong. Universities do lend opportunity to merit. They also reproduce the customary privileges of classes, races, genders, and professions. Sustaining the conviction that one operation remains viable in the face of the other requires constant effort.

Where familiar histories of the university consider the origination and institutionalization of bodies of knowledge, this book treats the establishment and transformation of audiences. Through that emphasis, we aim to supplement explanations of the university's role in reproducing (and challenging) social hierarchies. New players come into view. Although professors, students, policy makers, and university presidents remain important in our account, they are joined by athletic departments, publicists, providers of extension services, compilers of educational statistics, and student-services professionals. We include professors and students who worked (on campus and off) to make film, radio, television, and computer programs alongside those who limited themselves to papers and books. These newly visible actors bring with them a host of terms and concepts to specify public relations problems, communication strategies, and audience-cultivation techniques. However one may choose to define the university's lofty intellectual purpose or bemoan failures to achieve it, audience creation and management, we argue, describe how universities actually do business and maintain their social function.

The university's role in citizen formation, it turns out, has had little to do with the cultivation, *Bildung*-style, of self-determining individuals, although some commentators continue to imagine this as the university's ideal function. Ever since World War I established college as a key outlet for government propaganda, the college student has been the focus of efforts to promote ideological cohesion and, occasionally, awareness of how such cohesion is promoted. From the 1920s onward, policy leaders and campus activists alike staked the university's democratic contribution less on the moral fiber or rational capacities of individual students than on feats of mediation supposed to make what Dean Herbert Hawkes of Columbia College called citizens "who shall be safe for democracy."[2] Between the wars, general-education curricula ranked first among these mediating mechanisms. After World War II, concern with promulgating appropriately "democratic" attitudes found a complement in media experiences that encouraged student participation. Media making thus became equated with democratic action.

An emphasis on audience creation and management makes the relationship between the university and other media enterprises look strikingly different and revises customary understandings of what is proper to campus. Accounts in which mass media threaten the sanctity of university chambers fundamentally misunderstand the institution. American universities afford no refuge from commercial media and are not menaced by them: the academy offers commercial media a competitor and, often, a collaborator. Throughout this book, we find occasions to roll our eyes at the proposition that the latest new media will either imperil the university or revolutionize it. This perennial claim links examples ranging from massive open online courses (MOOCs) to correspondence courses propagated by land-grant universities in the late nineteenth century and television programming distributed by the National Educational Television network in the late 1950s. Twenty-first-century university administrators were not suddenly or newly inspired to reach far-flung students using cutting-edge technology. To various extents and in various ways, universities have embraced the new media of the day since cheaply reproducible print defined that category. No trope more reliably indicates the kind of history we oppose than the proposition that nonprint media fundamentally challenge, rather than alter and extend, the university's mission.

Given this reframing, it will be best for us to lay out our terms. According to received wisdom, "American research university" names a particular kind of institution devoted to research and doctoral studies, professional training, undergraduate experiences, and all manner of public services. US educators and philanthropists derived this organizational form from German and British precedents toward the end of the nineteenth century. They developed it in tandem with high schools, colleges, philanthropic foundations, professional organizations, business leaders, and government bureaus. By the 1920s, this multifaceted effort had fashioned something like the postsecondary-education sector that trained and employs us, the authors of this volume. That sector arose in the context of Progressive Era social reforms, participated in the growth of a professional managerial class, and developed its organizational techniques for making and disseminating knowledge in tandem with large business enterprises involved in marketing automobiles, pharmaceuticals, insurance policies, and more.[3] We have no disagreement with this basic description but see a need to supplement it. Because others have revealed how the rise of the US research university, Progressive social reform, and the growth of a professional managerial class relate as aspects of a historical shift, we are able to focus on the centrality of media initiatives to that change in, for instance, the convergence of World War I propaganda efforts, college general-education curricula, and the emerging profession of public relations. To the conventional description of the US academy, that is, we append our central proposition: the American research university is a media institution.

With the term "media" we indicate a method more than an object. The term describes a process of communicating to, and thereby connecting, audiences of varying sizes. This process differs from what happens when one person attempts to communicate with another. It involves a cluster of relations, which are linked through the multiple meanings of the term "media." In everyday speech, "media" names the material substrates or technologies through which this group connection occurs—the printed pages of textbooks, celluloid filmstrips shown in class, or electromagnetic waves broadcasting lectures over the air. The term also denotes the generic forms and contents typically conveyed by such carriers, even when circulated by other means. Initially projected through celluloid filmstrips onto big screens, *Casablanca* (1942), *Star Wars* (1977), and their ilk remain recognizable as "movies" when viewed by students on their mobile phones. The term "media" connotes, finally, conventional reception situations: theaters, classrooms, and living rooms. In practice, feats of mediation often involve a dense web of relations connecting substrates, forms, and reception situations. College football games simultaneously compel multitudes by means of stadiums, barroom televisions, domestic screens, and mobile phones. To investigate how university media mediate audiences is, thus, to consider not only the experiences those audiences share but also how their bodies have been arranged in time and space. This is why we emphasize the university's challenge of addressing multiple audiences by various means. The mediation entailed by students in classrooms watching filmstrips is part of the same general university project of audience address as the mediation of football fans enjoying a Saturday game. As new technologies and new forms and new reception settings accrue, so the work of mediating the university's audiences changes.

In the chapters that follow, we will sometimes use the term "information" as a synonym for mediation. By it, we will indicate knowledge that may be communicated, but we will emphasize the process allowing that feat, the process through which people and machines are informed and thereby arranged in relation to one another. When Marshall McLuhan describes electric light as "pure information" he uses the term in this way, highlighting in the process the technology's ability to alter patterns of human activity quite apart from any particular content it may or may not convey.[4] In just this way, the informational purity of the Carnegie unit underwrites course-distribution schemes that influence patterns of behavior for students, parents, faculty, and staff regardless of the courses in which students enroll. Universities inform high-school students that they will need a certain distribution of units to matriculate and then inform incoming students that they will need another distribution of units in order to graduate. Considered at scale, the formative effect lies not in the specific number of units required in this or that area by any given school but in the all-but-inescapable practice of treating course completions as counts.

The work of mediation does not stop at the classroom door, for classrooms, too, are situations for media reception. Some readers may recoil from our insistence on this matter. For many, the fetishization of pedagogical dialogue necessarily excludes the media that typically structure it. Teaching is rarely unmediated, which is why professors care not only about curricula but also about the platforms available to them in class, whether they be anthologies, lecture slides, or learning-management systems. For this reason, it makes sense to call students engaged in classroom conversations, note taking, and lecture appreciation "audiences" and thereby liken them to other media audiences of listeners, spectators, and readers. We explicitly refuse to oppose those activities held to distinguish the seminar room from the style of reception that takes place in movie theaters, as a long line of pedagogues are wont to do. Attending class, watching movies, and listening to radio broadcasts are obviously different activities, but none is a passive alternative to the others. Students are not always actively engaged in conversing with authority, just as film buffs talk back (sometimes out loud) to the screen. We might go even further. When today's students consult their cell phones or use their computers in the classroom, the same behaviors entailing class participation (tweeting to a course-designated hashtag, consulting the text of a downloaded article, watching a

YouTube video, etc.) are only distinguishable from the more general activities of surfing the web and engaging in social media if we consider the content of their interaction and the physical arrangement of the students themselves. The early-twenty-first-century classroom may seem hypermediated when retrospectively compared with its early-twentieth-century counterpart. Both "new media" moments, however, clarified not only that professors would need to compete for audiences with commercial media but equally that they could find new ways to exploit the media that make every classroom a connected one.

Universities, as institutions devoted to information, not only reproduce knowledge but also stabilize patterns of activity through which knowledge is created, communicated, and received. If they did not do this, they would fail to accomplish any of the social functions typically ascribed to them. Universities could not promote social mobility through meritocratic certification absent broad agreement that such certification has value. They could not buoy the economy by means of research innovation without disseminating the results of that innovation. They could not vouchsafe a cultural heritage without promulgating arts and humanities curricula and an array of public programs. US postsecondary education was expected to perform none of these functions before the research university built itself by attracting students and patrons with the promise to advance both individual prosperity and national well-being.

For the first half of the long twentieth century, American universities directed much of their work toward growing and organizing a mass audience. Most members of this audience were not expected to enroll in programs of study. It was hoped, nonetheless, that they would support postsecondary teaching and research through tuition checks, philanthropic contributions, and tax dollars. To generate this support, American schools needed to create a market for higher-education services, a market that, as late as the 1880s, did not really exist. This need to create a demand for its work distinguishes the American university from its European forebears and partly explains its media emphasis. Audiences for the German university were, effectively, captive. That institution had from the early nineteenth century prepared undergraduates for government service through something like what we would call a "liberal arts" education overseen by doctors of philosophy. To test into the university and complete a degree was to secure a position in the Prussian bureaucracy. Although late-nineteenth- and early-twentieth-century US educational leaders valued German curricula and particularly admired their support for advanced studies, they did not imagine a comparable connection between higher education and the state. In the absence of governmentally secured careers, American parents, students, and employers needed to be convinced that higher education offered a pathway to individual improvement and social progress. The first two chapters of the book chart attempts to anchor college in conventions of personal and national development ranging from the promotion of "campus life" in the late nineteenth century to arguments for general-education curricula after World War I to the mass-market adventures of Great Books in the 1930s, by which point universities had been making and teaching films for decades and had played a significant role in the development of radio.

Chapters 3 through 5 treat the midcentury changes that arguably propelled what Christopher Newfield has called the "genius" of "mass quality" higher education to its zenith—and also forecast the end of that ideal.[5] With World War II, the federal government altered its approach to funding research and directed large sums to universities. After the war, it also began to direct significant resources to student aid. Both in the research effort and in discussions of higher-education policy, planners paid unprecedented attention to the central coordination of nationally distributed undertakings. In this they were informed by theoretical work on communications, which had been accelerated by the war. They were also informed by television, which in the 1950s replaced Hollywood film as the medium universities most aspired to resemble (in their reach) and resist (in terms of programming content). A coordinated, mass address seemed a postwar imperative. Still, expansion brought variety in student populations as well as degree programs. It equally created an increasingly subdivided and specialized academic workforce. Particularly important to the subsequent development of university staffing models, for instance, was the growing postwar reliance on graduate student assistants, which altered the professor's role as well. On top of everything else, the GI Bill brought campuses adult learners with clear and practical goals, short-circuiting expectations that college should mark a passage to maturity under the tutelage of liberal arts professors.

By the mid-1960s, a different orientation held sway, one more focused on the differences within university audiences than their mass aggregation.

More granular statistical measures made the increasing variety in students and programs of study apprehensible and, to a degree, manageable. The Higher Education General Information Survey (HEGIS), which measured the 1965–66 academic year, provides a landmark as the earliest federal survey of institutional characteristics, enrollments, and degree completions available online. HEGIS and its successor, Integrated Postsecondary Education Data System (IPEDS), provided actionable information for university recruiting policies and federal antidiscrimination legislation alike. Although late-twentieth-century academic branding made "diversity" a buzzword, the decades immediately following the war laid the groundwork for the ability to perceive and value the student body as diverse demographically and in its academic interests. Universities faced greater competition from one another for students, who increasingly financed their degrees by taking on debt. Meanwhile, the proliferation of channels, the celebration (at both ends of the political spectrum) of DIY alternatives to establishment media, and partisan polarization all undercut the ambition of organizing national culture by means of mass media. Clark Kerr's 1963 coinage "multiversity" provided an early label for this tendency. The rhetorical hyperinflation of the 1980s' and 1990s' culture wars marked its fulfillment. From positions both inside and outside the university, culture warriors mobilized factions by granting English departments the authority to safeguard or destroy civilization, even as changing institutions encouraged English professors to conduct increasingly specialized research for niche audiences and a profusion of degree programs left English, along with every other field, with an ever-decreasing share of undergraduates. Chapters 6 through 9 flesh out these trends, and chapter 10 describes some of their most notable twenty-first-century extensions.

Although it organizes our argument through the following chapters, the shift from a mass to a manifold address, sometimes apprehensible as a passage from unification to fragmentation, belies a dynamic at work across the entire century. American research universities have always sought to multiply audiences as well as to bind them together. Accordingly, chapter 1 underscores that the institution took shape through the elective system, which made student choice the engine of its curricula, and then developed general-education and major-program requirements to constrain and direct students in their choice making. Similarly, chapter 2 emphasizes the different ideas of the university's public service entailed by, on the one hand,

the maturation of citizens via the "traditional" four-year college experience and, on the other, the self-improvement of adult learners via university extension. Before World War I, W. E. B. DuBois and Booker T.
Washington conducted a foundational version of the argument opposing
these two university missions, and they distinguished contending audiences in the process.

The desire to provide common knowledge has presented the nation's various universities with a century-spanning puzzle. Chapter 1 explains how
early-twentieth-century general-education planners came to promote expo-
sure to specific works and disciplines. At midcentury (chapter 4), the authors
of Harvard's landmark *General Education in a Free Society* prescribed more
general goals for courses such as "Western Thought and Institutions" and
areas such as "science and mathematics"—but they did not hesitate to recommend that particular books be read.[6] In the early twenty-first century (chapter 10), their visionary counterparts were likely to mandate competencies
(often called "learning outcomes") achievable by an unlimited variety of
means, only some of which might be standard courses earning credit by the
hour. The latter group envisioned that undergraduates would become familiar with particular styles or genres of knowledge. In contrast, the most
ambitious early-twentieth-century planners fancied that students would
all read from the same page. Since few early-twentieth-century universities could agree on what that page should be, however, this was only ever
an aspiration. How the university imagines (always) plural audiences is only
part of the puzzle of how it actually makes and maintains them.

In arguing, on the one hand, that concern with manifold audiences displaced the research university's early obsession with the masses and, on the
other, that manifold audiences have always mattered and the masses never
stopped being interesting, we demonstrate a pointed reluctance to embrace
the strident periodizations common in recent writing about the university.
A great many accounts place the university's late-twentieth-century transformation within a general political-economic trend known variously as
neoliberalism, financialization, privatization, post-Fordism, and the postindustrial service economy, with each of these terms opening a somewhat
different set of arguments over what constitutes the trend and when it
begins. They each have merits, and some readers will recognize a running,
if largely peripheral, engagement with arguments about neoliberalism
beginning in chapter 6. Our project on the whole, however, is to limn a less

familiar, perhaps less comfortable genealogy of the twenty-first-century university by refusing to subordinate problems of mediation to generalizations about economic organization.

The terms "corporatization" and "corporate university" are often used to name what has recently gone wrong with the university, but this usage invites confusion about how the university has changed. Lest we forget, universities were corporations under the law before businesses were. Far from indicating a historical shift, criticism of their businesslike features is an abiding refrain. Before World War I, Thorstein Veblen decried the university's corporate organization and mocked its leaders as "captains of erudition."[7] At midcentury, Theodor Adorno and Max Horkheimer did him one better when they identified the university and its experts as contributors to the culture industry writ large. They described contemporary culture as a totalizing operation dominated by the problem of producing variations on established genres. Designed to inform obedient consumer citizens, this operation involved intensive study as well as ceaseless repetition, which the Frankfurt School veterans scorned as equally distasteful varieties of "management."[8] The longevity of this type of critique offers a potent reminder that the American research university did not stand apart from the advanced capitalist society that created it. To the contrary, the research university invites serious comparison with contemporary businesses, nonprofits, and government organizations at any point in its history. As Adorno and Horkheimer recommend, comparison with media enterprise is often particularly fruitful. We are struck, for instance, by how well the sociologist Paul DiMaggio's influential account of "brokerage administration," developed to distinguish the managerial practices of mass-culture industries, accounts for key features of university administration, such as the reliance on reputation in evaluation.[9] We find it similarly notable that models for describing broadcasting audiences render intelligible changing patterns of baccalaureate degree completions (as we explain in chapter 8). Incorporation, however, will not provide the university with a historical "before" and "after."

We attend to the university's division of labor as an aspect of its audience-making and -managing activities. Universities did not first hire faculties and football coaches and then figure out how to promote their services. These roles developed in tandem with the media-relations strategies that explained whom and what universities were for. The more eagerly the university sought audiences for its work, the more specialized and subdivided its division of labor became. The creation of academic disciplines and their organization into university departments and divisions provide a major example of this dynamic across the book's chapters. Academic disciplines are nothing if not a mechanism for maintaining audiences. Much of any professor's research is addressed to her discipline; peer review is meant to uphold the discipline's standards, not the predilections of the individual reviewer. Some adventurous faculty members have always refused to paint within the lines, however, for scholars retain a habit of finding new audiences by hybridizing or subdividing prior approaches, which they predictably attempt to stabilize as new disciplines. Universities sometimes departmentalize those disciplines, typically shoehorning them into the existing organizational chart but sometimes reordering it. In the iterative process of departmental formation the compulsion to supplement or reshuffle the existing organizational scheme forever wars with the desire to defend it. Discipline making is a simultaneously audience-stabilizing and labor-subdividing activity.

Professors may be forgiven for seeing disciplinary audiences as all-important, since their careers depend on them, but the habit is myopic. Other forms of address matter too. When universities need to explain what they do to important constituencies such as students and parents, they do not typically lead with a list of disciplines. Nor are disciplinary affiliations the only way professors are given to understand their relation to colleagues in other fields. Chapter 1 points out that the division of American faculties into three parts—the physical sciences, the social sciences, and the humanities—solved a descriptive problem between the two world wars. It provided a shorthand for understanding what various electives might have in common and why general-education requirements were divided in the way they were. Managerial responsibility for a steadily increasing number of departments could be divided along these lines as well, and once that happened, the categories informed professional affiliations. Sociology professors might write primarily for other sociologists, but they could also understand themselves as allied with psychologists in arguments for funding "their" branch of the university. The conflation of discipline with branch—as if sociology could speak for the social sciences or English represented the humanities—encourages abiding confusion over who addresses whom.

Whenever a crisis is declared on behalf of "the humanities" or "science"—and such declarations are indeed perennial in the United States—a change in the division of labor through which the university attempts to maintain any and all of its audiences is typically at stake. To follow such changes, we will treat organizational labels such as "arts and humanities," "social sciences," "preprofessional degree programs," "STEM," "English," "sociology," and "biology" as bids to organize audiences and make them predictable. In observing how such terms work to slice up the university and reassemble it, we will be relatively unconcerned with their conceptual integrity. That is, we will not care whether "social science" rightly names all the disciplines grouped under the term and distinguishes them from others or whether advocates for "English" provide a true account of its methods and cultural value. Readers will have no difficulty finding discussion of these issues elsewhere. In contrast, we will care about what such groupings do to demarcate protected curricular zones, organize labor, aggregate enrollment numbers, and map the university's address to broader audiences.

An emphasis on the work performed by descriptive labels necessarily thwarts the reflex to frame advocacy for the university as a defense of one's own branch or discipline. Among the many examples of this reflex we might list, the anthropologist James Clifford's vision for a "Greater Humanities" provides the best occasion to apply this corrective to our own positions as scholars of film and media studies and English. Clifford laments that the humanities have lost their centrality in an increasingly subdivided university and calls for a "Greater Humanities" in response.[10] Into this category, he corrals all approaches that are "interpretive," "realist (not 'objective')," "historical," and "etho-political." In his accounting, this includes disciplines in literature, history, linguistics, "all the 'studies' and interdisciplines," "sociocultural anthropology," "embattled sectors of politics, economics, and psychology," as well as "what we might call the 'theoretical arts'—including theater arts, performance studies, film, and digital media." Although Clifford claims to describe "an already-existing reality," his "Greater Humanities," like the plain old-fashioned "humanities," is not an actual community so much as a hypothetical container for one—a bid to rally practitioners in these diverse fields under a common banner by conjuring a conceptual unity.[11]

By focusing on what Clifford hopes to accomplish with the category "Greater Humanities," it becomes easier to see what thwarts this ideal.

Professors and students across the broad constellation of fields Clifford invokes do not habitually constitute audiences for one another's work for reasons quite apart from whether he employs an appropriate conceptual sieve in grouping them. They work on different problems, have internalized different methods and disciplinary cultures, occupy offices in separate buildings, compete for institutional resources, and so on. For scholars in this wide array of fields to rise up as one would be a feat without precedent in the history of the American university—as Clifford well knows. His aim in setting an outrageously high bar is clearly to inspire a relatively small number of sympathetic readers to set an intellectual agenda. "All the devils in the details can be left for later," he allows. "There will always be plenty of time for them."[12] It fact, there is rarely enough time for all the detail work required for any vanguard to build a "Greater" academic community. That is one reason why it has been so much easier to proliferate niche audiences with competing claims to organize the university—and their own small plots of turf to defend—than it has been to unite them in a broad address. Collaborations work best, our subsequent chapters repeatedly demonstrate, when they start from concretely shared problems and conversations rather than from abstractions distinguishing disciplinary friends from enemies. To produce the combine known as "STEM" (science, technology, engineering, and math), for instance, required a decade of detail-oriented effort orchestrated by the National Science Foundation to link high schools and colleges (see chapter 9).

Clifford is not alone in perceiving that "the humanities" have lost their authority, but this supposed loss is better understood as a pyrrhic victory and a structural change. The last decades of the twentieth century witnessed a particularly energetic proliferation of audiences. The share of student attention lost by some of the fields Clifford names belies a rapid increase in the number of degree programs on offer, including some of the others he mentions. Every single part of the university experienced this transformation, which produced comparable opportunities and challenges across the disciplines. As subsequent chapters make clear, moreover, the American research university's humanities disciplines cannot have lost an ability to organize culture, because they never had it in first place. Not only have they competed and collaborated across the presumed divide between academic and commercial media enterprise, but they have also competed and collaborated with one another as well as with disciplines assigned to other university divisions. An old saw places the humanities at the heart of general education and presents the sciences as the engine of specialization. The evidence does not support this rhetoric, we will show. From the outset, any one of the research university's disciplines was likely to seek multiple audiences for its work, using different arguments in different circumstances to connect. Across the century, local variety, not central coordination, has been the rule.

In introducing our argument, we have so far proceeded by means of definitions, major themes, and examples where some readers may have appreciated attention to historiographical method. For those readers we note that our approach owes a debt to scholarship in any number of areas but has few direct precedents.[13] Most histories of American higher education avoid mediation in privileging intellectual, social, and institutional developments. For example, a number of histories emphasize the careers of academic disciplines. In such cases, the customary method combines intellectual and institutional history, assembling statements that assert or alter the discipline's core arguments while also charting the instantiation of departments, professional associations, journals, and the like, set against broader institutional trends. This bipolar methodology may partly explain why so many disciplinary histories share a plot in which heroic conceptualization leads to institutionalization followed by infighting, disillusionment, and boundary policing. Although institutionalizing a set of ideas always seems to be the goal, accomplishing that goal inevitably compromises them. If in taking such shape the story arc of English's institutionalization resembles that of women's studies, African American studies, or film and media studies, for example, this fact may ultimately tell us less about the way the university works than it does about the narrative limits of disciplinary history.[14]

When they eschew disciplinary history in favor of social history, chronicles of the university depict a different kind of institution, one more consistently connected to all manner of events beyond campus. For instance, John Thelin's *A History of American Higher Education* (2011) reminds professors that campus life rather than coursework has long constituted the main appeal for undergraduate applicants. To describe this fascination, Thelin looks to the magazines, movies, and football games that popularized college as a social scene. These media do not, however, cross over to touch his depiction of the university's educational and research functions. There, an intellectual-historical emphasis still holds sway. Thus, Thelin largely accepts a line drawn by more exclusively disciplinary histories as well, which almost always make mass media seem external to the educational part of higher education.

Because neither intellectual nor social historiography has been particularly interested in a more thoroughgoing account of mediation, the vast majority of academic histories have been ill-equipped to describe the media that structure everything from homecoming weekends to laboratory research, teaching, and extension services. This is not just an oversight. Rather, scholarship actively avoids such description by working to establish media's externality in two main ways.

First mistake: many historians describe how campus initiatives strive to compete with commercial media only to misunderstand this competition as straightforward antagonism. When professors set out to preserve high culture against the lowering effects of Hollywood, however, disgust with new mass appeals is rarely their primary motive. Often we find these defenders self-consciously playing catch-up, trying to figure out ways to woo audiences on scales rivaling those of the movies or, later on, television and the internet. Commercial media lead the way, in other words, often setting an agenda that the university follows.

Second mistake: historians are apt to conclude that because the academy is older, mass media must be an imposition from outside ivy-covered walls. The university precedes Hollywood, it seems to go without saying, modeled as it was in Europe by Greek and Renaissance practices of teaching established long before Americans started mucking about with problems of mass mediation. We will happily stipulate that the university is as old as Plato if we may also be permitted to describe his famous cave as a primordial mediation scenario.[15] Equally, we'd be perfectly willing to concede that the university has precedents in religious-educational apparatuses if we are allowed to describe them as institutions devoted to the project of audience mediation. In accepting a conventional periodization for the organizational form of the American research university, in other words, we do not deny that a much longer genealogy can be given. Rather, we wish to call attention to heretofore neglected family traits.

No history should fail to historicize the concepts that allow it to function. Therefore, we will pay particular attention to how the university has institutionalized, and failed to institutionalize, the study of mediation. This entails following a conversation from early-century discussions of publicity and propaganda through midcentury considerations of communication and information to late-century developments that established "media" as a disciplinary object and site of turf wars, often obscuring shared legacies of concern with this core institutional problematic. This type of attention to our own endeavor locates it within the human as opposed to the natural sciences. In this distinction, more familiar in Europe than in the United States, "the human sciences" comprise what American academics call the social sciences as well as the humanities.

As mentioned above, we take a nominalist and functionalist approach to disciplinary terminology throughout and generally suspect efforts to build allegiances around abstractions like "the humanities," so we wish to be especially clear about why we find it important to locate this approach within the human sciences. Nearly a half-century ago, Michel Foucault marveled at the fact that the human sciences demanded both interpretation ("one must understand a hidden meaning") and formalization ("one must . . . discover the system, the structural invariant, the network of simultaneities").[16] This was odd because interpretation and formalization can appear to be fundamentally different and even incompatible procedures: the one emphasizing our immanence within the field about which we produce knowledge and the other requiring a transcendent perspective. Foucault's investigation of this doubling in *The Order of Things* led him to the startling discovery that it was not an issue for the seventeenth- and eighteenth-century Europeans so often credited with making "man" the central preoccupation of science and philosophy.[17] Only in the nineteenth century did it begin to seem necessary to study human life as such, Foucault contends, in what amounted to a "change in the fundamental arrangements of knowledge."[18] This change generated distinctive epistemological dilemmas along with new disciplines. It subsequently became necessary to account for the fact that histories were written in history, that anthropologists came from particular cultures, and that literary interpretation disclosed truths about readers when it revealed operations of language (and vice versa). Although we have taken pains to be ecumenical in our treatment of the university's various disciplines, the arrangement of knowledge Foucault describes makes it impossible for us to approach our topic in a disciplinarily neutral fashion. We would not know how to write a natural history of the university.[19]

The later development of Foucault's method bears the burden of this kind of insight, even as it abandons the periodization of humanistic knowledge into epistemic strata.[20] With his turn from archeology to genealogy, Foucault describes humanist knowledge by means of its aims and effects— knowledge "made for cutting," a practice more than a form of consciousness.[21] He reminds us that it is not enough to describe the past. We also require an account of what it means to do so. Human scientists have proved eminently capable of recognizing that the knowledge they produce is situated and contingent while also potentially transformative of its situation and contingencies. Understood from such a perspective, "the university" will not appear as a fixed star but rather a shifting constellation. It cannot be understood by establishing an original instance. Rather, we should expect the look back through its present to disclose multiple trajectories that may not converge in the same way tomorrow.

Which is to say: any worthwhile history of the university should intervene in its practice. It should do so not as a good white paper might, by advocating specific policy changes, but rather as mass media do, by giving form to audiences, by presenting them with material worth arguing over. White papers work when their readers agree with them. Media work when their audiences agree to disagree about them. Although we will be happy to know that some readers agree with us, our primary goal is to help change the conversation. We have already noted that we consider declarations of crisis less useful than interrogations of how the university speaks to its audiences and what it expects from them. We have encouraged acknowledgment that nonprint media have long been used and studied by the American research university and the attendant realization that the hyperbole surrounding new media disruption is a symptom, not a description. Closest to home, perhaps, we aim to remind our faculty peers that few of their audiences are entirely intramural and to encourage them to reexamine the division of labor that allows audience engagement to occur. Faculty may discover unacknowledged collaborations with colleagues who are not professors but whose often specialized labor in student services, development, and athletics has done so much to shape relationships with parents, undergraduates, and football fans.

Chapter One

CAMPUS LIFE

American research universities flourished by engaging a mass-mediated society. Unthinkable without print, the American university took shape alongside large-circulation pictorial magazines, massive athletic spectacles, and the movies. These new media of the day were not external factors influencing the university's development. Rather, "mass mediation" names the problem set that distinguished American research universities from their domestic forebears and European prototypes. The questions of how large audiences could be organized through media, how audiences so organized could be directed or managed, and how such organization could be made compatible with capitalist democracy stamped American postsecondary education in all its parts.

Football addressed the first of these problems, namely, how to attract mass audiences to the university. The athletic contests mattered less than the campus culture for which they provided a synecdoche in magazines, newspapers, films, and, inevitably, on the radio and television. Football not only helped create and sustain higher education's major brands but also structured central arguments about the university's public mission. Though many Americans would never see the inside of any other campus building, they joined students and alumni in flocking to stadiums on Saturdays.

General-education advocates hoped that undergraduate curricula could have a similarly broad influence in forming ideologically appropriate citizens. Initiatives to develop general education as a project of citizen formation were energized by the extension of World War I propaganda efforts into university classrooms. Planners promoted the notion that university curricula could and should provide the basic intellectual equipment that would encourage students to act thoughtfully and ethically as members of a national community. Although enthusiasm for this project waxed and waned across the century, it continued to inspire influential voices. It also remains a noteworthy puzzle in that no coordinating body has ever been empowered to ensure that syllabi would in fact be nationally shared.[1] Although one can detect family resemblances, each school was free to develop and promote its own general-education scheme. Universities anchored general-education curricula in all sorts of specializations, in biology as well as in psychology, sociology, anthropology, philosophy, economics, political science, history, and English. By the 1930s, a widespread tripartite division of general education into humanities, social science, and natural science branches encouraged the fantasy that knowledge constituted an original unity, sundered by specialization, in which students might still receive a common grounding. Broad adoption of this organizational chart, however, did not constitute agreement on how to fill it.

Far more than shared syllabi, a shared measure of time spent in instruction held the US postsecondary-education sector together. Often maligned and underappreciated, the Carnegie Foundation's unit had awesome organizing power. It made commensurable the academic credentials supplied by various universities and the high schools that fed them students. If one high school's diploma could be seen as roughly equivalent to another's, if baccalaureate degrees from the University of Chicago and Harvard University could be perceived as more or less interchangeable markers of preparation for graduate school, it was not because they were understood to certify completion of identical programs of study. Rather, they represented the completion of numerically equivalent credit hours. The Carnegie unit, which made degree completions auditable as well as commensurable, also mediated the university as a workplace. It represented faculty as well as student labor and made it possible to equate a credit in any discipline with an hour in any other. In this way, the Carnegie unit provided a framework to accommodate the array of institutions that composed the higher-education sector. It equally enabled the management of work within those institutions and freed them to encourage specialized courses of proliferating variety. Perhaps most significantly, it facilitated the organization of disciplines into departments and made it possible to imagine a potentially infinite series of both degrees and the departmental containers where they would be administered.

The ability to see football, general education, and the Carnegie unit as similar kinds of efforts distinguishes our approach. More typically, football provides the mass-cultural foil for general education's soaring aspirations, while the credit hour seems to be the registrar's business, a managerial underbelly briefly glimpsed as the American research university takes flight. While we set these features in new relation, however, we are hardly the first to identify them as important.

Many agree that the period from the 1880s through the 1920s witnessed the development of a distinctively organized higher-education sector in the United States, one characterized, in the early days, by football and the elective system, which the Carnegie unit ordered after the turn of the century and general-education schemes reordered after World War I. To be sure, different accounts give different complexions to the era's change. Some, like Laurence Veysey's classic *The Emergence of the American University* (1965), strive to isolate major thoughts and thinkers, while others, like Frederick Rudolph's equally venerable *The American College and University: A History* (1962), emphasize the development of institutional forms and structures like departments and football programs.[2] Still other field shapers, like Burton Bledstein's *The Culture of Professionalism: The Middle Class and the Development of Higher Education in America* (1976), emphasize the university's credentialing work and role in reproducing class hierarchy. More recent scholarship expands, complicates, and sometimes synthesizes these perspectives, thickening our understanding of turn-of-the-century student life, institution formation, disciplinary struggles, and the relationship between the new American university and the older small college that transformed in tandem with it.[3] In sum, a half-century of work in this vein provides a general outline of changes brought by the university's rise.

In contrast to its British and Continental contemporaries, the American system would not assume that undergraduates arrived at university having completed their general liberal studies. Instead, it would expect them to finish that training, perhaps in the first two years, while also setting out on more specialized paths. New approaches to undergraduate curricula severed the link between "the classics" and the cultivation of student "character" formerly at the core of the American college experience. An emphasis on vernacular language, natural science, rapidly developing disciplines across the human sciences, and, above all, elective choice among these many subjects displaced the Greek- and Latin-intensive curriculum of the colonial college. Like their European precedents, the new American enterprises would include graduate schools to train PhDs. After the turn of the century, Americans would no longer seek such training in Germany. Although the architects of the American system invoked the German ideal, they built institutions that also promoted what the Germans considered to be "lower" professions. Alongside professional schools in the traditional areas of medicine, law, and theology, Americans built new ones in engineering, business, and agriculture. All were modernized to include theoretical as well as practical training. Professional certifications, which had been relatively autonomous from formal degree programs for most of the history of the republic, would be tied to the credentials higher education conferred. To secure a degree in medicine, for example, increasingly required first achieving a bachelor's degree. The result was a new American hybrid that expanded rapidly from 238,000 undergraduates enrolled at the turn of the century to 1.1 million in 1930.[4] By then, too, the first generation of American-trained PhDs had credentialed their successors.[5]

In the absence of established pathways from postsecondary education to careers, universities relied on mass media to promote their efforts and build their student bodies. For striving middle-class Americans of the late nineteenth century, illustrated weekly magazines such as the *Saturday Evening Post*, *Munsey's*, and *Cosmopolitan* spread the message that college offered upward mobility.[6] It also promised a good time. "The single most important change in American higher education at the end of the nineteenth century," explains the historian John Thelin, "was that collegegoing became fashionable and prestigious."[7] Turn-of-the-century media depicted a fascinating student lifestyle, one largely created by students themselves. Undergraduates made mascots, selected school colors, wrote alma maters, and, of course, staged athletic contests. "Courses were seen as a necessary evil," Thelin explains, "a price to be paid for admission to the greatest show on earth, campus life."[8] No aspect of the turn-of-the-century university better indicated its mass appeal than football, whose fans filled giant stadiums as salaried professionals assumed responsibility for orchestrating the sport.

FOOTBALL

Football and all its trappings made sense of "college" at a moment when the curriculum was challenged to do so. In the latter decades of the nineteenth century, many universities had adopted an elective system in which any two undergraduates might take two almost completely different sets of classes, and those classes competed with each other for enrollments.[9] Harvard, the standard bearer for this approach, removed subject requirements for all but freshmen in stages through the 1870s and 1880s. By 1897, their only required course was a year of rhetoric.[10] When Harvard installed Abbott Lawrence Lowell as its new president in 1909, it seemed clear to many faculty and administrators that the emphasis on student choice had gone too far.[11] They began to structure the options by adopting a system of majors. Nationally, as we will explain in greater detail, schemes for accommodating student choice within majors and general-education requirements soon prevailed. Students needed such rules, the University of Wisconsin's president Glenn Frank explained in a 1926 interview, to avoid narrowness that "destroys perspective" and to cultivate "an ability to correlate the knowledge gained in the specialist's field with the other facts and phases of life." To illustrate, Frank seized the obvious example: "One reason why football attracts so much more of the undergraduate's attention is that a football game is a vital, dramatic whole."[12] As consensus emerged that administrators and faculty needed to find new ways to address their student audiences, the rival and paradoxical model for unifying educational programming was clear: football.

Before college football provided university presidents with a model for addressing students en masse, its rituals were largely student made. In the 1890s, students tended to much of the organization of Saturday afternoon games, which also connected them with returning alumni.[13] By the 1920s, universities had transformed student-generated symbols and rituals into official campus culture, thereby making them available for wider usage in recruiting and marketing. School colors and mascots became official colors and mascots. Officially sanctioned college songs and societies, yearbooks, and festivals supplemented and sometimes replaced outright their student-made precursors.[14] Where "student managers" and alumni donors once ruled college sport, professional coaching staffs and powerful athletic directors held sway.

Even after the student body no longer organized these activities, however, it could still see itself as contributing to the institution by participating in them. Everyone understood that campus life, not classroom work, defined the school brand. "Who hears of a University as having a reputation for the number of hours the students study each day," Illinois's *Daily Illini* asked in 1921. "The youth of America is attracted to a university which has a strong football team, a talented band. . . . If a college has a strong faculty, that is good advertisement among the teaching profession but it has little or no weight with the high school graduate."[15] There is every reason to assume that some high-school students did care about the quality of instruction they might receive and may well have been unmoved by spectacular displays of school spirit. Still, the *Daily Illini*'s notion that football advertises the university can only seem prescient from an early-twenty-first-century perspective, when participation in the college football business—or celebration of the less commercial version of the sport that exists on some campuses—so clearly stamps institutional brands.

Football's mass address required stadiums, which were hardly built for students alone. Penn and Harvard launched a decades-long construction boom at around the turn of the century, setting the bar at structures capable of holding 40,000 fans. Yale upped the ante in 1914 with the 70,000-seat Yale Bowl. At the time, Yale's enrollment, including professional schools, totaled around 3,300 students.[16] Stanford, Penn, and Ohio State all built stadiums in the 60–65,000-seat range in the early 1920s. Cal completed its stadium (on top of a major geological fault) at 73,000 seats in 1923. Many more schools, including Northwestern, Minnesota, and Missouri, built more modest structures in the 40–50,000 seat range, and in 1927 Michigan constructed the Big House for as many as 84,000 fans.[17] For such schools, the game could be a profit center. In 1928, the nation's most elite program, Yale, reported a gross revenue of $1,119,000, with a net profit of $348,500 (almost five million in 2017 dollars).[18]

Monumental football stadiums also offered the spectacle of organized masses who filled them.[19] When tens of thousands of people sat or rose in unison, it was not entirely clear who or what directed that apparently spontaneous mass movement. Such demonstrations of masses in action posed a

FIGURE 1.1. The University of Pennsylvania's Franklin Field, as rebuilt in 1922 (photo c. 1945).
Source: Courtesy of University Archives, University of Pennsylvania.

problem simultaneously political, economic, and representational. How could the masses organized by the stadiums become more substantively involved in determining their own organization? Attending football spectacles looked a bit like civic engagement and a bit like losing oneself in a mindless crowd.

Various mass media extended the game's audience-organizing power beyond the stadium's stands. In his chronicle of college football's media-driven expansion, Michael Oriard credits the daily press with transforming it into a national sport, which also sold papers. In the first decades of the twentieth century, and particularly with the introduction of the tabloid in the 1920s, newspaper sports sections ballooned.[20] Radio quickly joined print. Advertisements for radio sets featuring listeners tuned to football appeared as early as 1923, and NBC radio scrambled to cover the Rose Bowl in 1927 when it emerged as the pioneering national commercial broadcast network. Meanwhile, at the movies college football provided a newsreel staple, and scores of feature-length musicals, dramas, and comedies centered on the sport.[21] *Time* put "Football's Public" on its cover not once but twice. "Once the crowd was one-quarter its present size," the magazine proclaimed in 1930. "It was composed of undergraduates, parents, alumni, their wives, sweethearts, cousins. For years it has been growing until it has come to include every element in the country."[22] As a cross-platform mass-media phenomenon, college football lent its patterns to—that is, informed—national culture.

As members of football's audience, students arrived on campuses mass media had already described. Just so, a movie inspires Harold Lloyd's college ambitions in *The Freshman* (1925).[23] His character, Harold Lamb, prepares for the experience by studying advice literature on college yells, fashions, and football. When the advice proves dated, upperclassmen relentlessly spoof the unwitting Lamb. Despite its outmoded particulars, however, mass culture proves correct in its basic premises: in the end, football actually does hold the key to popularity, which is all that counts as success on campus, which a title card describes as "a football stadium with a college attached." In playing well-established collegiate topoi for laughs, *The Freshman* finds no need to depict classrooms or professors. The curriculum proves no more compelling to the Freshman's more highly sexualized cinematic counterpart, the Co-Ed. She does attend class—but primarily to seduce

FIGURE 1.2. Harold Lloyd prepares for college in *The Freshman* (1925).

FIGURE 1.3. Clara Bow attends class in *The Wild Party* (1929).
Source: Courtesy of UCLA Film and Television Archive.

her professors, a project never better portrayed than by Clara Bow in Dorothy Arzner's *The Wild Party* (1929).[24] Although magazines, films, and radio broadcasts may not have depicted college life as it was, they generalized a framework for interpreting it.[25] Whatever students learned to be and do at college, they could expect to parse those experiences in relation to the stock scenarios and images media supplied.

Small wonder, then, that faculty and administrators came to resent the football audiences their universities had so successfully grown. In 1894, the University of Chicago's founding president, William Rainey Harper, proclaimed football violence a reasonable sacrifice to "the altar of vigorous and unsullied manhood," associating it with "moral purity" and "human self-restraint."[26] That same year, however, a range of football powers acknowledged a need to regulate the sport and met to start laying the groundwork for what, in 1910, would become the National Collegiate Athletic Association (NCAA). The nation's most elite program, Yale, joined in 1915. Already by the turn of century, a bevy of schools had set up oversight boards and committees to smooth relations between increasingly fractious faculty and their colleagues in football operations.[27] In 1908, for instance, Irving Babbitt found football a worthy adversary for the New Humanist standards he endorsed: "That a community like the college, which has met together to do homage to the things of the mind, should in practice worship at the feet of the successful athlete—this is an irony that no amount of beautiful effusions about the democratic spirit can disguise."[28] Such sentiment grew in intensity. In his 1921 annual report, Harvard's president Lowell observed with dismay, "The public interest in the sport, as a spectacle, has become general all over the country, and has increased markedly since the war." He questioned whether physical exercise and collegiate spirit could justify "a public spectacle attended by thousands of spectators every Saturday throughout the autumn," particularly given the high injury rates. He called upon "faculties, administrators and governing bodies to consider afresh the proper place of public intercollegiate athletic contests in the scheme of education."[29] As Lowell's remark suggests, faculty and administrative suspicion of the sport grew in proportion to its popularity.

By the 1920s, newspapers and magazines happily promoted football on one page while excoriating it on another. They chronicled on-field deaths, exposed corruption, and gave voice to irate faculty and administrators.[30] Increasingly, but not exclusively, commercialism became the focus of critique. For instance, Glenn E. Hoover, a University of Oregon economics professor, strikes a different note from Babbitt in a 1926 *New Republic* column, which calls upon universities to "trim the salary and dignity of the professional coach, that Colossus of the campus, and make him at least a little lower than the president." "The college boys are not the villains in this story," Hoover quickly adds. "They never deliberately resolve to compete with D. W. Griffith in the production of spectacles, but the local public demands a winning team and a stadium in which to stage them."[31] Concern with "salary and dignity"—that is, celebrity and also notoriety—here replaced Babbitt's lament for football's influence on the life of the mind.

Both emphases are evident in the results of a nationwide investigation launched by the Carnegie Foundation for the Advancement of Teaching in the mid-1920s. The research team crisscrossed the country conducting interviews and compiling statistics. In 1929, Howard Savage, a former Bryn Mawr English professor, wrote the final report. The investigation demonstrated that subsidizing football players was a widespread practice, that in a season on average 17 percent of college football players on any given team would sustain a serious injury, that schools including Harvard and Princeton maintained slush funds for recruiting, and that "unhygienic practices" were common. "The prime needs of our college athletics are two," Savage concluded: "Commercialism . . . must be diminished," and the "American college must renew within itself the force that will challenge the best intellectual capabilities of the undergraduate."[32] This appeal to tame the business of college sport and focus on student classroom audiences received front-page coverage in late October 1929, as the stock market crashed. "College Sports Tainted by Bounties," the *New York Times* declared.[33] Despite the bad press, however, football's business model held at any number of schools. College football rebounded before the stock market did.

The notion that athletics and academics are at odds is a consequence not only of the former's mass success but also of the latter's mass ambition. In the absence of any centrally coordinated plan to guide the growth of higher education in the United States, football's popularity could serve as a prototype for distinctly academic as well as athletic brands. The University of Chicago's history perhaps best exemplifies this dynamic. At the turn of the century, building a football program and beefing up specialized research seemed equally vital to the project of launching this Midwestern school. John D. Rockefeller tapped William Rainey Harper to be its first president in 1891. A prodigy who completed his Yale PhD in Semitic languages at the age of nineteen, Harper built Chicago by raiding competitors for talent. He plucked the soon-to-be–Nobel Prize–winning physicist Albert A. Michelson from Clark University, the philosopher John Dewey from the University of Michigan, the physiologist Jacques Loeb from the University of Strasbourg, and his former student, the football standout Amos Alonzo Stagg from Yale.

Stagg became the first tenured physical-education professor in the country and the first tenured football coach as well.[34] Harper viewed football as essential to the university's rapid growth and gave Stagg broad authority to oversee its development.[35] In return, Stagg made Chicago a powerhouse, a founding member of the Big Ten, and the national champion in 1905 and 1913. He aggressively recruited prospects from local high schools, cultivated alumni loyalty, and promoted the program in media ranging from billboards to radio.[36] In a pioneering "national" broadcast of 1922, telephone lines carried the Princeton game from Chicago to New York and northern New Jersey, where the locals doubtlessly appreciated Princeton's 21–18 victory.[37]

If building audiences for scholastics and football seemed necessary and compatible projects in the University of Chicago's first decades, they began to diverge around 1920 with the start of a decade-long curricular reform that yielded the "New Plan." A general-education approach including requirements for every year of the undergraduate experience, this core curriculum was modeled after a course called "The Nature of the World and Man," which had enrolled sixty students a year since 1924 and was staffed mainly by biologists.[38] The architect of the New Plan, Dean Chauncey Boucher, conceived of the overhaul as appealing particularly to a national audience of serious academic achievers. "If Chicago were to adopt such a plan as here outlined," he argued, "in a short time Chicago would have more applicants of better quality than ever before."[39] Sports had no place in this strategy: the New Plan dropped physical-education courses. Chicago's president Robert Maynard Hutchins argued that abolishing football would "confirm the pioneering reputation of the university and in one stroke do more to make clear what a university should be than we could do in any other way."[40] Meanwhile, crowds at Stagg's stadium thinned. He left Chicago in 1932 to become head coach at the University of the Pacific, and the athletic director who replaced him, hired from Oberlin College, did not care about mass athletic spectacles.[41] In 1939, Chicago canceled the football program that had helped call the university into being.[42]

The triumph of academics over athletics at Chicago presupposed an institutional field that comprised diverse colleges and universities; print, film, and broadcast media outlets; and policy-making agencies such as the NCAA and Carnegie Foundation. By the 1930s, if not before, this field was structured such that an institution's approach to football defined the kind of school it was, and for whom. When Chicago addressed the brainy strivers who would thrive in its rigorous New Plan, it abandoned an earlier strategy that insinuated the school into the city's secondary-education system and social calendar. Notre Dame, the University of Illinois, and other Midwestern institutions moved to fill that niche. What once had been a relatively autonomous student enterprise publicized by illustrated magazines now defined the university as a kind of media industry comparable to others—in both its athletic and its academic parts. The groups of professionals who supervised college football needed not only to coach the players but also to oversee press relations, marketing, and branding. If they were to provide a meaningful alternative, academics would need to be treated in a similar way, which is just how Chicago treated them in introducing the New Plan and trumpeting its capacity to attract students and retain the loyalty of alums. In this sense, football modeled the kind of pitch universities would need to make on behalf of more clearly educational initiatives like core curricula. Everywhere, albeit differently, these initiatives aimed to improve the student populations that football united. Nowhere, however, could they claim comparable reach.

GENERAL EDUCATION

The rise of the elective system established the classroom-audience problem as the flipside of the football problem: electives fragmented the student body; football united it. By the 1920s, most colleges and universities had defined the cohesiveness of the student body as an issue that the curriculum should manage. It was a matter of balancing general-education requirements with elective courses, of melding "liberal education" with field specialization. Mobilization for World War I gave the supradepartmental coordination of general education a major boost, bolstering the idea that a properly devised disciplinary blend would serve a national interest: college could train the undergraduate masses to behave as the citizenry of a democracy. Across the sector, institutions presented core curricula as a way to unify the student body and, by rhetorical extension, the nation. In so doing, they acted as if a coherent national public could be produced without anything like a common national curriculum. While some schools adapted precedents from other schools, and although widely used textbooks could provide some measure of cohesion, general-education schemes notably varied. For all that it expressed a shared goal, general education was not nearly as uniform in its address as football, wherein the fans of different teams nonetheless experienced the same game.

Among the postwar innovators, Columbia University has the distinction of developing and institutionalizing simultaneously two distinct and broadly influential approaches to general education. One, a course on Contemporary Civilization, is typically presented as the forebear of the Western Civilization survey that sprouted up across the country. The other, a course on Great Books, has had various heirs, some more closely tied to university classrooms than others. As we will explain, Encyclopedia Britannica mass marketed Great Books from the 1930s. In the 1980s, E. D. Hirsch revived the approach as a curated reading list (see chapter 9). Importantly, both of Columbia's initiatives learned from the mass mobilization of students as soldiers and supporters of the war effort.

Although it had prewar precedents, Columbia's Contemporary Civilization course took inspiration from the nationally implemented "War Issues" curriculum.[43] Overseen by the Federal Department of War and taught to uniformed student-soldiers at campuses across the land, War Issues had no nationally shared syllabus. By way of guidance, its national director explained that the course should conduct "a war of ideas" by providing "some understanding of the view of life and of society which they are called upon to defend and of that view against which we are fighting." Additionally, the War Department compelled interdisciplinarity by requiring colleges to assign "the best men available from the departments of history, government, philosophy, economics, and literature."[44] Columbia's version of War Issues emphasized politics, economics, and, importantly, the synthetic New History popularized by the Columbia professor James Harvey Robinson.[45]

After the war, the course provided reformers with an example of how teaching might take place across disciplines and how the elective system could be given focus through engagement with ripped-from-the-headlines world problems.[46] Dean Frederick Woodbridge claimed to speak for the campus in viewing it as the basis for "a liberal education for the youth of today."[47] In 1919, Columbia implemented Contemporary Civilization to fulfill this promise, at least for Columbia undergraduates. In contrast to the contemporaneous Harvard model, which programmed large lectures by prestigious professors and breakout discussion sections led by graduate student assistants, this course would be offered exclusively in small sections staffed by a specially selected instructional team drawn from different disciplines.[48] The Columbia University dean Herbert Hawkes described the course as mitigating the "destructive element in our society," aiding students in meeting "the arguments of the opponents of decency and sound government" while preparing each of them to be a "citizen who shall be safe for democracy."[49] Hawkes's bon mot aptly captures a premise shared by a number of period initiatives, which saw "democracy" not in terms of legal structures or electoral mechanics but as a culture or ethical orientation jeopardized by bureaucracy, mass media, and other features of capitalist modernity. Given this logic, education would be needed to protect democracy from its citizens.

A similar conviction led John Erskine to argue that citizens could be made good by requiring them to read the classics. Erskine emerged as an advocate for the Great Books approach from his wartime service chairing the Army Educational Commission and his postarmistice experience as academic director of the American Army University at Beaune. The Beaune post gave him the freedom to conduct "a bold experiment" that his Columbia colleagues had opposed before the war. He offered a required, classics-based Saturday-morning course on citizenship that espoused no modest aim. "We should be teaching every youth within our borders John Milton's large conception of citizenship," he wrote to General John J. Pershing in 1919, and then quoted from Milton's "Of Education": "I call therefore a complete and generous education that which fits a man to perform justly, skillfully, and magnanimously, all the offices, both private and public, of peace and war."[50] Erskine could not reach every youth, but he was able to implement his approach at Columbia the following year.

The Great Books course would become a kind of capstone seminar in Columbia's General Honors program. It was staffed from its beginning by a mixture of faculty and instructors, who in the early years worked in pairs—fractious ones being desirable, the better to model argument. Discussion was deemed essential to the project. As with Contemporary Civilization, the course was offered in sections of twenty-five to thirty students. "Perhaps for the first time they have the basis for an intellectual life in common," Erskine wrote of Columbia students, neatly conflating the pedagogical aims of the Great Books sections with the effects of the course on student life as a whole. "Meeting on the campus, they need not confine their talk to estimates of athletic prowess or school gossip." Erskine offered the process through which the "world chooses its great books" as an alternative to football.[51]

On campuses across the country, general education would take different forms depending on the particular constellations of administrators, faculty, and disciplines engaged in instituting it. Some universities, like Rutgers, appropriated Columbia's chronologically arranged Contemporary Civilization syllabus directly; others, like Stanford, reframed it as Citizenship, a course favoring economics and politics over history.[52] At many schools, professional historians succeeded in capturing one kind of Contemporary Civilization descendant: the Western Civilization survey, with its imperative to give Europe and the United States a shared past.[53] Nonetheless, some institutions, most famously the University of Chicago, rejected history as the unifying touchstone.

The War Department's expectation that "history, government, philosophy, economics, and literature" would be the disciplines most useful for propaganda purposes was not the only factor motivating the postwar development of general education. Many planners were enthralled by the proposition that knowledge constituted a unified domain sundered by specialization, which general education could make whole.[54] In this vein, and in contrast to Columbia's Contemporary Civilization and Great Books prototypes, Chicago's planners believed their core courses should emphasize the key premises and methods of analysis distinguishing natural science, social science, and the humanities. They supplemented a biology-heavy interdisciplinary course on "The Nature of the World of Man" with others including "Man and Society" and "The Meaning and Value of the Arts."

By the end of the 1920s, the conviction that general education should ideally unite three distinct branches of knowledge supplemented the citizen-building imperative proclaimed by Dean Hawkes a decade earlier. In 1929, Columbia recast Contemporary Civilization as a two-year sequence: part "A" had a historical-cultural pitch, while "B" focused on social science. Each drew staff from a different cluster of disciplines. Although Columbia planners hoped for a synthetic general-education course in natural science, they found the competing approaches of scientists in different departments an intractable problem as late as 1951.[55]

Despite such challenges of implementation, by the late 1930s most general-education schemes seemed willing to accept a tripartite categorization of disciplines as "natural science," "social science," and the "humanities."[56] These categories arguably did not organize postsecondary education in 1915, when the American Association of University Professors (AAUP) defended academic freedom by explaining that research advances in "natural science," "social science," and "philosophy and religion" required it. The postulation of branches that, taken together, constituted a whole offered a way to make diverse courses and disciplines cohere. As with the effort to inculcate ideological correctness, however, it failed to impose uniformity on general-education curricula nationwide. Everywhere, local differences and politics came into play, giving each institution's approach its own flavor.

Tripartite organizations of specializations supplied administrative coherence, not common knowledge or culture. As ways of mediating the undergraduate experience nationally, they worked more like the timeslots, day-parts, and genres of broadcast media than the wartime propaganda campaigns that, in no small part, provided their impetus. Given the branding of schools like Chicago, it is possible that some alumni felt more loyal to their general-education program than to their football mascot, although this does not seem to have been a widely shared phenomenon. Where general-education curricula did produce common experiences from campus to campus, textbook adoption, rather than a master plan, could claim credit. The Columbia historian James Harvey Robinson and his successor Charleton J. H. Hayes provided one such platform linking Western Civilization courses across the land.[57] Yet, as the historians Carolyn Lougee, Morris Rossibi, and William Woehrlin point out, "the single-volume, complete Western Civ textbook was not a matter of choice based on education theory but a simple matter of economic necessity. It took the paperback revolution, and postwar affluence among students in many schools, before faculties could even think about alternatives."[58] On campuses, general-education schemes may be credited with generalizing a tripartite division of knowledge as a way to manage disciplinary heterogeneity and providing a market for textbooks of particular sorts. Despite planners' aspirations, they did not displace college football—by 1930 a trans- and mass-media phenomenon—as a means of national address.

CARNEGIE UNITS AND ACADEMIC DEPARTMENTS

What bound the nation's schools into a system that could certify college graduates was not a curricular core but the Carnegie unit, "a medium without a message" if ever there was one, and the distinctive arrangement of departments and disciplines it monitored and maintained.[59] Although it never set policy directly, the Carnegie Foundation played a more important role in the development of national standards for higher education than any other organization. Beyond the influence of the credit hour, the foundation saturated the education sector with reports that informed not only on-campus decision makers but also the national press. It pioneered a remarkably effective, durable, and reproducible approach to higher-education administration when it determined that mediating institutions would be the best way to improve them.

Launched by Andrew Carnegie in 1906 with the idea of starting a pension plan for college teachers, the Carnegie Foundation used that program as a carrot. It allowed institutions to participate only if they adopted its standards for student admission, faculty appointment (all departments had to have PhD holders as chairs, for instance), and financial solvency (an endowment was mandated).[60] The approach succeeded all too well. The foundation's second annual report recounts that fifty-five schools signed up almost immediately.[61] A decade later, the number of participating institutions reached seventy-three, with more than five thousand teachers "associated in the enjoyment of these pension benefits."[62] This volume overwhelmed the foundation's assets, and the pension was spun off as the new Teachers Insurance and Annuity Association (TIAA). The Carnegie Foundation endured. It was not, its trustees asserted, a charity but "an educational agency" providing "a wholesome influence in education" by providing "outside criticism" and taking "into account the interests not alone of a community or of a section, but of a continent."[63] Although the value of Carnegie's influence has often been disputed, there is no question about the scope of its ambition.

In the name of a continental public's good, Carnegie standards sought to level a playing field on which individuals, institutions, and specializations might compete for attention and resources. An early challenge lay in determining what the word "college" would mean. In 1906, foundation officers found the term naming "institutions varying so widely in entrance requirements, standards of instruction, and facilities for work" as to have an "arbitrary" meaning.[64] To clear this up, the trustees proposed that a "college" should:

have at least six (6) professors giving their entire time to college and university work, a course of four full years in liberal arts and sciences, and should require for admission, not less than the usual four years of academic or high school preparation, or its equivalent, in addition to the preacademic or grammar school studies.[65]

Through their annual reports, the trustees would weigh in on every aspect of that definition, providing a wealth of data about not only the growing university sector but also the high schools that prepared its students. Most turn-of-the-century colleges admitted students from a list of schools they approved in advance, but variation in what high schools taught meant college admissions committees could not count on any particular preparation.[66] To provide guidance, the foundation borrowed a scheme for assessing high-school-graduation standards established by the New York State Board of Regents, which divided coursework into "counts." In the Carnegie scheme, these would be termed "units," with each one "being a course of five periods weekly throughout an academic year."[67] By standardizing the way high school appeared to college admissions officers, the foundation offered to order the intake side of higher education on a "national scale."[68] The unit proved equally effective in standardizing college courses and measuring degree completions.

Carnegie had partners and competitors in its efforts to bring order. The College Entrance Examination Board was launched in 1900 with a desire for comparable reach.[69] The Association of American Universities was formed the same year, initially serving as an effort to marshal the nation's top PhD-granting institutions (fourteen at conception) to compete with European schools. In 1913, the AAU would become an accrediting body, working with the Carnegie Foundation to produce an "Accepted List" of schools that met its criteria.[70]

The wider ramifications of standardization initiatives were ably imagined by early-twentieth-century detractors, who condemned the management of students and faculty through statistics and units and thereby started what would become a perennial refrain. "If quantitatively the American [university's] achievement is impressive," Babbitt averred, "qualitatively it is somewhat less satisfying."[71] The credit hour reduced university learning (and faculty work effort) to "units of time and volume," Thorstein Veblen declaimed, the better to "control and enforce it by a system of accountancy and surveillance."[72] Veblen's *The Higher Learning in America: A Memorandum on the Conduct of Universities by Businessmen* (published in 1918 but drafted earlier) lamented the drift of regulation that Carnegie enabled, along with the transformation of university "co-operation between teacher and student" into the more "mechanical" relationship between pupil and "schoolmaster."[73] Veblen's critique had been inspired in no small part by Chicago's football-loving, faculty-poaching President Harper, an exemplary "captain of erudition" if ever there was one.[74] Veblen was scandalized that universities had "Publicity Bureaus" and decried their "businesslike organization." So long as they were "guided by considerations of magnitude and statistical renown," he inveighed, they would be antipathetic to higher learning of the sort that could produce free-thinking citizens.[75]

In 1903, William James worried less about the numbers than he did about the kind of certification requirements that Carnegie would come to demand of pension-plan participants. The growing American system was yielding "a tyrannical Machine with unforeseen powers of exclusion and corruption," James asserted, because administrators required PhD certification of their professors, valuing that over the judgment of faculty specialists.[76] James saw early and well the new role academic specialization would give its faculty experts. On the one hand, administrators could not possibly have the expertise to recognize accomplishment in the range of research areas the university encompassed and would have to defer judgments of quality to in-field faculty. As in the system of "brokerage administration" that distinguishes mass-culture industries in Paul DiMaggio's important formulation, academic managers could only rely on reputation and track record to predict future success.[77] On the other hand, and again in parallel to other media-making corporations, peer reviewers would exercise their judgments within a framework of standard expectations regarding credentials, work product, and measures of reputation decided by administrators, often with reference to institutional placement within a broader organizational field.

The organizational field included professional associations that exerted their own standardizing pressures. The turn of the century had witnessed the establishment of the Modern Language Association (1883) and the devolution of the American Social Science Association (1865–1909) into more academically oriented and highly specialized groups such as the American Historical Association (1884), American Economics Association (1885), American Political Science Association (1903), and American Sociological Society (1905).[78] Through publications and conferences, each strove to coordinate and promote the efforts of its constituents, corralling in the process the examples and arguments that would delimit disciplines. This created a need for additional coordination. In 1919, when the American Council of Learned Societies was organized to represent the United States in the International Union of Academies, its continuing mission was to orchestrate the activities of proliferating disciplinary societies in the humanities and social sciences.

Professional associations succeeded by mediating the professorate, their print organs and conferences binding scholars into an audience for one another's work while at the same time distinguishing them from colleagues who did not read the same journals or attend the same meetings. On campuses, the academic department provided a home for the professionalized disciplines. At the same time, it offered an administrative solution to the problem of specialist professional autonomy within a standards-based university hierarchy. Borrowing an organizational form from contemporary business enterprise, the architects of the US research university organized departments into divisions, schools, colleges, and the like.[79] Perhaps nothing better distinguishes insider and outsider understandings of the university than familiarity with the department's role.

The department has often been seen as fragmenting intellectual life. In his 1962 history, Frederick Rudolph calls forth the nineteenth-century professor who "contained within himself the knowledge and the interests necessary to sustain him as a teacher of several subjects" and was made obsolete by "the concept of departmentalization, a symbolic statement of the disunity of knowledge which was never made by the old colleges."[80] Indictments of that symbolic statement abound. Rudolph cites the Princeton dean Andrew Fleming West's 1906 lament that "Many of our scholars seem to be subjects of some petty principality rather than freemen in the commonwealth of knowledge."[81] Writing in *Munsey's* in 1901, the president of Lafayette College Ethelbert Warfield assessed the growth of what he called the "Department Store Model," which made the American university structurally different from the European one. "The wide scope of such an institution makes it possible for it to give great service," he allowed, while worrying that "the highest service of university leadership" was imperiled by "an attempt to carry on too many of the departments."[82] Certainly, departments impeded efforts to develop general education, which typically added onto rather than replacing requirements in specialized majors (except in edge cases like St. John's College, which introduced an all-great-books curriculum in 1937). Inevitably, disciplines squabbled among themselves about whether and how to contribute to any synthetic project.

For all that it fragments universities into "petty principalities," departmental organization also secures faculty freedom in hiring and evaluating colleagues. As the peer-review-based system of tenure developed across US universities, one of its most pronounced effects was to strengthen further the hand of departmentalized disciplines, each of which specified its own tenure requirements within general guidelines.[83] Tenure's guarantee of independence from administrative fiat went hand in hand with an in-group professional address and an ever-increasing subdivision of scholarly labor. Biologists, sociologists, and philosophers labored to make themselves relatively free not only from administrative or political reprisal but also from interference by professors who were not biologists, sociologists, or philosophers.[84] Thus did "academic freedom," secured by tenure, proclaim a public interest while simultaneously strengthening specialization. The danger of this self-governance, as Richard Hofstadter and W. P. Metzger present it, was that "in fighting on the line of intramural law . . . the temptation is to make academic freedom coterminous with the security of professors in the guild."[85] Departmentalized, academic freedom was both public facing and inward looking.

Looking back on his three decades of experience with US universities in 1954, the art historian Erwin Panofsky underscored the Janus-faced quality of departmental organization—a feature that above all others distinguished the American system in which he taught from the German system that trained him. Panofsky was well aware that the American fortunes of his discipline had risen with departmental structure: "At the beginning, the new discipline had to fight its way out of an entanglement with practical art instruction, art appreciation, and that amorphous monster 'general education.'" Nonetheless, he preferred the European "chair" system, conceived as "a body of scholars, each surrounded by a cluster of *famuli*," to the American departmental system, conceived as "a body of students entrusted to a teaching staff." Departmentalization not only entailed "isolation and inbreeding" but also an emphasis on testing, certification, and productivity. Panofsky particularly lamented the effect of the system on his graduate students, whom he found haunted by the "specter of completeness." "Humanists cannot be 'trained,'" he declared, "they must be allowed to mature, or . . . to marinate." To this sentiment, he adduced the proverb, "*Liber non est qui non aliquando nihil agit*: 'He is not free who does not do nothing once in awhile.'"[86] As the organizational form that secured for faculty relative autonomy in research and teaching, departments did in fact balance the liberty to let one's mind wander with the requirement to be productive—however poor they may have been at marinating their graduate students.

For all the problems departments created and managed, they did not stabilize organizational charts. As Warfield and Panofsky each suggest, the university grew as academic departments proved adept at making new departments and sometimes at engendering new schools. In 1893, the University of Chicago's biology department spun off five departments: zoology, botany, anatomy, neurology, and physiology. Each had its own chair and internal hierarchy.[87] At Wisconsin in 1917, the Department of Political Economy, having ejected anthropology and sociology, was renamed the Department of Economics. At around this time too, Wisconsin's Department of English spun off journalism, which became a school unto itself, and public speaking, which conferred its first PhD in 1922.[88]

Insofar as academic disciplines do their jobs of producing new knowledge and engaging audiences interested in it, it is entirely reasonable to assume that they will, as a matter of course, subdivide, spin off new approaches, and occasionally enter promiscuous new combinations with one another. Increasing the number of departments has been one way the American academy has accommodated this essential characteristic of specialization. The leveling medium of the Carnegie unit has enabled this accommodation.

Far more than core curricula, then, football and the Carnegie unit made the American research university cohere and allowed it to flourish. Like indoor plumbing, the Carnegie unit has typically been taken for granted when not urgently needed. In contrast, football has often been denounced and admired as proof-positive of the university's mass effect. College football not only brought audiences but also supplied an important reference point in arguments presenting the university as a public good.

When they encountered a university divided into departments offering courses made interchangeable by the Carnegie unit, arguments presenting the university as a public good had to explain how, singly or in some combination, specializations could produce "general" knowledge. This category was built to reinforce the proposition that knowledge shared by undergraduates and professors would serve the interest of the nation as a whole. Arguments linking general education with the public good presupposed, and sometimes paused to explain, that mass improvement would result from providing postsecondary education to a relatively small proportion of the national population. Private universities, even, needed to win the public service argument to secure a tax exemption.[89] In the next chapter, we turn to the research university's mostly extramural public service operations. We hope to have made clear, however, that intramural audiences have never been entirely intramural: football crowds include fans other than students, the credit hour mediates relations between high schools and colleges, and general-education arguments have been pitched to policy makers and parents as much as to faculty and students.

Chapter Two

PUBLIC RELATIONS

Unlike the legends of campus life circulated by magazines and movies, university coursework could not, in and of itself, hope to inform the nation or provide it with a common culture. To do that, general education needed to leave campus and go on the road. Reincarnated as traveling lectures, popular digests, and trade publications, curricular initiatives succeeded in mediating large off-campus audiences. Great Books annexed itself first to the Lyceum and Chautauqua movements and then to a major publishing co-venture of the University of Chicago and Encyclopedia Britannica. Meanwhile, a reformist coalition of natural and social scientists set about popularizing science as a form of democratic participation. Contemporary with the primarily intramural curricular initiatives described in chapter 1, these efforts engaged distinct kinds of extramural audiences. These audiences could, by turns, be rhetorically lumped into a singular public, the target of attempts by university personnel to address the masses, or distinguished as constituencies that each demanded their own particular kinds of attention.

Through general education, popular science, and Great Books, universities both associated themselves with and distinguished themselves from religious authority. General-education curricula presented an array of scholarly disciplines, rather than the classics or the Bible, as a means of cultivating student "character." Yet in this new configuration, the virtues exemplified by classical literature (in translation) and the Bible might still be studied. Within an overarching trend toward secularization, intellectual historians seem to agree, the nineteenth-century college emphasis on Christian "moral education" would not be swept aside so much as nestled awkwardly alongside specialized knowledge production.[1] As translated by popular science writing, the research university's new knowledge more clearly competed with religion, worrying some that "science" had been mystified in the process. The Chautauqua movement, meanwhile, had long combined entertainment, education, and Protestant forms; it proved able to accommodate scholarly pitches willing to adjust to those parameters. Although the nature and strength of Americans' convictions is not our topic, it is important to note that efforts to inform extramural audiences by means of academic knowledge established universities and churches as distinct types of institutions that nonetheless had overlapping audiences and some comparable functions.

The movies also offered university classrooms an ally and extramural rival—one that often seemed more indicative of the moment. Hollywood, numerous studies of the 1910s and 1920s explained, could educate as well as distract, elevate as well as debase. Movies might sweeten classroom lessons through their entertainment properties, baiting students to read the literary works from which they were adapted. They might illustrate times and places students could not directly experience on campus. And they might deserve study in their own right, either as an art form or as an agent of social influence. While offering a tantalizing and sometimes deprecated object of study, Hollywood also provided a model for the lecturer's classroom address. In addition, universities produced movies to extend their educational reach. Although, as the media historian Gregory Waller argues, "educational film" had in this period no stable definition or institutional basis, university extension programs clearly provided a major site for its development and circulation.[2]

Extension programs preceded educational film production; the correspondence course flourished before slides, films, and radio programs supplemented it. Through such media extensions, a course might reach thousands of students. What distinguished this address was not the media involved (print, slides, and movies also featured in traditional classrooms) but rather the relationship between social improvement and self-improvement it called forth. The famed early-century debate between W. E. B.

Du Bois and Booker T. Washington made this difference a defining feature of arguments about social uplift and higher education. Unlike the undergraduate experience, extension was not associated with a particular student lifestyle, did not mark a passage to maturity, and did not aim to certify an elite. Its students took and completed courses as they felt benefited by them. Would this practical, self-help orientation reify social hierarchy (as Du Bois maintained) or transform it (as Washington argued)? The answer was yes.

Extension accommodated a traditionally liberal conception of the public good as aggregated individual benefit, in which students helped society by improving themselves. This approach always wanted to scale up. By the 1920s, however, extension also accommodated a tendency informed by the philosopher John Dewey that favored seminar-scale pedagogies designed to inform new publics by drawing out unarticulated community interests. This approach construed mass media and the lecture hall as its opposites. This opposition cannot be sustained as description of practice. Extension did not stabilize a distinction between face-to-face and point-to-mass pedagogies any better than traditional classrooms or the extracurricular adventures of Great Books. Rather, extension testifies to the multiplicity of university public service initiatives. Wherever adults aimed to improve themselves, there extension strove to be. Whatever media might compel them, universities strove to provide. In extension especially, university efforts to provision a broadly public service appeared to fracture a mass audience into distinct constituencies, for example, farmers, mechanics, and would-be screenplay writers—but also, especially in their Deweyan permutation, to constitute publics as communities of learners.

Defining the relationship between the "public" (imagined to govern itself) and the "mass" (imagined not to) ranked among the period's most vexing intellectual, political, and administrative challenges. Moreover, this way of framing the problem of democratic governance marked a major event in the history of the concept of mediation (and thus a condition of possibility for this book). Several academic specializations joined forces to theorize the challenge presented by what the Fabian social psychologist Graham Wallas influentially called the "Great Society," a global society interconnected by mass media and increasingly managed by bureaucracies and corporations.[3] The results of this interdisciplinary exchange ranged from the landmark 1920s debate between Dewey and Walter Lippmann, which established that mass democracy was not particularly democratic, to the new profession of public relations, which did not consult the public about its opinions so much as seek to intuit, research, and crystallize those opinions. Lessons learned from Great War propaganda efforts lent energy to these arguments. Overall, this set of developments made democracy seem a problem of managing information as opposed to one of extending the franchise, avoiding the "tyranny of the majority," or allowing for debate of the issues. That information problem stipulated, experts could agree to value "the public" without reaching consensus about how to fill the term.

The increasing subdivision of professional labor proliferated forms of public address. Developments off-campus advanced this trend. With the rise of popular science writing, for instance, different groups of university-trained professionals would explain science to the masses than would teach undergraduates and conduct research. Similarly, while turn-of-the-century universities asked English professors to compose promotional copy, by the 1930s those same schools were likely to employ public relations experts (and also offer degrees to credential them). Extension services led the university to hire an instructional staff separate from the traditional faculty and to maintain partnerships with all manner of government and community organizations. Popular science writers, English professors, and extension agents addressed distinct, if sometimes overlapping, audiences. Other kinds of experts flourished by securing the authority to describe the audiences that mass media informed. The media historian Shawn Shimpach proposes that the women volunteers of the Progressive Era's Social Survey Movement played a decisive role in defining what a "media audience" was by quantifying moviegoers' responses.[4] University-trained (mostly male) professionals would later co-opt these survey techniques, delegitimize the volunteers as amateurs, and provide their services to myriad initiatives to influence the masses by means of the movies. As this last example makes particularly clear, increases in the varieties of and possible roles for university-trained experts did not generalize expertise so much as make the university a partner in professional hierarchies of many different sorts. Although public service was the watchword, audience segmentation was arguably the result.

EDUTAINMENT

General education succeeded with off-campus masses by developing cultural forms that combined education and entertainment. General-education advocates leapt out of the classroom to address crowds small and large, in venues ranging from local libraries to Carnegie Hall. Meanwhile, the mass marketing of Great Books as a self-help pedagogy transformed living rooms into seminar rooms, and a new genre of introductions and "outlines" popularized academic research. This genre had a notably chiasmatic effect. It connected lay audiences with university specialists, but it also separated them, by defining "science" in particular as a rarefied domain that ordinary readers would need special interpreters to explain.

To popularize Great Books was to satisfy audience expectations cultivated by other mass-cultural phenomena, as John Erskine's career indicates. Erskine had a longstanding interest in multimedia performance. For instance, his wartime citizenship class at Beaune "consisted of an address followed by an hour of discussion and an hour of lantern-slide and motion picture demonstration."[5] In his history of film study, Dana Polan observes that Erskine, like others who followed him, "imagined Great Books as in a continuum with everyday commercial culture."[6] On this view, the classics could be popularized not against but rather as mass media. Over his career, Erskine increasingly devoted himself to this mission. In 1921, he set aside his scholarly monograph on Milton to finish a novel, *The Private Life of Helen of Troy* (1925), which became a bestseller and an Academy Award–nominated film directed by Alexander Korda. In 1937, he finally and fully disentangled himself from his position at Columbia to travel the lecture circuit. "To a certain extent," he wrote in his memoir, audiences imagined attending "a lecture by the author of a popular book for the purpose merely of spending an hour or so in his company—much as the motion picture audiences like to spend an evening with Clark Gable or with Errol Flynn." This goal was not incompatible, he concluded, with the kind of "lecture series organized by the community in the general hope of self-improvement."[7] He had in mind the legacy of the Lyceum and Chautauqua movements, which by 1900 had established the Protestant sermon, the topical lecture, and popular musical performance as genres related by a common programming strategy for white, middle-class American adults.[8] True to form, Erskine did not miss a beat when audiences requested a piano performance following his lecture on the classics. "Having a few pieces in my fingers," he reports, "I played for nearly half an hour. . . . The news spread that I would play if asked. For the rest of the tour I found myself putting on an elaborate show, first the lecture, then the brief recital."[9] Erskine had adapted his classroom approach to meet the expectations of audiences habituated to the popular lecture-plus-recital format.

The multitalented Erskine was hardly the only professor to take his academic show on the road. Erwin Panofsky, for instance, marveled at the decidedly un-German reception of art history among lecture-loving Americans in 1920s New York, with professors holding forth "not only in seats of learning but also in the homes of the wealthy, the audience arriving in twelve-cylinder Cadillacs, seasoned Rolls-Royces, Pierce-Arrows, and Locomobiles."[10] In 1930, when the then decades-old New Humanism finally enjoyed its fifteen minutes of national fame, Irving Babbitt, Henry Seidel Canby, and Carl Van Doren took to the stage at Carnegie Hall for a debate that drew three thousand spectators. It won predictably gossipy coverage in the *New Yorker*'s "Talk of the Town," which reported spectatorial interest in the cut of Babbitt's evening clothes and Van Doren's "ruddy" good health.[11] In various ways, professors could remain professors and also participate in edutainment forms nurtured by institutions like Chautauqua and social circuits like the New York art and intellectual sets.

For intellectual historians, two lines of argument intersect in the period's edutainment. One concerns the fate of scholarship under the pressure of popularization: there were costs as well as benefits. The other has to do with the authority of "religion" relative to "science" or "secular humanism." Although interpretations vary from historian to historian, the two lines of argument typically collide in concern over what became of science as it worked to displace religion: did popularization make science religion-like? Did it tend to become dogma in which the laity was encouraged to have faith, as opposed to the relentless program of interrogation, experiment, and testing engaged in by its adepts? We see this battle over the integrity of ideas, methods, and souls as part of process of audience formation and segmentation, one that also entailed a subdivision of professional labor.

In his intellectual history, Andrew Jewett usefully describes an early-twentieth-century contest between religiously minded professors and "scientific democrats," a broad and loose transdisciplinary constellation that encompassed many of the period's most prominent social scientists and philosophers as well as key biologists.[12] Rather than the "value-neutral" conception of science much bruited by its midcentury defenders, scientific democrats in the century's early decades promoted science as an ethical orientation capable of overcoming the sectarian religious divisions and checking the excesses of industrial capital. Although not all scientific democrats rejected religion, some, like Dewey, were adamant that organized religion had no role in democratic intellectual life. This placed them squarely at odds with figures like Babbitt and the neo-Thomist Mortimer Adler, who developed ways to accommodate secular expertise and religious conviction. Babbitt, for instance, worried less about social inequality than about the lack of "wisdom" and "character" among elites and proposed education in great books, including the Bible, as a means to stiffen the spines of a select few.

In what would become a familiar rhetorical gesture, Babbitt (in 1908) declared a "crisis" and responded by presenting his specialized approach as generally human intellectual equipment that, as such, could provide a counterpoint to the research university's instrumental knowledge production in the (supposedly more narrow) natural and social sciences.[13] The scientific democrats shared Babbitt's concern that the university would fail to provide an ethical compass, but they thought new knowledge in their specializations, rather than his, should provision it.

Neither camp could expect to sway multitudes without engaging off-campus audiences, but to do so demanded a specific kind of address. The scientific democrats could not expect to follow Erskine's path through the lecture circuit; the Lyceum and Chautauqua legacies required at least nominal observance of the Protestant forms to which they were indebted. Yet, to assert an ethical authority for scientific democracy, they did need to engage audiences already secured by religious sects. A spate of middlebrow books sought to resolve this problem by repackaging specialized research for 1920s audiences, which judging by their popularity surely must have included churchgoers (although in what proportion may be unknowable). In the natural sciences especially, such efforts began to formalize a division of labor in which popular science writer and professor were very different jobs.

Academic reception of the popularizers indicates a process of audience segmentation. Will Durant summed up Dewey's philosophical contribution, among others, in his 1926 bestseller *The Story of Philosophy: The Lives and Opinions of the Greater Philosophers.* Still in print almost a century later, the *Story* leads readers through a selection of continental philosophy from Plato to Nietzsche, pauses in Britain to include Bertrand Russell, and culminates by introducing the early-twentieth-century Americans William James, George Santayana, and Dewey. The psychology professor A. A. Roback began his appraisal for the *Philosophical Review* by observing that the "uncommon success" of the volume suggested the possibility of "other books in the philosophical or at any rate cultural field which could sell well if only sufficiently advertised." Advertising would be essential because the judgments of "professional philosophers . . . do not seem to impress the educated masses." After implicitly crediting Durant's success to his publicists, Roback nonetheless goes on to declare the *Story* "exceedingly stimulating." "It will help to awaken an interest in philosophy on the part of the layman and will be of value to the young student," he explained. In no sense, however, could the volume replace a college-level history of philosophy. In addition to the scandalous omission of Hegel and dubious inclusion of Voltaire, he points out errors of fact and interpretation. Durant had provided a trendy "appetizer" but not the main course.[14] To experience the full meal, one would need actually to major in philosophy. Although it was not for the most serious of academic readers, in short, the *Story* was on their side, underscoring the interest in and appeal of philosophical thought.

A similar combination of professional disdain and respect marked the reception of another 1926 publishing success (also still in print): Paul de Kruif's *Microbe Hunters*. Like Erskine and Durant, de Kruif, a University of Michigan trained microbiologist, left academe to pursue a writing career. Through chapters on Louis Pasteur's lab, Paul Ehrlich's discovery of the first chemotherapy agent, tsetse flies, and phagocytes, *Microbe Hunters* presents science as adventure. A lively stylist, de Kruif invented dialogue among famous medical researchers and so tortured the facts that one of his subjects, the malaria researcher Ronald Ross, saw fit to sue.[15] Nonetheless, *Microbe Hunters* has had plenty of academic fans. It "inspired a generation or more of budding young microbiologists," writes the historian of science and medicine William C. Summers, echoing Roback's sense that such appetizers had real value.[16]

When it came to promoting popularizations of their work, natural scientists were better organized than philosophers. In 1921, for example, the nonprofit Science Service, under the editorial guidance of the journalist and former chemist Edwin Slosson, began syndicating science stories to newspapers nationwide. Increasingly, the training of professional scientists and professional popularizers of science diverged, although the two groups maintained a symbiotic relationship. This may or may not have been good for "science," but it did effectively brand that domain as inaccessible to laymen, a sphere where an all-important "scientific method" generated counterintuitive, world-changing insights incomprehensible to those who could not do the math but that nonetheless could be realized in technologies and translated into simplified language by the press.[17] As the historian Daniel Patrick Thurs puts it, "descriptions of science that have infused it with power and authority have, when given a slight twist, also depicted it as a subject that could be safely ignored."[18] Or, as Jewett explains, popularization of science often communicated "that citizens should learn to defer to scientists and welcome the technological advances they generated."[19] From intellectual history's point of view, that formulation contravenes the main tenets of scientific democracy, which hoped to spread scientific reasoning, not encourage deference to experts.

From the vantage of media history, however, popular science reveals a dilemma likely to be faced by any academic effort to improve the nation. Namely, and by definition in fact, academic expertise is not easily generalized. To reach a broader audience, it requires supplementary forms of mediation and the division of labor required to produce them. By the 1930s, all parties to arguments about scientific democracy confronted an intellectual field in which religious authority vied with the authority not just of secular academic expertise but more specifically its popularized versions.

To offer one last example, Adler's first foray in Great Books outside the university drew on experience he acquired as a lecturer in the People's Institute of New York (a Chautauqua-style venue). With two years of funding from a Carnegie grant beginning in 1926, he brought in a group of "rising young Columbians" including Mark Van Doren and Jacques Barzun to run reading groups in and around Chicago.[20] Developing this approach in a second effort, Adler collaborated with the Chicago Public Library system and delegated instruction to trained lay leaders. Having handed off the instruction, however, Adler held tight to the reading list. Professors continued to determine which books counted as "great." This model appealed to Adler's boss at the University of Chicago, President Robert Maynard Hutchins. In the 1930s and 1940s the two would conspire in launching the Great Books Foundation, which they promoted in *Life*, and in cutting a deal with Encyclopedia Britannica to bring out a book series.[21] The Great Books were marketed to "voluntary groups of adults" in "reading circles" across the country.[22] In 1946 in Chicago, some two thousand people were enrolled in classes taught by faculty and laity in venues that included Marshall Field's department store downtown. Meanwhile, Hutchins and Adler served as discussion leaders for the city's rich, like Walter Paepcke, chairman of the Container Corporation of America, who would go on to found the Aspen Institute, a kind of think tank with public programs.[23] Adler (whom Hutchins was apparently fond of calling the "Great Bookie") hoped for nationwide enrollment of two million.[24] Although he fell short of this goal, nearly a million Great Books sets had sold by the end of the publication run in 1977. As a successful popularization effort, Adler's campaign demonstrated the efficacy of ceding control of the classroom and embracing mass-market publication as an alternative to the syllabus. Chicago eagerly ported the model to film and radio.

THE MOVIES

Lest we forget, movies entered Erskine's classroom well before he got into the screenplay business. One would never know this from the foundational histories of the American university written in the second half of the twentieth century. Although some of these accounts make passing reference to the use of visual aids, they typically represent the mainstream entertainment cinema produced by New York– and California-based firms as both an off-campus undertaking and a threat.

In the early twenty-first century, a different view started to take hold as scholars of film and media studies began to investigate (and complicate) the history of their discipline. Their investigations suggest that preoccupation with the movies informed many, if not most, of the research university's various parts. Polan's *Scenes of Instruction* (2007) disclosed that Hollywood films could be included among the Great Books, as Erskine and Adler proposed, or singled out for appreciation as a distinctive art form, as with Sawyer Faulk's cinema appreciation course at Syracuse University. They could anchor partnerships with industry, as with the University of Southern California's Academy of Motion Picture Arts and Sciences–sponsored curriculum, and also inspire extension-school programs in, for example, photoplay composition at Columbia University.[25] Meanwhile, contributors to the edited collection *Inventing Film Studies* (2008) revealed the university to be enmeshed in a host of initiatives to manipulate film as an instrument of social improvement. Before World War II, this effort connected the university and its professors with libraries, museums, and the League of Nations, in addition to various reform groups and the motion picture industry itself.[26] By compiling writing by women about cinema's first half-century, *The Red Velvet Seat* (2006) revealed the movies to be a key term in wide-ranging arguments about democratic self-governance, mass culture, and prospects for the aesthetic improvement of modern social life.[27] Although women were more likely to find outlets through the press than in university classrooms, they clearly participated in intellectual circuits that informed scholarship on campus.

In the first half of the twentieth century, this scholarship makes clear, the work of explaining the movies as an aesthetic, economic, and social phenomenon was not exclusive to the university, but it was partly based there. In *The Photoplay: A Psychological Study* (1916), the Harvard psychologist Hugo Münsterburg provided an account of cinema's hypnotic suggestion that ramified through a range of disciplines and underwrote the widely held conviction that to manage film content was to manage film audiences.[28] In *The Story of the Films* (1927), leading figures of the motion picture industry surveyed its operations for Harvard's Graduate School of Business Administration.[29] Professors contributed to publications such as the 1926 special issue of the *Annals of the American Academy of Political and Social Science*, in which an essay on "Our Foreign Trade in Motion Pictures" by C. J. North, chief of the Motion Picture Section, US Department of Commerce, appeared alongside articles on "Official Censorship Legislation," by Ford H. MacGregor, associate professor of political science and chief of the Municipal Information Bureau at the University of Wisconsin; "Motion Picture Lighting," by Alvin Wycoff, director of photography for the Famous Players–Lasky Corporation (aka Paramount); and "Public Library Motion Pictures," by the independent scholar (and social activist) Charlotte Perkins Gilman—among several other contributions.[30] Under the rubric of "film appreciation," educators launched campaigns that married analysis of commercial films to projects of civic engagement.[31] In 1933, the Ohio State University education professor Edgar Dale helped secondary schools extend this project by providing a widely used textbook:

How to Appreciate Motion Pictures.[32] The university that studied film was a porous and heterogeneous one in which academic expertise jostled against industrial expertise as well as the authority of government bureaus and social reformers.

Academic credentials mattered in this hierarchy of expertise, but they were not the only factor informing it. As Charlotte Perkins Gilman's scholarly independence indicates, American universities did not embrace women media experts as they did men. Nonetheless, women clearly helped chart the course for investigations of cinematic culture. Before the war, women involved in the Social Survey Movement arguably invented, through their techniques of quantification, the specific conception of audience these investigations typically employed.[33] After the war, it was not difficult to find women who spoke with authority on the movies. At New York's Museum of Modern Art, Iris Barry coached movie viewers in the proper attitude of contemplation and circulated exemplary films to universities for use in classes.[34] In the pages of the *New Republic*, Virginia Woolf described cinemagoers admiringly as "the savages of the twentieth century" and explained that for these primitives to evolve, the medium that entranced them would need to distinguish itself from prior literary forms.[35] Although neither Barry nor Woolf held a professorship, each clearly moved in academic circles.

Research focused on the university's involvement in educational film production and distribution complements the picture provided by histories of film study. The collections *Useful Cinema* (2011) and *Learning with the Lights Off* (2012) began to organize this scholarship, which reveals networks connecting universities with a web of government bureaus, educational associations, and commercial enterprises.[36] Although the various actors did not always agree on what an "educational film" was, they did seek to engage a wide range of on- and off-campus audiences. Educational films might show in traditional classrooms but also in sites as different as public libraries, churches, and farm bureaus.[37] Indicatively, university film production and distribution operations were typically housed in extension divisions, along with radio production facilities. In its efforts to produce and distribute radio as well as to produce, distribute, and study film, the university joined the broader distribution of labor through which these forms and technologies mediated masses.

Thus it should come as no surprise that in his landmark early treatise on the photoplay Münsterberg compares cinema's work with his own. "The greatest mission which the photoplay may have in our community is that of esthetic cultivation," he declares. Experience teaches him that "no training demands a more persistent and planful arousing of the mind than the esthetic training, and never is progress more difficult than when the teacher adjusts himself to the mere liking of the pupils."[38] Movies, like professors, should compel the attention of their audiences, not pander to it. So Harvard had conceived the professor's job in mapping out its approach to large lectures in 1902. The university's Committee on Improving Instruction tasked each professor "to stimulate thought and interest his hearers," while making the teaching assistants "responsible for seeing that the work is done, for helping and explaining, and for maintaining the standard of the course."[39] Of Münsterberg's own performance in this mode, a colleague reported: "When he read in a deep voice to represent the voice of God, the Radcliffe girls had to hide their faces from him and laugh."[40] Lectures, like Hollywood films, could fail on aesthetic grounds, and lecturers could find reason to envy photoplay audiences. "No art reaches a larger audience daily," Münsterberg writes of the movies, "no esthetic influence finds spectators in a more receptive frame of mind." One ought not to be distracted by the greater size and receptivity of motion picture audiences. The historically salient fact is that Radcliffe's and Harvard's student bodies can be compared with them.

By the twentieth century's end, the institutionalization of various forms of media study would make it difficult to perceive the extent to which university professors studied their own problems when they studied mainstream cinema's mass address. Münsterberg's legacy provides one indication of how this happened. Münsterberg held a PhD in psychology from the University of Leipzig. After joining Harvard's faculty in 1892, he helped train a generation of influential American intellectuals, including the sociologist Robert Ezra Park, who completed an MA at Harvard in 1899 before traveling to Germany for PhD work.[41] As a professor at the University of Chicago, Park credentialed Frederic Thrasher, who joined a Motion Picture Research Council team to conduct the landmark Payne Fund studies between 1928 and 1933. Disparate in method and, in the main, inconclusive as social science, reformers nonetheless pointed to these studies as documenting the effects of motion pictures on children. As the media historian Mark Lynn Anderson argues, the studies mattered most for their role in defining and developing the figure of the "media expert," a professional trained and employed by the social science branch of the university, whose work could supplement any number of bureaucratically orchestrated efforts to "improve" populations. As an NYU professor in the mid-1930s, Thrasher embodied this figure, yet his course, "The Motion Picture: Its Artistic, Educational, and Social Aspects," blended film history and appreciation with sociological examination of audiences (especially the students themselves).[42] The capture of media-effects research by the social sciences and film criticism by the arts and humanities may be regarded as an achievement of the interwar period. This remained a relatively porous border, however, before departments and PhDs in "mass communication" and "film studies" became prominent developers of curricula in the closing decades of the century. Then, these disciplines would seem new specializations outside and even alternative to the "core" fields comprised in general education. Historically, however, the problem of understanding mass media was inextricably entangled in the development of higher education's public-facing address to undergraduates—and beyond.

UNIVERSITY EXTENSION

It was by means of extension services that universities most clearly and directly cultivated their influence off campus. These efforts made particularly evident the push-pull of audience binding and audience segmentation as well as the tension between social improvement and hierarchical distinction. Addressed to the practical interests of adult learners, university extension accommodated high-touch as well as point-to-mass instructional models. Often associated with the agricultural programs of land-grant universities, extension services were also developed by elite privates and often pitched as means to diffuse their elitism. Extension was a transmedia undertaking. Incorporation of audiovisual materials did not, however, distinguish extension from traditional classrooms. Chicago's President Hutchins in 1931 advertised use of the university's educational film co-productions in its newly revised general-education curriculum, for instance.[43] Extension service departments did play a key role as distributors (on campus and off) of university-owned film prints and as radio producers and broadcasters. What mainly made extension different, however, was the issue exposed by one of the early twentieth century's major arguments linking democracy and higher education.

Before the war, W. E. B. Du Bois and Booker T. Washington conducted a defining version of the debate over the value of self-improvement as a goal of higher education. Du Bois criticized Washington's Tuskegee Normal and Industrial Institute for its emphasis on vocational training. The project of racial uplift would be better served, he argued, by educating a "Talented Tenth," who could vie for authority with white elites and shift the terms of national culture. For his part, Washington argued that progress in race relations would eventually be achieved not through cultural-political agitation but through the self-improved material circumstances of masses of Black folks. He aimed "not so much to educate a few hundred or a few thousand . . . as to change conditions among the masses of the Negro people."[44] To do this, Tuskegee aggressively set up extension programs, establishing, by the turn of the century, operations in twenty-eight states, four Caribbean territories, and Africa.[45] The Tuskegee curriculum, which had both occupational and normal tracks, facilitated this activity. Though destined for the classroom or pulpit, each four-year normal-school student also chose coursework in an occupational skill such as millinery, typesetting, or carpentry. Training in community leadership was also required. Du Bois trivialized Washington's project in a 1912 Indianapolis *Star* article when he found "no culture or uplift in washing clothes." He nonetheless gave a backhanded compliment in calling it the "Tuskegee Machine."[46] Washington's engine of social transformation appeared to Du Bois as a way to keep African Americans in their place, while Washington thought Du Bois's commitment to cultural uplift more likely to have that result.

Regardless of who was right, this argument made the question of how to revise American social hierarchy answerable in terms of competing educational models. Those models could be caricatured as "liberal arts" and "vocational" but also as "elite" and "practical." One seemed to entail polishing the character of brainy youths; the other addressed directly the material needs and interests of adults. The early-twentieth-century boom in extension programs guaranteed that the research university would embrace both approaches, along with the arguments defending each against the other. Universities did not generally organize themselves according to the Tuskegee model, in other words, nor did they adopt anything like its cohesive sense of mission. Rather, extension emerged as a typically parallel, often bureaucratically separate, part of the research university.

As more and more universities opened extension departments and schools, various national initiatives arose to facilitate their address to a widening array of public interests. Already by the early 1890s, Wisconsin had opened forty-seven centers of instruction in thirty-four towns, and New York offered extension courses throughout the state—in Yonkers, for example, three hundred students showed up for an astronomy class.[47] In 1914, the Smith-Lever Extension Act promoted this kind of activity by providing elevated levels of funding for extension schools and stations operated by the land-grant schools. The National University Extension Association formed in 1915, with twenty-two charter members attending the organization's first meeting at Wisconsin. The Carnegie Corporation supported the expansion of adult education through the American Association for Adult Education (AAAE), launched in 1926.[48] Often working in tandem with other professionalizing initiatives, extension services competed with proprietary schools in areas like law and business.[49]

Although extension played a key role in the land-grant universities, elite privates also helped develop the model. A founding member of the National Extension Association, Harvard hosted a collaborative adult education endeavor involving faculty from a range of Boston-area schools and the Museum of Fine Arts. The driver of this enterprise was Abbott Lawrence Lowell, a patriarchal trustee of the Lowell Institute from 1900 and president of Harvard from 1909.[50] From 1910, Harvard's university extension gave students the chance to earn a degree whose only distinction from a Harvard/Radcliffe credential was that it did not require residency. By 1922, twenty-nine courses were offered; some enrolled more than two hundred students.[51] At land-grant schools, meanwhile, services provided by farm stations and agricultural services played a different but not unrelated role in establishing public value. Experts oversaw quality control when a new state fertilizer law was introduced, supplied seed corn, and in other ways embedded the school in rural industry. Where Harvard's extension could claim to democratize the undergraduate experience, these other types of land-grant activities helped convince taxpayers that the state college worked for them, regardless of its more theoretical pursuits.[52]

Extension courses developed along two distinct tracks: discussion-based teaching in person and distance learning. Where Adler's Great Books

approach staked the improving power of discussion to professional determination of the curriculum, extension provided a forum for discussion-
based pedagogies that cast the ability to guide conversation, irrespective of
content, as the professor's most valuable skill. "Schoolmen" who "find their
center of interest in curriculum-making" are wasting their time, wrote the
professor of social work Edward Lindeman in *The Meaning of Adult Education* (1926).[53] A former student of Dewey, Lindeman maintained that a
good teacher would not cast "about with various kinds of bait until he gets
back his preconceived answer" but rather challenge students to test what
they know against what they encounter and to work with others to ask better questions.[54] Adult educators should "bridge the gap between experts
and experience," he argued.[55] Lindeman envisioned a manifold constitu-
ency for adult education, composed as often by scientists looking to learn
more about art as by farmers seeking the latest techniques for fertilization.
Such adult learners were fundamentally different from undergraduate
"credit-baggers" and "degree-hunters." They "attend classes voluntarily and
they leave whenever the teaching falls below the standard of interest."[56]
Adult education demanded that professors engage student interests as a
precondition to offering their expertise—this was its virtue.

Yet the small-group discussion idealized by Lindeman was not the predominant instructional mode. From the outset, universities were eager to
provide adult education through correspondence courses and other educational mass media. The correspondence course proved highly lucrative
for profit-making enterprises like the Scranton-based International Correspondence Schools (ICS), established in 1890. ICS served students nationwide and claimed more than four million alumni by 1930.[57] The young
research universities were quick to get in on the game, often seeking out
students far beyond any regional sphere of influence. The 1893 *Extension
Bulletin* of the New York State Regents observes that the University of Chicago's correspondence course operation was "taking active steps to carry
on this teaching in the state of New York," which alarmed Cornell and
other local schools "earnestly desirous that this teaching should be done
within our own state."[58] Wisconsin struck a deal with the Army and Navy
YMCA to distribute its classes.[59] Pennsylvania State University organized
a "Chautauqua course of home reading in agriculture" whose 1899 enrollment totaled more than 3,400 students from across the United States. Those
students collectively received more than 1,800 lessons by mail and returned

more than 1,200 optional examinations to be evaluated.[60] Still, this activity paled in comparison to that of for-profit services: by 1910 there were over two hundred proprietary correspondence schools in the United States offering classes that ranged from agriculture to mechanical engineering, home improvement, and academic preparation.[61] The courses could be general and also extraordinarily specialized: ICS offered distinct courses in steam engineering calibrated to different horsepower engines, for example.[62] This was, truly, teaching at scale.

Scaling up involved providing large numbers of students the same instructional materials as well as customizing approaches for specific audiences. This was a competitive market—in 1916, ICS projected spending two million dollars annually on advertising (around $44.5 million in 2017 dollars).[63] Like for-profits, land-grant universities constantly innovated new courses to satisfy a multifarious public demand. In 1915, the Wisconsin extension dean Louis Reber outlined a plan of "carrying the University to the homes of the people" and giving them "what they need—be it the last word in expert advice; courses of study carrying University credit; or easy lessons in cooking and sewing."[64] What they seemed to need most were business and engineering classes, but English, mathematics, and home economics were also popular. To recruit students and identify areas for course development, Wisconsin's pace-setting extension department relied on a team of field representatives.[65] At the other end of the spectrum, the recently hired University of Kentucky president Frank L. McVey tasked himself and his personal secretary with recruiting faculty and organizing correspondence courses, "general welfare work, debates and public forum[s]" in a 1919 push to expand Kentucky's extension services beyond agriculture.[66]

Film could be annexed to discussion-based pedagogies as well as mass-delivery schemes. Most notably, the 1915 innovation of the Columbia University Extension's photoplay composition course treated filmmaking as "craftsmanship" that, according to Polan, would improve pupils not via "the rush of emotion in the face of great art but from pride in learning a skill and participating in a job well done."[67] The film historian Kaveh Askari explains that, by administrative design, the course brought into the university extension the "picture study" approach that characterized discussions of art on the Lyceum circuit and especially at the Brooklyn Institute of Arts and Sciences, one of that circuit's major venues.[68] After two years, Francis Patterson took over the Columbia course from its creator, Victor Freeburg. Its emphasis shifted to producing commercially viable screenplays. Nonetheless, Patterson shared Freeburg's interest in elevating "the tastes of the public, which they contrast with 'the mass,' in desiring better films" as well as his conviction that a successful extension course could contribute to that project.[69]

The development of instructional film as a supplement to the distance- and distributed-learning track was coeval and put universities in the business of film production and distribution. As early as 1914, the University of Indiana's extension circulated films and lantern slides.[70] Just as the War Issues curriculum encouraged postwar development of general education, so too did federal mobilization spur university filmmaking. Indiana collaborated with extensions in Iowa and Wisconsin to produce *Gardening*, *Canning*, and *Drying*, three films that generated overwhelming requests for showings beginning in July 1917. The films supported the national effort to conserve resources needed for war. George Creel, the director of the Committee on Public Information, took note and called Indiana's extension director, J. J. Pettijohn, to join his staff in Washington. Pettijohn brought key members of Indiana's extension staff with him, and in the war's aftermath they joined him in his office when he was appointed director of the Federal Division of Educational Extension in the US Department of the Interior. The Indiana team successfully lobbied President Wilson and Congress to donate war-surplus films and lantern slides to university extension divisions nationwide, with the idea that these universities would then become regional distribution centers.[71] On average, each extension division received 113 reels.[72] Although federal support for visual aids quickly evaporated, the effort was critically important in regularizing the educational use of film nationally.

It became common for extension divisions to include a Bureau of Visual Instruction, an entity likely to provide instructional support on campus in addition to off-campus distribution. If the situation at the University of South Carolina is any indication, supplying that service posed an ongoing challenge. Describing the important work of the extension division amid financial difficulties in 1926, the student newspaper noted that the "Division plans to revive its Visual Education service as soon as practical" and went on to explain that the service "gives advice about all matters connected with visual instruction in the schools, and furnishes films upon historic, scientific, and other educational subjects."[73] Although their full story remains to be written, a number of imperatives seem to have collided in the Bureaus of Visual Instruction: to support learners on campus as well as off, to support any and all disciplines, to provide pedagogical advice as well as circulating film prints, and to do so on a budget appropriate to a peripheral as opposed to an essential service department.

In contrast to the Bureaus of Visual Instruction, which appear to have proliferated despite lackluster support, university production of educational films remained concentrated in a handful of institutions (although here again, much work remains to be done to provide a comprehensive picture). The expense and expertise involved in film production, particularly after the transition to synchronized sound, was likely a factor, but so too were institutional commitments and the ability to attract outside investment. Before the United States entered World War I, Midwestern land-grant schools led the field in film production, and the Ivies joined the game after the Treaty of Versailles. Yale, for instance, began making educational films in the early 1920s, including the noteworthy Chronicles of America series (1923–25), and Harvard established production operations in its Film Foundation (later renamed the Film Service) in 1928.[74] By the early 1930s, the University of Chicago had emerged as a leading producer through its partnerships with Electrical Research Products Inc. (ERPI), a subsidiary of AT&T's subsidiary Western Electric. ERPI did not draw its academic experts from Chicago alone. *The Wheat Farmer* (1938) was "produced in collaboration with Dr. H. P. Hartwig of Cornell University," for example. But Chicago was clearly the center of educational film production in the United States, with the University of Chicago a major partner.[75] In 1943, the advertising executive and University of Chicago vice president William Benton engineered a deal to acquire Encyclopedia Britannica, with the university as part owner. At the same time, he created Encyclopedia Britannica Films (EBF), the leading classroom film producer for the second half of the century, and acquired in the process its most important forebears, ERPI Classroom Films and Eastman Teaching Films.[76] As with the Britannica-linked Great Books initiative, EBF capitalized on decades of Chicago-based entrepreneurial zeal for educational mass media.

Among the period's new media, radio particularly appealed to federal and foundation partners for its ability to extend the university's reach. In the 1920s, land-grant universities in Wisconsin, Kansas, Michigan,

Minnesota, and Ohio launched especially significant early "schools of the air." Illinois, Iowa State, and Oklahoma developed important stations as well.[77] The Association of College and University Broadcasting Stations (later the National Association of Educational Broadcasters) attempted to orchestrate their efforts beginning in 1925. The US Department of Agriculture played an important role in radio production (as it did in film), where it saw an opportunity to build on university farming extension work. Working with the land-grant universities, the USDA encouraged farmers to construct their own inexpensive receivers.[78] The universities relied on the USDA for the market information they disseminated as well, solidifying a longstanding relationship between agricultural extension and governmental public service broadcasting. Corporate foundations also took an interest. In 1926, Carnegie, through its American Association for the Education of Adults, supported a National Advisory Council on Radio in Education (NACRE), which started work in 1930. In 1931, a Payne Fund grant to the National Committee on Education by Radio established the Institute for Education by Radio at Ohio State.

Over time, these efforts and others helped secure the notion that educational, public service radio might provide an alternative to commercial networks. The broadcast historian Michele Hilmes observes that university-produced radio programs (often on university-owned stations) provided one of two models for the development of public service broadcasting in the United States. The BBC provided the other, a nationally funded and managed broadcast system that made the American approach seem chaotic by comparison. Hilmes sees university radio and the BBC as "two competing poles between which US public broadcasting philosophy would swing" for much of the twentieth century.[79] Nor was there a bright line between public service and commercial broadcasting before the Public Broadcasting Act of 1967. For much of the century, commercial networks had good reasons to present themselves to audiences and federal regulators as airing programs that were in the nation's interest. Beginning in 1933, for example, NBC broadcast *University of Chicago Round Table*, an important public affairs discussion program that the edutainment pioneer Chicago created with Rockefeller Foundation support.

Whether it meant enrolling in a screenwriting seminar or listening to a radio program devoted to farming techniques, extension informed audiences different from undergraduate degree seekers. The difference did not reside in the varieties of media that informed them. True, correspondence courses, community film screenings, and radio broadcasts promoted different spatiotemporal arrangements than traditional classrooms, but extension students might be found in classrooms too, and the same films might show on campus and off. Moreover, just like the undergraduates who completed different versions of general education because they went to different schools, extension's various audiences can be distinguished from one another. If anything unites the category of "extension student," it is the promise of self-improvement. Depending on the approach and one's point of view, this promise either tacitly accepts the social hierarchy that provides the context for improvement or works to undermine it by constituting a community of learners.

MEDIA EXPERTS

In the 1920s, after constitutional amendments had provided the direct election of senators and expanded the franchise to women, and after the propaganda lessons of World War I, it seemed particularly notable that unelected experts were playing a greater role in national governance.[80] Those experts worked for relatively new government bureaus—such as the Federal Reserve (established 1913)—that set and oversaw policies directly. The Fed consigned to economists the monetary disputes that had been a focus of electoral politics.[81] Unelected experts also governed, as it were, through their work for what one might call influence industries—all manner of philanthropic foundations, cultural institutions, public relations operations, and, of course, mass-media producers that either aimed to shape policy or were seen as defining the environment on which policy would act and within which voters would vote. What could democratic self-governance mean in these circumstances? This was the question, and the challenge, of the Lippmann-Dewey debate.

Where prior arguments tended to present print as a means to extend democratic conversations, Lippmann and Dewey depicted mass media, including print, as a likely impediment to democracy, one that experts would need to manage. With one foot planted outside the university and another in it, this dispute theorized public opinion as a site of professional intervention by social scientists, journalists, publicists, and education experts while asking in what sense it could even be called "public." As such, the argument anchors much subsequent discussion about what it means to invoke "the public" in a mass-mediated republic.[82]

Lippmann launched the debate in *Public Opinion* (1922) by drawing attention to the difference between "the world outside" and "the pictures in our heads." Synthesizing recent trends in psychology, sociology, anthropology, semiology, and philosophy with his own study of the press, Lippmann developed "the stereotype" as a concept necessary for understanding our relation to the world. On this account, mass mediation and perceptual habit combined to predispose judgments in situations where traditional democratic theory expected decisions born of enlightened self-interest. As stereotype makers and tweakers grew more sophisticated and as global societies became more integrated and complex, ordinary citizens could not hope to acquire the knowledge necessary for meaningful determinations of their interests: they would necessarily make judgments based on stereotypes as opposed to the real environment. The only solution Lippmann could see for this problem was more deliberate intervention by professionals. Government bureaus would need not only social scientists capable of working out where the public interest lay but also experts capable of framing decisions in such a way that voters could make meaningful "yes" or "no" decisions about them. A working journalist throughout his career and not infrequently a presidential advisor, Lippmann was particularly concerned to specify an appropriate professional role for the commercial press.

Dewey's rebuttal took the form, first, of an exchange with Lippmann in the *New Republic* (which Lippmann had helped found in 1914) and then a series of lectures at Kenyon College, subsequently published as *The Public and Its Problems* (1927). Dewey, then a professor at Columbia University, shared Lippmann's premises and especially his critique of individual judgment, that ideal at the core of classical liberal democratic theory. His own philosophical work had informed Lippmann on this topic, and they had many of the same teachers. Dewey rejected Lippmann's technocratic solution, however. The answer to the public's problems, he thought, was an ongoing educational project that looked like a conversation.

Agreeing in the main with Lippman that "Symbols control sentiment and thought," Dewey proclaimed that "the new age has no symbols consonant with its activities."

We have the physical tools of communication as never before. The thoughts and aspirations congruous with them are not communicated, and hence are not common. Without such communication the public will remain shadowy and formless, seeking spasmodically for itself, but seizing and holding its shadow rather than its substance. Till the Great Society is converted into a Great Community, the Public will remain in eclipse. Communication can alone create a great community. Our Babel is not one of tongues but of the signs and symbols without which shared experience is impossible.[83]

Dewey saw "communication" as the opposite of the point-to-mass address typical of newspapers and especially movies. It was a fundamentally face-to-face phenomenon.[84] In *The Public and Its Problems*, this emphasis recalls that of the organizational theorist Mary Parker Follett, for whom the face-to-face encounter modeled both participatory democracy and a well-managed corporation.[85] Elsewhere, Dewey tended to place educators and educational institutions at the center of the democratic community-building project.[86] His community-as-classroom still privileged dialogue. Print might assist in but would not accomplish democratic communication.

For Dewey as well as Lippmann, the question whether the Great Society's masses could function as a self-determining public hinged on whether alternative forms of symbolic activity could be instituted. The public was shaped by the content that informed it. Individuals developed opinions through mediation.

It should be clear that our project in this book owes no small debt to this formulation. Considered in the theoretical terms that emerged from the Lippmann-Dewey debate, a self-governing public looked practically difficult, if not impossible. The public's problems were not, it turned out, of a sort the public could spontaneously understand on its own. Stereotypes circulated by mass media thwarted rather than enhanced understanding, yet the potential public at issue was much bigger than a face-to-face conversation could ever be. Some coordination would have to occur, but the agencies that might accomplish that did not yet exist. Lippmann and Dewey did not agree on what those agencies should be. They could agree, however, that democratic society would require the university and its experts. Although the debate did not resolve the question of how mass mediated society could be made democratic, it did establish "the public" as a practical and conceptual mediation problem on which a wide array of university-trained and -employed experts might go to work. This problem endured in the twenty-first century after social media—with its manifold communities, audience niches, and competing accusations of "fake news"—had displaced the figure of a mass public unified, for better or worse, by the press, movies, and radio.

From the start, public relations fit awkwardly into the professor's job description. Public service was, in the abstract, the profession's raison d'etre, but it was assumed that professors, as experts, would spend most of their time addressing smaller audiences of students and peers. When Erskine hit the road to promote Great Books, he clearly stepped out of his expected role as an English professor. Some English professors, however, were formally recruited for their universities' promotional efforts. In 1904, the University of Wisconsin enlisted its English Department to write bulletins conveying to newspapers "in an attractive way, the story of discoveries, inventions, and innovations" across campus.[87] This effort received national recognition. Numerous magazine articles established it as a model other schools hungry for press were quick to reproduce. Some, like the University of North Carolina, hired students to write dispatches. Others relied on their president to spread the word.[88] After the war, the University of Kentucky adopted another logical solution by turning to professors in its Journalism Department.[89] For a time, then, it seemed that expertise in fields like English and journalism might equip professors and students to double as university press agents.

By 1930, however, university public relations had become a function central administration assigned to specially trained experts. In his 1928 *Propaganda*, no less a figure than the public relations pioneer Edward Bernays recognized the universities as early adopters of PR methods. He reported that the American Association of College News Bureaus (established in 1917) then had some seventy-five members, including Yale, California, and Indiana. "It may surprise and shock some people," Bernays reported via a columnist in the magazine *Personality*, "to be told that the oldest and most dignified seats of learning in America now hire press agents, just as railroad companies, fraternal organizations, moving picture producers and political parties retain them. It is nevertheless a fact."[90] Working with societies like the National Education Association, Bernays noted, universities used publicity not only to promote themselves and their professors but also to redress more general concerns such as the prestige of teachers.

Bernays's 1920s volumes are theoretical statements explicitly in dialogue with the partly academic conversation captured in the Lippmann-Dewey debate. Consonant with that conversation in general, Bernays assumes that the public cannot explain itself or understand its best interests absent the guidance of university-trained professionals—professionals distinct, however, from professors of English or journalism. He introduced the "new" figure of the "public relations council" in *Crystallizing Public Opinion* (1923), noting "press agent," "publicity man," and "propagandist" as different names for basically the same job. That job was to be the person who "interprets the client to the public, which he is enabled to do in part because he interprets the public for the client." The public relations council blended "intuitive understanding" with "practical and psychological tests and surveys" in order to "crystallize" existing predispositions such that they might benefit, and also help define, a client's objectives.[91] Problem: "Cornell University discovers endowments are rare. Why? Because the people think the University is a state institution and therefore publicly supported." Solution: employ public relations experts to change the story.[92] Often these experts worked indirectly, relying on third parties to adjust public attitudes. The profession flourished by explaining the public as much as by influencing it.

In the turn to press agents—and as with football, Great Books, popular science, motion picture research, and extension services—universities discovered that to engage a broader public required more, not less, specialized expertise. Moreover, engagement required a division of labor in which experts explained the work of other experts in ways that different audiences could appreciate. Not infrequently, this work of explanation faced the challenge of identifying the eventual benefit of any research or teaching endeavor—especially one that appeared esoteric or obscure—and noting that its value might be inversely proportional to any immediate appeal. Wisconsin's President Van Hise provided an influential declaration of this principle in his 1905 inaugural address: "It cannot be predicted at what distant nook of knowledge, apparently remote from any practical service, a brilliantly useful stream may spring."[93] Through this artful turn of phrase, Van Hise established that knowledge deemed useless today might seem essential tomorrow and insinuated that brilliance shined most brightly out of public view.

Whatever their validity, appeals to the public value of specialized knowledge production may always be undercut by calling attention to the socioeconomic gap separating those who labor in Van Hise's "distant nook" from those supposed to benefit from their "brilliantly useful" knowledge. The socialist muckraker Upton Sinclair deftly exploited this opening when addressing New England workers in 1923:

Slaves in Boston's great department store, in which Harvard University owns twenty-five hundred shares of stock, be reconciled to your long hours and low wages and sentence to die of tuberculosis—because upon the wealth which you produce some learned person has prepared for mankind full data on "The Strong Verb in Chaucer." . . . Men who slave twelve hours a day in front of blazing white furnaces of Bethlehem, Midvale and Illinois Steel, cheer up and take a fresh grip on your shovels—you are making it possible for mankind to acquire exact knowledge concerning "The Beginnings of the Epistolary Novel in the Romance Languages."[94]

Sinclair doubtlessly demonstrates familiarity with his audience when he singles out research on Chaucer and epistolary novels. Nonetheless, his point would be equally valid had he selected correspondence courses in merchandising or advanced degrees in metallurgy. In its "cultural" as well as its "practical" specializations, the university was fully imbricated in an economic (and raced and gendered) system that benefited the few more than the many, and not necessarily because those few worked harder or were smarter than the rest. As ever in the neighborhood of the American Dream, fast footwork is needed to present the possibility of individual success—in Chaucer studies or anything else—as a broadly public value.

University experts addressed the public without being of the public. The public had as many guises as the university's experts could conceive audiences to improve. The "citizens safe for democracy" that Columbia's Contemporary Civilization aimed to incubate did not look like the curious movie-ticket- and book-buying adults whose attention Erskine, de Kruif, and Encyclopedia Britannica hoped to compel. Nor did they resemble Tuskegee's far-flung agents of uplift, Midwestern farmers tuning in university broadcasts on homebuilt receivers, or Columbia's aspiring screenplay writers. Across the disciplines, but with especially pronounced effects in the natural sciences, academic research came to rely on specialized popularizers to translate its import to a broad audience. Professors were likely to greet those more journalistic efforts with an admixture of suspicion and envy—they were not the real thing, but they whet student appetites nonetheless.

In the process of structuring a new national system of higher education and credentialing experts of various sorts, America's research universities succeeded in making themselves essential to defining and intervening in the public as an analytic problem. They did not, however, win the authority to manage it. Commercial media provided clearer examples of how the public could be influenced, and perhaps educated, by means of a centrally planned and massively distributed address. Universities found a model and a competitor in commercial motion pictures (as in organized religion). As we shall show, this pattern repeats itself.

As a sector, then, higher education secured its position among key American institutions by learning to address abstractly "general" and concretely plural publics through myriad media. In this, American schools departed from their precedents in Europe and distinguished themselves from the small colleges that dotted the nation's nineteenth-century landscape. As the federal government expanded its scope in the New Deal and World War II, the university's multifaceted address made it possible for federal dollars to transform higher education by organizing classrooms and research centers as major components of a midcentury communications complex.

Chapter Three

COMMUNICATIONS COMPLEX

A communications complex, far more than a military-industrial complex, connected the university with diverse and sometimes competing initiatives after World War II. This communications complex began to develop before the war under the auspices of philanthropies like the Rockefeller Foundation and through the efforts of trendsetters like the MIT engineer–turned–federal bureaucrat Vannevar Bush. The key players instituted a pattern of federal research investment very different from the previous war's. In World War I, federally funded efforts to develop new weapons and improve military medicine took place mainly inside government laboratories. In contrast, World War II planners distributed research tasks across universities and partners in private industry as well as federal departments. In so doing, they set a precedent for the wide array of new federal granting agencies that, in combination with the Serviceman's Readjustment Act of 1944 (the GI Bill), fueled rapid and dramatic university expansion after the war.

Communication ranked first among the topics of study caught up in this change: as a research problem it attracted significant federal as well as foundation investment and linked breakthroughs across the human and natural sciences. In the preceding chapters we described how President Wilson's administration, through its support for the War Issues curriculum as well as the sweeping domestic propaganda initiatives of the Committee on Public Information (CPI), lent impetus to general-education curricula, set up the landmark debate between Walter Lippmann and John Dewey, and helped define public relations as a distinct discipline. The federal government directly sponsored none of these postwar developments, however, and propaganda did not again become its priority until the United States formally entered the next world war. At that point, numerous agencies were tasked with analyzing propaganda, producing it directly, and orchestrating efforts involving nongovernmental outlets. In the preamble to war, the Rockefeller Foundation played a decisive role in organizing the effort, described by its Humanities Division head John Marshall as the quest for a "genuinely democratic propaganda."[1] After the war, the contradictions of "democratic propaganda" connected the Rockefeller Foundation's prewar agenda with myriad Cold War activities to understand and manage communications. As with investment in other research areas, the US government funded much of this work, which linked a web of fields dispersed across a network of universities and other institutions.

Researchers analyzed communications as a system, and communications systems connected them. Through efforts as much practical as theoretical, researchers of many stripes came to understand communication neither as an exchange of messages nor (per Lippmann and Dewey) as signs and symbols that informed mass opinions (although this function mattered). Rather, communication was reconceived as a complex system comprising several distinct components and functions. These components and functions could be studied discretely or in combination. They would likely include machines as well as human beings. Perhaps above all others, Harold Lasswell's name is associated with this schematization, which informed conversation starters as different as Claude Shannon and Warren Weaver's *The Mathematical Theory of Communication* (1949) and I. A. Richards's popular translation of *The Iliad: The Wrath of Achilles* (1950). Connecting work in the new disciplines of mass communications and computer science with New Critical literary studies, Lasswell's schema also informed key work in design and the interdiscipline of cybernetics, as we will discuss in chapter 4. The subsequent development of each of these disciplines has obscured their midcentury relation and occulted the degree to which they shared the problem of communication.

After the war, communications research informed the CIA's efforts abroad and domestically along with myriad other projects aimed at understanding and influencing conduct for economic and social purposes. These legacies of prewar work on "democratic propaganda" enmeshed the university's experts ever more tightly in the work of administering populations conceived as audiences. As elements in communications systems, citizens did not speak for themselves. Their predispositions could be studied and predicted. What they said might be lost in the noise or selected and magnified to promote particular effects. Some had much better access to communications channels than others. Different kinds of academic expertise would be required to model and shape their behavior as well as to question in what sense it could be called "democratic."

THE COMPLEX SCALES UP

To fight World War II, the US federal government scaled up its research effort not merely by increasing funding but also by developing the information management strategies necessary to outsource research to universities. In World War I, military and civilian leaders had called upon academic and corporate chemists for poison-gas research and physicists for work on machine guns and submarines. Typically, it seconded them to government agencies and laboratories.[2] As that war ended, Woodrow Wilson's administration chartered the National Research Council and then ignored it, quickly disengaging the federal government from scientific research outside its own bureaus.[3] In contrast, Harry Truman's post–World War II administration institutionalized and extended a model developed during the war to fund university-based research at unprecedented peacetime levels.

Between the world wars, universities began to develop institutional forms that allowed them to take, make, and reinvest funding from whatever source.[4] The Wisconsin Alumni Research Foundation (WARF) modeled an arrangement that would become ubiquitous by century's end. WARF was founded in 1925 to "manage the university's patents and invest the resulting revenue to support future research," a development prompted by a vitamin D discovery made by the Madison professor Harry Steenbock.[5] Other early success stories included the Wisconsin agriculture professor Karl Paul Link's anticoagulant warfarin (named after WARF), from which subsequent research derived the widely prescribed blood thinner

Coumadin.[6] By 2016, WARF could report an endowment of nearly $2.7 billion. In this model, the university acts as its own grant maker. It hopes to capitalize upon its faculty's inventions in order to fund future work.

In contrast, the development of a federal granting apparatus not only allowed the research enterprise to scale but also worked to subordinate local priorities to national needs. The new federal approach worked by managing information, not professors. Bureaucrats defined program goals, vetted proposals (often with the assistance of peer reviewers), and made awards. Universities built and maintained their own research infrastructure and sought to recover much of that cost through grants. Intramural research schemes, like those the federal government employed in World War I, could require that staff be hired and labs built to undertake new research. By taking advantage of existing university staffs and facilities, the new approach allowed research efforts to scale up almost as fast as checks could be written and paper pushed. To write those checks and push that paper, the federal government created an alphabet soup of postwar agencies, including the Atomic Energy Commission (AEC), the Office of Naval Research (ONR), the National Institutes of Health (NIH), and the National Science Foundation (NSF) in 1950 as well as, in 1965, the National Endowment for the Humanities (NEH) and the National Endowment for the Arts (NEA).[7] This approach developed and indeed required a massive communications capacity not only to publicize and review the grants but also to disseminate research results.

The federal research enterprise with the longest lineage provides perhaps the best example of how research scaled up. The National Institutes of Health descends from the Marine Hospital Service, established during the early years of the republic, and more directly from its Hygienic Laboratory, established in 1887 to investigate contagious diseases. Although Congress renamed it the Public Health Service in 1902, its staff physicians continued to be organized along military lines under the surgeon general. In 1930, the Ransdell Act renamed the US Hygienic Laboratory as the National Institute of Health, but the institution's emphasis remained overwhelmingly on funding research within Public Health Service laboratories. The 1931 fiscal-year appropriation for the NIH was $43,000, or around $661,000 in 2017 dollars. (In 2017, its fiscal-year budget was $33.1 billion.)[8]

To become the major supporter of university and corporate research familiar to twenty-first-century scholars, the NIH shifted its emphasis away from intramural research. The 1937 National Cancer Act provides a conventional marker; it established the National Cancer Institute and authorized it to provide research grants and fellowships to researchers at medical schools and other academic institutions.[9] This novel approach became the rule after the war, as the NIH was gradually pulled away from the Surgeon General's Office.[10] From a model that contained public research funding within a quasi-military organization, the NIH grew into a distributed arrangement wherein US government officials managed research efforts conducted by relatively autonomous institutions that eventually spanned the globe. The NIH was not simply orders of magnitude larger than the Public Health Service; it had been redesigned as an organization built to scale more easily.

At the NIH as elsewhere, the new bureaucratic approach required deliberate attention to the problem of sharing research questions and results. Accordingly, in the postwar period, the former Hygienic Laboratory itself began to act more clearly as an administrator and disseminator of information. Operating a sophisticated media service through its library became a key function.

The idea of a national medical library was an old one, but microfilm made it a reality. As early as 1870, the Hygienic Laboratory librarian John Shaw Billings (a surgeon by training) promoted the Army Medical Library as a national facility available for use by all physicians.[11] Between the two World Wars, the library's status followed the general trend in federal research support. By the late 1930s, it faced serious deficiencies of space, acquisitions, and cataloging. Its main bibliographic resource, the *Index-Catalogue*, was notoriously out of date.[12] This did not prevent the library from contributing to the war effort, however. In 1941, it began using microfilm to circulate its new *Current List of Medical Literature*, a rapidly produced index of recent articles in medical journals.[13] As its popular photoduplication service rapidly expanded, it began to look more and more like the Army Medical Library's central function. Although the bulk of the wartime orders came from military units, it also had civilian patrons.[14]

That balance shifted after the war, when military-surplus V-mail equipment allowed the library to provide print copies for civilian researchers who lacked film viewers.[15] By 1952, the service had expanded to fulfill 88,000 orders per year, nearly fifteen times as many as it had a decade earlier, and "microfilm copying amounted to more than half the use of the

Library."[16] Four years later, the Army Medical Library was recognized and renamed the National Library of Medicine under the Public Health Service. This led to its becoming a part of the NIH and enabled "the Library to rise to its full potential as the Nation's medical library and center of biomedical communications."[17] Although other placements for the library in the federal organizational chart were debated and might have succeeded, this solution acknowledged the centrality of "biomedical communications" to the continuation of research at the massive scale and wide institutional distribution modeled by the NIH.

In addition to its ability to scale by expanding the network of research institutions, the new federal funding arrangement had other notable information-handling features, such as the compartmentalization and hierarchical supervision through which distributed research was kept secret. As a leading architect of the system, Vannevar Bush built in such features as the head of the Office of Scientific Research and Development (OSRD), the grant-making parent for wartime science and technology research. Bush had tested a pyramidal and cellular organizational strategy at MIT in the mid-1930s, when he led an effort to build a computational machine for the Navy's cryptanalysis section, OP-20-G, using graduate student labor. The MIT effort largely failed because various mechanical subsystems could not perform as planned when integrated.[18] Solving individual problems was one thing, it seemed; combining solutions formulated in various research cells was another. To succeed, the cellular organization of research tasks required collaboration across different specializations. Deft information handling would send reports upward from discrete research locations. Administrators would also create enclosures, like the Manhattan Project site at Los Alamos, where researchers could more openly converse, as we will discuss in chapter 4.

In any event, by managing research as a communications problem rather than as an infrastructure or staffing problem, the federal government developed an unprecedented capacity to scale and coordinate a national research effort. Conceived as a complex communications system, the national research effort could be guided without being directly controlled. Federal bureaucracy would not itself generate research messages, nor would it design and manage every bit of infrastructure necessary to create, transmit, and receive them. It would strive, rather, to set agendas and provide channels whereby messages created by widely distributed researchers might inform others. This arrangement established a partnership between the government and the university far more extensive and durable than the one that briefly flowered during the First World War.

SYSTEMS ANALYSIS: ODYSSEY OF A DIAGRAM

Notably, midcentury researchers who theorized complex communications systems theorized their own working lives in the process, although it would not do to overemphasize the causality or suggest that it was unidirectional. While trying to make themselves heard in increasingly multifaceted, widely distributed, and hierarchical institutional settings, all manner of researchers learned to distinguish communication from the exchange of messages. Rather than focus on content exclusively, they would describe and strive to act upon anything that inhibited its transmission or limited its effects. Harold Lasswell's schema informed this scholarly direction. The historical import of this model derives less from its persuasiveness as an argument (or the fidelity with which others applied it) than it does from its capacity to mediate wide-ranging discussions.

Lasswell described a linear sequence in which each step entailed a distinct question that could be submitted to an appropriate flavor of analysis. Although not rendered graphically (so far as we have been able to determine) in Lasswell's key 1940s publications of the idea, the approach readily lends itself to diagrammatic expression. Over the years, numerous versions have been produced (see figure 3.1).

The question "Who communicates?" merited "control analysis." "What is said?" required "content analysis." "In which channel?" stipulated "media analysis." "To whom?" asked for "audience analysis." And "With what

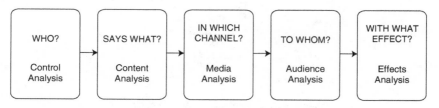

FIGURE 3.1. Diagram of schema described in Lasswell, "The Structure and Function of Communication in Society" (1948).
Source: Copyright 1949, 1998 by the Board of Trustees of the University of Illinois. Used with permission of the University of Illinois Press.

effect?" demanded "effects analysis."[19] The component parts of communication could thus be studied separately and in unexpected relations. For example, when radio gathered large groups of people around geographically dispersed receivers, that effect had little to do with any particular message or who was sending it. It had everything to do, however, with the medium employed. Whenever we distinguish the effects of mediation from its messages, in order to talk about audience segmentation, for example, we reveal a debt to this intervention.

In 1948, Claude Shannon, a mathematician, electrical engineer, and cryptographer employed by Bell Labs, and Warren Weaver, a machine translation pioneer and director of the Division of Natural Sciences at the Rockefeller Foundation, supplemented the Lasswellian schema to develop a shared formulation for mass-communication research and the new field of information theory.

Weaver's introduction to their coauthored volume reproduced this diagram from Shannon's original publication of "A Mathematical Theory of Communication."[20] With Lasswell, Shannon and Weaver emphasized that communication could be broken down into a series of component parts, each of which could be analyzed separately. They added complexity to

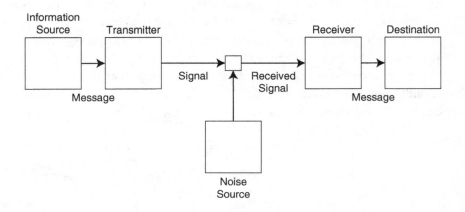

Fig. 1: Schematic diagram of a general communication system.

FIGURE 3.2. From *The Mathematical Theory of Communication.*
Source: Copyright 1949, 1998 by the Board of Trustees of the University of Illinois. Used with permission of the University of Illinois Press.

Lasswell's linear sequence by introducing the problem of "noise"—a component affecting the reception of the message but not anticipated in its selection. Weaver's introduction to Shannon's theory drew out the Lasswellian implication by extending Shannon's concern with the technical requirements for the accurate transmission of messages to the problems of how those messages are understood and with what effects on conduct. In this way, Weaver connected mass communications, mathematics, engineering, and the emerging discipline of computer science while explaining why this constellation mattered to a broader audience than the presumably discrete cohort that could follow Shannon's math.

This schematic of a "general communication system" depended on a specific definition of "information." It was not "meaning," Weaver underscored, but "a measure of one's freedom of choice when one selects a message."[21] This use of the term had roots in the physicist Ludwig Boltzmann's 1894 contention "that entropy is related to 'missing information.'"[22] In a state of maximum entropy, no information would be "missing," but also no message could be extracted from the random distribution. In simple instances, Weaver explains, "the amount of information" can be "measured by the logarithm of the number of available choices." Although Weaver labors to explain this formula to his late 1940s audiences, the approach to "information" he described would, in another few decades, become readily intelligible in measures of the storage and processing capacities of computing machines. Measured in logarithms to base two, that is, in "binary digits" or "bits," he writes: "If one has available say 16 alternative messages among which he is equally free to choose, then since $16 = 2^4$ so that $\log_2 16 = 4$, one says that this situation is characterized by 4 bits of information."[23] Within any communication system, then, any message would be related to the universe of its possible alternatives—the information from which the "information source" selects. Noise can be understood as undoing the selection involved in making the message, and it is no accident that Shannon and Weaver place it at the very center of the diagram.

The model assumes that the message will be transcoded and, at first glance, appears agnostic as to its content. "The selected message may consist of written or spoken words, or of pictures, music, etc. The *transmitter* changes this *message* into the *signal* which is actually sent over the *communication channel* from the transmitter to the *receiver*," which changes "the transmitted signal back into a message."[24] As a researcher for Bell

Labs, Shannon was centrally concerned with ways to minimize redundancy while retaining an ability to correct for noise. In this connection, however, he encounters a need to account for a variably dense (or free) information source. If some channels are noisier than others, some information sources are also much more dense. As the number of possible messages increases, more redundancy in the signal may be required to ensure that the message selected has been received. Defining "information" as "a measure of one's freedom of choice when one selects a message" allows Shannon to develop distinct functions to deal with various types of information sources—images transmitted by color television, for example, require a more complex function than sequences of letters transmitted by the telegraph.[25] The breakthrough lay not in seeing information as a quantity but rather in defining it as a variable relatable to other variables in the dynamic system being modeled.

Shannon and Weaver's diagram did not simply model communications systems but rather mediated their study and technological development. Their analytic approach is identifiable in any number of domains where it is (more or less deliberately) applied. Early-twenty-first-century readers may recognize Shannon's thinking in discussions of audio compression formats, for instance. In that case, algorithms identify the musical "message" within the information source such that it can be stored, transmitted, and reproduced using as few bits as possible. To do this, as the format historian Jonathan Sterne explains, software engineers rely on models of the information-handling capacities and habits of human hearing. At every step—from the original recording through encoding, decoding, and reception—compression technology assumes sounds captured, transcoded, and heard to be selections from among the sounds that might otherwise have been captured, transcoded, and, perhaps, heard. One does not need all of the audio information one could possibly have. Some of that information might not be audible to humans, for example, or some sounds may lead us to perceive sounds not actually in the signal, which can therefore be implied rather than stored and transmitted.

This assumption entails a corollary about the process of developing such complex communications systems. That process, somewhere along its path, typically involves university-based experts in addition to university-trained experts in private enterprise or government—but these researchers may not know one another or fully understand one another's work. As Sterne underscores, the ability to select which sounds constitute "the message" becomes an increasingly complex function that even its own engineers may not fully understand. Psychologists and physiologists schooled in midcentury approaches to information systems developed the perceptual encoding models these engineers employ, but that legacy of development need not concern them, just as the engineering remains opaque to the listener.[26] Compression constitutes a black box, which makes the relation between inputs and outputs predictable but the process relating them difficult, if not impossible, to discern. That process is not "technological" merely; it represents the congealed labor of generations of researchers with affiliations to midcentury communications research they may not even know they had.

Academic disciplines too can constitute black boxes of a sort, in which the congealed arguments of prior generations can simply appear as the way the discipline generates results. Lasswell's promiscuous diagram encouraged this kind of development, insofar as it seeded styles of analysis that soon forgot their kinship with one another. From a more global vantage, the application of a general model seems clear. Locally, however, the diagram's abstraction and modularity encouraged appropriation but provided no guarantee that those appropriations would remain conversant with one another. If they had, twenty-first-century scholars would more readily recognize literary New Criticism as a sibling of mass-communication studies.

I. A. Richards, a progenitor of the New Criticism, found good reason to reproduce the Shannon-Weaver diagram in the introduction to *Wrath of Achilles*, his 1950 translation of *The Iliad*, and to borrow its epigraph from Weaver's 1949 "Recent Contributions to the Mathematical Theory of Communications." As Richards would have it, translation is a feat of transcoding:

Here Homer (whatever that may be) is the *information source*. I (certain subsystems, rather, in me) am the *transmitter*. I encode certain things my information source seems to give me in a *signal*, which keeps up through the pages that follow. You (certain subsystems, rather, in you) are the *receiver*. You take in marks on the paper which you recode again in sentences and hand on to the *destination*.

Richards makes clear that this is less a generic description of translation than the theory informing his specific practice. His task, he tells us, involves selecting messages in Homer that remain receivable by Atomic Age readers.

Long lists are out, action sequences in, and all the ethical dilemmas of warfare are in with them. One of the epic's most essential messages even anticipates communication theory:

Whither, indeed, is all this directed? We have no better answer than Homer had. And as we wonder about that, the importance of the *noise source* needs no stressing—here, in the context of the first of all poems which
>have power to make
>Our noisy years seem moments in the being
>Of the eternal silence[27]

Here Richards and Homer lean on Wordsworth's "Ode: Intimations of Immortality from Recollections of Early Childhood" to characterize the ability to wrest significant "moments" from "noisy years" as poetry's abiding "power." Were we inclined to think of poems as pretty words, embellishments, the opposite of straight talk, we should think again. Rather, Richards claims for poetry the privilege of selecting durable messages about human existence, which constitutes an awesomely dense information source and destination. Poetic transmission, a history of transcodings of durable truths, secures those messages against the entropic "being / Of the eternal silence." Information theory thus explains poetry's specific value as a communication channel.

Richards was not in 1950 a newcomer to this way of thinking. Indeed, one can say that he had influenced its general development—although it is not clear exactly how much or in what way. As early as *Practical Criticism* (1929) Richards pitched poetry against the social effects of "mechanical" mass media, and he shared with a wide swath of interwar literary modernists a well-documented interest in communication as a problematic.[28] Before the war, he worked alongside Lasswell as a member of the Rockefeller Communication Seminar.[29] After it, he visited the pivotal Macy meetings on cybernetics, where Norbert Wiener did interesting things with Shannon's math. Lasswell's diagram did not invent a wholly new approach so much as it congealed a few decades' worth of transdisciplinary attention to the problem of communications.

The problem of medium specificity or "channel" preoccupied interwar literary critics as much as it did social psychologists like Lasswell (who wrote his 1927 University of Chicago doctoral dissertation on World War I propaganda). Notably, however, the literary critics tended to emphasize disciplinary borders where the social scientists debated generalizable schemes. Two texts that typically mark the start of the New Critical project clearly relate the work of policing disciplinary boundaries with that of defining medium specificity. In their 1938 textbook *Understanding Poetry*, Cleanth Brooks and Robert Penn Warren explained to readers that "The basic problem of communication in poetry is . . . of a totally different character from that involved in communication of matters of fact," for example, by newspapers.[30] That same year, John Crowe Ransom announced that criticism should neither encourage "appreciation" nor the "synopsis and paraphrase" favored by "women's clubs." Literary criticism should be "more scientific," "systematic," and "professional." It should distinguish itself from "historical" methodologies and the "moralizing" of Babbitt-style New Humanism. A good and proper task for professional literary critics would be to distinguish the communicative tendencies of prose from those of poetry. Prose reduces experience to communicate "a kind of story, character, thing, scene, or moral principle." Poetry compresses it, making selections calculated to inspire inferences about the totality in a "desperate ontological or metaphysical manoeuvre."[31] The New Critic's difference from historians and "women's clubs" depended on this ability to perceive and explain the distinct affordances of prose and poetry as communications channels.

New Criticism is typically (and rightly) understood as a successful campaign to distinguish literary analysis from other sorts of scholarly work. It interests us precisely because it also clearly borrowed from and contributed to a widely shared concern with communications. To school poetry audiences in their superiority to other audiences required a theory of medium specificity, which in turn presupposed a general model of communication. In midcentury descriptions of communication systems, multidisciplinary engagement combined with disciplinary formation. Uninformed by this process, later generations of scholars could imagine that their disciplines had evolved independently from one another. No matter how they appear from the inside, however, disciplines are not autochthonous. Sociological, mathematical, and New Critical efforts to schematize communication systems indicate vigorous borrowing across disciplines combined with equally energetic efforts to mark borders. Information theory became a field one could name. New Criticism poached it to defend its own disciplinary difference. Such efforts did not always agree on basic definitions. Weaver and Richards certainly share a concern with the problem of "possible messages," but this commonality belies differences. The contention that "poetry" (as opposed to text) constitutes a "signal" would be out of place in Weaver's discussion, just as description of poetic information in terms of bits would be foreign to Richards's. Sharing a communications diagram did not establish a shared research agenda, in short. It did, however, inform a shared passion for modeling complexity, for breaking communications down into component parts such that different analyses and experts might go to work on them.

DEMOCRATIC PROPAGANDA

To fight the Second World War, the federal government funded robust propaganda initiatives. After the war, these initiatives drew support from both covert and avowed federal investment, some of which was routed through the system of grants to universities that sustained research in other areas. In the years before the United States entered the conflict, propaganda research passed through a significant period of custodianship by the Rockefeller Foundation, which defined it as a subset of communications research. Rockefeller's communications projects all shared a twofold aim: they would develop methods for communications research in general while striving to understand and control Nazi propaganda in particular as the United States moved toward entering the war.[32]

Rockefeller researchers formulated propaganda as a problem that entailed a host of psychological, sociological, and semiological issues while raising core questions about the prospects for democratic governance. In this, they extended the Lippmann-Dewey debate.[33] That debate, we note in the previous chapter, established that mass-media circulation of stereotypes had an administrative function—it worked like propaganda even when not deliberately designed as such. Lippmann charged professionals with learning to direct this administration in support of democratic decision making. Dewey thought continuous pragmatic education should counter it. Both were informed by turn-of-the-century sociologists and psychologists who had emphasized that individuals do not exist prior to groups and that they have considerable perceptual limitations. Where classic liberal democratic theory defined public interest as

aggregated self-interest—expressible, for instance, in a majority vote—
Lippmann and Dewey concurred that perceived self-interest was shaped by
associations with others and was, in this sense, public. Everyone's opinion
had already been molded by group interactions and mediated by stereotypes that, Lippmann emphasized, were as essential to coping psychologically
with a complex world as they were hazardous to rational judgments about
it. Democracy, then, looked like a problem of how control over information
was distributed far more than it was a problem of who could vote on what.

Development of this line of argument became a major preoccupation for
the Rockefeller Foundation's Humanities Division, led by the medievalist
John Marshall. In 1936, Marshall helped launch the Princeton Radio
Research Project, which would quickly spin off numerous endeavors
involving diverse faculty and institutions. By 1940, representative Rocke-
feller mass-communication research initiatives included the Public Opin-
ion Research Project, led by Hadley Cantril at Princeton; the Office of
Radio Research, led by Paul Lazarsfeld at Columbia University; the Gradu-
ate Library Reading Project, led by Douglas Waples at the University of
Chicago; the American Film Center, led by Donald Slesinger; the Film
Library of the Museum of Modern Art, led by Iris Barry with Siegfried
Kracauer; the Totalitarian Communications Project, led by Ernst Kris and
Hans Speier at the New School for Social Research; and the Experimental
Division for the Study of Wartime Communications, led by Harold Lass-
well at the Library of Congress. To orchestrate this wide-ranging effort,
Marshall in 1938 created a Communications Seminar that included many
of these directors as well as selected others.[34] He did not much care for dis-
ciplinary turf wars: much of the research supported by his Humanities
Division was, in twenty-first-century terms, social scientific in nature.

When Marshall charged disciplinarily diverse experts to research
"genuinely democratic propaganda," he challenged them to reconcile imperatives that most of their contemporaries would have considered irrecon-
cilable. As the media historian Brett Gary explains, "propaganda" was
understood as an art of deceptive control by shadowy experts; democracy
was understood as an educational project aimed at equipping the masses
for self-determination.[35] Both positions assumed that some intervention
would be needed to create Americans capable of exercising democratic
judgment because modern social life made self-interest difficult to know.
In an effort to square the circle of "democratic propaganda," the Rockefeller

communication seminar strove simultaneously to "streamline decision-making (a Lippmannite position), facilitate public discussion of complicated problems (a Deweyan position), and take their scientific methods into the state's emerging surveillance apparatus on behalf of the long-term survival of an expert-guided democracy (a Lasswellian position)."[36] By 1941, then, Rockefeller's communication experts were inclined to see "propaganda" not only as a contest to control information in support of the war effort but also as a complex and contentious research problem on which the fate of liberal democracy depended, regardless of who won the war.

Communication research in this vein suffused federal bureaus during the war and universities after it. A remarkable range of scholars followed similar itineraries, moving from Rockefeller-funded projects to government offices to university positions. The archetypical traveler in this mode was Lasswell himself. A leading figure in Rockefeller communication research, he spent the war consulting with and training analysts for bureaus ranging from the Office of Fact and Figures and its successor Office of War Information (OWI) to the Office of Strategic Services (OSS), the Foreign Broadcast Monitoring Service of the Federal Communications Commission, and the US Army's Psychological Warfare Branch.[37] After the war, Lasswell joined the Yale School of Law, where he continued to collaborate with former colleagues such as Daniel Lerner, who moved from the Psychological Warfare Division to become a professor at Stanford, Columbia, and ultimately the Center for International Studies at MIT, establishing himself in the process as the leading light of "modernization theory."[38] Trace forward the career of any given Rockefeller participant or backward the career of any prominent postwar scholar of mass mediation—regardless of discipline—and one is likely to arrive at the same web of wartime propaganda research and operations.[39]

Connections of these sorts not only knit together the approaches of otherwise separate wartime initiatives at OWI, OSS, and numerous additional bureaus but also generated expanding professional networks that would shape many disciplines after the war, not least mass communication itself.[40] The experimental psychologist Carl Hovland left Yale to become chief psychologist and director of experimental studies for the Research Branch of the Information and Education Division of the War Department, where he conducted pathbreaking research on the effectiveness of military training films. Returning to Yale after the war, he founded its Program of Research on Communication and Attitude Change and established himself as one of the new discipline's pioneers.[41] The legendary Wilbur Schramm quit his job as director of the Iowa Writers Project to move to OWI, where he helped pen President Roosevelt's fireside chats. After the war, Schramm ran the nation's first PhD program in mass communication at Iowa (established in 1943), provided generations of national security experts with tools for distinguishing Soviet from authoritarian (but anticommunist) propaganda, consulted frequently on psychological operations, and helped develop educational television.[42]

New federal funding architectures supported the research networks that were dispersed among universities after the war. In his survey of the "first decade" of communication studies as an academic field after 1945, Christopher Simpson concludes that "U.S. military, propaganda, and intelligence agencies provided the large majority of all project funding for the field."[43] This funding entailed varying degrees of federal oversight.

Communications scholars joined classified military projects. For example, when the Air Force flew Wilbur Schramm, John W. Riley, and Frederick Williams to Seoul to interview anticommunist Korean refugees, some results of their investigation were classified, while others were used for propaganda purposes domestically in the form of a mass-market booklet, *The Reds Take a City*. Schramm and his coauthors explained with barely concealed admiration that "the program to control thought was the most pervasive part of Communist activity. Some form of propaganda was associated with literally everything the invaders did."[44] A "democratic" counterprogram would presumably need to be just as thorough.

In addition to projects with clear Cold War objectives, the national security apparatus supported basic research. It sustained publication of the field's leading journal, *Public Opinion Quarterly*, as well as Schramm's influential 1954 anthology *The Process and Effects of Mass Communication*, which outgrew its initial brief as a US Information Agency (USIA) training manual and went on to see long use as an introductory text.[45] Federal grants funded key institutes like the Bureau of Applied Social Research at Columbia, the Institute for Social Research at Michigan, the National Opinion Research Center at Chicago, the independent nonprofit Bureau of Social Science Research (in Washington, DC), the RAND Corporation, and the Center for International Studies at MIT, an effort that may have involved consulting contracts of dubious legality.[46]

It is worth lingering on the applied social research institute, which not only exemplified the new approach to federal investment in university research (as well as the continuing importance of foundation funding) but also guaranteed the survival of Marshall's "democratic propaganda" problem. The sociologist Allen Barton credits Lazarsfeld with introducing this institutional form to the US academy and with supplying its methodologies.[47] The Viennese émigré mathematician-cum-sociologist apparently excelled both at framing his findings for different audiences and at organizing collaborative work efforts.

Organizationally and theoretically Lazarsfeld encouraged the kind of large-scale surveys that became ubiquitous in late-twentieth-century discussions of electoral politics, consumer behavior, and media effects, among all manner of social phenomena. "He developed and clarified the multivariate analysis of sociological attributes," writes Barton, "and he was the inventor or major developer of the panel survey, the sociometric survey, and the contextual survey."[48] Each of these developed social scientific capacities to draw inferences about populations based on samples, with the panel survey providing insight into causal relations over time, the sociometric survey encouraging conclusions about social networks, and the contextual survey placing individual responses in the context of particular groups.

These techniques parsed and coded participants' responses to reveal patterns that were, by definition, imperceptible to the participants themselves. Amplification of the survey research approach could thus be expected to widen the gap between populations imagined to govern themselves as citizens and experts positioned to understand how those populations' responses could be predicted and their behaviors influenced. It did so, although without necessarily increasing expert confidence in the ability to influence the nation by means of its communications systems.

Lazarsfeld-inspired data collection and analysis is often credited with deflating the prewar contention that mass media had sweeping and powerful effects. Lazarsfeld pitched this claim in 1955's *Personal Influence*, coauthored with Elihu Katz. Katz and Lazarsfeld argued that mass media in themselves had limited direct effects on conduct and that the secondhand personal influence of "opinion leaders" proved more decisive. They represented this conclusion as the result of empirical research that had overturned ill-founded prewar speculations. In his reading of Lazarsfeld's prodigious output of the 1940s, however, Jefferson Pooley finds two very different ways of framing the "limited effects" insight that would go down in history as Lazarsfeld's signature contribution to media research. When Lazarsfeld addressed would-be propagandists, which he very frequently did, "the limits of direct media persuasion . . . are presented as a challenge for persuaders that, however, can be got around through messages that appeal to audiences' preexisting interests and through supplementary face-to-face persuasion." In other contexts, the same findings provide evidence "that the impact of media is happily negligible. Selectivity and interpersonal influence, in this second frame, are treated as reassuring buffers between man and media. Here, the message is a populist one, that media persuasion is very often ineffective."[49] After the war, this second framing appealed to Cold War advertisers and government agencies that wanted to calm public fears about media manipulation. Pooley views the difference between the two frames as a contradiction born of expediency. He depicts Lazarsfeld as an exquisite "packager" preternaturally attuned to where the funding would come from.

Be that as it may, both of Lazarsfeld's framings are equally enabled by a communications systems model. Each supposes communication to be a complex process linking and separating sending messages from the possibility of being affected by them. Such systems required study to be understood—and more study, insofar as the application of those studies would themselves require investigation to test results, hone future interventions, and so on. Whether media were best understood as powerful or limited in their effects, experts would be necessary to model and predict them. Absent sociopathy, these experts would be inclined to view their interventions with suspicion, since any prediction would be based on a model that itself was being tested in the application. (Lazarsfeld famously applied new methods to old data sets.) The research process could be called "democratic" when it placed its emphasis on testing (for example, of "what the people want") and "propaganda" when it emphasized application of the intervention (for example, to harden those predispositions). Thus, the applied social research institute, often affiliated with a university, continued Marshall's project after the war.

Outside academe, some wartime communication experts—particularly the women—followed roughly parallel trajectories to postwar careers in applied research. Lazarsfeld's Radio Project at Princeton and Columbia was home to the advertising researcher Rena Ross Bartos and the pioneering social psychology of the radio specialist Herta Herzog Massing, both of whom conducted research for the advertising giant McCann Erikson after the war. Helen Dinerman coauthored studies with Lazarsfeld and C. Wright Mills, was an OWI researcher during the war, and continued her work in the area afterward for International Research Associates, a firm providing public opinion data for the State Department. Similarly, Helen Gaudent moved from Princeton's Radio Project to the OWI, then after the war started the first Nevada ACLU chapter and wrote a column called "The Polls" in *Public Opinion Quarterly*.[50]

Later in the century, applied social survey research would often be construed as the opposite of the critical approach advocated by the Marxist Institute for Social Research, aka the Frankfurt School. Nonetheless, many members of the institute, like Lazarsfeld, escaped the Third Reich to become full participants in US communications research networks before and during the war. The institute developed its approach in tandem with American sociologists and psychologists and in the service of wartime propaganda efforts.[51] The Frankfurt School sociologist of literature Leo Lowenthal had a loose affiliation with Lazarsfeld's Columbia project before joining OWI and then, as research director, the Voice of America. After the war, he moved on to Stanford and UC Berkeley, where he chaired its sociology department.[52] Herbert Marcuse, Franz Neumann, and Otto Kirchheimer went to work for the Research and Analysis Branch (R&A) of the Office of Strategic Services (OSS), the precursor to the CIA. Their 1930s work on fascism as a dynamic internal to liberal democratic society informed reports on the situation inside Germany, suggestions for "psychological warfare" tactics to be deployed by OWI, and recommendations for rebuilding German society.[53] The Frankfurt School's understanding of authoritarianism as inherent in monopoly capitalism proved less interesting to US civilian and military planners after the war than during it. Nonetheless, key group members found a home in the American university. Twenty years later, Marcuse's *One-Dimensional Man* lent its analysis to the New Left, which in moments of poor judgment could fancy the university a space exempt from capitalist social relations.

The university's ability to shelter alternatives to arguments promoted by federal policy certainly does rank high among its virtues. But we should not fail to observe that alliances shift, that no theory has ever wholly determined the uses audiences would make of it, and, most emphatically, that wartime funding and interests shaped the communications complex left, right, and center.

After the war, left-wing intellectuals knowingly and unknowingly allied themselves with the CIA to position modernist difficulty as a bulwark against Soviet realism (and sometimes American popular culture). Music provides perhaps the clearest example from this long and winding Cold War battlefront. After a stint as a Rockefeller radio researcher and a period collaborating with empirical researchers at UC Berkeley to produce the broadly influential study *The Authoritarian Personality*, Theodor Adorno returned to Germany and published *Philosophie der nuen music* (1949). In it, he identified Arnold Schoenberg's prewar twelve-tone compositions as prototypes for "music that seemed incapable of being commandeered for purposes of propaganda," as the music historian Richard Taruskin puts it.[54] While US-led efforts to reshape Europe after the war shared neither Adorno's hostility to popular music nor this resistance to propaganda, the key players certainly understood that effective propaganda would not announce itself as such. They found it useful to promote difficult compositions, like Schoenberg's, that could be presented as both anti-Soviet and antifascist (Schoenberg had been banned by the Nazis, although other twelve-tone composers had not) as well as intellectually and culturally progressive without being self-evidently political.

In postwar Germany, this became an official program of the Occupying Military Government, United States (OMGUS), whose Information Control branches took over from the Psychological Warfare Division of the Allied Expeditionary Force.[55] In an old castle at Darmstadt, Information Control's Music Branch set up a summer school to reeducate Axis musicians and German listeners. Under the direction of the French composer Pierre Boulez, the school became a center for the postwar development of musical modernism. This was music made by experts for experts. Of the "total serialism" Boulez promoted, Taruskin notes that one could not discover the "algorithms governing a composition" by listening to it. A listener therefore could not hope to discern whether "the right notes" had been played. Only careful study of the musical notation would reveal the underlying logic of a score and enable evaluation of its correctness. Accordingly, serialism helped establish musical composition and musicology as professorial activities—something one might need a PhD to do—a change associated in the United States with the Princeton professor Milton Babbitt above all others.[56] On this front at least, US information-control agents were less concerned with winning the hearts and minds of the masses than they were to secure commitments from those perceived to be well positioned in key intellectual and cultural circuits. The CIA most craved the attention of tastemakers likely to engage the USSR's competing extension of Marxist intellectual traditions.

Although OMGUS's financial support for Darmstadt was not covert, the connections linking it to broader US efforts to mobilize the noncommunist left were.[57] The White Russian composer Nicolas Nabokov played a major role in those efforts, beginning with his participation in the Psychological Warfare Division in Germany during the war. In 1951, he became the general secretary of the Congress of Cultural Freedom, the main front through which the CIA covertly promoted US arts and culture abroad. At home, meanwhile, the CIA violated its legislative charter by supporting the American Committee for Cultural Freedom. This group of anticommunist New York intellectuals drawn from the old left included the New York University philosophy professor Sidney Hook, his former colleague James Burnham, the Columbia University English professor Lionel Trilling, his wife and scholarly collaborator Diana, and numerous prominent editors and journalists, among others.[58] When not busy working to keep the Congress of Cultural Freedom supplied with talent abroad, the group coordinated efforts to rescue small-circulation literary and critical magazines of the old left, such as the *Partisan Review* and the *New Leader*. Through publications, grants, and international conferences, CIA handlers and their confidants directed funds and suggestions to a much larger network of intellectuals—a mode of operation relying on pyramidal and cellular organizational structures similar to those that had managed secret wartime research. Decades later, many scholars who had participated in this network would be surprised to learn where the money and planning had come from.

In the postwar period, then, upscaled communication research proliferated sites of government intervention and amplified, without resolving, the conundrum of "genuinely democratic propaganda." Marshall's quest did not seem less contradictory after the war, just more difficult to speak about. The reasons were as much organizational as ideological. Communications had a become complex problem requiring complex solutions, such that any number of government bureaus might need to call upon university-based communications experts and the research they produced. Bureaucrats could hope to tune public opinion through initiatives as different as the propaganda classic *Reds Take a City*, serialist music, and the *Partisan Review*. Reincarnated as relatable variables, "message," "channel," and "effects" would require a massive and highly diversified, highly networked academic apparatus, one that produced new disciplinary distinctions along with new opportunities for transdisciplinary exchange. Through grants, federal agencies strove to direct these multifaceted efforts. Insofar as communication research was conducted in universities outside the government bureaus that often funded it, however, it retained a degree of autonomy—a pattern of information control that characterized scientific research as well. To prefer the communications complex as a description of the period to President Eisenhower's famous military-industrial framing is not to ignore the role of military spending and the industries it favored. It is, rather, to observe the generalization of a highly scalable systemic approach to expert intervention that distributed research efforts as much as it attempted to centralize management of them.

Chapter Four

NOT TWO CULTURES

In conventional accounts of the Second World War's academic legacies, federal funding ramified through university laboratories and transformed them into components of a military-industrial complex. Meanwhile, the Servicemen's Readjustment Act of 1944 (or GI Bill) directed unprecedented federal resources to student aid. Most of the money reached public universities, fueling their dramatic postwar growth and anchoring new commitments to what Christopher Newfield has called "mass quality" public education.[1] Thanks to a half-century of rhetorical manipulation, these two postwar developments can conjure dramatically opposed visions of the university, exemplifying the two cultures depicted by the British chemist (and novelist) C. P. Snow and his countryman, the literary critic F. R. Leavis. In their notorious early-1960s debate, academic science vied with literary criticism to save humanity from annihilation.

This Manichean view makes federal funding for scientific research seem the opposite of the federal tuition subsidy, which is supposed to have expanded access to educational approaches beloved by literary studies. It also hyperinflates the stakes involved in choosing between the two. Never mind that, at the federal level, the argument for democratic leveling through higher education was of a piece with postwar efforts to mobilize academic science to support the state. Never mind that research funding and student aid came with comparable reporting strings attached, which provided new channels through which federal policy could monitor and act upon postsecondary institutions. Never mind that GI Bill recipients sought business and engineering degrees more often than cultural heritage, and many humanists of the day complained that the mass influx lowered standards.[2] These facts aside, no early-twenty-first-century faculty member or administrator could fail to recognize the two-cultures opposition. Whatever may threaten—war, disease, famine, global warming, brutal conflicts over social identity, the depredations of global capitalism—early-twenty-first-century planners and patrons may be asked to make a life-or-death choice between two equally stereotypical midcentury universities: one funded by federal support for big science, the other funded by federal support for students interested in discovering culture through books.

We renounce this understanding of the university, its binary terms and its glamours. Contrary to the received view, Cold War scholarship in arts and letters was neither politically nor intellectually inimical to research in science and engineering. Nor did either of these supposed domains comprise an internally unified or consistent set of approaches. As the previous chapter recounted, in the middle of the twentieth century, the theory and practice of communication altered both what researchers studied and how research was conducted across various domains. Federal funding of science and engineering for military applications went hand in hand with military and CIA funding for professors of music, philosophy, art, and English. Understood in this context, the Snow-Leavis debate caricatured an academy that had become too complex to grasp as an array of disciplines and could thus find comfort in a simplification that reduced it to a matter of identities. Snow and Leavis agreed to mate a stereotypical condensation with the rhetorical inflation characteristic of action-adventure melodrama: the world's fate hung in the balance between the two cultures.

Cybernetics provides a better way to grasp the midcentury university's disciplinary profusion. Envisioned as an effort to synthesize and unify knowledge of machinic and human communications systems, it ended up (as usual) spinning off an array of distinct approaches. Some of these, such as the "democratic surrounds" informed by anthropology and design, took seriously the challenge of teaching audiences to understand themselves as vital components of communications systems and to engage those systems accordingly.

A comparable ambition, although with contrasting aims, informed the period's signature initiative to remake the nation's educational system as an engine of meritocratic sorting. The National Defense Research Committee (NDRC) chair and president of Harvard James Bryant Conant orchestrated Harvard's landmark master plan *General Education in a Free Society* while simultaneously overseeing the Manhattan Project. A similar administrative design and ambition informed each. Consistent with Conant's charge, the Harvard professors imagined the university as a collection of specializations capable of working in relative autonomy toward centrally defined goals. In this respect, development of a general-education curriculum resembled the process of inventing the atom bomb. Harvard's scheme systematically linked K–12 and postsecondary education and defined general education as the guarantor of both national unity and meritocracy while privileging New Critical literary studies as a counterweight to commercial mass culture. *General Education in a Free Society* (aka the Redbook) succeeded in reorganizing neither Harvard's curriculum nor the nation's. The scheme did, however, reinforce the conviction that higher education was essential to national and individual improvement and thereby helped justify a bigger role for the federal government in supporting it.

CYBERNETICS VERSUS THE TWO-BIT UNIVERSITY

In his 1970 memoir *Pieces of the Action*, the wartime science chief Vannevar Bush demonstrates how profoundly the problem of communications informed midcentury administration by describing the bomb as delivering a message when the United States dropped it. Bush explains that although US civilian and military planners knew they could win the war by conventional means, bombing Hiroshima and Nagasaki made an important point for the postwar era: "humanity" could either refrain from using new nuclear, chemical, and biological weapons or "thrust itself back into the dark ages." Vaporizing these cities and irradiating their inhabitants was, Bush contends, "the only way in which the dilemma could be presented with adequate impact on world consciousness."[3] On this account, the bomb solved a communications problem. It served as a channel in which the message "we can destroy civilization" could be communicated around the world with maximum persuasive effect.[4] This emphasis on the communications capacity of nuclear weaponry, and the belief that communications could be managed as effectively as the weapons themselves, provided the cornerstone of Cold War deterrence doctrine. It guaranteed funding for weapons science and mass-communications research alike, and it linked those enterprises with initiatives, such as funding for esoteric musical compositions, that proclaimed autonomy from military-industrial motives.

Vannevar Bush's message bomb informs C. P. Snow's 1959 Cambridge Rede Lecture, although it does not supply the lecture's primary world-historical menace. That role goes to the dangerously accelerating gap between rich and poor nations. To address this issue, Snow explains, a project comparable in scale to atom-bomb development will be necessary. He presents as an open question whether "Russia" or "the West" will fund this project and staff it with scientists, engineers, and linguists. He puts his faith in education, especially science education, as capable, hopefully, of bridging the Cold War divide. Snow writes in conclusion, "Closing the gap between our cultures is a necessity in the most abstract intellectual sense as well as the most practical."[5] Here, the "gap" in question might refer to the "mutual incomprehension" between "scientists" and "literary intellectuals" that supplies the lecture's pretext—but it might equally indicate the gulf between US and Soviet models, with impoverished African and Asian countries (and British intellectuals) caught in between. Humanity's future depends on getting education right, and getting education right depends on suturing the university's supposed halves.

Snow is well aware that his polarizing terms leave a lot out. "I was searching for something a little more than a dashing metaphor, a good deal less than a cultural map," he explains, "and for those purposes the two cultures is about right."[6] Pushed aside are "non-scientists of strong down-to-earth interests," "some of my American sociological friends," as well as scientific engagements with "long playing records" and "colour photography," which are artsy but not, Snow observes, "books."[7] Snow likes great books and thinks scientists should read more of them, just as he thinks literary types should be familiar with the Second Law of Thermodynamics.

What seems to annoy Snow most about literary experts is that "while no one was looking" they "took to referring to themselves as 'intellectuals' as though there were not others."[8] F. R. Leavis rose with alacrity to this particular bait. Agreeing, as professors often do, that it would be good to learn from one another, promote the university, and save the world, Leavis nonetheless insists that our common humanity is uniquely discoverable in "English literature, a living whole that can have its life only in the living present, in the creative response of individuals, who collaboratively renew and perpetuate what they participate in—a cultural community or consciousness."[9] By these lights, knowledge of the Second Law of Thermodynamics was not at all equivalent to knowledge of Shakespeare, as Snow proposed. The former was specialized, the latter, generally human. Professional literary critics like Leavis could thus claim custodianship of common culture. Inhabiting the stereotype Snow laid out for him, Leavis agreed to ignore much of the midcentury intellectual map. Reduction to two cultures served the interests of both parties. Each camp could lament their opposition while claiming for itself the half of the intellectual universe that mattered most.

Influential foundation and government reports from the midcentury forward often relied on such rhetoric, recounts Geoffrey Galt Harpham, the director of the National Humanities Center from 2003 to 2015. For instance, a 1964 American Council of Learned Societies committee went so far as to declare that "*only* the humanities can save us from external threats and from our own folly." Harpham finds it easy to parody the position that without the humanities "people would be . . . the prey of whatever barbarity is sweeping around the world," but he acknowledges the utility of thus raising the stakes of the argument.[10] Indeed, he too finds it difficult to avoid, arguing that to shake off self-interest and reconnect to larger social questions humanists "must resist any temptation to refashion their discipline along the lines of the natural or social sciences."[11] Like all functioning stereotypes, two-cultures thinking knows itself to be reductive but commands commitment anyway. This is so not because it posits a gap to be bridged—although that always seems like it would be a good idea—but because it provides the occasion to define and defend some fraction of the university as if it were the more important half.

The Columbia University English professor (and CIA stringer) Lionel Trilling was among the first to notice this function of the Snow-Leavis debate. In framing the British argument for US audiences, he called attention to its rhetorically supercharged stakes, declared his allegiance to literature, and then proceeded to take to task both Snow's "mistaken" lecture and Leavis's "failure" to rebut it: "both men set too much store by the idea of *culture* as a category of thought." They each attempt to normalize and elevate insular social groupings through preferences that strike Trilling as superficial. He likens adoption of one of these two cultures to "being the Person Who defines himself by wearing trousers without pleats." In other words, the "two cultures" offered little more than a marketing strategy, a bid to harden dispositions and polarize audiences.[12]

Trilling would know. A hard-line Cold Warrior and member of the American Committee for Cultural Freedom, he published regularly in the prominent British literary magazine *Encounter*, one of several supported by the Congress for Cultural Freedom after the war.[13] He well understood the CIA's postwar strategy, which relied on convincing skeptical Europeans that America could provide intellectual resources superior to those associated with Marxist traditions. He has no time whatsoever for Snow's fantasy that science might rise above politics and reconcile Cold War enemies. Yet he too strives for the moral high ground, yearning for a time when "mind" "belonged not to professions, or to social classes, or to cultural groups, but to man." In this once-upon-a-time of "mind," he continues, "it was possible for men, and becoming to them, to learn its proper use, for it was the means by which they could communicate with each other."[14] Homosocial idealization notwithstanding, the most striking feature of Trilling's nostalgia is that it makes man, professions, classes, and groups comparable communication problems, with the professions and their ilk presumed to limit exchanges that once flourished among the minds of men. This habit locates Trilling, along with Snow and Leavis, within the communications complex.

Which is to say, all three acknowledge that to work within any academic field entails challenges in speaking to any other, that specialization is distributed across the disciplines—including those that claim to be general— and that no professor can hope to sway the public without a communications strategy involving potentially tricky political alliances as well as rhetorical inflation and reduction. The "two cultures" did not try to map the British university, and it certainly did not describe the American one. In place of an explanation, Snow attempted to manage the university's increasingly dense and noisy communication channel. To the extent it succeeded, the "two cultures" did so by limiting the number of possible messages to four: "science," "literary intellectuals," "neither," or "both."

Cybernetics proposed one alternative to this two-bit university ($\mathrm{Log}_2 4 = 2$). More than any other midcentury effort, it aimed to synthesize knowledge of human and machinic communications systems into a unified theory. The effort floundered in its attempt to treat human audiences as systems components when mathematicians discovered limits to what they could model. This did not, however, discourage designers, artists, and anthropologists from taking up the charge. As with midcentury communications research more generally, cybernetics arguments yielded new disciplinary varieties through a process of cross-pollination. One variety did not need to threaten the others to thrive.

The era's major institutional effort to spur cybernetics research was designed specifically to foster exchange across incipient and established scholarly fields. In March 1946, the Josiah Macy Jr. Foundation launched seven years of meetings on cybernetics by sponsoring a discussion of the "computing machine of the nervous system" described by the neuroscientist Rafael Lorente de Nó as well as of the mathematician John von Neumann's "First Draft Report on the EDVAC," which employed a similar analogy in beginning to describe the computer architecture that would later bear his name.[15] Macy participants were inclined to believe that models capable of relating human cognitive systems with electromechanical ones should be able to encompass social systems as well. Thus, in addition to prominent neuroscientists, mathematicians, and psychologists the Macy meetings welcomed human scientists such as the anthropologists Margaret Mead and Gregory Bateson, the linguist Roman Jakobson, and (every foundation's favorite) the literary critic I. A. Richards.

As the historian of science Steve Heims explains, the problem of "feedback," and particularly the negative feedback loop, ran through the Macy meetings and provided a key means of analogizing (and organizing) human cognitive, machinic, and social systems.[16] In a negative feedback loop, a system's output, fed back as an input, affects subsequent output, generally by stabilizing the system. The effect of heat on a thermostat is a classic example of this "negative" information in action. The very mechanism that calls a furnace to heat a room stops it from doing so when the room exceeds a preset temperature. Macy regulars set about finding negative feedback in all kinds of systems that involved information but conceded that it was difficult or impossible to find mathematical ways to describe social systems in these terms. The MIT mathematician Norbert Wiener lamented this limit in his 1948 bestseller *Cybernetics*. He explained that though "the social system is an organization . . . in which circular processes of a feedback nature play an important part," the heterogeneity of social life meant "the human sciences are very poor testing-grounds for a new mathematical technique."[17] That he and his colleagues could not see a way for information theory to guide social scientific research left much, "whether we like it or not," wrote Wiener, "to the un-'scientific,' narrative method of the professional historian."[18] Cybernetics informed other approaches in the "un-'scientific'" human sciences despite that acknowledgment.

The design legends Charles and Ray Eames were among those who took up the challenge to extend cybernetics research into social domains, as their 1953 educational film *A Communication Primer* attests. The film works through Shannon and Weaver's *The Mathematical Theory of Communication*. To the famed Shannon-Weaver diagram (described in the previous chapter) the Eameses add two cross-filled boxes (see figures 4.1 and 4.2). These highlight the theory's treatment of communications as a matter of selecting from a set of possible messages and recovering that selection post-transmission. The Eameses develop the complexity of the model by multiplying examples, beginning with the transmission of an instruction to "buy"

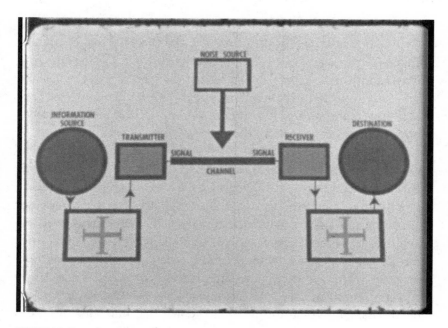

FIGURE 4.1. Frame from Charles and Ray Eames, *Communications Primer* (1953).

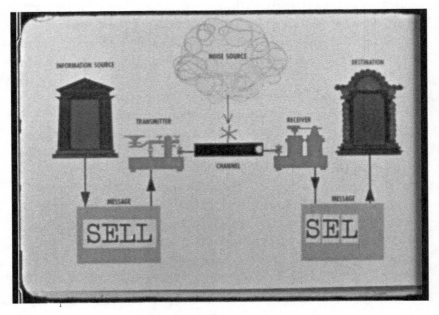

FIGURE 4.2. Frame from Charles and Ray Eames, *Communications Primer* (1953).

or "sell" communicated between two banks by telegraph and continuing through the message "I love you," which can be encoded, as the film demonstrates, in words, sounds, or images but must remain distinguishable from "I hate you" to function as a message. Within minutes of this basic lesson, viewers are prepared to scrutinize swirling flocks of birds and human crowds crossing busy streets for the messages they may encode.

The Eameses' film reaches a cybernetically informed conclusion by visually comparing halftone screen printing and computer punch tapes while the narrator describes each as aggregations of binary "decisions." We learn how a halftone image works through a series of dissolves and a voiceover explanation. The camera pulls back from the halftone screen to reveal the result that the systemic aggregation of such "decisions" can produce (see figures 4.3 and 4.4). Social communications systems are likened to the halftone image, which is likened to the pattern of dots on the punch tape. When the total system is considered, the interaction of the elements may be unclear. Nonetheless, any system can be broken down into individual decisions that are repeated or rejected over time within feedback loops.

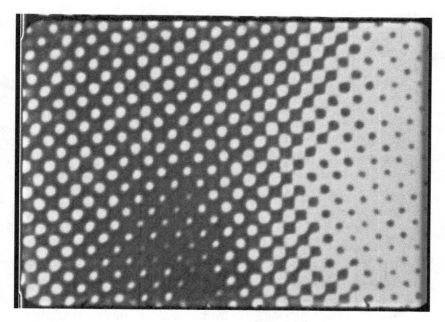

FIGURE 4.3. Frame from Charles and Ray Eames, *A Communications Primer* (1953).

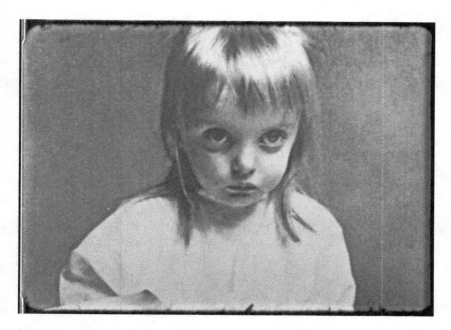

FIGURE 4.4. Frame from Charles and Ray Eames, *A Communications Primer* (1953).

In their willingness to move from register to register—from bank transactions to romantic exchanges, birds to crowds, halftones to punch tapes—the Eameses make a leap where Wiener marks a limit. To end the film, they present a control tower, an airplane, and a cockpit; the narrator explains that each component in this system bears a responsibility for the whole. "No matter what the technique," the voiceover proclaims, "communication means the responsibility of decision." The human component of the aviation system, represented by a hand, enters the montage for the first and only time, and the voice intones "right down the line" as a brush paints that line, graphically miming the human finger, diagonally across the screen (see figures 4.5 and 4.6).

With these final words and images, the Eameses find a substitute for the mathematical model of social feedback loops that Wiener failed to produce: namely, a viewer schooled in the ability to recognize actions as coded messages. By these lights, good communications will be maintained not by comprehensive modeling but by individual responsibility for the function of the whole.

FIGURE 4.5. Frame from Charles and Ray Eames, *A Communications Primer* (1953).

FIGURE 4.6. Frame from Charles and Ray Eames, *A Communications Primer* (1953).

The Eameses' film amplifies, extends, and accelerates a message across symbolic registers—writing, sounds, and images—and conceptual domains—finance, romance, ornithology, and sociology. As the media studies scholar Orit Halpern observes, the film performs "the idea of redundancy, the production of noise, and the concept of information, by giving multiple examples of the same idea." In its presentation, the film demonstrates an aspiration "to produce a new type of informatic spectator and designer—both the consumer and the producer of such communication systems" that Halpern finds equally evident in the designer George Nelson's contemporaneous class for UCLA business and engineering students.[19] Along with the design professor György Kepes (New Bauhaus, MIT), Nelson and the Eameses exemplify a much broader set of efforts to develop and institutionalize new art and design pedagogies for the midcentury university.[20] Simply put, through their efforts design entered the university via the elaboration of communication systems.

Anthropology was a key part of the midcentury constellation linking cybernetics and design and training audiences to act as components of communications systems. That training was a hallmark of the postwar media form Fred Turner dubs "the democratic surround." As Turner explains, Mead and Bateson's anthropology moved on from jostling with cybernetics to join forces with Bauhaus émigrés in producing "multi-image, multi-sound-source media environments" designed to bolster "the democratic personality" and counter "single-source mass media."[21] Turner finds a prototype in *The Balinese Character: A Photographic Analysis* (1942), wherein Mead and Bateson's selection, arrangement, and captioning of photographs present "their own ethnographic tactics as models of the sort of apperceptive habits that could produce democratic personalities."[22] Such uses of mixed media encouraged audiences to perceive reception as a meaning-making activity—as part of the work of maintaining culture. Democratic freedom required this habit, argued the diverse collection of scholars and artists grouped by Turner.

An imperative to retrain perceptual habits clearly informed *The Family of Man*, the blockbuster 1955 show at the Museum of Modern Art in New York that provides Turner with a mature example of the surround. Curated by Edward Steichen and filling the museum's entire second floor, the show guided visitors through more than five hundred photographs taken by nearly three hundred photographers from around the world. Organized to encourage viewers to rediscover themselves as part of a globally various but nonetheless shared human lifecycle, the exhibit's layout created open spaces in which visitors might pool for discussion, observe one another in relation to the images, and choose different pathways through the installation.[23] The surround thus constituted an information system in which gallery visitors were not simply addressees of the curatorial message but also participants in its creation. The US Information Agency (USIA) took notice of this effort to enact the human family and found it consistent with the perceptual habits that they hoped would create American allies abroad. They exported the show and developed its format globally. The democratic surround thereby joined the US Cold War propaganda toolkit.[24] Meanwhile, the same confluence of anthropology, systems theory, and Bauhaus design concurrently informed the practice of experimentalists such as the composer John Cage and his partner, the choreographer Merce

Cunningham, who began to develop the participatory multimedia "happening" at North Carolina's Black Mountain College in the early 1950s.

To divide the midcentury university that sustained Weiner, the Eameses, Mead, and Cage into two opposing camps is fundamentally to misconstrue how diverse and sometimes competing academic experts act on populations outside the university. A "culture" of science will no more save us than a "culture" of literature—or some fancied marriage of the two. As Snow and Leavis agreed to produce them, these stereotypical identities offered professors a way to explain an increasingly complex university to themselves, promoting the fantasy of an embattled and heroic posture. In contrast, the Macy meetings, like the Rockefeller Communications Seminar before them, encouraged professors to engage one another, to discover shared problems as well as limits to synthesis. This kind of work had farreaching applications in engineering as well as in democratic surrounds.

For readers schooled to think of the 1950s as conformist, Turner's argument about the democratic surround generates frisson by providing a genealogy connecting swinging 1960s happenings and state-sponsored Cold War art installations. Both flavors of surround made audience participation seem crucial to the cultivation of democratic perceptual habits. Despite that emphasis, however, neither flavor could dispense with expert guidance. Expert guidance meant, in part, professorial guidance—albeit sometimes by occasional professors like Cage, for whom university teaching was clearly a day job. Although participants were free to choose multiple paths through the surround, the possibilities were still constrained in advance by its design, with its assumption that democracy would require the cultivation of new perceptual habits. Nonetheless, the design ambitions and parameters of the democratic surround, and particularly the conception of "democracy" involved, differed from the period's other signature efforts to organize multidisciplinary teams of scholars in service of the state.

A MANHATTAN PROJECT FOR GENERAL EDUCATION

James Bryant Conant knew how to set a conference table. He also knew how to ensure that what happened at a conference table would secure the attention of many more people than the expert teams he called to order, whether those teams were researching new ways to structure undergraduate curricula or to exploit nuclear fission. A chemist by training, Conant had conducted poison-gas research during World War I. While presiding over Harvard University (from 1933 to 1953), he served alongside Vannevar Bush as one of the eight original members of the National Defense Research Committee (NDRC). In 1941, he became NDRC chair when the council was made advisory to the newly formed Office of Scientific Research and Development (OSRD) helmed by Bush. As Bush's lieutenant, Conant oversaw the Manhattan Project. Meanwhile, as Harvard's president in 1943, he charged a team of professors to devise a system of "general education—a liberal education—not for the relatively few, but for a multitude."[25] This charge produced *General Education in a Free Society*, or the Harvard Redbook. Published in 1945, it offers one of the most elaborately conceived and fully articulated schemes for organizing US education as a whole, making sweeping recommendations for compulsory primary and secondary education as well voluntary postsecondary institutions of various stripes. The special role it accords literary studies won enduring admiration from the likes of the literature scholar Geoffrey Galt Harpham, who calls it "the single most important document in the history of 'the humanities.'"[26] Like the Manhattan Project and any number of other wartime initiatives, Conant's curriculum project treated national welfare as a problem requiring multidisciplinary research expertise and administrative control over communication systems.

To produce the Redbook, Conant charged "a Committee largely composed of members of the Faculty of Arts and Sciences . . . men of distinction in special fields of learning."[27] He provided his professors with a budget: $60,000 (nearly $870,000 in 2017 dollars).[28] And then he left them to it. The faculty understood the responsibility implied by this division of labor well enough. The "Letter of Transmittal" written by the authors to Conant describes their work as a "quest" requiring intense meetings, exhaustive networking, and the attendant issues of information management and sequestration: the group "periodically secluded itself for sessions of several days' duration."[29] Developed behind closed committee doors, a comprehensive plan for K–12 and postsecondary education was then disseminated.

The NDRC employed a similar bureaucratic method to produce the atom bomb, although on a much larger scale. Teams of scientists and engineers were assembled, charged, and given relative autonomy to pursue their

work. In keeping with Bush's preference for pyramidal and cellular organizations, each original NDRC member had his own area of operations
(Conant's was "chemistry and explosives") and then "built under him a system of sections to deal with explicit problems, and each recruited his personnel for the purpose. Soon these sections became groups of specialists."[30]
To help secure research results, Bush instituted highly compartmentalized
work assignments and outcomes evaluation. Researchers were given only
the information necessary to the task at hand.[31] This organizational scheme
allowed the NDRC, and then the OSRD, to contain secrets, distribute work,
and coordinate project labs from above. It was the direct precursor to the
federal funding and grants administration architecture that flourished
after the war, and Bush played a key role in establishing this architecture
as a strong advocate for the NSF.

Atomic-weapons research presents a particularly clear instance of the
kinds of communications problems such administrative structures aimed
to resolve. Before the war, information about new discoveries had no clearly
defined way to reach the scientists who contributed to nuclear research.
Ernest Lawrence at UC Berkeley might wait a long time to learn what Niels
Bohr was up to in Denmark, and he might learn it via academic gossip—
hardly a reliable channel. Nor was it easy for the physicists grinding away
at fission to get the attention of government funders. After Pearl Harbor,
Bush was far more interested in radar than in what seemed to him open-
ended and overly expensive nuclear physics, and there was no formal channel through which to change his mind.[32] The British sent the Australian
physicist Mark Oliphant to the United States to lobby him. Oliphant updated
Lawrence (who was also involved in the radar research being conducted at
MIT), who pulled in Arthur Compton (a Nobel Prize winner for his research
on X-rays), who was assisted by the Harvard chemist George Kistiakowsky
in getting Conant to persuade Bush to secure support from President Roosevelt.[33] The resulting Manhattan Project was less a secret plan hatched by
Bush, Conant, Oppenheimer, or anyone else than it was a means to coordinate, secure, fund, and expand a preexisting but loosely organized research
network. It was a communications initiative, in other words, every bit as
much as a physics and engineering effort.

Successful bomb building required collaboration across different
research specializations. Secrecy, however, militated in favor of a cellular
subdivision of research tasks such that individual teams of scientists could

not know, and thus could not reveal, the whole to which they contributed. Los Alamos offered a solution to this dilemma by bringing the relevant scientists together in one compound and regulating interactions among them. Nonetheless, bomb research was never entirely pulled away from universities and their habitual ways of handling important information through publication and gossip rather than secure channels. Even after their relocation to the desert, Los Alamos physicists and engineers continued to rely on colleagues at the University of Chicago, Columbia, and (until Germany invaded Denmark) Bohr's Institute for Theoretical Physics at the University of Copenhagen. Von Neumann, whose expertise in detonation waves and growing interest in computational machines had value to several ORDC projects, was one of a few experts who traveled among them.[34] Beyond the academy, the Manhattan Project also incorporated reactors—DuPont ran the one at Hanford, in Washington State—and offices in both civilian and military bureaucracies. Each of these networked cells would ideally report their discoveries up the pyramid to Washington, DC, which would then disseminate them back down on a need-to-know basis.[35]

Conant's charge to his Cambridge, Massachusetts, faculty made a small-scale Los Alamos, minus the security checkpoints, out of Harvard conference rooms. It should not surprise us, then, that the Redbook's recommendations for Harvard's curriculum reproduced an emphasis on organization, delegation, and distributed specialization. Anticipating the logic of postwar federal grant funding, it envisioned a cellular array made up of classrooms rather than research labs, whose general aims and systems of operation would be decided by means of central planners. The document outlines a philosophy and proposes a distribution of courses while delegating important decisions about content and pedagogy to the faculty. "There is not one best way of introducing people to Homer or Plato or Dante," the Redbook authors opined. "Or, if there is, which it is is not known. Freedom for the instructor is essential."[36] Similarly, in recommending a course on "Western Thought and Institutions," the authors found it "inappropriate . . . to outline in detail a scheme of this course, or even to indicate all the topics with which it would be concerned."[37] In the area of "science and mathematics," where the authors perceived the hazard of excessive specialization most keenly, they proposed general-education courses offering "reasonably broad syntheses within the areas of science and mathematics . . . taught so as to convey some integrative viewpoint, scientific method, or the development of scientific concepts, or the scientific world-view."[38] Diverse experts were called to put flesh on the bones of this master plan.

They had only to accept the skeleton. Literature professors could accomplish their task as they saw fit, for instance, so long as they accepted the information theory known as New Critical close reading and did not wander off into discussions of "Western Institutions" or the scientific worldview. Drawing the lines within which their colleagues were free to paint, without stipulating what exactly they painted there, the committee nonetheless opined that eight volumes would probably suffice for the course on "Great Texts of Literature" and offered that a "list from which a selection would be made might include Homer, one or two of the Greek tragedies, Plato, the Bible, Virgil, Dante, Shakespeare, Milton, Tolstoy." Suggestions for "Western Thought and Institutions," meanwhile, included "Aquinas, Machiavelli, Luther, Bodin, Locke, Montesquieu, Rousseau, Adam Smith, Bentham, and Mill, to mention no others."[39] One appeal of general education on this model is a fantasy of efficient organization in which the members of the faculty all understand their jobs (as contributions to a whole) and are given autonomy to do them.

More compelling to Conant, however, was the dream of large-scale social engineering according to which education can be made an effective "instrument of national policy."[40] Conant was well versed in the contradictory proposition that democracy requires expert supervision. As he explained in *Education in a Divided World* (1948), "A set of common beliefs is essential for the health and vigor of a free society. And it is through education that these beliefs are developed in the young and carried forward in later life."[41] Conant portrayed the American "political, social, and economic system" as "on trial in the grim world of the mid-twentieth century" and presented general education as a means to win it.[42] This appeal, Gerald Graff subsequently noted, was a "frank expression of Cold War anti-Communism."[43] Higher education, on Conant's view, would be an instrument of what John Marshall had called "democratic propaganda," with all the contradictions that entailed.

The Redbook's democracy is emphatically an expert-guided one. In its core assumptions, it has little in common with early-twentieth-century defenses of humanistic training as the cultivation of character necessary for self-governing citizens, despite rhetoric calculated to evoke those connotations. Although the Harvard professors frequently proclaim a need to balance a "Jeffersonian" hierarchizing imperative with a "Jacksonian" impetus to level, neither provides their strongest precursor. That honor might be claimed by the Wilsonian effort to use universities to instruct the First World War's student soldiers, an effort to define national values that seeded Western Civilization and Great Books requirements after the war. Or, better, it could be claimed by students of World War I propaganda like Harold Lasswell, that pillar of the Rockefeller communications group, who so effectively advocated for expert guidance of democracy by means of communications systems.

The Redbook borrows its communications theory from New Criticism at the expense of many other approaches that Lasswell's schema also informed (see chapter 3). While "philosophy," "fine arts," and even "music" are allowed contributions to general education in the "humanities," and while general education also requires work in "the social sciences" and "science and mathematics," the professors elevate literary studies as allowing students "direct access to the potentialities and norms of living as they are presented to the mental eye by the best authors."[44] By "direct," they did not mean untrained: students would need to be schooled in "intensive, close study of well-written paragraphs and poems which are saying important things compactly." But this sort of study needed no help from other fields to unveil ways of life: "Strained correlation with civics, social studies" should be avoided in literature instruction, the Redbook cautions.[45] In issuing these precepts, the Redbook authors proposed John Crowe Ransom's "scientific" reading practice as general intellectual equipment. That is, they privilege this specialization among the others comprised in general education by presenting its aims and methods as uniquely generalizable to "the potentialities and norms of living."

As the only English professor among the Redbook's authors, Richards typically receives the credit for its emphasis on literary training. That explanation will not suffice. While Richards's persuasive powers are not in question, the Redbook committee was chock-a-block with prominent professors from other fields. Fully a quarter of its members, including Chairman Paul Buck, were historians by training. Whatever the force of Richards's authority, the prominence of New Criticism may be explained by the urgency of the communication problem it poses and resolves. While generalizing efforts in the social and natural sciences are likewise valued as a means to counter research specialization, a New Critical approach to

literature is pitched as uniquely capable of countering the centrifugal influence of demographic variety and the debasing effects of commercial mass
media. This approach only makes sense if we understand the Redbook as
applying communications theory with one hand and writing it out of the
curriculum with the other. Both moves are required to privilege literary
education as the solution to "a centrifugal culture in extreme need of unifying forces."[46]

To remediate such a "centrifugal culture in extreme need of unifying
forces," the Redbook authors continued a pattern set by general-education
planners after World War I: they presented commercial mass media as
competition that educators would need to appropriate as well as counter in
the service of "democracy." Radio, for example, had recovered "the power
to attend to and criticize the spoken word," endowing it with "a public
importance it has not enjoyed since the invention of printing."[47] Professors
could take advantage of the new prestige for the voice in encouraging their
students to read poems aloud. At the same time, they could rest assured
that those feats of reading would inculcate a critical faculty that radio listening did not. The Redbook authors cast a suspicious eye on the "judgments of publishers, journalists, advertisers, radio-program directors, and
motion-picture producers as to the capacities and interest of their publics"
and proposed that "schooling better aware of its aims may come to see in
contemporary distractions some of its major opponents." The classroom's
superiority over the "juke box" had to do with the way it encouraged students "to talk things over or think things out."[48] By promoting academic
expertise over that of the professionals working in media more generally,
the Redbook authors proposed simultaneously to seize the opportunity
presented by radio and to turn back the threat posed by its "distractions."
Opposition to mass culture thus provides the Redbook with both an animating mission and a double bind: think like the creators and theorists
of mass media do, but distinguish the apparatus of education from all
other media institutions.

The Redbook ends with this paradoxical craving for an educational system capable of curating a shared culture like, but opposed to, the one commercial mass media was credited with creating. "General education is the
sole means by which communities can protect themselves from the ill
effects of overrapid change," the authors contend. It is not entirely clear
what worries them most. On the one hand, they present all mass media as

**In a world of strife,
there's peace in beer**

FIGURE 4.7. United Brewers Industrial Foundation Advertisement
(1941).

threat vectors: "The press, radio, photography, television—our progressive disembodiment—and indeed all increased means of mass communication have their dangers."[49] The specter of "progressive disembodiment" would seem calculated to reinforce the prestige of face-to-face instruction and equate it with democratic deliberation conceived as "protection" from "overrapid change." On the other hand, what really gets the authors' goat is "the degradation which language undergoes when the greatest words are most often met in servitude to mean or trivial purposes. 'In a world of strife, there is peace in beer.'" To counter this supposed debasement of language by an advertisement that "adorned many a newspaper in the days before Pearl Harbor," the authors marshal quotations from *Troilus and Cressida* and *Richard II* ("He that is secure is not safe").[50] The gesture encapsulates the core contradiction of the Redbook program: to organize society, "general education" would need to make its slogans as familiar as those of beer advertisers while simultaneously promoting antipathy to all such sloganeering and the media channels through which it finds audiences.

In "The Culture Industry: Enlightenment as Mass Deception," Max Horkheimer and Theodor Adorno notably explode this contradiction by disallowing its foundational distinction between commercial media and the classics vouchsafed by academe. The Frankfurt School veterans identify a totalizing project that cuts across institutions and that depends on the manipulation of style through recourse to established prototypes. The rise of commercial mass media has in no way dampened enthusiasm for this project, they argue. To the contrary. "The complaints of art historians and cultural attorneys over the exhaustion of the energy which created artistic style in the West are frighteningly unfounded," they write. "No medieval patron of architecture can have scrutinised the subjects of church windows and sculptures more suspiciously than the studio hierarchies examine a plot by Balzac or Victor Hugo before it receives the imprimatur of feasibility."[51] The problem for Horkheimer and Adorno is not any lack of interest in style but rather the way such attention typically eschews social reality in favor of "late liberal taste threateningly imposed as a norm." Here, the academy and Hollywood are clear collaborators, "culture agencies, who work harmoniously with others of their kind as only managers do, whether they come from the ready-to-wear trade or college."[52] The Frankfurt theorists are not interested in identifying a "democratic" or "human" "culture" that might be preserved in the face of beer advertisements; instead they observe the collapse of autonomy from the market that Enlightenment thinking once claimed. Commercial mass media redefine the terms according to which cultural interventions take place, including any attempts from the academy. The project of improving the quality of the models consumers imitate cannot be expected to alter a social world administered in this fashion. Nor, finally, would replacing "studio hierarchies" with the Redbook's general-education experts result in more meaningfully democratic self-governance. Adorno and Horkheimer's critique thus discloses the authoritarian underbelly of Conant's project to instill "common beliefs" through education.

Conant's ambition notwithstanding, *General Education in a Free Society* cannot be credited with cultivating common beliefs alternative to those the culture industries supplied. It did find favor with policy makers. As Harpham observes, the Truman Report, *Higher Education for American*

Democracy (1947), established that postsecondary education deserved federal dollars and endorsed "a unified general education for American youth." The report echoed the Redbook: "College must find the right relationship between specialized training on the one hand, aiming at a thousand different careers, and the transmission of a common cultural heritage toward a common citizenship on the other."[53] Many advocates of higher education have reprised this appeal along with its construal of specialization as a threat that "transmission of a common cultural heritage" can counter.[54] For all their rhetorical appeal, these recommendations have never really acquired the force of policy. No federal bureau has been formed to mandate and manage the kind of curricular scheme the Redbook prescribed. In the 1960s, the Truman report did help provide the rationale for the dramatic expansion of federal financial aid to students, a story we tell in chapter 6. But as usual, decisions about university curricula were reserved for individual schools and audited by accrediting bodies. Federal agencies collected and disseminated data about programs of study, but policies designed to support meritocratic leveling based their interventions on student demographics, not general-education curricula. The form of Conant's multidisciplinary undertaking proved more reproducible than the content it recommended.

Despite its ambition to provision ideological coherence, the Redbook ended up recommending administrative initiatives that focused more on distinguishing populations. The Harvard professors set "unity conditioned by difference" as an overarching goal, but they also identified and advocated for a stratified higher-education sector. Their emphasis on meritocracy as a counterweight to inherited privilege belies their rhetoric of community and self-determination. The authors underscore that students differ in ability, in interest, in the opportunities available to them, and in the geography that shapes them. To create a national situation in which merit can be recognized therefore required a scheme of general education to balance opposing imperatives: "give scope to ability and raise the average."[55] The authors emphasize the need for "greater diversity than exists at present" in higher education, "since nothing else will match the actual range of intelligence and background among students."[56] The nation would waste youths that could succeed in college if it could not identify them and somehow fund their educations. Equally, the nation would waste college if it presumed that everyone needed to attend. The Harvard professors agreed that high school properly marked the end of compulsory education and viewed trade school as an appropriate option for many high-school graduates. The argument does not favor college for all when it insists that America needs talent. Democratizing gestures in this influential volume are indistinguishable, in the end, from the procedures of normalization required for meritocratic appraisal.

This conception of a tiered but centrally coordinated educational system also resembled the media marketplace the Redbook zealously denounced. That diversified media market unified national audiences not by exposing everyone to identical content but by reproducing genres, establishing broadcast schedules, and cultivating interpretive habits. Not everyone experienced the same program, in other words, but broadcasters could expect them to distinguish various kinds of entertainment programs from one another—and from the news. Similarly, university curricula in the Redbook model worked not by enforcing reading lists but by dividing curricula into similar types of required courses. Thus, it should come as no surprise that for all their antipathy to commercial mass culture, the Redbook authors found it easy to imagine how universities might use media not only to extend their reach but also to distinguish the populations that tuned in.

Although the Redbook saves its last breath to spit Shakespeare back at beer advertising, it arrives at this point by way of a discussion about "New Media of Education." Here, the Harvard professors sound like early-twenty-first-century EdTech disruptors. "Something of a revolution is indeed taking place through these new means of bringing the world itself, and clarified versions of it, to us," they write of film, radio, and television. True, the audiovisual revolution threatens the relative prestige of words. "Instead of words having to explain or represent things, it is rather things, and actual processes taking place before us, which explain words or call them in question." But this is not necessarily bad news: "Numberless opportunities in fact await producers aware of educational aims and with enough imagination to pursue them."[57] On cinematic adaptations of great books they write: "As a rule the values which gave the book its permanent interest are replaced by more instant and transitory lures." Nonetheless they insist: "There is nothing in the nature of the medium, however, to cause this. The fault is with the director's defective ideas of his function."[58] Like the advocates of extension services before them and MOOC enthusiasts after, the Redbook authors are keen to present audiovisual media as a wide-open field for educational research and experimentation.[59]

In making the case that media's dangers lay not in the media themselves so much as those who controlled them, the Redbook authors promote a bigger role for educators like themselves. They also argue—to sympathetic readers in the Truman administration and others—that media should be seen as part of the national educational infrastructure. To function properly as such, the reasoning goes, educational media would need to be protected from commercial competitors and made responsive to universities. After the war, as the Redbook forecasts, the argument focused on television. Television reached a relatively small viewership in 1945, but the three major networks (ABC, CBS, and NBC) would connect nearly every American household by the late 1950s. The Federal Communications Commission (FCC) deliberately slowed network expansion by imposing a freeze on new station licenses from 1948 to 1952. Among other issues, the FCC felt it needed to study whether and how the broadcast spectrum should be reserved for noncommercial, educational television (they decided it should). The Redbook clearly ranks among the arguments lending urgency to that issue.

The Redbook's ambitions for educational television typically disappear from accounts like Harpham's, which praise its defense of "the humanities." Such characterizations are liable to construe the humanities as a literary tradition to be defended rather an evolving project newer media might be enlisted to extend. Both aims are clearly discernable in the Redbook. *General Education in a Free Society* builds upon the general-education project spurred by the War Issues curriculum of the First World War and updated by the distinctive approaches to managing multidisciplinary research teams and the ambition to vouchsafe the nation through expert administration of communications that characterized the Second World War. In all these senses, the Redbook was a Manhattan Project for general education.

The Redbook's recapitulation of partitions labeled "science and mathematics," "social sciences," and "humanities" provided a poor map for the university that flourished in its wake. The "two cultures," as Snow and Trilling both acknowledged, was not even a serious attempt at such a description but rather operated as a promotional pitch that made some professors feel like the fate of the world depended on their work. The period's production of new approaches that crossed and relocated customary disciplinary boundaries is more noteworthy than this self-aggrandizing polemic. Disciplines cross-pollinated, tested themselves against their neighbors, and spun off new approaches. Wiener discovered a limit to math's ability to model human systems after spending significant time in Macy seminar rooms with human scientists like Mead, Bateson, and Richards. The Eameses continued to find cybernetics an appealing model for social communication despite that acknowledgment. Far more than allegiance to "science" or to "literature," the shared problem of communications explains what in retrospect may seem like surprising combinations of disciplinary specialization and universalizing ambition across design, neurobiology, information theory, mass communications, and New Criticism. More than object or discipline, method and mode of address distinguished efforts to study and shape communications under the atom bomb's shadow. The midcentury specializations that proposed, each in its own way, to describe the systems through which humans communicated also proposed to intervene in those systems, as the Redbook's interest in "New Media of Education," Wiener's *Cybernetics*, and the Eameses' film *A Communications Primer* all attest.

From an audience-organizing perspective, the major contrast was not to be found between literature and science but between Redbook-style general education and the para-academic pop-up installations known as "democratic surrounds." The former proposed a leveling organization of knowledge, the establishment of standards against which meritorious individuals might stand out. The latter drew attention to communications systems in action and encouraged participants to take responsibility for their roles as system components. Both styles of endeavor argued that "democracy" would require university-based communications experts to guide the interpretive habits of audiences. Both types of efforts would, by turns, identify dangers presented by commercial media while also attempting to exploit their affordances.

As ever, professors and educational planners coveted mass media's reach. In received portraits of the conformist 1950s, mainstream media, especially television, often appear as agents of ideological consensus. In setting a comparable goal for higher education, ambitious planners like Conant put the university in competition with this supposedly unifying mass effect. Yet Conant's administrative strategy, continued mutatis mutandis by the Redbook's curricular plan, did not aim primarily to craft a message for the masses. It allowed multidisciplinary teams to collaborate—sometimes intentionally, sometimes unaware of one another's work—to identify and engage distinct audience segments. For all its talk of a common core, the Redbook demanded no shared reading list. It acknowledged demographic variety and proposed replacing it with meritocratic variety; acceptance of broad goals and categories would allow general education to inform different high-school, trade-school, and college audiences. University planners would subsequently learn to perceive the demographic variety of the student body as a positive quality to be cultivated and managed along with merit, rather than being replaced by it. As arguments like Turner's reveal, that development was less a repudiation of midcentury arguments than is often supposed. By the end of the war, researchers had revealed mass-media messaging as a system involving many variables: from whom, to whom, and in what medium the message was sent mattered as much as the message itself. As radio and television audiences also knew, if one did not like the message, one could always change the channel. It logically followed, then, that interest in what made, or might make, channels and audiences different from one another would rival considerations of what they had, or should have, in common.

Chapter Five

TELEVISION, OR NEW MEDIA

In the decades following World War II, television replaced Hollywood film as the medium that ambitious universities aspired to resemble (in reach) and resist (in content). The Public Broadcasting Act of 1967 established the Corporation for Public Broadcasting as a federal grant maker, which in turn created the Public Broadcasting System (PBS). That network went live in 1970. By then, viewers could be expected to distinguish the types of programs shown by "public" (often called "educational") television from commercial options as well as from "instructional" television tailored specifically for classroom use.[1] Universities played a key role in developing both "public" and "instructional" genres as well as in securing a noncommercial television network option. Many of the noncommercial stations comprising PBS and the precursor National Educational Television (NET) network were owned and operated by universities.[2] Other "community" stations, like WGBH-Boston, were configured as independent nonprofits but had significant, longstanding partnerships with area schools. In the 1950s, the university's extension by means of television promised the kind of elevating and unifying national address fancied by James Bryan Conant. In the studios of WGBH, I. A. Richards, a Redbook contributor, lent his energy to the development of an educational television station. By 1970, when PBS supplemented, without replacing, both commercial and instructional options, Richards's student Marshall McLuhan had set the problem of "democratic propaganda" aside in favor of a bracing account of what made television radically new.

EDUCATIONAL TELEVISION AND NATIONAL WELFARE

First among other philanthropies, the Ford Foundation sustained the growth of educational television and connected it to arguments about national welfare. It supported pioneering programs through grants and, in 1952, set up NET, which linked stations and classrooms as a film distributor.[3] (Kinescopes made at the time of broadcast were the only distribution option for live programming before the introduction of videotape in the late 1950s, and they remained the only cost-effective option though the 1960s.) In 1955, Indiana University's well-established Audio-Visual Center won the contract to distribute NET films as part of a broader effort to "identify groups that can employ educational television materials," maintain a distribution network, and seed research on the medium's teaching capacities.[4] NET kinescopes could thus reach movie screens in college classrooms as easily as they could reach TV screens served by NET stations.

In chapter 1, we introduced Robert Maynard Hutchins as the University of Chicago president who disdained football crowds and advocated the New Plan as alternative branding. In 1951, as Chicago's chancellor, Hutchins revealed a comparable disdain for television viewers, describing them as "indistinguishable from the lower forms of plant life."[5] Across the sector, college football was deemed essential yet was often disparaged. Television took on a comparable role. The media historian Anna McCarthy explains that Hutchins managed both to belittle TV viewers and see the medium as "a crucial tool for raising awareness of the ongoing erosion of civil liberties precipitated by domestic anticommunism, and for educating citizens about the issues at stake in the ongoing fight for racial justice in the South."[6] He had some experience with such issues. As Chicago's chancellor, he had overseen the wartime Commission on Freedom of the Press (the Hutchins Commission), a body that drew on Rockefeller-seminar talent including Harold Lasswell and Archibald MacLeish and that helped pave the way for the Chicago Committee on Communication (1947–1960)—an early effort to organize training in mass communication at the school. Under his leadership, the Ford Foundation sought to tap the medium's potential to reach populations its other efforts could not, although as McCarthy notes, "they were unwilling to relinquish the idea that the people were part of the problem."[7] These attitudes were consistent with the commitment to expert-guided democracy that had characterized Rockefeller-funded communications research before the war and repeatedly surfaced as a tension within Cold War liberalism.[8]

Ford Foundation policy, with federal regulatory approval and in partnership with a wide range of private and public institutions, ran ahead of federal law in key areas like civil rights and public broadcasting. The foundation's nominally democratic television initiatives, however, delighted in the point-to-mass potential of broadcasting technologies and strove to educate audiences in ways that did not often require listening to them. Then again, the period's communications research had established that it was not easy to listen. One of its major results was to define media effects as a complex problem requiring professional analysis and intervention, whether the aim was to persuade people or to empower their decisions. Professional intervention could take the form of applied social survey research, which aimed to reveal patterns defining groups, patterns that those groups could not perceive on their own. It could look like the Redbook's centrally planned general-education scheme, which aimed to sort populations by merit rather than demographic contingency. Or it could look like the democratic surround, that is, open-ended media events designed to school new perceptual habits and guide participants to "their own" conclusions.

Although the Redbook and democratic surround both pitched themselves against mainstream mass media, they were more likely to segment the audiences those media had won than to replace one kind of mass experience with another. Similarly, educational television in the United States, instituted as a supplement to the commercial networks, would be unlikely to have the same kind of mass effect as government broadcasting monopolies like the BBC, which provided a model for public service broadcasting in the United States.[9] Although imagined as an alternative means of informing a national audience, American public media would be more likely to fracture it further by introducing yet another channel. The distinction between "public" and "instructional" television similarly segmented audiences and gave the university a different role to play with respect to each.

Even as the Ford Foundation collaborated with universities to invent a distinctly American variety of noncommercial television and secure it federal support, it also funded Marshall McLuhan, whose famous assertion that "the medium is the message" could make the difference between commercial and noncommercial options seem irrelevant. McLuhan developed this proposition in the decade after his successful 1953 Ford Foundation proposal (with his University of Toronto colleague Ted Carpenter) to investigate "Changing Patterns of Language and Behavior and the New Media of Communication." McLuhan and Carpenter gathered an interdisciplinary research group and reported, among other findings, that students could learn the same content better through televised lectures than through print.[10] McLuhan's 1964 *Understanding Media*, which popularized the phrase "the medium is the message," pulled from information theory and anthropology to define television as the exemplary "cool" medium. Compared with a "hot" medium like film, its relatively low information density demanded greater participation by audiences to "complete" its message, while the simultaneity of its broadcast connected a global village. Audiences joined TV's global village in something like the way visitors to *The Family of Man* participated in that exhibit: they completed possible messages allowed, but not determined, by the program. Although many eagerly seized on the communitarian connotations of this "village," McLuhan presented it as atavistic, violent, and antipathetic to individual privacy.[11] For a viewership so conceived, distinguishing the programs of NBC, ABC, and CBS from those of NET was largely beside the point. TV in general was cool. Its effects included supplanting prior media forms by incorporating them. Through this sweeping style of argument, explains the TV historian Aniko Bodroghkozy, McLuhan became "guru to the television generation." He supplied media theory to the student counterculture's underground press and succeeded as a popularizer worth interviewing in *Playboy*, quoting in the *New York Times*, and casting for a cameo in *Annie Hall* (1977).[12] "American educationalists were especially early adopters," the historian Charles Acland observes, of McLuhan's "ideas about the new literacies supposedly needed for the contemporary media environment"—a legacy, we would add, that continued into the twenty-first century.[13]

A media revolution might seem to separate Hutchins's derisory comments about TV viewers from McLuhan's iconoclastic prognostications about the medium, and in one way it does. Television changed dramatically between 1951, when it could not be said to address a national viewership, and 1964, when it clearly did. Because Hutchins helped guide that transition at the helm of the Ford Foundation, however, we cannot regard him as the "before" to McLuhan's "after." Nor should the presumed contrast between Cold War liberalism and counterculture style allow us to overlook the fact that McLuhan too was a creature of big foundations, corporations, and the state, as well as the University of Toronto. In 1958, for example, the (US) National Association of Educational Broadcasters invited him to deliver a keynote in Omaha and later recruited him to create a high-school syllabus for media training, an effort funded by the US National Defense Education Act. Starting in 1959, he also taught a course on communication to executives from General Electric.[14] There are continuities, in short, as well as differences between Hutchins's "lower forms of plant life" and McLuhan's "global village."

What most distinguished McLuhan's moment was its ability to set the problem of "democratic propaganda" aside. McLuhan lightened the load John Marshall had given media theorists as they prepared for jobs as wartime propagandists by strongly separating media effects from specific messages. (In this, his work has something in common with the very different work of Paul Lazarsfeld and Elihu Katz, who, as chapter 3 notes, also lightened the burden through their 1955 argument that media had limited direct influence on opinion.) McLuhan defined a new role for the media expert as a "guru" who provoked insights through koans like "the future of the future is the present"—"probes," McLuhan called them, that worked by provoking auditors rather than by providing comprehensive, actionable models.[15] In this role, he simultaneously diagnosed "the new" and attempted to call it into being, a project that earned him a place in Alvin Toffler's 1972 collection of "futurists" and established him as *Wired* magazine's "patron saint."[16]

The period of change that links and separates Hutchins and McLuhan might be observed in microcosm through the television career of McLuhan's former professor, I. A. Richards, who worked on no fewer than three shows with WGBH in the late 1950s. Although a prominent advocate for educational uses of mass media, Richards throughout his career derided film, radio, and TV for producing what he once called "dehumanized social animals" instead of "self-controlled, self-judging, self-ruling men and women."[17] McLuhan's reputation as a television advocate notwithstanding, Richards's emphasis echoes his pupil's equation of reading with privacy and individual goal orientation in contrast to the "groupy, trendy," "third-world" quality of the "post-literate" youth McLuhan described to TV Ontario's Mike McManus in 1977.[18] McLuhan's celebrity, however, failed to disturb his teacher's confidence that electronic media could be appropriated for other purposes by guarding against their affordances.[19] In *Design for Escape* (1968), Richards ranked TV among the best available means to conduct global education in English, particularly if enhanced by computer.[20] He cautioned, however, that a "severe, and most exacting puritanism of purpose is needed to keep the distracting temptations of these media at bay" and specifically to counter TV's "powerfully sedative action."[21] If this dangerous, narcotic television looked opposite to McLuhan's cool communal but also "third world" and privacy-denying medium, that was in large part because Richards continued to see television as something one might use to study other media, that is, use to say something else. McLuhan, in contrast, made his living as a *new media expert*, a prophet of the kinds of social relations recent media innovations might produce. Expanding its ranks to include jobs for the likes of McLuhan, the university did not sunset opportunities for the likes of Richards. Both styles of argument continued to flourish in twenty-first-century arguments over EdTech.

RICHARDS: TELEVISION PRESENTER

At WGBH, Richards sought to discover whether and how the New Critical approach to poetry might be translated for television audiences. As the station began making television in 1955, Richards collaborated with Christine Gibson and M. H. Ilsey to produce the surprisingly successful *French Through Television*, which aired 159 half-hour broadcasts.[22] Then, as "Professor and Lowell Television Lecturer at Harvard University," he launched two series devoted specifically to literature: *Sense of Poetry* (October–December 1957) and *Wrath of Achilles* (January–March 1958). Produced by Lewis Barlow, Richards's shows belong to a pioneering set of televised lectures, funded by the Ford Foundation, that featured professors from a range of disciplines.[23]

In 1970, WGBH would become a major node in the new Public Broadcasting System. As an NET station in the 1950s, it played a key role in developing the genres that would later distinguish public from commercial and instructional television. WGBH was formally connected to Harvard and other Boston-area universities and cultural organizations via the Lowell Institute Cooperative Broadcasting Council (LICBC). Established to sponsor public lectures in 1836, the Lowell Institute had, by the 1950s, decades of experience working with the extension services of Boston-area universities. Before television, its Broadcasting Council had connected these partners with WGBH radio. Television was merely the latest new medium to support its mission to "to inform the populace regardless of gender, race or economic status."[24] Accordingly, through its participation in the LICBC and the NET, Harvard's role as media maker was tested, extended, qualified, and confirmed.

Although pioneering, Richards's shows were not great television. Richards has a certain retro charm, but his performances could not be called dynamic. He gets little help from the camera. In *Sense of Poetry*, relief from a relentless medium close-up is provided mainly by text. He reads poems at length as they scroll in white characters down a black screen. On rare but memorable occasions, Richards offers a chart, a device also employed in his classroom lectures at Harvard, according to the *Crimson*, which references his "famous diagrammatic slides."[25] The vococentrism of these series is partly the point. In episode 6 of *Sense of Poetry*, which discusses Keats's "Ode on a Grecian Urn," Richards explains that "poetry, like music, is a sound art." Hearing this, one cannot but wonder whether *Sense* might have worked better on the radio, where Richards's memorable diction for favored terms like "beauty" would not have competed for attention with his unruly hair and cramped visage. (WGBH-FM radio did rebroadcast *Wrath* on Monday nights at 10:00.) Although WGBH-TV (Channel 2) clearly found an audience in 1957, it seems likely that Richards would have had difficulty drawing viewers from NBC's *Dragnet* on WBZ (Channel 4), with which he shared the Thursday 8:30 p.m. timeslot. Richards's shows were kinescoped to allow NET distribution, but it is not clear to what extent they were shown on other NET stations or in classrooms after their Boston airdates.[26]

Roughly contemporary LICBC science and art series are notably more televisual in style than Richards's poetry-appreciation classes. The early 1960s art program *Museum Open House*, for example, took advantage of Boston's Museum of Fine Arts, which had been wired and lit for

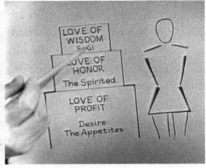

FIGURE 5.1. Frame from *Sense of Poetry* (1957). *Source*: Courtesy of the WGBH Media Library & Archives.

FIGURE 5.2. Frame from *Sense of Poetry* (1957). *Source*: Courtesy of the WGBH Media Library & Archives.

television broadcasting by 1956. The artist Russell Connor, an employee of the museum, played host. In this show, the camera is free to guide the viewer's attention by roaming the surface of the artworks being described—a technique later termed the "Ken Burns effect." In contrast, when *Wrath* offers Greek sculptures as "springboards for the imagination," these appear as still slides projected alongside Richards's talking head. The production values of Richards's shows look particularly low when compared with its contemporary *Of Science and Scientists*. Hosted by the Harvard professor of applied physics and general education Philippe Le Corbeiller, its episodes used stock footage to illustrate key points, employed a rotating cast of scientists as opposed to a single lecturer, and staged dynamic lab experiments to punctuate the professors' explanations. These presenters have memorized their pitches or follow cue cards held off screen. They look into the camera; Richards reads from crumpled notes.

Some Lowell television lecturers probably worked harder than others to accommodate the medium. Faced with the dire results of his early attempts to perform for the camera, Richards's colleague Edwin Boring, whose lectures composed the thirty-eight episodes of the late-1950s show *Psychology One*, created a more intimate address to the viewer by "imagining the three television cameras were three different people: Poppa, Mamma, and little August."[27] This does make a difference on screen.

As the LICBC partners worked to build audiences and attract funding for educational television broadcasting, they found themselves reevaluating the quality of the Harvard professors for their capacity to serve as on-air talent. In 1959, Harvard faculty appraised and ranked by WGBH included the historians John K. Fairbank, Edwin O. Reischauer, and Arthur Meier Schlesinger Jr.; the poet, professor of rhetoric, and former Librarian of Congress Archibald MacLeish; the economist John Kenneth Galbraith; and the political scientist Louis Hartz.[28] Harvard Extension's director Reginald Phelps wrote of his desire for shows that "balance . . . the attractive and the substantial."[29] A 1962 WGBH memorandum by Program Manager Robert Larsen speaks of the need for "balanced programming" as well, which in his mind means locating fields such as area studies, "Africa, South America, India and the Orient," which "could be done much better as television lectureships if sufficient funds were available."[30] With respect to public broadcasting, topical interest and professors' audience appeal were early and constant concerns.

Although Boring's psychology lectures seem more attuned to the demands and affordances of the medium than Richards's, they remain clearly recognizable as lectures, whereas *Museum Open House* and *Of Science and Scientists* also look like something else: public television. In their presentation styles, the art and science shows seem to extend traditions of educational and documentary filmmaking and, rough as these early programs were at times, to anticipate PBS staples like *NOVA*, which are designed to capture broader television audiences. In contrast, in their clunky use of visual supplements like "diagrammatic slides" and images of Greek sculptures, Richards's programs place themselves in what we now perceive to be a different genre: the canned lecture of instructional videos.

These genres diverged. If in the 1950s classroom and broadcast audiences for educational television could seem to overlap, *The French Chef* (1963–1973) with Julia Child helped establish different expectations. Although Child's kitchen mimicked the classroom in certain respects, WGBH quickly began to treat her performance in a manner that audiences would recognize as a distinct kind of show.[31] Serving as an early-evening lead-in both to *Museum Open House* and *Arts of Japan, The French Chef* was rebroadcast in the afternoon too, thus making it easily available to potentially distinct primetime and daytime audiences.[32] Instead of being driven by course requirements and academic reputations, WGBH behaved more like a commercial broadcaster driven by viewer demographics, dayparts, and televisual charisma.

Broadcast television was not, however, the station's sole focus. WGBH and Harvard extension collaborated, for instance, to produce telecourses for Navy nuclear submarine crews, among whom the historian Crane Brinton's telecourse *The Anatomy of a Revolution* was a notably popular offering.[33] The station continued to support K–12 classroom instruction as well. By the mid-1960s, however, WGBH had farmed out most instructional offerings to its UHF sister station. WGBH's station manager Hartford Gunn explained to Director of Harvard Extension Phelps that WGBH primetime belonged to shows "that an entire family could watch and enjoy," such as *Meet the Arts* and *Exploring the Crafts*.[34]

Although significant points of contact between universities and public broadcasters would remain, their notions of educational programming were clearly different when PBS replaced NET in 1970 with Gunn at the helm. Certainly by the time the first episode of *Sesame Street* appeared (on NET) in November 1969, public television could claim to provide shows as innovative as its private competition, but with different aims and audiences in mind. *Sesame Street* addressed itself to children and their parents (primarily their mothers) while tapping significant ongoing funding from foundations, federal government, and "viewers like you." Produced by the independent nonprofit Children's Television Workshop (CTW), the show's first episode borrowed Carol Burnett from her long-running CBS show (1967–1978). CTW employed academic consultants to help design and legitimate its on-screen product, but it kept them safely out of view. Meanwhile, Harvard extension continued, as it had since 1910, to use the latest new media to extend the reach of campus offerings.[35]

Richards's television foray indicates how the Redbook's ambition to capture "New Media of Instruction" encountered and transformed media-making institutions. It would be an exaggeration to claim PBS as the Redbook's most important legacy. Federal financial aid to students probably deserves that recognition. But public television may well outrank the Redbook's scheme of general education as a concrete accomplishment. When the volume made clear that the university competes with commercial media for the attention of students (and anyone else), it joined forces with powerful funders, like the Ford Foundation, to advocate a noncommercial television option. That argument prevailed and established universities as major players in the development of public television. As one might expect, Ford, Harvard, WGBH, and Richards tried to use television to extend the Redbook's privileged communications theory: New Criticism. This effort produced new distinctions between public/educational and instructional shows and audiences. It also distinguished professors who consulted off screen from those who might serve as on-air talent.

MCLUHAN: NEW MEDIA GURU

Where Richards took to the airwaves to spread the word about Keats and Homer, McLuhan talked mainly about his own ideas. His style was often the story. To pick just one example, the producers of the Canadian Broadcasting Corporation's television documentary series *Telescope* in 1967 asked McLuhan to explain the type of statement they called "McLuhanism." The documentarians staged a confessional moment. McLuhan lies on a couch in a tie and suspenders, framed from the chest up, an open book perched on the couch-back above him. The camera zooms in tight to a close-up as he explains, "there's a sign hanging on a Toronto junkyard: 'Help beautify junkyards, throw something lovely away today.' This kind of bizarre, would-be cynical, and, uh, paradoxical sort of remark has I think some of the characteristics of a McLuhanism" in that it makes unexpected connections. The McLuhanism is "a form of circuitry," he concludes.[36] As befits a guru, McLuhan was evidently comfortable talking about himself on TV. Unlike Richards, he clearly perceived that its documentary and talk-show formats required a style of performance different from the lecture or seminar address.[37] Better even than lines from Shakespeare, McLuhanism answered the Redbook's call for antiadvertising slogans that could circulate like advertising did. This facility helped establish him as one of those exceptional professors who could bridge on- and off-campus audiences.

We began this chapter by proposing that, as a media theorist, McLuhan's major contribution lay in his procedure for establishing what it meant for a medium to be "new." In "The Medium Is the Message," he famously explains that media alter the form, scale, and speed of human interaction and that this ability matters more than any specific content such media carry. He presents history as a succession of "new" media technologies that "extend" human capacities in revolutionary ways. In the twenty-first century, this notion thrived in messianic accounts—both celebratory and apocalyptic—that presented networked digital information as a sweeping novelty that rendered everything else hopelessly out of date. McLuhan's view is less technologically determinist than that of many who appropriate him. From his Toronto colleague the political economist Harold Innis, he had learned to embed technology in a thicker history of material social relations. Media novelty, for him, also involved a kind of dialectic: a new medium absorbed prior media as content and prepared itself to be "flipped" in turn into an even newer form.[38] Nonetheless, and despite persistent cageyness about "the future of the present," the sense that new media make older media "obsolete," also rendering obsolete a set of social relationships along with them, characterizes McLuhan's approach.

This emphasis may have stamped McLuhan's home discipline of English more profoundly than it did the study of television. McLuhan's *The Gutenberg Galaxy* (1962) developed precedents including Innis's *Empire and Communications* (1950) to make generally available the contention that print had been a radically new mass medium. This idea underwrote any number of histories of the book, not to mention sweeping studies like Elizabeth L. Eisenstein's massive two-volume survey *The Printing Press as an Agent of Change* (1979) and Benedict Anderson's *Imagined Communities* (1983), both of which credited print with replacing one world-historical order in favor of another.[39] It should not surprise us that scholars do not typically track these innovative arguments back to McLuhan and, through him, the less discipline-bound universe of midcentury communications research in which Richards sat across seminar tables from Lasswell and Norbert Wiener.[40] (Nor do they typically invoke the distinctly Canadian intellectual space from which Innis's *Empire and Communications* launched itself against US neocolonialism.) Disciplines, like Anderson's nations, habitually erase the historical field of operations that gives them life.

Television, meanwhile, would be studied in various ways by relatively new disciplines, like mass communications, and established ones, like sociology. The 1970 publication of Eric Barnow's *The Image Empire: A History of Broadcasting in the United States from 1953* provides one customary marker for TV's emergence as a discrete field of scholarly inquiry in the United States.[41] In method, Barnow's narrative history, which interweaves considerations of industrial organization and economics, government regulation, program innovation, and social context, seems a world removed from McLuhan's contemporary speculations about electronic media's revolutionary powers. The university had room for both types—and it continued to employ specialists in metaphysical poetry and the classics.

Although some schools continued to own and operate stations, by the 1970s the production of television by universities had fallen into a pattern that recalled the disposition of film and radio between the world wars. Extension divisions produced instructional television (often on film) for limited audiences. As with film and radio, the university would explain the audience relations the new medium afforded while leaving the task of maintaining those audiences primarily to commercial broadcasters and the new noncommercial public option. Where interwar educational film production had drawn investment from the likes of AT&T's subsidiary ERPI, the 1960s witnessed intense new interest by such firms as IBM, Raytheon, and Xerox, who aimed to deploy cutting-edge, electronic educational technologies to supplement classroom instruction through applications of "systems thinking." The EdTech historian Curtis Fletcher notes that "essentially, the nation's entire electronics industry moved en masse into the schoolroom."[42] There was a wrinkle, however, in that college students began to demand training in film and television production.

Chapter Six

COOPTATION

After World War II, federal dollars restructured the university's relationship to the state. This had consequences more profound and sweeping than the funding of specific research projects and groups of students. Federal dollars for research and student financial aid opened a dense two-way communications channel. For every grant check issued in Washington, reports would flow back from recipient institutions. Washington could use this information to describe higher education as a milieu on which policy could act. In the previous three chapters, we concentrated on the institutional and individual actors that developed and extended this midcentury communications complex. Now we turn to the students of the 1960s, whose increasing numbers, diversity, and do-it-yourself ethos inspired new programs of study as well as new practices of data collection. The media of biopolitics—tables and charts measuring the health and well-being of multifarious student populations—are the oft-ignored counterparts to the more familiar stars of the 1960s university, student activists. In the next chapter, we will consider how students both added value to and inflected the politics of contemporary media industries. Here, we are concerned with how they transformed universities as institutions.

From positions on both the right and left, student activists presented the midcentury university as a core institution of an oppressive establishment that would nonetheless be particularly susceptible to change. This emphasis on remaking the university arguably distinguishes the period's college-goers from upstream movements such as the American Student Union (1935–1941) and the Southern Negro Youth Congress (1937–1949) as well as from efforts to organize student governments such as the National Student Federation of America (est. 1925). Although they resembled prior movements in working to connect students with broader struggles to oppose wars or redress economic and racial injustice, student movements after World War II notably focused on the university itself as a target of intervention. That emphasis made them more a part of the communications complex than their antiestablishment rhetoric suggests.

As several early-twenty-first-century commentators have noted, the students-versus-the-establishment plot urges a reductive understanding of the 1960s and a misleading notion of what made that decade different from the 1950s.[1] Hallmarks of the 1960s from the civil rights struggle to counter-cultural happenings have clear antecedents in the preceding decade. Mainstream media of the 1960s learned to conjure campus radicals along with college lettermen and to address youths as a distinct (and highly profitable) demographic. Antiestablishment postures could be good for business at the university as well, if administrators could learn to appropriate and repurpose them. It diminishes neither the commitment of student radicals nor the violence with which universities sometimes confronted them to point out that change happened differently than the various actors envisioned at the time.

Students successfully agitated for new degree programs in areas like film studies, women's studies, and African American studies, and they won voices for minority and marginalized communities in university decision making. Although students did not dominate the university's curriculum or its committee rooms, decision makers in both domains learned to take their interests into account, particularly when it seemed those interests might take an organized and oppositional form. This dynamic, described at the time as "cooptation" by the sociologist Philip Selznick, is one way to characterize institutional change.

In part, universities learned to anticipate and co-opt students' interests by collecting more and more data about them. Federal enumerators played a major role here, and in some ways they supported the agendas of student activists more than those of university administrations. Civil rights legislation in particular both increased the demand for more granular demographic data about students and required that universities change in response to it. Students claimed a role in defining whom universities should educate and how they should go about it. At the same time, federal and university policy, mediated by statistics, worked to redefine students as adult consumers (and potential litigants). This shift effectively reframed the student-university relationship in contractual terms. It equally provided the university with a new priority of improving its responsiveness to student demands by co-opting them as its own.

This new orientation replaced the in loco parentis model that the influx of adult students under the GI Bill had already strained. In student affairs the earlier approach had mandated features like single-sex dormitories, while in general education it anchored the idea that a specific set of classes would allow any student whatsoever to mature into a good citizen. Treating students as adults meant engaging "traditional" undergraduates in something like the way universities had long addressed extension students. As audiences for educational services, students were expected to know what they wanted. Student interests were presumed to be various—while mass appeals might succeed, everything about the system favored niche marketing. Remediated as a statistical puzzle and politico-economic agent, the student body was a different kind of actor than the one that had cheered for football teams earlier in the century.

COMMUNITIES OF CONTROVERSY

Cooptation of student protest by university officialdom provides evidence of dissent's effectiveness rather than its neutralization. This is not to suggest that either students or administrators got what they wanted. The University of California at Berkeley provides a customary reference point in discussions of campus struggle. Its "FSM 50" (Free Speech Movement at Fifty) site indicates the extent to which student activism redefined that university's brand. In 1964, Mario Savio famously denounced the Cal "machine."[2] Fifty years later, university marketing appropriated his image to locate "activism" in the institution's "DNA," as the website's banner proudly declared above a picture of Savio and Martin Luther King Jr. hailing multitudes in Sproul Plaza.[3] The page associates Savio's likeness not only with King's but also with that of Mohandas "Mahatma" Gandhi. It does not picture his antagonist, the UC system's president Clark Kerr.

"Berkeley radicals" are, in fact, iconic. The university's publicists are not wrong to claim activism as a defining feature of the institution. Moreover, it would undervalue student contributions to present publicity as neutralizing their critique. The challenge of student radicalism is not erased when PR blunts its sharper edges. To the contrary, in the movement's wake, generations of campus activists could be expected to fill Sproul Plaza just as generations of Cal football fans could be expected to crowd California Memorial Stadium. Both audiences help Berkeley remain Berkeley.

If Yale showed the way for the football-centric schools of the early twentieth century, and if Chicago in the 1930s modeled a more scholarly address, so student activism Berkeley-style became a hallmark of campus life. This is so despite the fact that the aims and demographic composition of the Free Speech Movement were hardly isomorphic with all student activism in the period. Student protest and its sometimes violent repression stamped institutional identities at schools ranging from Columbia University to Kent State and Florida State—known for a time as the "Berkeley of the South." At UC San Diego, protests helped launch a minority-focused Third College, while Black studies departments at the University of Colorado, Cornell University, the University of Minnesota, and elsewhere trace their origins to student activism. Within constraints imposed by public and donor relations, twenty-first-century schools often find it worthwhile to memorialize these legacies. As much as the FSM set a paradigm for 1960s protest, Berkeley's splashy website also exemplifies a trend discernable on university web pages and in alumni magazines across the country.[4]

Selznick developed the term "coöptation" to describe "the process of absorbing new elements into the leadership or policy-determining structure of an organization as a means of averting threats to its stability or existence."[5] Importantly, he distinguished formal versions of the process from informal ones. In the formal variety, an organization shores up its legitimacy by incorporating publicly what otherwise would be opposing voices. Such cooptation typically involves no significant redistribution of power. Selznick's study of the Tennessee Valley Authority shows, for example, that although voluntary associations of valley residents were touted as a means to satisfy the core policy objective of decentralized "grassroots" participation in the project, in practice they worked to strengthen bureaucracy's hand in decision making. Informal cooptation, in contrast, actually does redistribute authority. It is concerned not with appearances but with "meeting the pressure of specific individuals or interest groups which are in a position to enforce demands."[6] For example, because they were well positioned to advise farmers and to communicate their concerns, the extension officers of land-grant colleges played a decisive role in brokering fertilizer distribution for the TVA's agricultural program, although they did not serve officially in that capacity.

Selznick underscores that whereas formal cooptation always looks like public relations, informal cooptation is "covert." Because the power of informally co-opted actors comes from a potentially competing organization (for example, the land-grant college or the FSM), to acknowledge informal cooptation would expose the limits of the co-opting organization's authority. It might further disclose that some parties have more clout than others, suggesting that institutional rules granting every member of a committee one vote, for instance, do not apply to actual circumstances, in which some constituencies must be satisfied and others may be ignored. Admitting that the institution relies upon outside authority and that it cannot function according to the letter of its own bureaucratic law tends to undermine organizational legitimacy and thus impair function.

Informal and formal mechanisms are not opposites, however, in that formal cooptation cannot be merely for show and still be effective. "Consequently, formal coöptation requires informal control over the coöpted elements lest the unity of command and decision be imperiled."[7] Formally co-opted outsiders cannot simply be treated as insiders if they really do represent divergent interests. Successfully co-opted actors find themselves paradoxically included in the organization's decision-making hierarchy even while remaining outside it.[8]

To deal with the annoying fact that the public (or customers, or students) has interests different from those that bureaucracy anticipates, leadership may try any number of formal ploys. It can, for instance, include dissenters on committees or invite them to public forums, thereby involving them in decision making while ceding little authority to shape outcomes. Unless, however, bureaucrats can develop informal arrangements that really do accommodate competing interests and accept limits on their own power in the process, they will find it difficult to get anything done. For Selznick, then, cooptation holds the key to understanding how bureaucratic organizations function and change in relation to other social assemblages.

In universities of the 1960s and 1970s, such a process did in fact change formal governance structures. Universities found informal ways to accommodate charismatic and strident student spokespersons like Savio who seemed in every way opposed to establishment administrators like Kerr. At the same time, student activists retained constituencies outside and often antagonistic to campus policies and administrative structures. Importantly, students often handled their own public relations when addressing audiences off campus.

The 1960s were not the first time universities co-opted energetic student organizations. In chapter 1, we described how the American university's early-twentieth-century flowering stemmed from its successful incorporation of the forms of campus life that students created around athletic contests. The US higher-education sector could not have grown as rapidly as it did absent an ability to attract and organize football crowds by appropriating this student-made culture. Remarkably, students continued to treat this culture as theirs even after the authority to administer it passed to professional coaches and publicists. Football's cooptation, moreover, profoundly shaped faculty members' and administrators' approaches to undergraduate education. Even as they disparaged the sport for threatening the academic mission, they *hoped* curricula might generate similar mass effects.

The 1950s further frustrated the dream of higher education competing with commercial mass media. As described in the previous chapter, television enabled new synergies of mass spectacle and mass education, but it also created distinctions among types of audiences, making it more difficult than ever to conceive "the university" as having a coherent mass address. Alongside academic programming as television content, college football underwent parallel program differentiation. After World War II, football grew along with higher education and the nation's burgeoning television networks. The GI Bill enabled numerous talented athletes to afford university education, and nearly half of these students headed to large public schools with football programs.[9] Although NBC pioneered football broadcasts with a 1939 contest between Fordham and Waynesburg, college football did not promise a mass viewership before 1950. Then, in anticipation of the boom in receiver ownership that would follow the end of the FCC's freeze on new station licenses in 1952, networks hungry for programming began to contract with schools in major media markets as well as those, like Notre Dame, with potentially national fan bases.[10] Television contracts changed business models that had relied on gate sales, and a marked division emerged between the TV revenue haves and have-nots. In 1951, the NCAA intervened to organize broadcasting, establishing a cartel that would resist deregulation until the 1980s. As the historian Jeffrey Montez de Oca observes, the NCAA attempted to define broadcast rules that would protect smaller schools' football programs from a "TV aristocracy" of big-time schools.[11] Nonetheless, many small colleges decided that they could no longer afford the sport.[12] As the 1950s drew to a close, the national market for college football broadcasts distinguished not only individual school brands, then, but also separated schools willing and able to compete for Nielsen ratings from those that were not. From the perspective of the higher-education sector as a whole, a mass TV viewership for college football had the paradoxical effect of further segmenting university audiences even as it grew them.

Before the publication of William F. Buckley's *God and Man at Yale* in 1951, students tended not to claim the curriculum as "theirs" in the same way that football was. As a Yale undergraduate in the late 1940s, Buckley developed in the pages of the *Yale Daily News* and at the Yale Political Union a type of critique that would become available, mutatis mutandis, to students of diverse political orientations. He identified the university as a space that capitalist Christians could reclaim from liberal professors and their complacent student followers. The culmination of this critique, *God and Man at Yale*, portrayed an academy in which the campus president's office and boards of trustees needed to ally themselves more forcefully with the fathers who were "paying for the transmission of knowledge and values" occurring at the university. These paternal forces had effectively betrayed their class interest by allowing professors to pursue a liberal establishment agenda that, for example, mainstreamed Keynesian economics.[13]

Buckley hoped an alliance between conservative students and alumni groups would prompt presidents, trustees, and donors to own their privilege and use their power to ensure that the values transmitted by the university were more properly capitalist and more explicitly Christian. In order to challenge university administration to confront its professorial establishment, he embraced the notion of the university as a communications channel. He also conceived it as a base for an ongoing political strategy. "I believe that if and when the menace of Communism is gone," he wrote, "other vital battles, at present subordinated, will emerge to the foreground. And the winner must have help from the classroom."[14] As it turned out, the student left found more help from the classroom than the right, insofar as curricula were not generally refocused on Christian and capitalist messaging but rather opened up to a wider array of approaches.

Activism in the 1960s made student claims on the curriculum routine. To linger a bit longer with the iconic instance, FSM radicalism distinguished itself as a confluence of curricular experiment and media engagement. Speaking from the steps of Berkeley's Sproul Hall in December 1964, Savio whipped up the crowd by quoting President Kerr: "Would you ever imagine the manager of a firm making a statement publicly in opposition to his board of directors?" Savio claimed to have hoped for more public support from the president—"a well-meaning liberal"—and seized upon the remark to declare opposition to a university in which "Kerr in fact is the manager . . . the faculty are a bunch of employees and we're the raw materials!"[15] Students "don't mean to be made into any product," he argued, "don't mean . . . to end up being bought by some clients of the university, be they the government, be they industry, be they organized labor, be they anyone! We're human beings!"[16] To demonstrate their humanity, Savio explained, his fellow students would return to Sproul Hall, organize classes on "freedom," and screen some movies.[17] "We're going to have classes on [the] 1st and 14th amendments!" he declared. "We're going to spend our time learning about the things this University is afraid that we know. We're going to learn about freedom up there. And we're going to learn by doing!" Under the banner of a "Free University of California," graduate students and others (including the area poet Gary Snyder) taught lessons drawn from sociology, mathematics, history, literature, and film.[18] Of these, film was the only plausible candidate for a subject the university actually feared teaching, since Berkeley at the time had entire departments devoted to each of the others, a topic to which we will return.

For the moment, it bears underscoring that although student activism at Berkeley certainly disrupted normal campus operations, it proved far from antithetical to master planner Kerr's signature statement in *The Uses of the University* (1963). Here, Kerr defined the contemporary university as less an organism than a mechanism, a "city of infinite variety" rather than a "village with its priests."[19] As it grew and became multiple, the university linked itself more securely into "the world of work," Kerr argued. The professor was "taking on the characteristics of an entrepreneur," as industry and academy merged "physically and psychologically."[20] Although his mechanical metaphors and seeming affinity for industry proved troubling to Savio and other activists, all agreed that the contemporary university could not be understood as an enclosed ivory tower; it was a public-facing enterprise. Kerr emphasized the multiplicity of publics the university addressed and found that variety mirrored within what he termed the "multiversity." Such institutions' "edges are fuzzy," he wrote, in that they reach "out to alumni, legislators, farmers, businessmen, who are all related to one or more . . . internal communities." Although strikingly lacking in central coordination, he found, the multiversity serves those external communities and also criticizes them. It can in no way ignore them.[21]

The students' public performances aptly demonstrated Kerr's central argument that contemporary multiversities were incapable of coordinated action across their many parts and were only manageable as an ensemble of divergent functions necessarily addressing external audiences. According to Kerr's 1965 commencement address, FSM rebellion gave "a new urgency to efforts for educational and organizational reform."[22] Their headline-grabbing insistence on social and political autonomy coincided with university managers' attempts to grapple with the institution's ever-increasing heterogeneity. Neither camp could accept "raw materials" as a metaphor for "students." Kerr, who depicted the multiversity as "not one community but several," acknowledged that it could be "a confusing place for the student." "It offers him a vast range of choices," he wrote, "enough literally to stagger the mind. In this range of choices he encounters the opportunities and the dilemmas of freedom. The casualty rate is high. The walking wounded are many."[23] The FSM's emphasis on the whole "human being" revealed a kindred concern with fragmentation. The intellectual historian Andrew Jewett observes that the movement advocated a "thoroughly old-fashioned model of liberal education" that proposed the university's autonomy as a precondition for social critique.[24] Old-fashioned though it may have been, FSM's postprotest screening series and self-guided freedom curriculum also indicated student preferences that the multiversity could accommodate by expanding its curriculum and curating an heterogeneous array of course and degree options. Together, Kerr and the FSM imagined an undergraduate who would need to function as a mature political and intellectual agent in order to navigate the multiversity. This revision would eventually establish terms like "stakeholder," "client," and "customer" as functional substitutes for "student," a development the FSM clearly would have abhorred.

FSM activism can no more be disentangled from establishment media than from the establishment curriculum it opposed. In its moment, the FSM found audiences through the listener-supported local radio station KPFA as well as advertiser-supported local and national newspapers and television. Now, YouTube circulates Savio's speeches. At the time, Savio is said to have been inspired by materials the Redbook authors would have welcomed on college syllabi—Melville, Kant, Thucydides, and Thoreau.[25] His fellow activist Bettina Aptheker also alleges that the famous "bodies upon the gears" speech owes its emphasis on civil disobedience to the kind of Hollywood fare those same Harvard professors feared—Richard Burton and Peter O'Toole's Oscar-winning movie *Becket*, which dramatized the twelfth-century conflict between Henry II and his archbishop of Canterbury.[26] The Redbook's proposed media hierarchy guided neither Savio's intervention nor many of the innovative approaches to the study of culture that emerged alongside the FSM.

Awareness that universities were in the business of mass mediation distinguished this period's emblematic student manifesto: the Port Huron Statement. Written by the Students for a Democratic Society in 1962, the year before Kerr's *Uses of the University* was published, the Port Huron Statement joins Kerr in upending key assumptions that guided midcentury planners. Unlike the Redbook authors, but like Max Horkheimer and Theodor Adorno, SDS saw little difference between mass media and the university's custodians of tradition. "Tragically," they wrote in the Port Huron Statement,

the actual intellectual effect of the college experience is hardly distinguishable from that of any other communications channel—say, a television set—passing on the stock truths of the day. Students leave college somewhat more "tolerant" than when they arrived, but basically unchallenged in their values and political orientations. With administrators ordering the institutions, and faculty the curriculum, the student learns by his isolation to accept elite rule within the university, which prepares him to accept later forms of minority control.

The similarity between TV and college lay not only in their content—both "pass on stock truths"—but also in their form—both organized messages from above and sought to "communicate" rather than to "challenge" them. In contrast, the SDS envisioned its ideal university as "a community of controversy, within itself and in its effects on communities beyond."[27] Although deeply enmeshed in the military-industrial complex, the university was nonetheless "the only mainstream institution that is open to participation by individuals of nearly any viewpoint" and thus uniquely available to those seeking to codify alternatives. While staunchly critical of the university, then, the Port Huron Statement nonetheless echoed generations of advocates in portraying it as "a potential base and agency in a movement of social change."[28] In other words, SDS thought more like the advocates of educational television than like James Bryant Conant. The point was to not remake the university such that it could secure a national ideology (they thought it was already of a piece with one). Rather, the point was to reimagine the university as a channel capable of nurturing alternatives to the mainstream.

The SDS developed its media critique from C. Wright Mills. In *The Power Elite* (1956), Mills extends the argument of Walter Lippman's *Public Opinion* (1922) to conclude that "in a mass society, the dominant type of communication is the formal media, and the publics become mere *media markets*: all those exposed to the contents of given mass media."[29] Although education might be expected to cultivate an enlightened, self-aware public, Mills declared that it had failed that task: "mass education, in many respects, has become—another mass medium." It reinforced elite rule by encouraging "intellectual mediocrity, vocational training, nationalistic loyalties, and little else."[30] Although Mills believed that true forms of public life remained in America, he held out little hope that these scattered and marginalized publics could out-organize established elites and their institutions. The SDS found hope in the project of transforming the university, which would obviously require not simply openness to different viewpoints but also programming strategies designed to upend "stock truths" and challenge established communication channels.

As we have already observed, these counterprogramming strategies would be susceptible to cooptation as *additional* communications channels. New channels segmented audiences, sometimes further subdividing them, sometimes producing new constellations. This eventually altered the geometry of publicity imagined by Mills, in which truer, marginal publics stood on the edges of a strongly centralizing, inauthentic, mass-mediated public. In the area of curriculum, for instance, once universities had institutionalized a procession of new majors for which students agitated in African American studies, film studies, women's studies, and many, many others, it became difficult to imagine that each opposed the same central node. Instead, the upstarts often collaborated and sometimes competed with one another as well as with existing departments and disciplines. The new majors recruited students who might also be considering a major in history, communications, or English. They might share faculty with departments in which such majors were housed even as they sought to distinguish their research and course offerings as interdisciplinary. Each new alternative, moreover, might purport to provide a generalizable vantage that all the others excluded. There could be as many construals of what defined "mainstream mass culture" as there were disciplines concerned with that problem, overloading of the category of "mass" to entropic effect and diminishing the utility of the term.

When mainstream media targeted college-going youth, they too tried to distinguish themselves from the establishment. Hollywood had studiously addressed itself to capturing the fifteen-to-twenty-four-year-old demographic in the 1950s—an effort in which new independent producers such as American International Pictures found notable success.[31] In the 1960s, the Hollywood majors and television producers alike pegged their fortunes to the youth market. After all, it was widely understood that by 1967 more than half of the American population would be under twenty-five. As the media historian Aniko Bodroghkozy explains, "prime time attempted to turn itself into a 'groove tube,' incorporating significant amounts of (admittedly simplified and sanitized) countercultural and campus politico values and critiques."[32] Filmmakers found college audiences with new "youth classics" such as *The Graduate* (1966), *Bonnie and Clyde* (1967), and *Easy Rider* (1969). Hollywood also attempted to engage campus protest directly. In the tumultuous year of 1970, it released a cycle of films about student radicalism including *Zabriskie Point*, *Getting Straight*, and *The Strawberry Statement*. The latter film generated especially lively debate in the underground student press, with some writers maintaining that sensationalized riot imagery trivialized the political struggle and others declaring that it could prove effective in radicalizing the unconverted.[33]

Examination of mainstream film and television thus reveals sustained efforts to engage and manage the controversies of the day, a dynamic ill-described as a project of disseminating "stock truths" or exposing "mere media markets" to "content."

The antinomy between "mass-media communications" and the "community of controversy" is performative. As a description, it cannot be sustained. The SDS rightly affirmed that the university was media-like through and through while demonstrating that it also included student dissenters. By co-opting disruptive student behavior, universities, like movie producers, could redefine it as innovation. This process made it impossible to understand higher education as a singular counterweight to mass media. It required, rather, that the university be grasped as a mixed-media enterprise that included national network television starring the football team as well as avant-garde cinema screened by the movie club. Read together, Savio's Sproul Plaza performances, SDS's "community of controversy," and Kerr's "multiversity" announced that this manifold address would henceforth characterize the American research university.

CURRICULAR AND ORGANIZATIONAL CHANGE

Not all roads to cooptation lead through Sproul Plaza. If Savio provides an iconic face of student activism, he cannot front the diverse student-inspired curricular changes of the 1960s and 1970s. No female FSM leaders joined Savio on stage for the "bodies upon the gears" speech, which must challenge anyone to construe it as a moment in the struggle to establish women's studies programs.[34] Years later, Savio lamented the divergence of the New Left and Black nationalism in the aftermath of the FSM; the freedom curriculum's attention to the Fourteenth Amendment was not the same thing as agitation for African American studies.[35] In one area only was the classroom agenda Savio proclaimed both significantly new and of piece with student demands elsewhere: it seemed important to study films. The development of degree programs in this area cannot stand in for all the other new "studies," each of which followed its own path. Nonetheless, film studies provides a particularly clear and relatively widespread example of how colleges co-opted student energies.

Although a wide range of media had been included in academic curricula for many decades, large numbers of courses and degree programs devoted specifically to film study—production as well as history and criticism—did not exist before students agitated for them in the 1960s. Berkeley, for instance, did not offer a BA in film until 1976 (film and media studies achieved departmental status there in 2010).[36] A survey conducted by the American Film Institute for its college guide documents that courses in film production and criticism increased from 244 at seventy-one institutions in 1964 to 9,228 courses at 1,067 institutions by 1978, by which time the guide considered courses in television production and criticism as well. The number of students (including graduate students) grew from 5,300 in 1969 to 40,596 by 1978—a rate far outpacing the growth of student populations as a whole.[37] (Federal agencies did not count degrees in the field before the late 1980s.) The media historian Michael Zryd observes that "the expansion of film study in the 1960s was largely a student-led phenomenon." University administrations, he shows, "rarely initiated and only reluctantly responded to student interest."[38] Campus film societies, which grew in number from "two hundred in the early 1950s to five thousand by the late 1960s," played a key role. They not only spurred courses but also helped develop national distribution networks and exhibition venues for alternatives to commercial theatrical releases.[39]

The University of South Carolina provides an interesting case in point. A new period of student involvement in campus film programming arguably began in 1947, when an English exchange student and "other persons interested in . . . high-class foreign film" established the University Film Society. By 1950, the society claimed regular audiences of 350 to 500 persons.[40] In 1955, its programs included faculty speakers who offered brief comments on films of "historic or cultural interest."[41] Two years later, however, it disbanded, citing "competition from television" as well as from numerous screening venues and series on campus and off.[42] In its wake, the community-based Columbia Fine Films Society proved a durable organizer of art-film screenings, although there were signs that it had begun to lose touch with student audiences by 1963.[43] Nonetheless, in 1965 a commentator in the student newspaper extolled both the community group and the student union's unnamed programmer for bringing excellent films to town. He found film "one of the few cultural areas where Columbia is equal, or perhaps superior, to cities of comparable status."[44] From 1947 to 1965, then, responsibility for programming film alternatives in Columbia shifted from the student-led University Film Society (which had a faculty advisory board) to the community-based Columbia Fine Films Society and the student union. Throughout this period, the student newspaper (*The Gamecock*) recorded little disagreement over the definition of "fine films" or the value of screening them in the Columbia area. This would soon change.

In the fall of 1967, University of South Carolina students formed the Celluloid Society to "study" experimental films in a local coffee house—student memberships were $1.50; faculty could join for $3.00.[45] This proved a pivotal moment in the politicization of campus film culture.[46] In addition to the experimentalists of the Celluloid Society, other student groups showed interest in building constituencies through screenings. In December 1967, for instance, the local Young Americans for Freedom chapter planned to screen a series of documentaries to prompt discussion of "Red China and the United Nations."[47] Meanwhile, the student union ran a series of "popular films," which showed midweek, and "fine films," which showed on weekends. As was typical at the time, campus film culture included sharply divergent interests.

In the fall of 1969, a tension between the audiences addressed by different student film series boiled over. "For a long time," wrote William W. Byler in a letter to the *Gamecock*'s editor, "there has been a quietly smoldering controversy over the Russell House film programs." That controversy erupted at a Monday-night screening of the Michael Caine thriller *The Ipcress File* (1965) and *Les Portes du Silence* (1966), a short subject "which dealt with the polyphonic music of the Renaissance." The short had been scheduled for the previous Thursday's "fine film" program, but the print had not arrived in time, so the Films Committee had added it to the Monday "popular film" screening. "The audience immediately showed its dissatisfaction," Byler reported. "By the middle of the short there was intermittent hissing and booing; and by the end, the jeers and catcalls were so intense that the soundtrack was virtually drowned out." He recommended that the Films Committee take greater care to distinguish audiences in the future: "For the 'popular' film audiences, who succumb so easily to the mass-mediocrity psychosis, it is time for the Committee to reconsider its objectives. Give them what they obviously want (and deserve)—the very worst movies available."[48] Byler's letter not only indicates the polarization of campus film culture but also underscores that control of the student union's series had passed to a student Films Committee, the leadership of which was hotly contested.[49] Controversy over the student union's film series erupted again 1971, when 726 students signed a petition demanding something other than "popular" American films.[50]

In its taste for student and experimental work, its ambition to supplant preexisting organizations, its embrace of film programming as a kind of political activity, and its inspiration of more formal programs of study, the University of South Carolina's Celluloid Society exemplifies the general tendencies of 1960s campus film societies identified by Zryd. The Celluloid Society claimed to have taken over from the "defunct" Columbia Fine Films Society in February 1969. By the fall, its members ran the Russell House Films Committee as well.[51] In addition to the established "fine films" programs, Celluloid Society types organized screenings of student work dealing with "social issues" as well as "underground films." Expressly created as a forum to study films, the Celluloid Society conducted a "short course on film" that inspired student filmmakers in 1969.[52] By the fall of 1971, students could enroll in "The Film Experience," a course offered in English and journalism by the professors Benjamin Dunlap and George P. Garrett. Dunlap "seems to exude a charisma like that which surrounds other media freaks," the *Gamecock* reported in 1973, noting also that the course enrolled one thousand students annually.[53]

Administrative moves to co-opt student interest by formalizing a program of film study swiftly followed. The university president created a Media Arts Institute under the directorship of the composer Don Gillis, which claimed to enroll three hundred students in production courses by 1974.[54] In 1975, the Faculty Senate's Committee on Curriculum and Courses recommended creation of two baccalaureate degrees in media arts—one a liberal arts degree, the other a preprofessional program—as well as two master's degrees—a master of media arts and a master of education in media instruction. "The Media Arts include all electronic, electrographic, photographic, and graphic media," explained the proposal. "One needs only to open his eyes and ears to realize the tremendous impact of these forces on our lives and society."[55] For whatever reasons, the administration decided to keep "media" in the vocational space. Only the preprofessional bachelor of media arts and the two master's degrees were approved. The university would not launch a liberal arts BA in film and media study until the new millennium, producing its first graduates in 2004.[56] The creation of that program would be driven primarily by faculty, not students, and would respond to curricular norms set by similar programs at other schools. To be sure, faculty advocates needed to demonstrate student interest in the new major, but the impetus to create new curricula no longer came from student agitators in the Celluloid Society.

As this pattern repeated itself nationally, it yielded a remarkable variety of programs. As at the University of South Carolina, the local talents, ambitions, and professional interests of faculty and administrators, as opposed to a nationally recognized prototype or plan, initially determined how various institutions co-opted student interest. In 1967, New York University did indicate one overarching trend when it moved its longstanding film program from the "Communication Arts Group," which served education students, to a new "School of the Arts." As this tendency to place film within the arts may suggest, much of the frisson of student film work came from the personal appropriation of glossy corporate forms. Many new and revised programs of study eschewed training for established industries in favor of low-budget, hands-on approaches that lent themselves to self-expression, documentary, and experimental forms.[57] But this was not the case everywhere. Surveying the "Student Film World" in 1970, Thomas Frensch found an industry-inspired "crew concept" entrenched at the University of Southern California's decades-old program, for example. Meanwhile, an "experimental and free-wheelin'" emphasis prevailed amid the cornfields at the University of Iowa, which was then building a "multi-million dollar arts complex" to include film. The University of Michigan in Ann Arbor offered few courses but hosted a thriving film festival; West Virginia University's eager students faced a recalcitrant "19th-century administration"; Temple was home to a new and rapidly growing program emphasizing " 'creative documentary' "; and so on.[58] Frensch's report captures a moment when various universities' decisions to co-opt student interest in film had produced an array of loosely coupled initiatives.

This distinctive pattern of development has had durable consequences, but these are easily misunderstood. In its 2015 "State of the Field" report, the Society for Cinema and Media Studies (SCMS) cites as major challenges the "lack of consistency in how units operate, what kinds of courses they offer, and how they define themselves" as well as the range of possible institutional configurations for degree programs. Some are standalone units, while others might be tracks in art history, English, communications, or theater, and still others might be located in interdisciplinary humanities programs.[59] The SCMS report emphasizes immature disciplinary coordination relative, for example, to disciplines that were departmentalized nationwide before World War II. We would emphasize, rather, that the institutional variety indexes dynamics of formal and informal cooptation, which played out differently on different campuses and shaped many of this period's new degrees. These are pointers to a new mode of university operation, in other words, rather than indicators of a stage in a disciplinary lifestyle modeled by history or English.

Student-inspired curricula in film and other areas did not simply add new degree pathways but also altered the organizational logic that distinguished disciplines and linked coursework to student demand. In 1969, 269 student protests across the country proclaimed the need for new Black studies, Chicano studies, and women's studies programs.[60] As these programs started to appear, they made older efforts to mold students seem unresponsive to their interests. As Roderick Ferguson observes, "the universalizing names of canonicity, nationality, or economy" bespoke an elder generation.[61] Requirements were reduced and new majors formed, reversing the post–World War I impulse to constrain the student choices that the elective system and Carnegie unit had introduced in the 1890s. In its aims and effects, co-opting organized student interests was fundamentally different from the task of trying to organize those interests through core curricula.

Where SCMS perceives that field's legacy of cooptation as a "challenge," ethnic studies and women's studies practitioners are more likely to perceive a contradiction. As Ferguson puts it, ethnic studies and women's studies interdisciplines came to represent "an instance in which minoritized differences negotiate and maneuver agreements with and estrangements from institutionalization."[62] The process of institutionalization has generated significant commentary from within the interdisciplines. As Lisa Lowe explains, ethnic studies matched a "transformative critique of traditional disciplines" with the establishment of its own often equally "orthodox objects and methods."[63] Accordingly, many of the new programs challenged the authority of institutionalized disciplines while simultaneously structuring themselves in the way any degree program would. For example, they might define the field for students in foundational courses while pulling electives from various departments. In this way, institutionalization created a paradox Wendy Brown called the "impossibility of Women's

Studies" because that effort inevitably "circumscribes uncircumscribable 'women' as an object of study."[64] "Canon formation has become one of the thorny dilemmas for the black feminist critic," elaborated Barbara Christian: "We may be imitating the very structure that shut our literatures out in the first place."[65] Similarly, Evelyn Hu-DeHart finds that faculty and their students continue to struggle in reconciling "the academic goal of ethnic studies—the production of knowledge—with its original commitment to liberating and empowering the communities of color."[66] Histories of women's studies offer a comparable "suspicion," as Robyn Wiegman puts it, "that what needs to be changed (in the wider political world) may be beyond our control" as professors.[67] As these and other assessments by practitioners in the interdisciplines suggest, to do this work is to confront the limits of what Selznick described as formal cooptation—which prefers to restaff committees while conceding little real power. By holding onto what Ferguson calls "visions that are in the institution but not of it," the anti-/interdisciplines insist that attention to extrainstitutional interests continue.[68] In so doing, they lend new energy to the very cooptation that vexes them and make clear how much this process has been responsible for changing what happens in post-1960s universities.

The new interdisciplines changed the student body as a whole, but to see how we need to look beyond the classroom. Ferguson notes the importance of considering new admissions policies, campus cultural centers, and faculty-recruitment efforts alongside curriculum. Developments across these sites created "the minority" as "a new institutional being," he argues.[69] Campuses learned to value and even celebrate "diversity" as a way of managing "insurgent articulations of minority difference, without absolute suppression but through selective revision and deployment."[70] A certain amount of minority discontent, effectively co-opted, signaled that campuses were doing their job to ameliorate longstanding injustices.

By redescribing this process as one of co-opting marginalized student interests, we can see better its relation to contemporary developments in areas like film studies, which were less about revaluing minority differences. Such an approach might also take in changes to degree programs not attributable to student dissent but indebted, perhaps, to the multiversity's need to co-opt other constituencies (Kerr mentions "alumni, legislators, farmers, businessmen"). The history of bioengineering, for example, is generally narrated as a series of technological discoveries (of dialysis, the pacemaker, the artificial heart, and so forth), but one might propose a consideration of university relations with industry and government granting agencies. Such an account would place biotech along with experimental film and Black Power as participants, albeit very different ones, in processes of cooptation that revised the university's relationship to organized outside interests.

In her autobiography, Angela Davis provides an instructive example. In the summer of 1967, Davis and a fellow UC San Diego student were jailed for asking police why fellow antiwar activists were being arrested. Quickly, this campus incident became a regional news story. She explained: "A rock station based in Los Angeles was running a spot every hour: 'Have you heard about the people down south [in San Diego] who got arrested because they wanted to know about the law?'" Desiring to stay in the media spotlight, Davis realized the importance of involving employees as well as students in efforts to start a Black Student Union. She recalled, "if we hadn't we would have been too small to get the attention we needed to function."[71] Radio abets activism here not only by spreading the message but also by demonstrating that the message was spreadable, that student efforts might find an audience that includes university employees and, equally, rock fans.

The resulting coalition of students and employees left behind a durable organizational model at UCSD. The UJIMA network formed in the 1960s continues to promote "opportunities for African-American staff, faculty, students, alumni, and community members" through its support of "all programs and services aimed at advancing the educational, cultural, and professional conditions of African-American individuals internal and external to the campus community." UJIMA supplies a representative to the University's Diversity Council, whose twenty-four members comprise senior administrators and faculty as well as representatives of staff and student organizations.[72] This sort of council, some version of which now exists on many, if not most, campuses, does the work both of managing internal heterogeneity and of cultivating a relationship between the academy and its outside.

In making such participation seem possible and ensuring that such bodies as a University Diversity Council appeared necessary, student activism helped encourage universities to understand demographic inclusion as a problem to be managed. With its focus on the academic institution, to be clear, such a project was different from the bolder project, no doubt embraced by some Diversity Council members, of deinstitutionalizing racism throughout the land. Yet, this kind of co-optation cannot have been merely "formal" in Selznick's terms in that merely pro-forma inclusion cannot durably succeed. To seem legitimately to have heard such activists, an organization must eventually engage them, a process that may well happen informally behind closed doors rather than out in the open at a center like UJIMA. This combination of formal and informal cooptation strategies may partly explain why universities continue to confront significant challenges of diversity and inclusion despite decades of attention to the problem. Many of the mechanisms for managing demographic differences are for show, and some ways of redistributing power cannot be avowed.

In lobbying for a Black Student Union at UC San Diego, Davis and her peers clearly wanted to change university policy in ways the State of California considered threatening. Ronald Reagan's famous vendetta against Davis personified a hostile governmental response to radical action. After failing to have her fired in 1969 because of her membership in the Communist Party, the California Regents succeeded in removing her a year later for "inflammatory" language.[73] That drama, however, occludes another in which Davis shared the stage with bureaucrats at the Office of Civil Rights and the Department of Education. Episodes from the story of state repression—the Free Speech Movement, Florida State University's 1969 "Night of the Bayonets," Yale's occupation by the National Guard, and the massacre at Kent State in 1970—have tended to obscure this durable legacy of institutional transformation and alliance, more in itself than for itself, of student activists and bureaucrats. Violent intervention by state and federal authorities prompted, in part, what Ferguson describes as the "convergence of administrative and police powers" in the post-1960s university. Through the addition of campus police to their bureaucracies and classrooms, he contends, academic institutions became more "statelike."[74] Campus police would secure safe spaces for student dissent as well as suppress its disruptions. Adjudicating between disruptive and nondisruptive, co-optable and not co-optable students became a regular administrative function. Post-1960s administrations could take it for granted that running a university meant managing a student body composed of diverse populations with often sharply divergent backgrounds, interests, and needs and, further, that these populations might act in their own interests to challenge and change the university.

STUDENT POPULATIONS

The institutionalization of new student powers went hand in hand with more intensive management of student populations via statistical media. This is not a contradiction but rather the kind of relation Michel Foucault trained us to appreciate when he identified the specification of populations as an organizing rubric, alongside liberty and discipline, for modern governance. More than any particular policy shift and underwriting all of them, more intensive collection and presentation of data by federal agencies changed how the postsecondary education sector was regulated. Statisticians complemented the work of student activists when they built survey instruments that made new segments of the student population countable and charted their progress in relation to prior norms. Such measures set up controversies over how schools could or should make use of demographic data in admissions. In this, they interacted with another relatively new statistical initiative led by the private sector: the standardized test score. In turn, demographics and test scores played important roles in the allocation of federal financial aid to students. With rising costs and an increasing emphasis on loans, as opposed to grant aid, students and parents became important audiences for all manner of data about higher ed. School choice required decisions not only about experiential "fit" but also about management of the risks that debt financing entailed. Thus, while students acquired unprecedented freedoms to determine what paths they might take through college, they also found that schools and government bureaus became more capable of anticipating and categorizing those choices, of imposing their own meaning on them, and turning those interpretations into policy. This numbers game was itself a means of cooptation.

Counting students has long been a core function of the federal bureaucracy. Apart from a spurt of funding to support World War I propaganda operations on campuses, this was the primary role the federal government played in postsecondary education before World War II. In 1867, when Congress created the office from which the current Department of Education descends, it intended to "collect" and "diffuse" statistical information to show the "condition and progress" of education in the United States and its territories and to work for the betterment of education throughout the land.[75] Of a piece with myriad nineteenth-century uses of statistical explanation in administration, this kind of bureaucratic gesture distinguishes biopolitical governance from its antecedents, as several scholars note.[76] Nonetheless, as we noted in chapter 1, it was not a federal bureau but rather a nongovernmental philanthropy, the Carnegie Foundation, that established the system of "counts" that made undergraduate degree completions at different institutions appear roughly equivalent and allowed them to be audited by nongovernmental accrediting agencies. For their part, federal enumerators attended to demographic variety, starting with measures of degree completions by sex in the early twentieth century. As succeeding waves of government and nongovernment actors identified inherited inequalities of race, sex, and class as national problems that higher education should help solve, they looked to federal numbers to specify those problems and appraise progress in addressing them.

It was not until the mid-1960s, however, that survey data detailing the composition of the student body acquired statutory force, as new federal laws aimed to level the playing field for diverse American populations. Federal numbers have arguably succeeded better in describing that playing field than federal policy has in leveling it. Myriad activists, politicians, and bureaucrats have debated whether the demographic composition of the student body is a problem Washington should fix. They have not agreed on what a solution would entail. In the early twenty-first century, education policy had not removed barriers set by inherited inequalities, particularly of race and class. But everyone relied on the same data. In this way, federal enumerators created (by informing, that is, mediating) a new administrative reality that politics could interpret and upon which policy could act.

Two landmark laws—the Civil Rights Act of 1964 and the Higher Education Act of 1965—made federal data actionable. The former declared that "No person in the United States shall, on the ground of race, color, or national origin, be excluded from participation in, be denied the benefits of, or be subjected to discrimination under any program or activity receiving Federal financial assistance" (Title VI). The latter directed significant federal financial assistance to an array of higher-education projects, including one to "assist in raising the academic quality of colleges . . . which for financial and other reasons are struggling for survival and are isolated from the main currents of academic life" (Title III).[77] These laws pushed higher education in a different direction than, for instance, the Carnegie unit, which normalized student accomplishments across the sector. In contrast, the 1960s legislation sought to optimize differences both in student populations and in the types of schools composing higher education as a whole.[78] In this shift, outliers could have positive value. The Higher Education Act, with its provision of assistance to those "isolated from the main currents," exemplified this even more clearly than the Civil Rights Act, with its prohibition of exclusion, denial of benefits, and discrimination—assertions of a general norm that simultaneously sought to redress its failures (were preexisting laws equitably applied, the prohibitions would not be necessary). Readers of twentieth-century social theory will recognize this as a tendency described by Michel Foucault. Foucault presents both the unification of a society by norms and the organization of ever more highly visible internal differences as equally within the historical purview of the biopolitical state. However, he sees a shifting of emphasis away from normalization over the course of the twentieth century.[79] US postsecondary education followed that trend. In making it possible to act on data that represented students in all their demographic variety, the new laws urged more intensive efforts to gather and analyze it.

The introduction of a new survey instrument for the school year ending June 30, 1966, marks a great leap forward for federal collection of data about postsecondary education. The Higher Education General Information Survey (HEGIS) tabulated associate's as well as bachelor's and graduate degree completions by major field of study at postsecondary institutions in the United States and its territories.[80] It is the earliest such survey readily available as a digital dataset. HEGIS tabulated completions in particular fields by sex. It accounted racial difference only at the level of the student body as a whole. The 1966 survey, for example, asked institutions to declare the "predominant race of the student body" as either "white" or "black." Institutions reporting for the first time were assumed to be "white" unless otherwise indicated. Comprehensive annual statistics about specific degrees earned by race did not become readily available until the 1976–77 academic year. Then, the Office of Education acted to require institutions to enumerate completions in the HEGIS using these categories: "Non-resident alien, Black, non-Hispanic, American Indian or Alaskan Native, Asian or Pacific Islander, Hispanic, White, non-Hispanic." In a gesture perceivable as schadenfreude, the Office of Education framed its new requirement as a paperwork reduction.

In recent years, the Office for Civil Rights (OCR) has collected some data on degrees conferred by racial/ethnic category from selected States. In order to lighten the burden on reporting institutions by eliminating the considerable duplication of effort in reporting to two separate agencies, the OCR survey has been combined with this survey form and integrated into the HEGIS program.[81]

As a result, it became possible after 1977 to compare comprehensively the composition of particular degree programs by race/ethnicity as well as by sex at federally funded institutions. The demographics of particular degrees could then be compared not only with one another but also with any number of other variables captured in regular surveys of fall enrollments and institutional characteristics, not to mention census data, employment figures, and so on.

In her 1983 history *The Troubled Crusade*, Diane Ravitch describes the new number-driven policies as revolutionary in their effects; she also bemoans them. When the Office for Civil Rights began compliance reviews of higher education in 1971, she argues, "it no longer meant that contractors should hire and treat employees *without regard* to their race, color, religion, sex, or national origin, but that they should act *with regard* to those factors."[82] Ravitch contends that enumerating populations introduces discrimination where otherwise employees might be judged on their merits. One might reply that the Office of Education's earlier policy of counting all schools as predominantly "white" unless otherwise notified indicates the limitations of color blindness as an antidiscrimination policy. Positive attention to differences has seemed to many, ourselves included, necessary to counter the privilege assumed by the norm. In any event, new awareness of the relative numbers of students when measured by race/ethnicity and sex inaugurated decades of strident argument over the proper use of such numbers in admissions.

The 1978 US Supreme Court decision in *Regents of the University of California v. Bakke* set the precedent for allowing race to be a factor in admissions policies while rejecting the use of specific quotas. This determination—in which racial difference counted, but it was improper to say exactly how much—made demographic categories full participants in arguments about the need to balance higher education's meritocratic and democratizing effects. Even as some worried that affirmative action undermined meritocracy, others defended the proposition that democracy required positive action to level an unequal playing field. The racial composition of the student body was a central issue but not the only issue. Survey data encouraged planners to correlate the demographics of particular degrees with any number of other variables describing educational institutions and the nation's population as a whole. Federal enumeration and statistical normalization of the student body thus cut at least two ways. As much as it measured progress in broadening access, it also intensified attention to higher education's sorting function.

When it came to sorting, high-school graduates were far more likely to be aware of another relatively new quantifying strategy, in which the federal government did not directly participate. The machine-scored multiple-choice aptitude test began to assume something like its current role in college admissions around 1958. The test now known as the SAT had origins in IQ testing developed in the first half of the century, but most college admissions were still not competitive in 1948 when the Educational Testing Service (ETS) began to administer it.[83] A decade later, more than half a million students took the SAT each year, and, for the first time, students were shown their scores.[84] Beginning in 1959, college aspirants could also take the ACT, the SAT's Midwestern competitor. The choice of test instrument itself distinguished types of student populations. Whereas the SAT emphasized ranking applicants and was favored by elite private institutions, the ACT emphasized screening out unqualified applicants and was used mainly by expanding public universities—with notable exceptions. In 1960, California guaranteed ETS a future when it began using the SAT as part of President Kerr's Master Plan. Test scores made the difference between admission to one of the prestigious, research oriented, Universities of California and matriculation at one of the California State Universities. The test thus insinuated a powerful distinguishing mechanism into a system that promised broad access to public higher education.

The comparative fields created by student demographics and standardized testing were essential to the growth of federal financial-aid programs, which required measures of need as well as qualification. In 1958, the National Defense Education Act had created the National Defense Student Loan as a signature "space race" initiative to promote, especially, training in science and engineering. At that time, state residents paid an "incidental fee" of $120 per year to attend the tuition-free University of California, and tuition at Harvard cost around $1,250, approximately $10,700 in 2017 dollars.[85] By the mid-1960s, a series of federal laws had configured student financial aid as a "package" of grants, loans, and student work programs.[86] Although the causation is complex and in dispute, tuition and loan packages grew in tandem over the next several decades.[87]

In 1972, the Basic Educational Opportunities Grant (BEOG, later the Pell Grant) marked a notable shift in the federal approach to student financial aid. The Pell program continued the pattern set by earlier "War on Poverty" programs in conceiving aid as a flexible package, directed toward lower-income students, and with many more students qualifying.[88] Unlike earlier grants, however, Pell funding was "portable": it followed the student, not the institution.[89] This approach not only increased options for students but also incentivized institutions to recruit them. It proved popular. By 1990, about one in five enrolled students received Pell funding.[90] Even as Pell rose, however, the federal funding emphasis shifted to loans. In 1978, President Carter signed the Middle Income Student Assistance Act. The law expanded the Pell Grant program and extended eligibility to families with incomes up to around $25,000 (more than $97,000 in 2017 dollars).[91] At the same time, it opened the Guaranteed Student Loan program to all students, regardless of need.

The historian John Thelin loosely connects the post-1972 trend to channel federal financial aid to individual students (as opposed to making grants to institutions) with several tendencies. Many institutions placed new emphasis on attracting "nontraditional students," particularly by articulating two-year, off-campus, and evening-school programs with more traditional four-year degree programs. To attract the core undergraduate demographic, many campuses renovated their physical plants, particularly their fitness centers and residence halls (campuses seemed suddenly to require rock-climbing walls). In an acknowledgment that undergraduates might be treated as adults, housing went coed. Administrators placed new emphasis on retention and completion rates, which called attention to the lack of connection between high-school and university curricula. Even highly selective institutions found it necessary to remediate the writing and math skills of matriculating students in order to improve their chances of completion. And faculty registered a change in student attitudes, noting "a 'new vocationalism'—in particular, an obsession with preprofessional studies" at the undergraduate level.[92] In all these developments, one sees the influence of numbers in objectifying new problems. Recruitment and retention rates, the proportion of in-state and out-of-state tuition in the funding mix, the ethnic diversity of the student body, investment in student services relative to instruction, and so on could all be compared with one another and with national norms by size, type, and location of institution.

New metrics revised old arguments. The 1966 "Equality of Educational Opportunity Study," aka the "Coleman Report," solicited by the Department of Education employed statistical analysis to assess the schooling options available to different demographics. The report established benchmarks that continue to ground debate about whether updated numbers show improvements in "achievement gaps" across various groups, about what means of amelioration are most effective, and about whether statistical measures provide the most accurate means of assessment in the first place.[93] Where the Coleman Report assumed that federal intervention would have succeeded when achievement was evenly distributed across a given set of demographic segments, other voices distinguished equality of opportunity from the measurement of merit. "The great university is of necessity elitist—the elite of merit," Kerr asserts in *The Uses of the University*, "but it operates in an environment dedicated to an egalitarian philosophy."[94] Measures of merit are no less controversial than stats on "achievement gaps." The most readily available data—course grades and test scores—have routinely had their validity questioned. Audiences for the Coleman Report found that ambiguities in its numbers made them highly interpretable by divergent cadres of policy wonks, while Kerr and subsequent defenders of meritocracy yearned for a pitch that could ensure that "the contribution of the elite [would] be made clear to the egalitarians."[95] The oh-so-American problem of harmonizing merit and access endured, but after the 1960s numerical representation would play a far more important role in mediating it.

The new style of metric-driven administration inspired detractors, including supporters of big-time football. The effects on athletics of the 1972 Education Amendments caught many by surprise, Thelin observes.[96] The law's Title IX antidiscrimination clause is written in the most general of terms to guarantee no one "shall, on the basis of sex, be excluded from participation in, be denied the benefits of, or be subjected to discrimination under any education program or activity receiving Federal financial assistance."[97] In congressional hearings that followed the 1975 publishing of the regulations in the *Federal Register*, however, it became clear that implementation of Title IX had the potential to affect sports in general and football in particular. Panicked senators worried that in order to equalize support for men's and women's athletics, universities would be all but forced to redistribute money allocated to their football programs. The legislators proposed amendments and publicly denounced the policy. "Are we going to let Title IX kill the goose that lays the golden eggs in those colleges and universities with a major revenue-producing sport?" asked Nebraska senator Roman Hruska.[98] As the historian Susan Ware observes, there were not many profitable programs at the time; the NCAA reported that only one in five football teams actually made money for their schools.[99] For those schools, however, a lot seemed to ride on protecting college football's (increasingly television-centric) business model.[100] Just so, the Javits Amendment to Title IX allowed "reasonable (regulatory) provisions" for sports that had special requirements, including the "nature/replacement of equipment, rates of injury resulting from participation, nature of facilities required for competition, and the maintenance/upkeep requirements of those facilities."[101] These coded exceptions for big-time football programs threw competing imperatives into relief. Where television worked to sort schools according to the ratings their football programs could command, Title IX provided a contrasting, student-centered metric, where the value was measured in terms not of market share but of equal opportunity to participate in college athletics. Diversity in sports is every bit as countable as diversity in curriculum: both yield actionable data and had the potential to alter economic calculations around, for instance, the costs and benefits of running expensive but alumni-friendly gridiron spectacles.

New metrics not only described student participation but also addressed students themselves as increasingly attentive consumers. Undergraduates and parents paid a growing proportion of the cost of an expanding postsecondary sector. Moreover, they were expected to calculate and manage the risk involved in their investment. Seen throughout the century as a vehicle of upward mobility, the value of attending any particular college could now be appraised in more individual terms according to a differential grid that compared types of institutions and their costs with aid packages that included future obligations. Students could theoretically turn to the same rich field of publicly available statistical information that informed federal policy. After 1983, they could simply pick up the *US News* annual report on "America's Best Colleges." It may have appeared to *US News* editors that students "shopping" in a marketplace of institutions needed decent consumer advice. But this was no trip to the mall. Rather, in shopping for their higher education students entered a universe defined by the ebb and flow of various sorts of statistical predictions. Would institutions realize the value that an individual's SAT score predicted? Would this or that school or major result in employment that would allow the student to repay her loans? For students, it was not simply a matter of affording college but of self-assessment that took into account the institutions that might wish to attract and select them.

For institutions, increasing student variety brought a range of retention problems, financial-aid issues, and social needs—but also public relations benefits. Institutions advertised the diversity of their incoming classes in direct-mail flyers and, later, on splashy websites. Marketing diversity added another potential metric to the return on investment calculations encouraged by the US News rankings. As institutions vied to brand themselves "diverse," some prospective students might ask which school would best expand their social networks. Others might worry about the burden of being asked to embody and represent the new diversity. Faced with competing criteria, students mulled early decision, considered what constituted a "safety school," and availed themselves of application coaches. All of these practices presupposed calculations of chance made possible by data. The 1980s revealed in full flower the consequences of data-driven policies innovated in the 1960s and 1970s.

Students "spoke" through their stats as well as their megaphones. Quantifications of fall enrollments, retention rates, degree completions by major field, average standardized test scores, and percentages of students receiving financial aid—all these and more indicated students' needs and preferences. Students confronting choices about what and where to study could expect to consult statistical representations of their predecessors' decisions, along with interpretations of what those numbers might portend for their own futures. The updated version of turn-of-the-century campus life had a ranking—one could in fact attend the top party school.[102] School choice also entailed a supplemental means-ends calculation, as loans assumed a more prominent role in college financing. In addition to recording and guiding students' decisions, data also mediated debate about whether and how changing student demographics altered established social hierarchies. When numbers made it possible to track progress in credentialing students from previously excluded groups or in involving them in college sports, those numbers invited discussion of whether such progress changed the way power was conducted more broadly. Student data and student protest did not always urge the same conclusions—although sometimes they did. They nonethless conspired to establish student decisions as a focus of institutional concern. Schools as well as the students themselves would be held accountable for the choices students made.

Downstream in the 2000s, some on the left discovered a frightening neoliberal turn in the fact that decisions freighted with economic consequences had been delegated to undergraduates. Meanwhile, conservatives proudly advocated "student choice." Both sides might have been better at remembering the 1960s roots of this emphasis. Student movements on the left as well as the right promoted student choice when they successfully agitated for new programs of study and more formal roles in campus governance. In effect if not always intent, federal enumerators joined forces with these students when they began intensively to collect data about increasingly diverse student populations. "Student choice" means not only conceiving students as decision makers but also conceiving schools and curricula as an expansive menu of options from which one might choose. Cooptation remains a useful concept for avoiding either a romantic tale in which 1960s radicalism briefly flowered or a millenarian account of how data-driven policy corrupts the academy.

Chapter Seven

STUDENT IMMATERIAL LABOR

In effect if not intent, 1960s students rebranded the American research university. While university administrators doubtlessly conceived of student activism as a problem to be contained, they also learned to treat it as a potentially positive contribution, as innovation. This dynamic incorporated several different varieties of student organization, as we noted in the previous chapter. Some, like Berkeley's Free Speech Movement and San Diego's UJIMA network, staged media events. Others, like the University of South Carolina's Celluloid Society, experimented with new forms of media education. Alongside more intensive measurement of student populations, cooptation of these sorts of student media work modified the research university's institutional form, creating new administrative offices, departments, and centers as well as new connections to communities outside their walls. Through this multifaceted process, we have argued, students energized a shift, already underway, from a university conceivable as an organic whole that aspired to address a national public to the multiversity, best grasped as a loosely coupled network of often disparate functions addressing plural audiences.

Through their media experiments as well as their habits of listening, viewing, and reading, student dissenters demonstrated the value of "immaterial labor." By this term, economic theory following Maurizio Lazzarato designates "the kinds of activities involved in defining and fixing cultural and artistic standards, fashions, tastes, consumer norms, and, more strategically, public opinion."[1] Rebellious (and often unpaid) students added value by arranging readings and screenings as much as by programming computers, writing underground newspapers, and making videos. "The particularity of the commodity produced through immaterial labor," Lazzarato writes, "consists in the fact that it is not destroyed in the act of consumption, but rather it enlarges, transforms, and creates the 'ideological' and cultural environment of the consumer."[2] In this broader sense, student immaterial labor underwrote the off-campus ventures of advertisers, publishers, and film distributors, as well as the personal computer industry.

We began to describe the ascent of this form of work in chapter 4, when we noted that midcentury systems thinking supported two different approaches to the problem of mass communications. One, perhaps best exemplified by Vannevar Bush's admiration for the statement made by the Hiroshima and Nagasaki bombs, emphasized cutting through a noisy channel to impress a clear message on populations worldwide. The other, the democratic surround, urged masses to embrace their roles as participants in communications systems through events like the *Family of Man* exhibit, which encouraged visitors to see themselves as part of the show and as necessary to complete its message. Across several domains in the 1960s and 1970s, the latter strand prevailed. It seemed increasingly important to draw a bright line between "doing" and "consuming" media and to find positive political value in artworks and institutions that encouraged the former.[3] This notion linked initiatives as various as designing a computer that would encourage users to "Think Different," staging a "happening," engaging a televised political debate, teaching community members to use Portapak video, and marketing *Lady Chatterley's Lover* as a membership card for "the underground."[4] Inasmuch as each of these projects extended the trajectory of the democratic surround, however, they also lent the energy of youth to approaches hatched by professors of design, music, mathematics, media, biology, and anthropology.

Campus counterculture buoyed media enterprises that the university did not control along with some that it did. For instance, where new degrees in film studies co-opted student interest in something like the way colleges had earlier taken control of football, distributors of experimental film strongly asserted their autonomy from the universities that constituted their primary rental market. Students added value to experimental film by arbitrating its grooviness, but their schools did not capture all of this value when they created courses in it. Some of the added value was realized by filmmakers and distributors when they marketed films to nonstudent audiences as well as to students at other institutions. Similarly, classrooms, studios, and labs could incubate off-campus startups or connect student media workers with nonprofit organizations. In these ways, student immaterial labor supported new networks linking universities to off-campus media enterprises of widely various sorts. Lazzarato may be correct to suggest that tastemaking practices previously "the privileged domain of the bourgeoisie and its children" were diffused through the polity into various trendsetting niches in the 1970s.[5] If he is, then student immaterial labor contributed significantly to that change.

PERSONAL COMPUTING: A COUNTERCULTURE SUCCESS STORY

The success of the personal computing industry can take credit for an emerging and heavily revised consensus about the student counterculture, one that effectively upends the narrative supplied by the first wave of descriptions. Consider, for example, the evolution of the historian Timothy Roszak's position on the topic. In his 1969 *The Making of a Counter Culture*, Roszak urged readers to understand mass mediation as the misrepresentation of a more authentic youth culture that somehow existed apart from it. Opening a vast chasm between rock concerts and underground newspapers on the one hand and "mainstream media" on the other, he declared that young people "have done a miserably bad job of dealing with the distortive publicity with which the mass media have burdened their embryonic experiments. . . . Whatever these things called 'beatniks' and 'hippies' originally were, or still are, may have nothing to do with what *Time, Esquire, Cheeta*, CBSNBCABC, Broadway comedy, and Hollywood have decided to make of them."[6] The tragically misrepresented youths of 1969 look very different in Roszak's introduction to the book's 1995 edition. There we find the counterculture "transforming IBM's gargantuan computational engines into funky, but cunningly hand-crafted communications devices that worked from a typewriter keyboard and adapted the television monitor to the strange new use of displaying the coded meaning of binary numbers."[7] With this shift in emphasis, a history of mediation begins to replace a history of representation. Rather than being asked to consider if "hippies" resembled the characters depicted by "CBSNBCABC," we are made to wonder how hippie dropouts came to fill the world with iPhones.[8]

More emphatically than Roszak, Fred Turner takes advantage of the retrospection ubiquitous computing affords to complicate historical periodizations separating the grey bureaucratic 1950s from 1960s youth rebellion as well as from 1980s corporate beige. In his sequel to *The Democratic Surround*, *From Counterculture to Cyberculture*, Turner presents the *Whole Earth Catalog* author Stewart Brand as the figure bridging Silicon Valley to the legacies of midcentury systems theory as expressed in the widely read work of Norbert Wiener, Marshall McLuhan, and Buckminster Fuller as well as in the less well-known work of the biologist Paul Erhlich, with whom Brand studied biology at Stanford.[9] For Turner, Brand also connects systems thinking with the milieu of 1950s experimental music and art exemplified by John Cage and Robert Rauschenberg, which traveled from its Black Mountain College incubator to become Manhattan "happenings" in the 1960s.[10] All these precedents, Turner argues, are necessary to understand the love/hate relationship with technology that inspired the likes of Steve Wozniak and Steve Jobs to conceive personal computing as a form of political rebellion and empowering self-expression.[11] Blending intellectual- and media-history approaches, Turner reveals a series of colleges and universities to have been key nodes in a network that includes enterprises as various as the San Francisco Trips Festival, the Portola Institute (a nonprofit educational foundation and *Whole Earth Catalog* publisher), and Apple Computer, Inc.[12]

Where Turner weaves a rich academic history around Brand, many journalists are apt to make hacker-CEOs their main characters.[13] This version of the 1960s legacy begins not with systems theory but with MIT students who had grown up hacking telephone networks and found themselves well positioned to do something unexpected with the Department of Defense funding flowing onto their campus. With fellow members of the Tech Model Railroad Club, Steve Russell completed the legendary video game *Spacewar!* in 1962. Although the MIT students did not profit from the game, the computer manufacturer DEC was happy to include it as shareware with its PDP-1. Through Russell, the game is often said to have seeded the career of PONG's pioneer Nolan Bushnell and fueled the fortunes of the console maker Atari.[14] In the 1970s, as computer science and industry began the move west to Silicon Valley, journalistic accounts make counterculture dropouts and campus activists even more important to a story of business innovation. The dropouts loom particularly large. Bill Gates left Harvard in 1975 without completing his degree. Steve Wozniak famously met Steve Jobs in 1971 while the former was an undergrad at Berkeley and the latter was getting in trouble for pulling pranks at Homestead High School (Jobs would become a Reed College dropout a few years later). The two were members of the Homebrew Computer Club, which thrived in the orbit of Stanford. The club benefited from the contributions of programming experimenters like Fred Moore, who in 1959 went on a hunger strike to protest compulsory ROTC training while a Berkeley student and inspired the likes of David Horowitz to become politically active undergraduates.[15]

Campus counterculture, to which McLuhan made no small contribution, developed the technique of branding media alternatives as revolutionary. This trope, more than any specific technological breakthrough, has proved the university's lasting contribution to societies newly informed by personal computing. Early-twenty-first-century EdTech celebrants, for instance, often reprised the epochal tenor of such gestures while abandoning their politics. They cast Silicon Valley's male executives as outsiders prepared to deploy "technology" to "disrupt" higher education's stodgy ways. As we argue in chapter 10, the university no more fails to "keep up" with these mock revolutionaries than it failed to educate Gates and Jobs.

To appreciate what gets lost in the account that abstracts technology from its institutional mediation, we might pause briefly to consider what technological innovation actually looks like. Lynn Conway has described in some detail the decades-long process through which she made key contributions to Very Large Scale Integration (VLSI), which became essential to integrated circuit design. She traces her career from the early 1960s, when she minored in cultural anthropology while training as an electrical engineer at Columbia University, through positions at IBM and Xerox PARC, a key teaching stint at MIT in 1978, recognition in the 1980s for major contributions to the field, and more recent recognition as a transgender role model. Conway's story features eureka moments—"Suddenly it beamed down to me: MOS design rules should not be framed as sets of lengths but as sets of ratios of lengths. Such dimensionless rules could then be scaled to any process as multiples of a basic length unit in microns, a unit I called Lambda (λ)." Overall, however, she emphasizes teamwork and the institutional circumstances that afford or constrain it.[16] In contrast to IBM, which fired her for undertaking a gender transition in the late 1960s, a "vibrant counter culture within PARC helped brace us against all doubts; it seemed everyone there was reaching for dreams."[17] In addition to this enabling corporate culture, Conway credits success to an ability to spread information about VSLI through a textbook coauthored with Carver Mead, the journal *Lambda*, and the ARPANET (the Defense Department's pioneering TCP/IP network that linked university and corporate researchers). "The emerging internet and PC technology enabled me to operate in wholly new ways as an architect of disruptive change," she writes, adding that "Almost no one at the time could visualize what I was actually doing, thus I needed no 'permission' to do it and no one was power-positioned to stop it. As a corollary, few folks later understood what had really happened—much less who had done it."[18] In Conway's account, technological change is as much an effect of mediation as a cause of it, universities and tech companies plainly participate in the same information networks, and revolutions cannot be chalked up to the rebellions of famous young men.

When Roszak, Turner, and others teach us to see Apple and Microsoft as counterculture success stories, they upend the still familiar narrative in which 1960s youth movements, failing in their grand project to change the world, grew up or burned out. In place of this tale they limn a richly ironic story in which hippie college dropouts give birth to the emblematic twenty-first-century corporate technoculture. The historian Thomas Frank claims an equally sweeping and counterintuitive role for the counterculture in transforming business-management philosophy. He points to *Up the Organization: How to Stop the Corporation from Stifling People and Strangling Profits*, a seminal business text of 1970 that treats Ho Chi Minh as a management guru and helped end the midcentury obsession with micromanaging Taylorist control in favor of the flexibility, creativity, and agility valued by post-1970s business administration.[19] Such appropriations are not what students had in mind when building new audiences for Ho's revolutionary manifesto and its ilk. Nonetheless, they testify to the scope of that intervention. In the wake of this revision, it still makes sense to question whether and how the counterculture actually worked to redistribute social privileges. Whether student movements lived up to their own rhetoric, however, is ultimately less important than how they remediated audiences.

ACTIVIST MEDIA, LEFT AND RIGHT

Student-assisted remediation segmented audiences and created sometimes surprising new combinations. It informed new factional audiences for the paraeducational apparatus of conservative think tanks, progressive community organizations, and self-described outsider artists employed by the university. It also led to arresting mash-ups of antiestablishment constituencies.

Although Turner does not mention William F. Buckley in *The Democratic Surround*, he could have. With his patrician, paternalistic demeanor and clear ties to the establishment institutions he frequently abhorred, this student provocateur turned public-affairs television host embodied a style very different from the hip self-presentations of McLuhan, Cage, and Brand. For this difference, perhaps, he merits backhanded acknowledgment in Turner's follow-up, *From Counterculture to Cyberculture*. There, Turner quotes *Wired* magazine's cofounder Louis Rossetto as recalling "it wasn't a Buckleyite conservatism that got me—it was the individualist, anti-statist conservatism that got me."[20] Rossetto is explaining, some thirty years later, his emergence in the early 1970s as a flag bearer for a libertarian "New Right." He joins Turner's colorful cast of characters as an advocate of technological disruption, and his example helps Turner explain how that commitment afforded a convergence of left- and right-wing activist stances. It is likely, however, that subsequent development of Buckley's television persona, a somewhat stale fixture by the time he finally went off the air in 1999, skews Rossetto's recollection of Buckley's historical relationship with "individualist, anti-state conservatism." In the 1960s and 1970s, that relationship was hardly one of straightforward antagonism.

By 1966, the author of *God and Man at Yale* had shifted his attention away from appropriating the university as a conservative communications channel to engaging television audiences through his talk show *Firing Line*. Although it first appeared on commercial television via New York's independent station WOR, Buckley's program became a staple of public television after moving to South Carolina's PBS affiliate, SCETV, in 1971. While the show aimed to convert viewers to the Christian conservative cause, Buckley's commitment to a postcollege community of controversy turned his set into a space for encounters that may seem surprising in retrospect. The media historian Heather Hendershot concludes, for instance, that *Firing Line* may well have been "the single venue in the 'mainstream' American mass media where Black Power got a fair shake in the late 1960s and early 1970s," in no small part because the program gave movement leaders sufficient airtime to make their case.[21] Rather than pandering to preexisting political identifications, *Firing Line* notably expected viewers to develop their political commitments through intellectual engagement in its debates. In its first decade, the show remained conversant with campus movements on the left and the right, not infrequently featuring authors who had written about campus struggles and sometimes featuring students (or recent graduates) as interviewees and members of studio audiences.[22] *Firing Line* was participatory media.

While Buckley took to the airwaves, the Young Americans for Freedom (YAF), the conservative counterpart to the SDS, took up his interest in using educational institutions to transmit "knowledge and values" (see chapter 6). These were compatible strategies: Buckley featured YAF members on his show at least three times before 1978.[23]

In the 1970s, YAF alumnae created the organizing strategies that yielded the "Reagan Revolution" of the 1980s and, in the process, dramatically revised the style, demographic base, and policy positions of the Republican Party. They did so, in part, by building a parallel educational establishment in the form of think tanks such as the Heritage Foundation and the American Enterprise Institute.[24] This parallel academy sustained conservative research, publication, and advocacy without the myriad obligations imposed by teaching and certification. Like professors but with public relations savvy, these wonks issued reports, plugged stories to the news media, and by the 1980s were playing a central role in campaigns to restructure higher education and defund federally supported cultural organizations such as PBS and the NEA.

While the right built think tanks, some left-leaning students remade television. Along with relatively cheap 16mm film and offset-printing technologies, the introduction in 1967 of Sony's half-inch Portapak video recorder facilitated broader media access. Although Portapak's low resolution presented difficulties for standard-definition television broadcast, its portability and the ability immediately to review and rerecord program content lent itself to projects that involved training communities to represent themselves. Such was the mission outlined in the 1972 manifesto *Guerrilla Television*, by Michael Shamberg and the Raindance Corporation, which envisioned the democratizing power of "narrowcast" video as an antidote to the mass conformism of commercial broadcast media. The historian Deirdre Boyle identifies exponents of the community video movement ranging from the Alternate Media Center at New York University, founded by George Stoney and Red Burns in 1971, to Ted Carpenter's Appalachian Broadside TV, founded the following year. In her account, however, the University of Minnesota's Community Video Access Center perhaps best indicates the possibilities and constraints of university involvement.

Funded by the university's student government, the University Community Video Access Center (UCV) offered a for-credit course whose alumni helped staff free monthly workshops for students and community members. By 1974, UCV was teaching 1,200 community members per year how to use video.[25] Also beginning that year, the center leveraged the university's relationship with local PBS station KTCA to air the innovative *Communitube*, a magazine show featuring content supplied by community groups as well as UCV students and staffers.[26] Although the show's often edgy style and choice of subject matter clashed with the broadcast-journalism conventions regnant at KTCA, *Communitube* led to the critically acclaimed biweekly series *Changing Channels*, which ran on that station for four seasons. As this project matured, the difference between staff and community-produced content become more notable. National attention to the show and a shift in its funding model (from student government to federal grant support) caused further drift away from the university. In the 1980s, UCV spun off from the university and was reincarnated as Intermedia Arts Minnesota, which received funding from memberships as well as federal grants and promoted visual and performing arts alongside video.

Boyle plots UCV's trajectory, and that of the video movement more broadly, as a failure to achieve the radical democratic vision that inspired it. Yet her account also reveals the profound influence of UCV's startup. "UCV's alumni is like a who's who in television, covering broadcast news, documentary, and entertainment," she observes.[27] Moreover, while Boyle disparages Intermedia Arts for abandoning a locally oriented activist program in favor of national artists and arts funding in the 1980s, a look at the organization's website in the 2010s reveals its Up and Out festival for "LGBTQIA+" filmmakers; its ongoing Catalyst Series, which aims to spark "dialogue and social change with new performing arts, visual arts and film presentations"; and its Media Active project, which connects local organizations and business with teenage media producers.[28] We ought not to let the story of UCV's failure to provoke the revolution (so far) obviate the fact that students led the university to spin off a now solidly established community arts organization. Like the Heritage Foundation, Intermedia Arts exists, in no small part, thanks to student immaterial labor.

DISTRIBUTION NETWORKS

If startups like UCV encouraged students to experiment with audiences outside the university, students also provided audiences for extramural experimenters. In the preceding chapter, we pointed to the University of South Carolina's Celluloid Society as an example of the campus film society movement, which programmed experimental films and thereby spurred the creation of courses in which students could learn to make films and analyze them. Such screening programs depended on distributors and vice versa. Academic film study and experimental-film distribution grew up together in the 1960s, Michael Zryd demonstrates, countering a received narrative that describes avant-garde filmmaking as autonomous before the university captured it in the 1970s.

Examination of the distribution network linking academic and nonacademic makers and audiences allows Zryd to recontextualize the avant-garde's hostility toward academe. ("To be 'academic' is an insult even for the academics," he observes).[29] As independent institutions, distributors like the Film-Makers' Cooperative (Coop) secured the proposition that an avant-garde could engage audiences without the university's help. At the same time, however, these distributors relied on universities for most of their revenue.[30] Moreover, university screenings secured more geographically diverse audiences than the avant-garde could otherwise reach. As the 1960s became the 1980s, Zryd shows, distributors like the Coop increasingly linked university-based filmmakers and audiences across the country. This tendency effectively decentralized avant-garde production and reception, dispersing it away from New York and San Francisco, which nonetheless remained home base for the major distributors. This network configuration encouraged experimental filmmakers in their belief that extra-academic exhibition (curated by New York or San Francisco) offered a more authentic and political forum for the kinds of work that universities paid them to make and for which universities provided the core audience.

Similar patterns can be observed in theater, dance, and music—all areas in which "experimental," "avant-garde," or "alternative" forms came to depend on university-based networks. The dance historian Sally Banes underscores that arguments on behalf of noncommercial media attracted university support in tandem with funding from corporate foundations and federal grant agencies (for example, the NEA and the NEH, established in 1965). That is, university support for the avant-garde in the 1960s was not sui generis but part of a national advocacy and grant-making network that positioned the university as an ideal patron of experimental art.[31] The space for art that this network carved out of the university was not an entirely comfortable one. It was unclear, for example, how tenure and promotion processes would judge creative effort, as the dance historian Timothy Hagood explains.[32] At the beginning of the 1960s, Hagood observes, "dance educators still questioned whether or not dance was . . . an academic discipline." Professional dance organizations ran a "Dance as a Discipline" conference in 1965 to prepare what the organizers called "the case for dance as a full partner in the academic enterprise."[33] By the end of the decade, they had convinced themselves and an increasing number of colleges and universities that it could be. Nonetheless, Banes and Hagood agree, they perceived that accomplishment with ambivalence. Like other university-based experimental artists, they worried that academic cooptation would limit their ability to provoke and that the tendency toward standard curricula would discourage innovation. They also had to manage the increasing number of students enrolled during what Hagood calls the "Dance Boom" of the 1970s.[34]

Increasing student enrollments in departments and programs generating experimental media, along with the proliferation of networks that tied on-campus activities with off-campus production and distribution, conspired to institutionalize a love-hate relationship in which artists supported by the academy often preferred to think of themselves as "outsiders" and reproduced this ethos in the students they trained.[35] Nothing epitomized this tendency more than creative writing, as the literary critic Mark McGurl has influentially argued. Student demand drove "a tenfold multiplication of creative writing programs" in the 1960s, according to McGurl, as other universities adapted models established by "Iowa, Stanford, Johns Hopkins, Denver, and a handful of other early movers."[36] "Consecrated to the unpredictable value of 'creativity' and the 'art of voice,'" McGurl shows, "these programs embodied an institutional aspiration to be open to 'outside influences' that would keep them alive and lively and new. They were also, more simply, a way of giving students what they intensely wanted: a chance to express themselves."[37] Creative writing professors, like other faculty artists, could behave as if unaware that their outsider posture made them valuable to their university employers. Embracing that posture, universities found a way both to compel student attention and to connect with the literary marketplace, which, like the movies, bent toward the youth during that decade.[38]

We have proposed that the Film-Makers Coop exemplifies a network configuration in which professors and students, that is, canonical university insiders, could perceive themselves as doing outsider work insofar as the distributor functioned as a node that appeared relatively autonomous from the university. The Coop's power to curate and promote experimental film could seem alternative, even opposed, to the university's authority. This kind of relation could be reversed in a way that allowed readers outside the university to feel part of the student underground.

Grove Press perhaps best exemplifies this reversible relation. The literary historian Loren Glass describes the press as a "quilting point" that enabled "authors, academics, editors, readers, and activists around the world . . . to coalesce around a distinct set of aesthetic sensibilities and political affiliations."[39] It accomplished this by embracing the cheap paperback, a medium then being exploited by the large publishing houses to reach a mass market. Grove used it to cultivate "a series of cultural and generic niches" extending well beyond campus boundaries.[40] To these niches, student dissenters lent their luster and their labor.

From the late 1950s, Grove's Evergreen imprint acted like the Film-Makers Coop when it populated syllabi with authors such as Samuel Beckett, Alain Robbe-Grillet, Jean Genet, Khuswat Singh, Kenzaburo Oe, Amos Tutuola, and Octavio Paz. Beginning in 1962, its Black Cat series filled campus bookstores with titles including Frantz Fanon's *Wretched of the Earth*, Che

Guevara's *Reminiscences of the Cuban Revolutionary War*, Julius Lester's *Look Out, Whitey! Black Power's Gon' Get Your Mama!*, *The Autobiography of Malcolm X*, and *The Bust Book: What to Do Until the Lawyer Comes*, by the SDS activists Kathy Boudin, Brian Glick, Eleanor Raskin, and Gustin Reichbach. Although it was something of a vanity project for its publisher, Barney Rosset Jr., Grove added film production and distribution to its publishing operations in the late 1960s, and Grove films were not infrequently shown on college campuses. In 1967, Grove distributed the controversial, and profitable, Swedish film *I Am Curious (Yellow)*. The film showed nationally in art houses, not porn theaters, but an ultimately unsuccessful attempt by Massachusetts to ban the film as pornographic contributed to its allure.

The audience Grove built around material describable as pornography was different from on-campus audiences for its literary Evergreen and political Black Cat booklists, although these audiences overlapped. The erotically oriented audience grew significantly as a result of Grove's 1966 "Join the Underground Campaign," which addressed readers "over 21" who had "grown up with the underground writers of the fifties and sixties who've reshaped the literary landscape" and wanted "to share in the new freedoms that book and magazine publishers are winning in the courts."[41] The campaign promoted titles controversial for their depictions of sexuality, many of which had been subjected to censorship, and it succeeded in nearly doubling the circulation of Grove's literary magazine, the *Evergreen Review*, in the first half of 1966. The press hired Marketing Data, Inc., to survey these subscribers and determined that "the average member of the 'under-ground' is a 39-year-old male, married, two children, a college graduate who holds a managerial position in business or industry, and has a median family income of $12,875."[42] To cultivate further this off-campus constituency, Grove developed its offerings in "pornography and erotica exhumed from the Edwardian and Victorian undergrounds."[43] The "underground" one "joined" by purchasing D. H. Lawrence's *Lady Chatterley's Lover* (1928) thus anchored itself both in the alluring rebellious styles of 1960s youth and in the curation of literary classics by New York publishers. Insofar as Grove's advertising campaign capitalized on campus dissent to promote its selections, one must also conclude that the press monetized students' immaterial labor.

Grove's high-profile porn profiteering made it a superb target for feminist protest. Activists led by Robin Morgan occupied Grove's offices in

April 1970. They demanded recognition of an employee union, denounced its exploitative emphasis on "sado-masochistic literature" and "pornographic films," and indicted a workplace "oppressive" to female employees.[44] Glass sees this as evidence that the moral discourse around pornography occasioned broader political contests.[45] One should add that here, as elsewhere, feminist intervention upset the counterculture's oppositional stance by insisting that any alternatives reproducing the same old sexism were poor ones.[46] Third parties could still profit from this immaterial labor. In *The World Split Open*, for instance, Ruth Rosen offers a peek into "a feminist guerrilla action" in which members of her Berkeley-based group "invaded" listener-supported radio station KPFA to demand better attention to women's issues and more participation by women in media making. The group "melted back into polite and respectable womanhood," and "the station began producing programs on women's history, poetry, literature, music, news, and public affairs," which presumably helped it engage politicized female listeners.[47]

For media activists who wanted to retain autonomy from the university, maintaining a distribution channel that remained relevant to campus audiences proved crucial. Women Make Movies (WMM) provides a notably successful example. Organized in 1969 by Ariel Dougherty, Sheila Paige, and Dolores Bargowski to promote the creation of films by and about women, WMM incorporated as a nonprofit in 1972. Dougherty had studied filmmaking at Sarah Lawrence College in its first course on the subject, while Bargowski had been active in feminist organizations at Detroit's Monteith College. The three met in New York, where Dougherty and Page taught filmmaking classes to youths via community organizations, museums, and schools. Such programs pursued imperatives similar to that animating UCV and numerous other participatory-media initiatives. WMM adapted the approach to train women in filmmaking and to screen and promote their films, circulating them to festivals and to other women's groups. After Dougherty and Paige stepped down in 1975, WMM regrouped as a production and distribution collective, but with declining grant funding this model could not be sustained. At decade's end, WMM began to circulate films by nonmembers, and by the early 1980s distribution provided its main source of income.[48] Debra Zimmerman, who became WMM's director in 1983, observed in the 2010s that despite success at international festivals and with the Academy Awards, the organization "wouldn't exist" without rental income from academia.[49] Although it resembled Film-Makers Coop in this respect, WMM nonetheless functioned differently as a node in a network connecting filmmakers with student and other audiences, both in the variety of initiatives to which it contributed and in its political posture vis-à-vis the university.

The scope of its feminist ambition probably explains why WMM's production and distribution network suffered less from the schizoid love-hate relationship with the academy that generally beset the avant-garde. While WMM sustained experimental work, early on it also engaged consciousness-raising efforts in areas like healthcare, notably releasing *Healthcaring: From Our End of the Speculum* (dir. Denise Bostrom and Jane Warrenbrand) in 1976. According to the historian Kristen Fallica, the film was "used by scores of community centers and health organizations and helped fuel the growth of women's health groups and alternative clinics."[50] In its twenty-first-century incarnation, WMM's catalog supports curricula in areas ranging from film history to public health, anthropology, and linguistics.[51] The organization's production-assistance program continues to offer workshops, but it also provides a nonprofit financial services umbrella for filmmakers who attract funding from other sources. This program supported films such as Laura Poitras's Edward Snowden documentary *Citizenfour* (2014) and Marielle Heller's sexual coming-of-age story *Diary of Teenage Girl* (2015)—each of which aimed to engage broad audiences. WMM thus offers an example of a durable organization that has been able to distinguish as well as link feminist interventions in media form, public health advocacy, and the gendered division of media labor. It does so by drawing on several distinct academic audiences for its substantial catalog of educational, documentary, and experimental films to help support production efforts outside academe.

It mattered to the success of programs in creative writing, dance, experimental film, women's students, and all the other new fields that students lent their energies to them. Professors contributed their immaterial labor too, but universities paid them for it. Students (and their parents) paid universities. Not only did their enrollments drive university investment in professors and facilities, but students' creative and political work, both in class and out, contributed to the "'ideological' and cultural environment of the consumer." Students attuned to political uses of media supplied Buckley's show not only with object lessons in the depredations of wayward youth but also with examples of fit interlocutors. They inspired conservative think tanks and informed community organizations like Intermedia Arts. They branded computer technologies as "disruptive." Each of these developments coupled the university, sometimes loosely, sometimes tightly, with external organizations and audiences. In the process, they helped remake the whole mediasphere to which universities belong.

Each group was likely to portray itself as uniquely oppositional. Feminist activists saw Grove's underground posture as more of the same sexism. The experimental filmmaking crowd wanted nothing to do with the community video people, and vice versa. Creative writers thought books were best. *Wired*'s Rossetto could not, in retrospect, imagine having anything in common with Buckley, just as the YAF and SDS espoused opposing styles and aims. Despite this, the changes student media workers provoked are best appraised in aggregate. The revolution they made was different from the revolutions they proclaimed, and the cultivation of niche audiences was one of its effects.

The participatory-media revolution meant that universities would nurture, often deliberately, sometimes quite by accident, spaces in which students could experiment on their peers as well as on extramural audiences. Conversely, they could be understood as spaces where extramural experimentalists might recruit talent, whether for feminist filmmaking or for computer coding, and where they might find audiences and influencers to drive the next wave of media experimentation and activism. Administrators figured out not only that students would pay tuition for such opportunities but also how better to manage the value students added—along with the sometimes uncomfortable controversies they created.

Far more clearly than ever before, student immaterial labor connected campuses with networks universities sustained but did not control. The shift has antecedents, to be sure, in the rise of popular science books (chapter 1), federal grant apparatuses (chapter 3), and educational television (chapter 5). None of these precedents, however, allied themselves with on-campus factions that opposed university policies or questioned the university's relevance, as post-1960s constellations were wont to do. Over the long haul, independent distribution held the key to sustaining an activist stance while maintaining on-campus audiences. Although it stretches the traditional definition of "distribution," we imagine this as a function performed not only by the likes of WMM and Grove but also by conservative think tanks when they promulgate talking points for campus activists and by Twitter hashtags like #BlackLivesMatter.

The proliferation of audience segments and the dispersal of relatively autonomous distribution nodes diminished confidence in the university's ability to manage national welfare. Clark Kerr's multiversity reimagined this loss as a virtue. As Kerr correctly perceived, the inability to manage the university's many connections from on high testified, in the aggregate, to its increased importance in social reproduction. Higher education mattered more broadly than ever before, albeit to constituencies that often ignored, and sometimes hated, one another. There was, however, at least one vantage from which the new shape of US postsecondary education could be perceived: the numbers solicited and reported by the federal government, which became increasingly important to managing the multiversity and to which we now turn.

BY THE NUMBERS

Should anyone imagine they can understand how the American university changed after 1970 without accounting for its reliance on quantitative mediation, they should think again. In chapter 6, we observed the importance of student demographic data to redefining the student body. Universities and government bureaucracies learned to approach student diversity as a positive quality they would agree to manage. We also showed that such data, supplemented by financial information and test scores, anchored new programs of financial aid to students. We further connected federal data-collection efforts with the proliferation of new degree programs that, often but not always, co-opted students' interests. We offered as one milestone the introduction of a new federal survey instrument, the Higher Education General Information Survey (HEGIS), which first captured student-body profiles for the school year ending in June 1966. Notably, the Association for Institutional Research, which connected offices doing such research at universities across the country, was founded the same year. In this chapter, we continue our line of argument about the centrality of academic numbers. We show, first, that the most commonly circulated representations of the data describing undergraduate-degree completions are dangerously misleading and, second, that different statistics will better explain what happened to the university's division of labor.

Degree "share" names the most commonly cited metric of supply and demand. Share measures the proportion of undergraduate completions falling to particular programs of study. As a metric of what universities supply, it is frequently used to demonstrate that they underproduce, for example, nurses, teachers, or engineers relative to current workforce requirements. As a metric of what students demand, it typically testifies to changing undergraduate interest in broad areas like "the humanities" or "the sciences" as well as in specific fields that may be proposed as bellwethers of enrollment trends. Particularly among those concerned to meet enrollment targets, degree share is sometimes likened to "market share." We argue that the specific conception of share used by media industries is more relevant. Television producers, advertisers, and ratings agencies treat share as a measure fundamental to the process of making programming decisions and selling advertising spots. Consideration of this process illuminates how universities work better than more generic invocations of a "market." Comparison with media industries also suggests new ways of measuring student audiences.

People who work in (or study) broadcast media will be familiar with measures of program "reach." Below, we develop a reach measure for universities' degree programs. Considered in tandem with share, this measure significantly complicates familiar narratives of national supply and demand by capturing both the proliferation of degree offerings and their uneven distribution. Most majors are not widespread. To a list of familiar majors like "History" or "Physics," universities have added many, many more in areas as different as "Bioengineering and Biomedical Engineering" and "Tourism and Travel Services Management." As they increased in number, new majors did not show up at every school, but everywhere more majors meant a smaller share for each. The reach metric demonstrates how university curricula transitioned from a "broadcast" era in which majors were fewer to a "narrowcast" era of the sort often associated with cable TV's proliferation of channels. Among other features, this shift sundered the relationship between discipline and department that characterized the American research university at its inception (see chapter 1). Majors increased faster than the number of departments to manage them.

To describe reach and complicate commonplace depictions of share requires us to call upon publicly available datasets as well as simple math.

We recognize this could test the patience of some readers, but we cannot recommend that they skip over our discussion. We would hope, rather, that the potentially alienating encounter with quantitative assessment itself makes a point. Avoiding numbers as incomprehensible or rejecting them out of hand as invalid is all too common in some quarters. Insofar as data inform academic policies, this posture of innumeracy is a posture of disengagement. Stakeholders in the university need to be capable of understanding the media through which it communicates. In many circumstances, it communicates through numbers. Readers well aware of this fact may be impatient with our discussion for a different reason. To them, it will be obvious that we are not statisticians. We can only hope that they will find it possible to complement our effort by challenging and improving upon it.

The volatility generated by larger numbers of degree programs, the decoupling of department and discipline, and the need to see a more diverse student body through to completion spurred an increasing subdivision of academic labor. Although one might not know it from numerous accounts denouncing the ballooning growth of campus administration, the rise of student services was the single largest contributor to that phenomenon. In addition to student-services professionals, instructional demand meant employment for graduate students, who became a newly significant part of the academic workforce. Programmatic specialization helped place tenure-track faculty members at a further remove from the "whole student," whom many faculty, especially perhaps those in the humanities, continued to describe as their target. A growing array of student-services occupations in effect replaced those faculty, while graduate students became their colleagues in the classroom.

Perhaps more than our other chapters, we expect this one will serve different purposes for different kinds of readers. We aim to assist our faculty readers in rethinking their relationship to the array of student-services professionals who are their colleagues and who may understand the university and its quantitative media better than they do. For these readers as well as colleagues in university administration, we want to refocus the alarm that sometimes accompanies news of declining share. Our account underscores that the department has become a precarious container for the functions traditionally bundled in it. We also provide a different frame for understanding the boom in graduate student and temporary lecturer employment. For readers outside the university who may have no idea why universities now employ so many more nonfaculty personnel than they used to, or what it means that they offer degrees in subjects that did not exist when they went to school, we aim to reveal the internal complexity of the workplace from a novel point of view. This is not a pitch for additional public funding or an appeal to cut costs. Nor is it an argument that students should be choosing different majors. Rather, we mean to inform those engaged in such conversations that different numbers should mediate them.

REACH VERSUS SHARE

Annual reporting of federal survey data has emphasized the share of completions awarded not in the specific majors students actually complete but in categories aggregating those majors. That is, those writing the reports bundle completions into broader and more recognizable categories that are not themselves in the underlying data. This approach, urged by the complexity of the survey results, is bound to be misleading. It makes the extent of the variation in degree programs disappear, and it can easily tip the scale to alter perceptions of the share won by different areas.

For example, the National Science Foundation (NSF) employs a scheme that distinguishes eight different kinds of engineering degrees but lumps together an array of discrete majors into amalgams like "Biological Sciences" and "Arts and Music."[1] This may imply that American universities allow students to major in "Arts and Music," when in fact no such major could have been recorded (no code for it exists). Further, the NSF data may suggest that engineering has undergone a process of specialization when "Biological Sciences" has not—this is untrue. When the National Center for Education Statistics (NCES) depicts the same underlying data, it presents a differently inaccurate picture. It groups all engineering degrees together, while reporting total completions in "Biological and Biomedical Sciences" and "Visual and Performing Arts." Consumers of both reports could be forgiven for thinking that the addition of "Biomedical" does not much change the NSF's category and that "Visual and Performing Arts" is just another name for "Arts and Music." Such assumptions are unwarranted. To pick just one example, the NSF includes degrees in "Religious/Sacred Music" in "Arts and Music," but NCES counts them under "Theology and Religious Vocations."[2] Perceptions of share will vary accordingly. Neither agency, we stipulate, sets out to deceive its readers. Misprision results from the generic conventions of the share report, where intelligibility demands that the many hundreds of fields in which a college student might actually major be reduced to a few bundles—perhaps as many as fifty if the data is presented in tabular form, far fewer if a pie chart or time-series plot presents it. The cost of representing share in this manner is obfuscation of the university's actual structure.

Journalists come closer to lying than the federal agencies do when they ignore this highly contestable process of aggregation and use NCES or NSF results to make alarmist charts and tell the stories that go with them (see figure 8.1).[3] Though ill-considered, this kind of presentation is to be expected. Newspapers understand what will grab readers' attention, and sensational pictures of degree share compel faculty members, administrators, and policy makers for much the same reason as they attract the general readership. Share appears to measure what undergraduates favor. As such, it informs arguments over funding as well as campaigns to redirect student interest. Precisely because numbers have this power, responsible journalists and readers should ask more questions about them, questions like: What exactly is included in this category of "the humanities"? With how many other categories does it compete for share over the term of its supposed decline? It is in fact possible, and not even particularly difficult, to know the share of completions falling to fields in which students actually major. It is also possible to plot changing shares in relation to the average share of all programs, which, as one would expect, has steadily declined as the number of degrees on offer has increased.

Once disaggregated, share of degree completions can be likened to television "channel share": "the share one channel has of all viewing for particular time period . . . calculated by dividing the channel's average audience by the average audience of all channels."[4] This differs from a "rating," which represents the viewing audience as a percentage of the total possible universe of viewers (for example, Households Using Television [HUT]). According to the Nielsen agency, networks care more about share because it tells them how well they are competing with other networks (for example, if FX has more or less of a share than TNT).[5] Advertisers care more about the proportion of a given demographic they might influence—thus, ratings.

Although he does not employ these terms, the historian and higher-education blogger Ben Schmidt argues for a ratings-like measure of baccalaureate completions.[6] He proposes charting majors not as a percentage

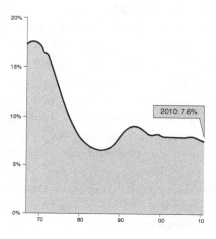

Decline and Fall

Percentage of bachelor's degrees at U.S. colleges
and universities awarded in the humanities

Source: American Academy of Arts and Sciences. *Wall Street Journal.*

FIGURE 8.1. Alarmist chart published by the *Wall Street Journal* in June 2013.

of degrees earned (or share) but as a percentage of all twenty-three-year-olds—because not completing a degree is also an option for this demographic. If we are interested in what higher education does for our society, Schmidt reasons, we might better care about the proportion of young people receiving particular types of degrees rather than the proportion of degree earners choosing one path as opposed to some other. Whether employment or civic life concerns us, it is ultimately more important what proportion of all adults have training in a particular field than what percentage of recent graduates do. Schmidt has a point. Both measures should inform us, not least because the contrast between the two might remind professors and administrators of their positions in the division of labor.

Although university financing, budgeting, and scheduling are considerably different from such activities in television, professors are in a position similar to TV producers. They seek student interest among those enrolled at their institution and hope that increasing their proportion of majors will increase, or at least maintain, administrative investment in program development. Like television producers, moreover, faculty members reveal their self-interest in a preoccupation with share, even if, as Schmidt suggests, an interest in ratings would be more civic-minded. Were faculty more civic-minded, we would think like advertisers do and care about the proportion of *potential* college-goers that complete majors in our areas. Most faculty, however, do not have roles that allow or encourage them to act on such a concern. They are not involved in outreach and recruitment but rather develop and execute the program content recruiters promote. Insofar as degree programs compete with one another for an institution's limited resources, administrative models favor share—faster growing programs may expect more frequent faculty hires, for instance; those in decline may lose lines. Especially because postsecondary education lacks a ratings-like measure of the sort Schmidt proposes, it can be easy for professors to overlook the fact that the potential audience is always much larger than the current student body and to become overly focused on besting the major housed in the building next door.

If the contrast between share and ratings can be seen in the different discussions they produce about student completions, consideration of yet another audience measure reveals profound changes in the organization of university curricula that are invisible to both share and ratings. In broadcast industries, "reach" is the percentage of a total target audience exposed to programming at least once during a given period (for example, the percentage of Households Using Television [HUT] or People Using Television [PUT] who could have seen a particular show in a particular time slot). To explore the relevance of reach for the academy, one must grapple with the fact that instructional programs are different from television programs in key ways. Duration is one obvious difference—the notion of a time slot does not fit completions measured at annual intervals. Moreover, the statistical universe needs specification. Postsecondary institutions can be grouped and distinguished in any number of ways. TV markets can too, but the categories differ: for example, the "major metropolitan areas" referenced in television reach are not the same kind of category as "research, very high activity," which defines a particular kind of school (also known as an R1). Recognizing these differences, it seems reasonable to accept the annual total of baccalaureate completions at a specific set of institutions as a fair measure of the target audience, that is, undergraduates completing university (UCU).

Defining the audience in this way takes into consideration the fact that program availability may guide students' selections of schools. The data would allow us to delimit target audiences geographically, in the way that TV markets are traditionally specified, but such an approach would not account for the fact that students may travel far to enroll in the particular programs they desire (and to which they gain admission). Although program availability is hardly the only factor motivating school choice, that fact that it is one argues in favor of a definition of audience as broad as the data will allow. Degrees reach unevenly across the entire US system of higher education, as students and parents will likely discover when they begin to shop for schools. Measures of reach will not, however, encompass the potential students who avoided college or those who did not complete degrees. For that, again, one would need a ratings-like measure.

As we define it, reach measures the percentage of students who could have chosen to finish a given program because it was available at their institutions. Because we are particularly interested in the research university, we have narrowed the statistical universe somewhat to consider only undergraduates completing baccalaureate degrees at institutions that also confer the PhD. The number of students who *might have* completed a degree in any given field (as identified by the federal Classification of Instructional Programs code, or CIP) can be found by adding up baccalaureate completions at those schools awarding degrees in that field to provide a total of potential completions (PC). To arrive at the percentage of reach, divide by UCU (Reach $= PC_{(CIP)} / UCU$). This statistic reveals that the vast majority of instructional programs have been available only to a very small proportion of students completing baccalaureate degrees. Moreover, calculating average reach for odd years from 1967 to 2015 indicates a consistently downward trend. After 1985, the average program reached around 10 percent of completers; it would drop off again in the new century.

No single institution could possibly offer all the programs listed in the Classification of Instructional Programs (CIP)—the federally mandated taxonomy through which US institutions report major completions. According to the Integrated Postsecondary Education Data System (IPEDS) survey for 2015, the number of different degrees offered at PhD institutions had grown to almost a thousand.[7] The change over time has been dramatic: the 1967 HEGIS survey recorded baccalaureate awards in a mere 187 distinct programs of study.

Reach numbers reveal that the more majors there were to choose from, the less evenly distributed those majors became. Although relative numbers of students reached does not translate directly into numbers of schools (because schools vary in size), it is possible to infer relative ubiquity. Majors with very high reach, exceptions to the general rule, are necessarily available almost everywhere in the United States. Majors with average reach, the vast majority, might be peppered throughout the country or clustered geographically. Regardless of spatial distribution, however, the average major is available to a very limited proportion of students. If this seems surprising, one may credit overemphasis on aggregation and the idealization of an earlier form of the university.

As one might expect, decline in average reach correlates with expansion of the curricular taxonomy employed by the federal government. Figure 8.2 shows the number of distinct degree programs in which baccalaureate completions were recorded (again, at PhD-granting institutions) as well as the mean reach of programs awarding those completions. The elaboration of HEGIS codes after 1970 seems decisive, as does the introduction of the CIP schema in 1985. Both dates show a significant bump in the number of degrees registered by the federal data and, correspondingly, a declining average reach. CIP revisions in 1990, 2000, and 2010 had a less dramatic but still discernible effect. Each update expanded the "menu" of degrees from which institutions could choose to record completions.[8] Notably,

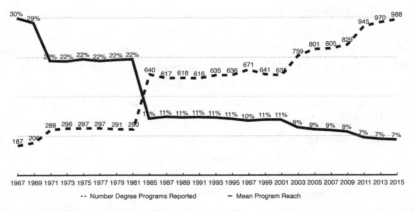

FIGURE 8.2. Programs reported and mean reach, 1967–2015, odd years.
Source: Compiled by the authors from publicly available HEGIS and IPEDS data.

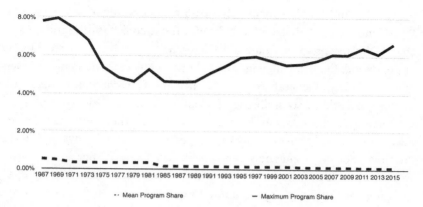

FIGURE 8.3. Mean and maximum program share of total completions, 1967–2015, odd years.
Source: Compiled by the authors from publicly available HEGIS and IPEDS data.

these changes had a less marked effect on share numbers (see figure 8.3). Mean share of completions did decline as the number of programs increased, leaving a slimmer slice for each. More striking, however, is how low the average has been: starting at .53 percent in 1967, it hovered around .16 percent from 1985 to 2001 and declined to .10 percent by 2011. Nonetheless, a few programs could claim a relatively large share. The 1970 HEGIS reclassification clearly affected the maximum share any given program could expect, but across subsequent taxonomic changes, that number has defied the downward trend. In 2015, it rebounded to almost 7 percent.

The share leaders in 2015 were Registered Nursing/Registered Nurse (70 percent reach, 6.7 percent share) and Psychology, General (93 percent reach, 5.9 percent share). For every ten students in the country, that is, seven could major in Registered Nursing, while fewer than seven in one hundred actually did so. Psychology, General had an even more impressive reach: nine in ten students could have majored in it. Fewer students selected that option—but still a considerable number, far more than most majors. The top percentile of share started at 1.9 percent, which is to say that 99 percent of major programs of study had less than 2 percent share. The reach measure indicates one reason why this might be the case. After 1985, any given program of study could, on average, expect to reach 11 percent or less of graduating undergraduates. In 2015 the average major was available to one student in ten. Psychology, General, available to just about everyone, was not the norm.

The few and familiar majors that commentators might name tended to be the most widely distributed ones, not those commanding the greatest share. Only five programs maintained a reach of more than 90 percent for the entire period: English Language and Literature, General; Mathematics, General; Psychology, General; Political Science and Government, General; and History, General. A sixth, Biology/Biological Sciences, General, leapt above 90 percent reach in 1975 and stayed there; some other high-reach majors have more recently fallen below the 90 percent threshold: Physics, General after 1995; Sociology after 2007; and Chemistry, General after 2011. In other words, after 2011, whether you went to a small and specialized PhD-granting institution or to a gigantic university, you could expect to find someone majoring in English, Biology, Mathematics, Psychology, Political Science, or History. Out of nearly one thousand baccalaureate programs tracked at PhD-granting institutions, these six degrees, and only these degrees, can be regarded as ubiquitous. They are the basic-cable channels of higher education.

Outside these familiar basic-cable channels, one finds an array of majors and an equally broad range of explanations for declining average reach. In 1991, the following examples clustered around the average reach of 11 percent:

- Japanese Language and Literature (CIP 16.0302)—11.8 percent at twenty-one institutions
- Bioengineering and Biomedical Engineering (CIP 14.0501)—11.6 percent at twenty-eight institutions
- English Languages and Literatures, Other (CIP 23.9999)—11.4 percent at twenty-eight institutions
- Tourism and Travel Services Management (CIP 52.0903)—11.2 percent at eighteen institutions
- East Asian Studies (CIP 05.0104)—11.1 percent at twenty-six institutions
- Ecology (CIP 26.1301)—10.9 percent at twenty institutions
- Dental Hygiene/Hygienist (CIP 51.0602)—10.8 percent at forty-one institutions
- Physical Sciences (CIP 40.0101)—10.5 percent at twenty-four institutions

Even this limited sample suggests several reasons for the generally low average of reach.

- Tourism and Travel Services Management, for example, looks like a specialized preprofessional degree that might be more typically offered at the graduate level, while baccalaureate degrees (again, at PhD-granting institutions) in Dental Hygiene/Hygienist look like more robust versions of preprofessional degrees offered at the associate level.[9] These are exactly the sorts of programs a school might launch if it wanted to market specialized degrees to undergraduates anxious about their employment prospects.

- Japanese Language and Literature and East Asian Studies, in contrast, look like different flavors of liberal arts BAs that might be attracting students with similar interests but that are institutionalized differently at different schools. The former might be housed in a modern languages or comparative literature department, for example; the latter is likely set up as an interdisciplinary program. Schools might have one and not the other primarily because of local faculty (and administrative) strengths and interests. Something similar is probably going on with English Languages and Literatures, Other. English departments in those twenty-eight schools have likely set up degree paths that look fairly different from traditional offerings and may resemble degree programs classified otherwise elsewhere.

- Bioengineering, like East Asian Studies, could be seen as an "emerging" interdisciplinary degree program. And quite a mover! By 2015, it would have a 30 percent reach, more than four times the mean reach that year (7 percent).

- Ecology, in contrast, after slowly extending itself from a far-below-average reach of 1 percent in 1967 to the average in 1991, remained average, following the gradual downward trend in reach for majors in general to 7 percent in 2015.

- Physical Sciences also followed the declining average—but probably for different reasons. If East Asian Studies, Bioengineering, and Ecology all represented relatively new ways of combining methodologies and problems that might otherwise belong to comparative languages or history, biology or mechanical engineering, evolutionary biology or earth science, the CIP code in Physical Science identified a residual general rubric. Most students interested in physical science were by 1991 choosing from more specialized degrees in Chemistry, Geology/Earth Science, or Physics.

This short list of examples, then, points to at least three major tendencies driving the proliferation of degree programs and, thus, the downward trend in reach:

1. Niche marketing to students concerned about their employment prospects
2. Uneven success in attracting student (and administrative) interest to new versions of liberal arts and sciences degrees
3. Local variety in configuring new degree programs amid established departments and disciplines

As the appearance of English Languages and Literatures, Other in our short list suggests, this manifold dynamic transformed even the basic-cable majors.[10]

To reckon with such curious categories as English Languages and Literatures, Other, it helps to understand the taxonomic structure. CIP codes begin with two-digit "families" followed by four-digit extensions indicating their more specialized children, which are themselves often grouped into series. For example, after the 2010 round of reclassification, CIP family 23, English Language and Literature/Letters, included four distinct series: 23.01 English Language and Literature, General; 23.13 Rhetoric and Composition/Writing Studies; 23.14 Literature; and 23.99 English Language and Literature/Letters, Other. All told, these four series contain thirteen distinct degree programs. The vast majority of BA completions are recorded in 23.0101 (English Language and Literature, General), but many English departments credential students in more specific ways. For example, 23.1302, Creative Writing, had a 5 percent reach in 1970, which had doubled to around 10 percent by 2005, then rising again to 13 percent in 2015, when 1,639 students completed the degree at ninety-eight institutions.[11]

Notably, CIP codes are assigned according to curricular content, not departmental home. Creative writing, for instance, is sometimes part of English and sometimes a standalone department. Regardless, the degree can be reported to the federal government the same way, as 23.1302, Creative Writing. Measures of its reach will not be affected by its departmental location. It is, however, also possible that an English department offering a major track or emphasis in creative writing, one that would look very similar to a creative writing degree elsewhere, would record those degrees as English Languages and Literatures, General. In this case, measures of reach would be affected. Students completing that track would appear to have been reached by English Languages and Literatures, General and not by Creative Writing. Although they may share a name like "English," degrees are not departments.

Measures based on CIP codes do not directly indicate departmental organization, but the reach metric does reveal patterns that suggest how university organizational charts changed. Speech and Rhetorical Studies (23.1001) offers an example. This degree saw its reach plummet to 26 percent in 2011 from nearly 70 percent in 1971. Back then, it was known to HEGIS as Speech, Debate & Forensic Science (Rhetoric & Public Address). Administrative and student interest in this area most likely shifted to CIP family 09: Communication, Journalism, and Related Programs. Just so, Speech Communication and Rhetoric (09.0101) saw its reach grow from 17 percent in 1971 to over 50 percent by 1985, when it had a respectable 2 percent share of all baccalaureate completions. It is possible, even likely, that during this migration many students earned 09 (Communication) degrees from professors who had 23 (English) PhDs. Conversely, English departments that cling to Speech and Rhetorical Studies (23.1001) may find themselves employing Speech Communication and Rhetoric (09.0101) PhDs. English was hardly the only basic-cable channel to witness such changes. In the sciences, for example, Biological and Biomedical Sciences (CIP family 26) has been particularly dynamic, with degree programs subdividing, merging, fading, and expanding. To pick just one fast riser that now seems relatively stable: Biochemistry's 21 percent reach (.08 percent share) in 1967 grew to around 49 percent (.4 percent share) by 2007. Taxonomic changes, along with metrics of reach and share, thus indicate the centrifugal force of program development, which spins off new departments and internally fractures existing ones.

Beyond the basic-cable channels, it is easier to see the countervailing centripetal force exerted by the taxonomy as it attempts to order programs that, at ground level on campus, may seem far flung and distinct. For example, CIP family 50, Visual and Performing Arts, includes degree programs ranging from Dance, General (50.0301) to Art History, Criticism and Conservation (50.0703) and Arts, Entertainment, and Media Management, General (50.1001)—degrees likely to be administered by different programs, departments, and perhaps even different colleges or schools within a university. CIP family 05, Area, Ethnic, Cultural, Gender, and Group Studies, offers a similar gallimaufry of programs, ranging from American/United States Studies/Civilization to Ukrainian Studies, African-American/Black Studies, Women's Studies, Folklore Studies, and so on. These are not in any meaningful sense disciplinary families with specialized children, nor will their practitioners understand them as such. Ukrainian studies and women's studies, for example, are not more specialized versions of a common approach but rather represent distinct efforts to bring arrays of methodologies to bear on shared concerns. The taxonomy builders, rather than disciplines or universities, create these categorical umbrellas for otherwise unrelated fields.

The taxonomy enforces its family structure at the expense of alternatives. It is not simply that it would be possible to bundle degrees differently, which schematic revisions have done. Rather, emphasis on the parent-child hierarchy militates against horizontal consideration of the siblings. Dance and art history, for instance, could be said to differ just as creative writing and speech and rhetoric do. Their professors may have different terminal degrees (MFAs for dance and creative writing, PhDs for art history and speech and rhetoric) and different criteria for tenure and promotion. Moreover, faculty in each will have professional colleagues working within an array of organizational structures nationwide: some in standalone departments, some in specialized schools or programs, others as parts of departments called something else. If dance and creative writing are in this sense close cousins, the scheme thwarts consideration of that family resemblance in favor of the hierarchy that places dance under Visual and Performing Arts and creative writing under English Language and Literatures.

The CIP family plan facilitates aggregation in a way that distorts both perceptions of share and our understanding of what it means for an area to be expanding or declining. Film and media studies provides a particularly clear example. Today, members of its major professional organization, the Society for Cinema and Media Studies, could point to schools with strong reputations in the field that reported undergraduate degrees under Mass Communications/Media Studies (09.0102), Film/Cinema/Video Studies (50.0601), and English Language and Literatures, General (23.0101)—that is, some schools offered recognizably strong programs in film and media studies as an emphasis within an English degree and counted them that way. Although perceivable by the profession, this cluster disappears when aggregated into the different buckets of Communication, Journalism, and Related Programs (CIP 09); Visual and Performing Arts (CIP 50); or English Languages and Literatures (CIP 05). After they were added to the taxonomy in 1985, both Mass Communications/Media Studies and Film/Cinema/Video Studies grew faster than average—they exceeded the mean standard

TABLE 8.1

Degree	1985		2015	
	% Reach	% Share	% Reach	% Share
Mass Communications/Media Studies (09.0102)	0.10	—	19.43	0.52
Film/Cinema/Video Studies (50.0601)	5.86	0.04	20.48	0.18
09.0102 and 50.0601 Combined	**5.96**	**0.04**	**39.91**	**0.7**
English, Languages and Literatures, General (23.0101)	91.44	2.31	90.71	1.98
Mean	**10.82**	**0.16**	**6.76**	**0.10**

deviation of reach (see table 8.1).[12] Considered together, they had a respectable reach and share by 2015.

Importantly, the data does not allow us to know what proportion of English degrees might have resembled the degrees recorded in the other majors. The reach of basic-cable English held steady and exceeded the cumulative reach of the newer degrees. Its share reflected that much greater reach. There can be no doubt, however, that a different method of aggregation would give film and media studies a much larger share than the one revealed by the default grouping of the 09, 50, and 23 fields. The reach number, a new metric, provides an entirely different perspective on which fields are growing. According to it, film and media studies was not the fastest mover but certainly did rank among a wide range of expanding fields. The ubiquitous basic-cable channels, which had nowhere to expand, were outliers to that trend. Everyone should have expected them to lose share to the upstarts.

Despite what local organizational charts may envision, department, discipline, and degree have clearly diverged. By 1990, if not before, the panoply of programs loosely grouped into areas like "Visual and Performing Arts" constituted the norm system-wide. Most students learned to grapple with this norm as they tried to make sense of the degree offerings and requirements at their institutions, and faculty members who served on curriculum committees or participated in advising outside the major also confronted it.

However, because departments retain their organizational role as the individual faculty member's employer in the important matters of tenure, promotion, and merit recognition, professors (and their graduate students) were apt to mistake the department for the default form of curricular organization as well. Faculty teaching mainly in "interdisciplinary" programs often aspired to departmental status with the relative autonomy in hiring and promotion that brings, while faculty teaching primarily through large departments often touted them as uniting diverse approaches under a single rubric.

Names and numbers conjure the realities they describe. They mediate discussions about the university that guide its possible futures. The tripartite schema that, in the 1930s, divided general education in "natural science," "social science," and "humanities" is hardly the only possible way to cluster the very wide array of programs and approaches that universities foster. In the early twenty-first century, the instability of that still recognizable schema revealed itself in combinations like "arts and humanities," "humanities and social science," and "science, technology, engineering, and math" (STEM). The later grouping owes its success to the National Science Foundation's (NSF) Education and Human Resources Directorate, which took an extraordinarily comprehensive approach to the problem of STEM education, from primary school through the doctorate.[13] NSF, we would be remiss not to recall, was initially chartered to fund research in social as well as natural science—*except* in biomedical fields, where it was envisioned that the National Institutes of Health (NIH) would be the primary federal grant maker. Depending on who is counting, then, biomedicine may not be "science." Numerical aggregation establishes each of these kinds of groupings as a reality on which institutions can go to work. Names and numbers orient funding streams, inform curricular distributions, and set administrative hierarchies. Disaggregating such abstract assemblages into the most granular data available discloses a very different reality. A thousand degrees jostle together. The organization chart does not contain them. They compete for attention and have the potential to enter into productive new combinations. Their progeny will be more likely to add options than to winnow the field.

STUDENT SERVICES AND "PART-TIME" INSTRUCTORS

In 1965, just before HEGIS marked the start of the period of disciplinary profusion we have described above, Clark Kerr observed that the multiversity's mind-boggling array of choices had created many "walking wounded" undergraduates.[14] By the end of the 1980s, when those choices had dramatically increased, it was clear that faculty would not, and probably could not, treat these wounds. They would be salved instead by student-services professionals. This change occurred alongside another, which distinguished the roles of tenure-line and term-contract faculty. The different actors caught up in these changes—faculty of all sorts, student-services professionals, and students—were positioned to perceive them differently.

Growing numbers of student-services professionals brought faculty the unwelcome news that they did not understand the students for which they competed. The 1960s and 1970s empowered student-services professionals along with students, Paul Bloland and his fellow chroniclers of *Reform in Student Affairs* (1994) explain. Institutions of higher education turned to student-affairs staff to manage student dissent while satisfying new legal requirements that they be treated as adults.[15] In the process, student affairs secured its claim to expertise about student behavior—expertise that faculty lacked. It soon began to help them navigate course offerings. "Faculty members frequently feel quite uncomfortable" advising new populations of students facing newly open post-1960s curricula, alleged the architects of Academic Advising at the University of Wisconsin, Green Bay, which launched outreach programs in the 1970s to help "first-generation college students who commute to the campus and who seem unaware of the helping services available to them."[16] The University of South Carolina, meanwhile, launched a national trend in 1972 with its "University 101," a first-year seminar overseen by professional staff in the division of Student Affairs and Academic Support with no fixed content and, as of 2014, three broad goals: "Foster Academic Success," "Help Students Discover and Connect with the University of South Carolina," and "Prepare Students for Responsible Lives in a Diverse, Interconnected, and Changing World."[17] Faculty failure to understand and engage a changing student body looms large in the accounts student services provide of its own success.

Be that as it may, changes to the faculty and student services in the 1970s and 1980s alike could be characterized by a tendency toward the diversification of expertise. Just as new majors could require new kinds of professors to teach them, so new approaches to student services mandated new sorts of professionals. A wide array of health experts, crisis counseling officers, career advisors, financial-aid consultants, and sundry others took on the job of completing the transformation of undergraduates begun in the 1960s. These experts took the diversity of the student body and its developmental needs as a given. Student populations had to be understood in all their multiplicity such that they could be counseled toward academic success as well as healthy and productive behaviors outside the classroom. The new student-services professionals held themselves responsible for addressing and developing the "whole student."[18] Although it connected with classroom work occasionally—when students faced health crises, for example, seriously breached campus discipline, or dramatically underperformed—the student-services apparatus in its most robust form managed a dense web of relations guiding students from their first campus visits through their class reunions.

Like their professional counterparts in health and financial services outside the university, student-services professionals addressed individual student clients as members of the distinct sorts of populations categorized, explained, and monitored by their specialties. The students addressed by coaches were athletes; those hailed by financial-aid experts were borrowers and grant recipients; mental health counselors had patients, and so on. Each professional specialty subdivided "students" into more finely grained types, measured potential, monitored deviance, and sought to intervene appropriately. But no two specialties did this in precisely the same way. If, for example, we imagine "the student" as a junior swimmer and Pell Grant recipient who needs six credit hours in foreign languages to graduate with her engineering major and is about to discover an unplanned pregnancy but for right now is focused on getting tickets for the concert next weekend, then we might also begin to imagine how her coach, financial-aid officer, academic advisor, and student crisis center staffer could each engage her to the best of their abilities without understanding her in the same way as their peers. The new teams of professionals could claim to serve "whole students" only retrospectively and in the aggregate. In this respect, the treatment of student-services clients is not that different from how various clinical and financial services professions address other adults as, simultaneously, individuals and members of specific types of populations.

Student services differs, however, in that students also belong to institutional populations: entering and graduating cohorts; majors by subject; campus-wide demographic divisions by race, ethnicity, sex, gender, family income, region of origin, generation in college, GPA, SAT or ACT score, and so on. The student-services boom in the 1970s was a beneficiary of the biopolitical initiatives of the 1960s, wherein universities and the federal government gathered more and more finely grained statistics about their changing demographics, collaborating in the process with student activists to identify and incorporate minority differences within the undergraduate student body. This broad effort defined the variegated population that student services addressed.

Effectiveness of the student-services sector, like that of the faculty, could be rendered through institution-wide metrics like admissions ratios, diversity measures, and four-year completion rates. These data could circulate as part of marketing pitches and would in later decades figure in various schemes for ranking colleges and universities across the nation. Wesleyan University, to pick just one example, adopted "Diversity University" as its brand, which required it to gather and publicize measures of student populations that demonstrated this commitment.[19] Developing in tandem, the student-services sector and these metrics conceived classroom teaching as one kind of client service among the many that universities provide.

Student services boomed. For three decades after 1975, it was the "fastest-growing category of professional employment in higher education," far outpacing both the growth of faculty positions and the increase in "administrative, managerial and executive positions" (a category with which it was often misleadingly conflated).[20] As the sociologists Larry Leslie and Gary Rhoades further note, no centrally coordinated strategy guided this expansion.[21] Rather, it stemmed from a diverse array of causes, each of which added a new feature to university bureaucracy. Governmental regulation (Title IX, perhaps most famously) compelled some student-services hires in areas of intramural athletics. Positions emerged with the student loan industry and its compliance requirements. Others were tied to competition among schools vying to fund the widest range of activities, study-abroad opportunities, and career-making internships. Still others responded to the new demographics of undergraduate enrollments, as women eclipsed men among undergraduates in the 1980s and as more diverse populations became the norm at a wider range of schools.

Although commentators observe that the rise of student services followed an era of elevated enrollments (and it did), changing staff-to-student ratios reveal that hiring increased far more rapidly than student enrollment during the 1980s at all sorts of schools. In 1976, according to the *Digest of*

Education Statistics, there were 50.9 students (full-time equivalents) for every "non-faculty professional." A decade later, in 1987, that ratio declined to 28.8, and it continued to creep downward even as undergraduate student enrollment increased by 13 percent to around 12.8 million students in 1987.[22] Hiring professional staff was evidently an economical way to enlarge student-development efforts, although the numbers suggest this strategy played out differently at publics and privates.[23] At public institutions, investment in student services may have partly compensated for decreased funding for classroom instruction.[24] At private colleges and universities, in contrast, funds for teaching rose more or less in sync with those for advising, counseling, coaching, and so forth.[25] In sum, student services appeared an increasingly integral part of growth strategies at private colleges and universities and a key element in plans to maintain growth while decreasing instructional cost at the publics.

Whether they perceived themselves to have lost authority or gained help, faculty found themselves deferring to more and more varied sorts of professionals who were not professors when it came to the project of student development. In his American Association for Higher Education report "Academic Advising: Getting Us Through the Eighties," Thomas Grites proclaimed, "Academic advising in American higher education has evolved from a routine, isolated, single-purpose, faculty activity to a comprehensive process of academic, career, and personal development performed by personnel from most elements of the campus community."[26] This innovation so effectively complicated communication between professor and student that education professionals became embroiled in a "national dialogue" about how to help faculty get to know their students, which probably further complicated it. Faculty-in-residence programs, faculty participation in campus orientation proceedings, and faculty/student-affairs "planning teams" were tested as ways to reengage professors in the process of addressing students and their developmental needs.[27] The division of labor had changed.[28]

Professional responsibility for providing educational experiences not only extended beyond the classroom but preceded any on-campus encounter. Universities frequently attempted to stoke their reputations for educational quality by presenting average test scores and measures of the socioeconomic diversity of the incoming class. In this pitch, a student's peers were deemed as important to the overall educational experience as the faculty's instructional contribution. Faculty could not influence incoming class composition in any clear or direct fashion. Recruiters and admissions officers more directly moved the dial on those numbers.

Faculty thus failed to perceive the nature of their relationship with student-services experts whenever they considered them to be support staff existing primarily to aid professorial work in the classroom or, even less charitably, as bureaucratic functionaries who imposed constraints on instructional freedom. Such a blind spot, moreover, implicated a wider set of working relationships. The challenge of understanding what student services did was akin to the challenge of collaborating with colleagues outside one's department or of trying to grapple with the very real inequities involved in instructional labor.

Although it did not make national headlines until the 1990s, the process of shifting instructional responsibility from tenure-line faculty to far less well compensated term-contract instructors began in the 1960s alongside the growth in student-services professionals. Universities addressed post–World War II enrollment spikes by increasing the ranks of graduate instructors along with tenure-line faculty. As early as 1967, the sociologists Robert Dubin and Frederic Beisse argued that reliance on graduate students at large public universities followed a well-known rule:

Whenever there is pressure on an established occupation or profession to provide more services, and the demand cannot be met through normal expansion of the supply of certified experts, then portions of the skill will be shifted, by a division of labor, to lower skilled and lower status work colleagues.[29]

After 1976, as NCES data compiled and arranged by the American Association of University Professors demonstrate, graduate student employees remained a relatively stable percentage of the workforce system-wide. Meanwhile, the ranks of part-time faculty grew dramatically (see figure 8.4). As with the complementary student-services boom, different sorts of institutions navigated significantly distinct pathways through this shift. Public four-year institutions saw significant growth in the percentage of graduate student employees, for example, whereas the increasing proportion of part-time faculty was more dramatic at private nonprofits and most dramatic at private for-profits.[30] Nonetheless, despite variation prompted by

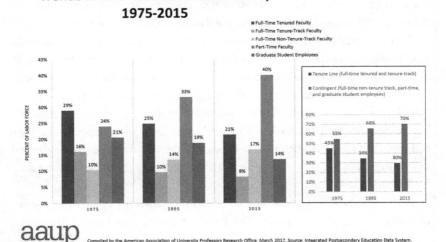

FIGURE 8.4. Trends in the academic labor force, 1976–2015.
Compiled by the American Association of University Professors Research Office, http://research.aaup
.org, March 2017. Source: Courtesy AAUP.

disparate revenue models, fluctuations in the type and amount of state and federal funding, and differences of institutional mission, the overall shape of the revised division of instructional labor is clear.

At the research university, increasing reliance on term-contract instructors—graduate students and adjuncts—did not mean less student-teacher contact overall, just less contact between students and tenure-line professors. Adjuncts paid to teach were not expected to devote time to research and service as tenure-line faculty were. Graduate assistant responsibilities for grading and leading discussion sections involved closer contact with undergraduates than the supervising professor might typically have. Although professorial instructional responsibilities might remain constant—at, say, two courses per term—there were fewer professors to go around. Particularly at large research institutions, faculty might get to know students as individuals only in their junior or senior years. It was easy for full-timers living through this change to grasp that they were being pushed away from relationships with students (graduate and undergraduate) in favor, especially, of research productivity.

If faculty perceived the change, however, they were slow to grasp and respond to its systemic character. In retrospect, polemics about the plight of humanities graduate students make this blind spot especially notable. The general response of professional associations to this period's employment crisis was not to engage the new division of labor but to defend the tenure system.[31] The emphasis may be detected even among those who pushed the issue relatively early on, in the context of the culture wars. In their 1995 collection *Higher Education Under Fire: Politics, Economics, and the Crisis of the Humanities*, Michael Bérubé and Cary Nelson linked attacks on "the humanities" (especially English) with campaigns to reduce its funding, ratchet up expectations for research productivity, and shift the instructional burden from tenure-line faculty to adjuncts and graduate instructors. Among all these issues, they chose to emphasize the pipeline problem. "It is time to say, bluntly, that graduate education is losing its moral foundation," they wrote, because professors continued to prepare graduate student "apprentices" for jobs like theirs that had been declining in number while turning a blind eye to their institutions' increasing reliance on relatively cheap graduate student labor to do the teaching.[32] "For decades American universities have fostered a kind of *idiot savant* academic culture," Bérubé and Nelson observe. "Faculty members maintain expertise in their disciplines but remain mostly ignorant about how the university works."[33] This blunt point took some time to sink in.

Only after 2010 did it begin to seem legitimate to train English graduate students for the division of labor created in the last decades of the twentieth century by, for example, reducing time to degree, shifting requirements to acknowledge that many graduates would serve long tours in the contingent labor pool, and exploring training for careers outside academe.[34] Although early-twenty-first-century faculty continue to supervise graduate student teaching assistants, we suspect that the role of tenured faculty "mentor" to untenured junior colleagues more closely approximates the master-apprentice relation that 1960s professors had with their graduate students. For most graduate students, we further suspect, learning to act in a tenure-line role—juggling the teaching, research, and managerial ("service") responsibilities this involves—begins in earnest after the tenure-line position is secure.

The ranks of term-contract instructors and student-services professionals increased in tandem with the programmatic shifts we have revealed by disaggregating share and developing a metric for reach. Non-tenure-track instructors—graduate students and part-timers—were both an economical means to deliver that curriculum and a response to its volatility, since student interest might develop faster than the pipelines that credentialed and tenured faculty. Student services sought to address the challenge of advising increasingly diverse students through an increasingly diverse curriculum.

The habit of aggregating myriad degrees into conglomerations like STEM or "the humanities" obscures the relationship among these changes and encourages faculty and administrators to act on a university different from the one they actually inhabit. Circulating the right numbers would help observers see majors as majors, not as departments. It would also help everyone reckon with the university's division of labor by clarifying that the growing ranks of student-services professionals and term-contract instructors addressed, in part, the complexity generated by increasingly diverse degrees and students.

In the same period this chapter has described, the culture wars mobilized key factions by avoiding discussion of structural changes in favor of wedge issues. Remarkably, what English departments taught ranked high among these. Voices on the left as well as the right stridently declared that universities would fail unless English professors changed their ways. Looking back on this period in 2011, the intellectual historian Peter Uwe Hohendahl rightly remarks "that the conservative and neoconservative critics of the 1980s did not notice or respond to the actual transformations of the American university," which, for him, had less to with literature curricula than with the proliferation of new business models. While cultural warriors battled over the meaning, content, and value of an humanistic education, Hohendahl contends, the opponent of such learning "was no longer the radical student or the left-leaning professor but an administrator who defines curriculum reforms in terms of student enrollment and credit output"—with little concern about content.[35] Left-leaning humanists, he argues, understood the period better because they correctly perceived the university's newly corporate qualities.

Hohendahl is right that this period's superheated rhetoric often turned on a model of liberal learning that institutional renovation had made obsolete. He is wrong to propose administrative villains as primary agents of this change. The use of enrollments and Carnegie units as administrative measures was hardly new. Before the First World War, such measures inspired Thorstein Veblen to chastise the university for "businesslike organization" (see chapter 1). It is true that new budget approaches, like Activity-Based Budgeting and Responsibility-Centered Management, more closely matched resource allocation with student credit-hour production. The perception that English was somehow at risk did not, however, derive from a wholly new concern with how many students took its classes. That perception had as much to do with the new competitive environment produced by proliferating degree programs as it did with any particular approach to the budget. This long-term trend, for which faculty and students were as responsible as administrators, altered the entire university, not just English.

Chapter Nine

BAD ENGLISH

The Culture Wars Reconsidered

It is remarkable how much attention English departments commanded during the culture wars of the 1980s and 1990s. Although commentators inside the university and out could not agree about what was wrong with the nation or with its educational system, a peculiar consensus emerged that changes to English would be necessary to fix both. More peculiar still, "English" often appeared as a bad object among its most vocal supporters. Its professors could do nothing right: either they did not properly uphold tradition or they stubbornly refused to supplant it. Bad English came to figure many, perhaps most, of the university's post-1960s troubles. The fate of the liberal arts, the future of character building, the problem of research "excellence," prospects for detente between the humanities and the sciences—English managed to pull these problems and more into its increasingly erratic orbit.

Three trends converged to define English as this period's leading negative example. First, as we described in the previous chapter and like all other undergraduate majors, English faced a more competitive environment. It did so in the manner peculiar to the "basic cable" degrees, which had no way to expand their reach and which found themselves sometimes spinning off, sometimes co-opting, degrees that competed with the traditional literature major. Second, again as described previously and like all other disciplines, English underwent a subdivision of labor that created new relationships among tenure-line faculty, graduate students, term-contract instructors, and student-services professionals. Literary scholarship became increasingly specialized, and professors were required to produce more of it. New forums, such as the invited lecture and the humanities center, encouraged an emphasis on specialized research and cultivated new forms of academic celebrity.

The third major trend was the presentation of English as the proper custodian of common culture, the font of general education after the fashion of Great Books or Redbook-style New Criticism. Propelled by a conservative policy agenda, this description of English cast increasing specialization as a fall from grace, a dramatic decline from an era when English purportedly organized the undergraduate curriculum as a whole. Though this pitch found both support and opposition on campus, it was doubly misleading. First, English had never justly claimed the power to curate national culture. Second, attempts to claim that power were not generalist. When partisans of English made the case, they relied precisely on their specialization, identifying lists of Great Books or employing methods of New Criticism, which purported to inculcate specific reading habits that uniquely served the commonweal. As ever, misrecognition underwrote nostalgia. Repeated denunciations of English made it seem that, once upon a time, it had actually vouchsafed a lettered citizenry. Such a gesture tells us more about the 1980s and 1990s than it does about any moment in the university's past.

William Bennett led the charge against English; Bill Readings wrote its epitaph. In 1984, Bennett, President Ronald Reagan's appointee to lead the National Endowment for the Humanities and then the Department of Education, delivered *To Reclaim a Legacy: A Report on the Humanities in Higher Education*. In 1996, Readings, an associate professor of comparative literature, posthumously published *The University in Ruins*. These two works provide conventional bookends for a period of "warfare" in which the forces of Reaganite reaction (or revolution) vied with an exhausted (or deeply entrenched) academic left to control "culture."[1] They do not agree on a definition of "culture." For Bennett, it could be indicated by a book list. For Readings, it resembled a pedagogy. Yet each told a story of ruin and redemption with literature at its center.

Above all, the late-century badness of English testified to the difference between Bennett's broad audience and Readings's narrower one. Their efforts ought to remind us that a successfully broad address is not the same as a generalizing rhetoric. At the end of the period, the "Sokal affair," in which a physicist trolled the cultural studies journal *Social Text* and, by implication, theory-crazed humanists at large, confirmed the importance of taking audience into account.[2]

FACULTY STARS, PUBLIC INTELLECTUALS, AND HUMANITIES CENTERS

The university, we have repeatedly insisted, does not first develop a division of labor and then, only after, learn to promote its services. The work of connecting people by means of college football, general-education curricula, educational television, statistics describing undergraduate completions, and esoteric theoretical treatises evolves in tandem with the variety of job titles for those conducting such work. In the 1980s, tenure-line faculty increasingly found that their most important performances would be addressed to faculty outside their home institutions. As some professorial duties were passed off to term-contract instructors and others to student-services professionals, the new norm for faculty on the tenure track increasingly emphasized research, which was appraised both quantitatively and qualitatively, in terms of reputation.

The academic star system exemplified this new state of affairs and was indicatively conflated with the recent history of literary criticism by the very English professor who identified it. "Since the rise of theory in the 1970s," David Shumway argued in 1997, "a star system, a new form of intellectual authority and professional status, has become significant and perhaps dominant in literary studies."[3] Shumway's list of luminaries includes Judith Butler, Jacques Derrida, Stanley Fish, Henry Louis Gates, Fredric Jameson, and Gayatri Chakravorty Spivak—each of whom names a theoretical brand, but only some of whom are trained in or known for producing "literary studies." Shumway's remark thus indicates that "theory" allowed prominent scholars to transcend discipline, and he also repeats the culture wars' habit of identifying the notorious humanist as a literature scholar. In this, if in nothing else, he followed a precedent set a decade earlier by the conservative culture warrior Allan Bloom, who denounced Derrida for creating a "fad" that devalued the great books—a category that for him bundled classic works of literature and philosophy.[4] Although they clearly have different aims and commitments, Shumway and Bloom each fueled the machinery of professorial celebrity that they critiqued. They were far from alone in doing so.

The celebrity machine was not, we must insist, located only in English departments. As the *New York Times* reported in 1997, concern extended outside the humanities to encompass culture change in the social and natural sciences. "Bidding wars break out regularly over molecular biologists, African-American historians, mathematicians, whoever university administrators believe possess the reputation and scholarly heft to lift a department or a school up a rung in the national rankings," the newspaper observed with alarm.[5] Moreover, stars like Derrida were more at home in humanities centers than they were in any specific department. They belonged with fellow travelers, in heady conversations with peers and graduate students, not in dreary meetings devoted to reforming the undergraduate British literature survey. Stardom, Shumway explains, brought heightened visibility, higher salaries, a perch at the top of the scholarly hierarchy, and an ability to seek advantage by moving from one institution to another.[6] The new scholarly jet-set traversed a world that extended far beyond their home universities while remaining largely within the academy.

In their prominence and ability to engage conversations across different institutional and disciplinary domains, the stars of the 1980s recalled the adventurers of earlier eras of humanist experiment. But in most other ways, the glittering life that Shumway details looks very different from, say, John Erskine's lecturing roadshow with periodic piano performances, John von Neumann's name-branded computer architecture, or Marshall McLuhan's gnomic television persona. This period's academic celebrity dovetailed with an evolving subdivision of labor and institutionalized a structure of professional aspiration. Like the star system of Hollywood's "studio era," Shumway contends, the academic system "involves identification with a person who represents an ideal. Most academics . . . cannot hope to follow the stars' career paths," but that ideal shaped expectations nonetheless.[7] Ambitious young professors might take an interest not only in the stars' scholarship, which they would need to displace or surmount in their rise, but also in stars' biographies, personalities, and sense of style, which offered prototypes for the posture of the celebrity academic.

The supreme star turn was therefore not the widely read book but the plenary lecture—a form of public performance that presupposed publication and was addressed primarily to other faculty and graduate students. The Johns Hopkins University's 1966 "Languages of Criticism and the Sciences of Man" symposium, which introduced Derrida to US academic audiences, would go down in history as the prototypical star-studded theory conference (Roland Barthes, Jacques Lacan, and Tzvetan Todorov were also among those who gave talks). In truth, the event is perhaps best described as star making, since it both secured US reputations for its participants and established a programming strategy others would imitate. The generalization of this approach, the extension of personal and institutional commitments of time and money to lecture series, conferences, and travel, gave academic stardom a systemic quality. As Shumway points out, such investment was unheard of before the 1970s. While it may have adapted a model as old as Hollywood, the institutional support systems allowing an academic star system to thrive were relatively new.

The humanities center gave institutional stability to the kind of celebrity engagement cultivated by occasional symposia and lectures. The 1980s witnessed a new wave of commitments to this established form, which had been designed to promote advanced work bridging humanities disciplines. Wesleyan University and the University of Wisconsin had founded such centers as early as 1959 but arguably did not herald a trend before the late 1970s. The National Humanities Center was launched in 1978 with support from the American Academy of Arts and Sciences. The Whitney Humanities Center at Yale University appeared in 1981. Yale needed a center because of "specific concerns like departmentalization, the lack of an intellectual community and the University becoming increasingly atomized and privatized," according to its first director, the comparative literature and legal scholar Peter Brooks, who added, "My own thinking was most influenced by a remark that Yale was an exceptional place for students but did little for faculty."[8] The University of California Humanities Research Institute, which linked system campuses from its home at UC Irvine, was founded in 1987.

In the culture wars, the centers played a key role in specifying threats to the humanities and organizing a faculty response to them. In the fall of 1988, the UC center invited its first group of faculty researchers to answer the question, "How Does Collaborative Research Work in the Humanities?" The group's convener, the philosopher Bernd Magnus from UC Riverside, described "the call for collaboration . . . as an adaptive response by humanists to a changed and changing cultural environment," the hostility of which he summed up by invoking the troika "Bennett, Bloom, and [NEH chair Lynne] Cheney."[9] By 1989, a panel of humanities center directors convened by the American Council of Learned Societies could confidently assert that the "proliferation of interdisciplinary humanities centers" amounted to the recent development most capable of responding "to negative criticisms" and revealing "the range and importance of the humanities."[10] Citing a probably incomplete list of some three hundred such centers nationwide, the panelists found them fostering interdisciplinary conversations that required faculty to "move beyond the constraints of narrowly conceived specialization" to reexamine "the assumptions that govern their thought" and to bring "fresh perspectives to bear on issues of deep concern to society."

As a cure for what ailed "the humanities"—attacks from outside, specialization, atomization of the faculty, loss of relevance—these centers offered a haven for experiment within the confines of the university. Yet the centers' ability to change a national conversation about the humanities (or anything else) was limited by their audiences. As Julie Thompson Klein observes, "The word 'center' is ironic, since many are not central to the mission of an institution. They are peripheral enclaves." In these sheltered spaces, she adds, "the emphasis has been on individual research and paper reading rather than collaborative work."[11] Exerting a compelling pull on the intellectual life of the period, humanities centers supported grand agenda-setting projects for the humanities, but they addressed niche audiences habituated to the academic star system.

The extent to which the new academic protocols represented a withdrawal from more generally public discussions became a leitmotif in the culture wars. The humanities churned out work that energetically engaged contemporary social and political issues but often wondered who was listening. Our own development as scholars was shaped by this dynamic. As graduate students, we joined enthusiastic humanities center audiences and were often enthralled by speakers from across the disciplines and around the world—our role models. Inevitably, or so it seems in retrospect, discussions of the theoretical consistency and political value of any visitor's contribution confronted the issue of whether it could travel outside academic circles. Could new work that aspired to be like the star's, but different and maybe better, establish its currency with the humanities center set and also make good on a commitment to challenge extra-academic culture?

Not infrequently, this concern took the form of finger-wagging that tended to ignore the restructuring of the workplace. The intellectual historian Russell Jacoby provided perhaps the definitive instance in *The Last Intellectuals* (1989). "Younger intellectuals," he wrote, "are almost exclusively professors. Campuses are their homes; colleagues their audience; monographs and specialized journals their media."[12] Although a decade later (in writing a new preface for his book) Jacoby found it easy to come up with examples of scientists (Carl Sagan, Stephen Jay Gould) and African American studies professors (Adolph Reed, Cornel West) who regularly addressed a more general public, he continued to lament that in the main humanists and social scientists "theorize . . . at academic conferences."[13] Left intellectuals particularly disappointed Jacoby in this regard. Under attack during the culture wars, they "growled and scowled," lamely "collected conference papers," and if they deigned to address antagonists in public their books invariably "lacked bite."[14] Right-wing intellectuals knew better than to content themselves with plenary lectures: they aroused the masses.

Those right-wing public intellectuals, like Roger Kimball and Dinesh D'Souza, did not work primarily for universities or haunt humanities centers. They worked for the think tanks whose rise we attributed, in part, to student immaterial labor in chapter 7. With support from conservative organizations like the Manhattan Institute for Policy Research (Kimball) and the American Enterprise Institute (D'Souza), they made their livings not by teaching surveys or striving for tenure-worthy reputations but by interpreting the university for the mainstream press and inciting controversies that would benefit conservative causes. Right and left intellectuals did their rabblerousing from very different positions in an intellectual division of labor. Thus, it is not surprising that they would seek different audiences for their work.

Faculty members trained after 1980 may find it almost impossible to imagine a professoriate not generally required to publish for tenure. Yet so it was before the buyer's market of the 1970s allowed departments to demand more research productivity. This is the conclusion of a 2006 Modern Language Association report that locates "the emergence of expectations oriented more toward publication than toward teaching in the period between 1968 and 1995."[15] Not all schools or departments experienced this phenomenon to the same extent or on the same timetable. Nonetheless, unlike generations before them, post-1970 graduate students in most humanities disciplines were wise to behave as if they would be expected to publish to succeed on the job market and, further, to presume that a scholarly book from a reputable academic press would be required for them to achieve tenure.

The MLA appeared justifiably ambivalent about this drift toward an emphasis on research publication. Dispiritingly, the trend ratcheted up expectations for its members, suggested an emphasis on quantity over quality, and shifted professorial attention away from the classroom. More hopefully, counting articles and books and appraising their contributions provided a clearer rubric for assessing merit than had existed previously. At a time when legal changes and challenges were clarifying the need to make hiring and promotion decisions on the basis of something other than homophily, the MLA saw value in replacing "a system of promotion and reward that had few procedures of accountability." Instead of an old boy's network, in which the department chair was sometimes the major arbiter of tenure and promotion decisions, "bureaucratic equity" promised that personnel actions might "enact (or at least appear to enact) institutional rules and procedures rather than personal inclinations and biases."[16] With the prospect of greater parity came more paperwork, as the economist Barbara Bergmann observed in 1991: "progress reports, form filling-in, projections, and mission statements"—these were the media through which the faculty addressed the audience of committees, deans, provosts, and presidents whose approval was necessary to secure new hires as well as tenure and promote them.[17] To survive the long period of intense scrutiny preceding tenure, faculty members would need to become adept, first, at explaining their research contributions to an audience of specialists in their fields and, second, at explaining the value of this contribution to an institutional audience of academics and administrators from different subfields and disciplines.

Here the logic of the star system was integrated with bureaucratized evaluation procedures. "Name recognition" provided actionable information. Particularly for the audience of academic but out-of-field appraisers, it provided evidence that a scholar had addressed the audience that really mattered: other specialists. "In the multiversity literary scholars rarely attain expertise beyond one field or subfield," Jeffrey Williams observes of his colleagues, "and their merit is assessed autonomously by those within their particular areas."[18] For purposes of internal review, however, the tokens of stardom—"an oft-cited Oxford book or prestigious speaking engagements"—vouched for the scholar under review in a manner that other faculty and administrators alike could appreciate.[19]

Across the disciplines scholarly activity developed as a media market. All manner of professors were criticized for cultivating niche audiences and embracing celebrity cults. But they were also evaluated more stringently than before on the basis of their publications and reputation with in-field peers outside their home institutions. In the sciences, for instance, success in national grant competitions and journal impact factors emerged as (controversial) performance criteria.[20] Readings and his successors largely miss this story in damning the "university of excellence" through association with the business corporation. For Readings, the university ran to ruin when it devoted itself to churning out profit maximizers and consumers, for whom "excellence," irrespective of content or aim, seemed self-evidently valuable. He depicts a university that has been overrun by its business school, much to the detriment of its beleaguered humanities departments. Readings rightly observes that "excellence" was no mere marketing scheme but also a thoroughly mediated bureaucratic quality that emphasized numerical rankings. He underreports, however, the centrality of peer review and reputation.[21] Peer-reviewed articles were counted separately from those that were not. Qualitative assessment mattered as well, in recommendation letters, for instance, as well as in reputational surveys of departments and schools. Nor was the ratcheting up of documentation and expectations motivated solely by the ambition to "excel." These changes were also urged by the imperative to ensure meritocratic evaluation of an academic workforce that was increasingly diverse both demographically and in terms of research specialization. More than a cult of celebrity or "excellence" fetish, then, the academic star system was one way thoroughly transformed relations of intellectual production and reception could be named and apprehended.

No blockbuster polemic or revision of general education could hope to halt the proliferation of disciplines or undo the increasing subdivision of academic labor. Indeed, the culture wars arguably furthered those trends. Partisans skirmished over whether reading certain books would make college worth it, whether "women's," "African American," and "film" named legitimate fields of undergraduate studies, and whether "theory" was a boon or a menace. New programs flourished; lines hardened as often as they blurred. To specify certain philosophical and literary texts as "core" knowledge—as some culture warriors sought to do—was to offer yet another specialized approach as general—a fact other culture warriors had no problem detecting. Framing arguments in terms of whether English departments properly curated cultural value, then, meant miseducating taxpayers, parents, and students about the institution.

THE CULTURE WARS RECONSIDERED

Public opinion was certainly at stake when, in November 1984, William Bennett, then director of the National Endowment for the Humanities, released the report of a thirty-one-member blue-ribbon panel, *To Reclaim a Legacy: A Report on the Humanities in Higher Education*. A front-page story in the *New York Times* summarized the report's conclusions: "American colleges and universities are failing to give students 'an adequate education in the culture and civilization of which they are members.'" The report went on to identify the culprits: "College faculties have caved in to vocational and other pressures from students and abdicated their authority over what students should study and learn."[22] The *New York Times* did not mention two additional recommendations made by the panel: "college and university presidents must take responsibility for the educational needs of *all* students by making plain what the institution stands for and what knowledge it regards as essential to a good education," and "excellent teaching" should be rewarded in "hiring, promotion, and tenure decisions."[23] Mention of these proposals would have opened a different can of worms and perhaps suggested a need for explanations of how contemporary universities actually arrived at decisions about what would be taught. Curricular catastrophe prompted by delinquent faculty made a better story.

Bennett crowned content king and, in so doing, reactivated old themes for a new audience. His report emphasizes how the humanities "contribute to an informed sense of community by enabling us to learn about and become participants in a common culture, shareholders in our civilization. But," he cautions, "our goal should be more than just a common culture—even television and the comics can give us that."[24] Counting on readers to find "television and comics" uniformly debasing, Bennett's preferred curriculum emphasizes literature and political philosophy (the area of his

PhD) penned by well-known European and American authors as the chosen "landmarks of human achievement."[25] Although this recommendation was directed at academic audiences, the report addressed itself primarily to opinion leaders—editorial boards, journalists, pundits, and press agents—capable of advancing a story professors could be expected to hate in the service of reforms that would need to be imposed from without.

In this, *To Reclaim a Legacy* exemplified the type of policy and public relations initiative funded and coordinated by conservative think tanks. Writing for the liberal watchdog National Committee for Responsive Philanthropy, David Callahan describes a sophisticated array of fundraising, organizing, lobbying, and policy-analysis organizations following a model set by the powerful Heritage Foundation. "There is no mainstream or left-of-center parallel to the critical mass of conservative policy institutions currently operating in the United States today," he reported in 1999.[26] This well-oiled apparatus helped frame coverage of events including Bennett's confirmation as Reagan's secretary of education in February 1985, routinely providing columnists and reporters with quotes and guidance. Writing in the *Washington Post*, for instance, the book critic Jonathan Yardley echoed conservative talking points when he celebrated Bennett's recognition that "the odd fellow out in higher education today is the student: the bright, ambitious student whose needs are not met by the academic bureaucracy and its irrelevant courses, and the equally bright ambitious student whose needs would be better served in trade school or the marketplace."[27] This position aligned with the trends identified by the professor of composition and rhetoric Ira Shor, who explains that attacks on "illiteracy" and the proclamation of a need to go "back to basics" predominated in conservative circles from 1975 to 1982. Toward the end of Reagan's first term (1982–84), the think tanks shifted rhetorical gears to oppose "mediocrity" and favor "excellence." Both strategies supported policies that sought to reduce public funding for education overall and redirect resources away from Great Society projects aimed at "leveling the playing field."[28] Among neoconservatives, hierarchy was in, and attacking curricula provided a way to promote it.

In 1987 two surprising publishing successes, both from trade presses, energized this strategy. Simon and Schuster published *The Closing of the American Mind: How Higher Education Has Failed Democracy and Impoverished the Souls of Today's Students*, wherein the University of Chicago professor of philosophy Allan Bloom lent his gravitas to the conservative mission. For parents eager to take matters into their own hands, Random House offered the University of Virginia professor of English E. D. Hirsch's *Cultural Literacy: What Every American Needs to Know*. Where Hirsch had crafted an advice book, Bloom addressed parents and voters who had learned from conservative PR that disordered humanities curricula imperiled the nation's future.

Although Bloom's polemic connected with this audience, it is difficult in retrospect to appraise how well he actually understood the institution he critiques. He does perceive programmatic expansion: "when a student arrives at the university, he finds a bewildering variety of departments and a bewildering variety of courses."[29] Where student-services advisers were stepping into the breach, Bloom instead offered his favorite books as a guide. Ignore the mess of interdisciplines and new concentrations, he counseled. Stay clear of "Black Studies and Women's or Gender Studies, along with Learn Another Culture."[30] Look to "the humanities": "the specialty that now exclusively possesses the books that are not specialized, that insist upon asking the questions about the whole that are excluded from the rest of the university."[31] Bloom reveals his ignorance in characterizing Black studies and women's or gender studies as unconcerned with "the whole." Moreover, students would have found it practically difficult to follow his advice—the federal taxonomy did not at the time include a major called "Humanities."

Hirsch's list-making activities had received favorable mention in the Bennett report. In *Cultural Literacy*, he maintained that education could not produce socially leveling effects absent strict standardization of content. While his account of names "every American needs to know" did not descend to "television and comics," it did reveal a more capacious sense of the essentials than Bennett's. It includes, for example, "Hepburn, Katharine" next to "Hera (Juno)" and "Hitchcock, Alfred" alongside "Hobbes, John."[32] Above all, Hirsch sought to overleap institutional impediments to building curricula around reading lists and tell parents directly what their children should "know." He succeeded in creating a popular series of advice books as opposed to a general-education curriculum.

Bloom and Hirsch established 1987 as a pivotal year in the culture wars not because their arguments changed minds on campus but because they garnered so much off-campus attention. They did not inaugurate a substantially new debate about curriculum, harkening back as they did to post–World War I efforts to anchor core curricula in Great Books and to the Redbook's New Critical variation on the theme. Rather, the main lesson these books taught was that the topic of general-education curricula allowed professors to address a trade audience. Thanks in part to sustained efforts to mold opinion by means of the popular press (at which the conservative think tanks excelled), this audience seemed willing to grant university humanities coursework something like the attention it gave other hot-button culture-wars issues like abortion, gun politics, gay rights, creationism, "welfare queens," and public funding for the arts.

Such publicity horrified and inspired English professors in equal measure. In giving literature pride of place in their arguments, Bennett, Bloom, and Hirsch put a spotlight on contemporary efforts to expand and/or displace literary canons in favor of minor literatures and an array of theoretical approaches. They also recapitulated a legacy of conflating English with the humanities in these kinds of discussions while elevating the stakes of that category error. There can be no doubt that "wars" over "culture" were a boon to English, inasmuch as there is no such thing as bad press, but they were equally a burden, inasmuch as literature faculty found themselves drawn into a battle whose terms had already been set, that misrepresented their institutions, and that put many of them very much on defense.

Left-wing humanist responses typically attended to the content of conservative polemics rather than Bloom's and Hirsch's success in addressing political and parental audiences. They operated in the scholarly mode of rebuttal, that is, rather than embracing Edward Bernays's foundational PR lesson that one should interpret the public before attempting to offer it a different interpretation. Pulling the debate back into the academy seemed exactly the right approach to Gerald Graff, whose 1991 *Beyond the Culture Wars*, which contended that canon-loving professors and allied pundits had "wildly inflated" "the extent of curricular change." There was, in fact, no good evidence that the classics had disappeared from English-department curricula, although new materials had been added.[33] Accordingly, he relocated the culture wars to "the English department faculty lounge at Middle America University" and reframed it as conflict between "Older Male Professor" and "Young Female Professor" over whether Matthew Arnold's poem "Dover Beach" should be taught.[34] By bringing this conflict into the classroom as a pedagogical problem, he argued, English could keep both Arnold's poem and the critique of its inclusion. Even as he exposed the distortion involved in conservatives' framing of the university's troubled "humanities," that is, he acceded to their agenda and sought to moderate the conflict by treating it as a problem of disciplinary history, pedagogy, and above all content.

According to Bennett Lovett-Graff's meticulous review of the literature, *Beyond the Culture Wars* was precisely the breakthrough academic opponents of the conservative account had long awaited. Throughout the 1980s, publishers, newspaper reviewers, and the conservative Olin Foundation sustained the attack, Lovett-Graff narrates, while "academic rebuttal tended toward the ephemeral, appearing as the usual flurry of articles in, if not obscure, certainly not popular journals." Into this fray, Graff launched "an extended defense and rebuttal . . . finally written for a lay audience and published by a major publisher [Norton]."[35] Written for a lay audience yet framing the problem as an academic one, to be clear. As Lovett-Graff explains, Graff's intervention did little to alter the terms of debate outside English departments. This was because it centered the debate within the classroom and the faculty lounge rather than connecting those academic venues to audiences beyond the university.

Nor did Graff's commitment to the classroom connect with the think-tank intellectuals who pushed the conservative agenda. Students were not the primary audience for the likes of Kimball and D'Souza, who continued to aim at policy makers like Bennett and addressed multitudes by means of mainstream media outlets. Notably, in 1991 and 1992 D'Souza went on tour with the Milton scholar Stanley Fish, staging for standing-room-only crowds campus debates about political correctness in which literary studies provided a central example. Their spectacular public disputation of First Amendment issues touched a topical concern, affirmed that English professors could in fact pack them in, and offered a pointed contrast to Graff's contemporary effort to calm the faculty lounge. It turned out that specialized training in English did not preclude one from engaging in a hotly public debate, as Jacoby had suggested in 1989. As the examples of Bloom and Hirsch (a lifelong Democrat) should have testified, it was neither specialization nor political affiliation per se that limited one's ability to cause trouble. Nor was writerly acumen the determining factor, as anyone attempting to navigate Bloom's overblown and repetitive prose could soon discover.[36]

Instead, the issue was connecting with and mediating among different audiences, which often required working with gatekeepers who moderated mainstream distribution channels.

Partly acknowledging this audience problem, some voices of authority on the left cautioned their colleagues against engaging in a battle of the books. In 1992, the African American studies professor Hazel Carby questioned any institutional politics that limited itself to decolonizing the canon, asking readers of *Radical History Review*, "Have we, as a society, successfully eliminated the desire for achieving integration through political agitation for civil rights and opted instead for knowing each other through cultural texts?"[37] Segregation, she observed, was a bigger obstacle to common curricula than the content of reading lists. In other words, here was a way to reframe the issue, to not follow the right in privileging syllabi above questions of access and integration, and to reinterpret the public so as to offer it a different interpretation.

Meanwhile, the English professor Richard Ohmann continued to remind his colleagues that the mechanisms for reproducing literary capital were alive and well, just unevenly distributed. Only at elite schools like his employer Wesleyan University was it possible to imagine that English might offer a "humane and pleasant activity of reading good books and trying to understand the world."[38] Such activity, he had argued a decade earlier in *English in America* (1976), played a central role in reproducing class relations by confirming elite students' sense of their humanity and entitlement, while making clear to the rest that they were ignorant of "the best that has been thought and said."[39] Ohmann echoed Bennett's observation that if all one wanted was shared knowledge, television offered an up-to-date repository, but he refused the secretary's offhand dismissal of that knowledge. "Why not base the SATs on that," he archly asked, "and watch scores shoot up?"[40] Indeed, if common culture is the point, why not?

In the Bloom-Hirsch year of 1987, the Yale literature professor John Guillory supplemented Ohmann's point and anticipated Carby's. The battle to conserve or "open" the canon, he argued, both under- and overestimated the role of the school in social reproduction. Underestimated, in that, as Ohmann argued, it gave little attention to the school's institutional form and its historical function of conserving established social relations. Overestimated, as Carby would later elaborate, in the conviction that social relations could be acted upon directly by changing syllabi.[41] In contrast to those who argued ferociously that adding books by women and people of color to a mostly white, male canon would have either a disastrous or a salutary effect on American society, Guillory limns a history that makes the idea of controlling culture "from within literature" seem preposterous. If there is common culture anymore, he explains, "the center of the system of social reproduction has moved elsewhere, into the domain of mass culture." In this environment, literary norms have "the anachronistic aura of 'old money'"—once powerful, still rich, no longer central.[42] The canon wars looked like a symptom of literature's belatedness, inasmuch as they demonstrated that those authorities charged with transmitting literary tradition could no longer agree on what it was. In this way, debate over the canon promised to delegitimize the whole enterprise of literary studies, which Guillory did not appear to regard as bad news.[43]

Among the literature professors, then, the sharpest observers of this moment lamented the fact that their colleagues' professional stake in keeping the argument focused on the content and manner of literary instruction undermined projects that understood professors as agents of social reproduction and thus, potentially, change. In effect if not intent, however, their often wide-ranging critiques of contemporary culture and politics nonetheless retained the category of "literature" as the core problem. This emphasis on medium specificity necessarily limited the scope of their interventions.

Indicatively, Ohmann and Guillory reproduced the assumption that "literature" and "mass culture" were opposites while also presenting them as comparable. This allowed them to recenter discussion on the problem of how the university's curation of "culture" maintained social hierarchy without hanging up their literature professor hats and becoming, for instance, sociologists or historians. Many in English departments took this "cultural turn."[44] Their arguments introduced new problems in asserting and then conflating differences among kinds of mediation. For example, once poems and sitcoms were rendered as opposing forms, representing a succession of historical dominants, it became difficult to explain how it was that poems and sitcoms shared some audiences while dividing others or how these types of works could organize such different types of exchanges in classrooms, humanities centers, and the *New York Times*. Wherever literature remained the prototype of culture, it would prove difficult to grasp the breadth, depth, and variety of the American research university's audience-making legacies, which included football, the movies, radio, et al.

The notion that English departments could provide a "big tent" welcoming anyone who studied "culture" emblematized the category error. Klein explains: "The success of Theory justified including 'literary everything' from film, romances, and hip-hop to museums and sexuality." She might have added primatology, physiology, cartography, and any number of other sciences. This aggressive expansion "put English in direct competition with other disciplines."[45] Rather than welcoming new friends, that is, big-tent English was more likely to generate an us-them distinction that militated against alliance building across the university. Klein narrates this primarily as a problem for intellectual history, that is, as an issue of how theory, discipline, and interdisciplinarity were understood and practiced. It was also plainly an audience problem. While it was clear what big-tent English wanted to talk about—anything and everything—it was often much less clear how it planned to engage diverse audiences, inside the university and out, that might have a stake in its ruminations.

As disciplines outside the basic-cable channels engaged the problem of extending their reach, it was tempting to follow the precedent English set and argue that one's particular specialization might provide the essence of general education. If it seemed like English became powerful at midcentury by asserting that its expertise in reading poetry provided a sure way to understand culture, other disciplines might put forward similar claims. Comparative literature provided similar cultural reading skills while also acknowledging the polyphony of the modern word. Art history, particularly in its visual culture studies offshoot, was uniquely positioned to offer a global historical synthesis that also provided a means of decoding contemporary imagery of all kinds. And so on.

The audience problem looked very different outside of English departments, however. From basic-cable history to new discipline-defying clusters and emerging disciplines, the entire operation of speaking for the "humanities" by taking a position on "the canon" seemed simply beside the point. In 1988, the historian Peter Novick explained that his colleagues confronted "a sweeping challenge to the objectivist program of the founding fathers of the historical profession."[46] From this point of view, the post-1960 theory revolution looked like a challenge not to "great books" but to founding disciplinary epistemologies—which had fractured into an array of historiographical approaches. Epistemological challenge was, perhaps, the primary aim that united the faculty gathered in the History of

Consciousness program at UC Santa Cruz, which included, at various moments and in various overlapping configurations, the historian Hayden White, the biologist Donna Haraway, the anthropologist James Clifford, the semiotician Teresa de Lauretis, the literary critic Fredric Jameson, and the philosopher Angela Davis.[47] This was a PhD program built on the model of the humanities center, complete with highly mobile stars who built bridges across disciplines by disturbing their central tenets. For none of them could the problem of "culture" be encompassed in a reading list. Meanwhile, film studies built itself a more strongly disciplinary foundation in the form of weighty tomes like David Bordwell, Kristin Thompson, and Janet Staiger's *The Classical Hollywood Cinema* (1985), which deliberately turned its back on analyses of individual works to focus on "group style" and the industrial history that sustained it. These departments and disciplines simply did not see the 1980s as a decade defined by battles over which literature to read and how to read it. Across the humanities, diverse operations—sometimes discipline organizing, sometimes transcending discipline—constelled new kinds of faculty and student audiences. In so doing, they anticipated futures for research and teaching unimaginable to those litigating literature.

STEM VERSUS THE SCIENCE WARS

By 2010, whatever lingering passion Bad English aroused paled in comparison with enthusiasm for (and resentment of) Science, Technology, Engineering, and Mathematics (STEM). The coinage is credited to Rita Colwell, the first woman to serve as director of the National Science Foundation. One of its first applications was STEMTEC, an NSF-funded teacher-education project launched in 1998 involving Amherst, Hampshire, Mount Holyoke, Smith, and UMass Amherst, who coordinated the education of future science teachers with the Greenfield, Holyoke, and Springfield Technical Community Colleges as well as several Massachusetts school districts. Presidents including George W. Bush and Barack Obama joined nonprofits like the Gates Foundation in seeking to recenter both K–12 and collegiate general education around STEM curricula. The 2007 report "Rising Above the Gathering Storm," published by the National Academy of Sciences, Engineering, and Medicine, congealed resources through an alarmist narrative in which globalization threatened the vitality of the US economy.

Only the "productivity of well-trained people and the steady stream of scientific and technical innovations they produce" could save it.[48] It would be difficult to find a better example of how well-coordinated action across a number of domains—disciplines and institutions that might easily have understood themselves to be in competition with one another—could, in relatively short order, create an effective new assemblage. Before STEM, the 1990s science wars offered a striking counterexample.

The science wars should finally have made clear to academics that while attacking someone else's discipline might be a good way to start a broadly public argument about the university, it was a bad way to end one. Such, at any rate, is the lesson of the storied Sokal affair. In 1994, Paul Gross and Norman Levitt's *Higher Superstition* had extended the conservative public relations campaign against humanities professors to a battle that had been brewing around a largely social scientific specialty, "Science and Technology Studies," which had descended directly from C. P. Snow's interest in science as a "culture."[49] Flattening a wide range of scholars into what they called "the cultural left," Gross and Levitt characterized a uniformly science-denying "postmodernist" relativism. Developing this gesture, the physicist Alan Sokal spoofed the leftist cultural studies journal *Social Text* in 1996. He mimicked the rhetoric of cultural theory in propounding spectacular falsehoods regarding his nominal topic, quantum gravity. Out-of-discipline *Social Text* editors recognized the rhetoric as appropriate to their theme issue on "the science wars" but did not detect the errors of fact. Exposing his deception, Sokal offered it as proof that postmodernist jargon—which anyone could parrot—trumped scientific reason for the *Social Text* crowd.[50]

This event demonstrated the distance between the kind of arguments that played well in the press and those valued inside the university, where specialization had long been the norm.[51] A working physicist like Sokal considered the validity of specific scientific protocols and epistemologies to have serious intellectual and professional stakes, but those protocols and epistemologies were plainly not the story for the journalists who reported on the hoax. Steve Fuller observes:

The public uptake . . . followed the example of Gross and Levitt's book in playing into the right's call for greater scrutiny of academic practices more generally, a conclusion that Sokal himself had not wished to draw, given that his own work is largely theoretical and hence unlikely to attract the large grants that increasingly pass for "relevance" in market-driven public accounting schemes.[52]

Moreover, Sokal's campaign to embarrass "the cultural left" by stereotyping them as science opponents ignored any number of scholars who worked across that supposed divide including, for example, the environmental studies expert and feminist scholar Sandra Harding; the atheist polemicist and evolutionary biologist Richard Dawkins; and Dawkins's sometimes combatant in evolutionary biology, the paleontologist Stephen Jay Gould, whose 1981 *The Mismeasure of Man* offered a scathing critique of the racism inherent in intelligence and psychological testing.[53] Unlike the work of such figures, which cleared common ground for debates that crossed disciplines, Sokal's spoof did little to help scholars in the natural and human sciences understand one another, inhabit the same institutions, or fix whatever they thought was wrong with them. Here, as throughout the culture wars, a desire to go public with important arguments about teaching and research meant acceding to the terms set by the editors, journalists, and pundits in a position to shape the story.

Sokal's gambit exposed a rift not between science and the humanities but between headline-grabbing polemics and disciplinarily focused scholarship. This is actionable information, Fuller argues, which implies a radically different way to distinguish faculty than Sokal's effort to pitch "science" against "postmodernism." Fuller suggests drawing lines between "scientists and STSers who wish to protect the academy from the rest of society . . . on one side" and "those who wish to use the academy as a vehicle for reforming society . . . on the other."[54] He invites "academics to seek constituencies outside academia for whom alternative conceptions of the social role of academics could make a difference to their own activities." Although Fuller addressed his colleagues in STS with his exhortation, it might have easily been adapted to those English professors most concerned to avoid the reduction of culture to lists of great books.[55] Indeed, Carby made something like this point in urging her colleagues to commit to desegregation beyond the classroom and its texts. Whatever Sokal's hoax may have done to promote a sense of public urgency around science—soon to be STEM—education, it was not good PR for science on campus, where it only confirmed that English professors and physicists should view one another with suspicion and could find no common cause.

In 1996, as the Sokal affair broke, Readings argued that saving the university must involve faculty renewing their dedication to teaching "knowledge acquisition as a *process* rather than acquisition of knowledge as a product."[56] He found hope for a wrecked university in attention to pedagogy, starting with a new role for literary studies. He lamented "the end of the reign of literary culture as the organizing discipline of the University's cultural mission" and thereby repeated the myth that literature had once had such a central role.[57] Literature scholars would need to dispense with the German idealism that had, he argued, legitimated cultural curation as national service. Rather than cultivate individual citizen-subjects, literature professors should nurture student counterpublics. He hoped they would not be alone. His concluding chapters sought converts across disciplines, wherever opponents of the instrumentalist University of Excellence could be found.

After Readings, many were eager to claim this oppositional task. Numerous commentators sought to unravel and then retie the knot imagined to have once bound young citizens to core texts of philosophy and literature at the heart of the university.[58] In *The Humanities and the Dream of America* (2011), National Humanities Center Director Geoffrey Galt Harpham describes the fall from a "postwar national self-understanding" in which "the humanities" and, particularly, "English" provided the institutional center for a general education geared to developing the "whole man."[59] Harpham advocates reengaging this mission of *Bildung* but with a difference: to discard normalizing expectations about the particular kind of person the virtuous citizen would be, humanists would need to attend to the demographic variety of student populations.[60] In *The University in a Corporate Culture* (2003), Eric Gould picks up a different thread from Readings to argue that humanities faculties lost their capacity to oversee student development as a whole when they were "thrust into a service role at the undergraduate level"—that is, held responsible for requirements like writing and little else—and were therefore "forced to find ways to make themselves useful to professional and vocational interests."[61] Dreams of once-upon-a-time humanities cultivating virtuous, self-governing (albeit normatively white, male, and well-off) individuals run through these arguments. To regain their relevance, humanities professors would need to reclaim their lost mission but improve it by sharpening polemics and retheorizing key terms. We hope to have demonstrated the futility of this argument and, frankly, its narrow-mindedness.

Neither the reprisal of the two-cultures thesis in the Sokal affair, nor Graff's bid to teach conflicts through English syllabi, nor Readings's critique of the "university of excellence" helped anyone understand the major changes roiling the universities where they worked, studied, or paid tuition. Even at the height of Great Books's mass-market success, the humanities had never managed to curate national culture in the way Bennett imagined they should or Readings imagined they had. To promote or accept that framing performed a fundamental misrecognition. Although English had a broad reach, its 3.25 percent share of undergraduate degree completions by 1991 hardly recommended it as *the* place where a national battle for the future of higher education would be decided. Similarly, the college students supposedly threatened by postmodernism could not turn to science for a rebuttal, for the simple reason that they took no classes in "science." Rather, at most schools each student chose a certain number of units from disciplines as different as mathematics and geology, chemistry and computer science. These disciplines, like all degree programs, competed for increasingly slender shares of undergraduate degree seekers. The careers of tenure-line faculty everywhere did depend on winning student attention, but that task also could be shuffled off to graduate students and term-contract instructors. It was more important to win the attention of in-field peers at other institutions, and in a way that peers from different fields in their home institutions could recognize and legitimate. Some scholars followed the path laid out by early-twentieth-century popularizers and translated new research in their fields for broader audiences. The public intellectuals of the culture wars did something different, however, when they sought to explain what the university should be and do. More and less knowingly, they engaged in the effort to predispose audiences, thus recalling what became known in the 1920s as public relations, for which the uglier name was propaganda.

Chapter Ten

THE LONG TWENTIETH CENTURY

As we wrote this book over the course of the 2010s, a stunning array of commentators argued that the American university had lost the ability to fulfill its public service mission. In the presidential election of 2016, both political parties emphasized the burden of student loan debt.[1] Candidates sought to motivate voters who feared that college would no longer be able to provide an upward path. In the months after President Trump's election, White House proclamations banned visitors from foreign countries, proposed steep cuts to federal research dollars, and signaled a new era of antagonism between universities and the executive branch. University presidents signed letters of protest.[2] University scientists marched.[3] Some faculty considered running for office.[4] Meanwhile, conservative students, journalists, politicians, and foundations pushed free speech on campus as a wedge issue, often pitching it against initiatives designed to make campuses feel safer for people who were not white men. College was clearly a partisan issue. The Pew Research Center reported in 2017 that 58 percent of Republicans viewed colleges and universities as having a negative effect on the country's direction, a sharp increase since 2015 and a dramatic contrast with the view among Democrats, 72 percent of whom thought colleges and universities made a positive difference.[5] Such controversies updated familiar challenges for a higher-education sector that had always needed to secure the support of diverse audiences.

To conclude our examination of this century-spanning project, we identify four controversies that both indicate continuities and distinguish our twenty-first-century present. We begin by noting that numerous actors vied to establish new measures of institutional and individual accomplishment. Proliferating measures both responded to and fueled concern over the value of college. Although they shared this preoccupation with value, different metrics addressed different groups and thereby further segmented potential audiences for higher education. An emphasis on "outcomes"— right-sized for every kind of student—began to displace the Carnegie unit, which had helped call the US system of postsecondary education into being.

Second, we observe that media technology again promised a revolution in higher education—and again proved less inherently disruptive than advocates hoped and detractors feared. Database-driven educational media reprised a familiar pattern when they appropriated commercial media platforms to engage students and scale up the university's address. They differed from correspondence courses, movies, radio, and television, however, in the way they captured the collective intelligence and demographic variety of student masses.

Third, we turn to the figure of the debt-ridden, itinerant adjunct instructor who emblematized the university's dysfunctional division of labor in a wide range of media outlets. The adjunct's plight demanded new public-facing arguments about how the university worked. Among faculty and administrators, it lent urgency to discussions about the faculty's role in managing, governing, or "designing" their universities. As with the arguments that defined and promoted faculty tenure at the start of the century, this new wave of concern did not represent a division of labor so much as it attempted to mediate one. The faculty played catch-up: asked to own their complicity in adjunctification and defend the value of their research expertise, they struggled to reanimate arguments that presented faculty "freedom" as a public benefit. They also formulated new arguments, which sloughed off their presumed special status as faculty and sought new alliances inside the university and out.

Finally, students protested. Evan as American universities grew accustomed to treating undergraduates as clients, students continued to see campus as a forum for and target of political activity. Campus outsiders fully expected students to act in this way and complicated their performances by seeking to harness their immaterial labor. Predictably, students took advantage of the latest media affordances when they staged protests, demonstrating in turn what those platforms could do. Combined with social media, college football became a locus of campus struggle. Smart college presidents remained capable of co-opting student ideas and energies; those who could not were liable to lose their jobs. Student action confirmed both that the university remained capable of informing American social order and that no consensus guided its audience-building operations.

ASSESSMENT CONTROVERSIES AND THE FUTURE OF MERIT

Of all the truisms that have guided higher education in the United States, few can seem more fragile than the axiom that college should allow merit to overcome the circumstances of one's birth. "The country's most powerful engine of upward mobility is under assault," proclaimed the opinion page of the *New York Times* in May 2017.[6] Across the nation, state funding for public higher education had declined, often sharply, even as state governments continued to mandate that universities fulfill a public service mission. Public schools increasingly funded themselves as privates did, through grants, donations, and auxiliary enterprises. Above all, they relied on tuition dollars—for which they competed with every other college and university in the country.[7] To afford college, 70 percent of students borrowed, and delinquency rates were rising.[8] The Federal Reserve Bank of New York in 2017 observed that student loan payments had more than tripled as a share of total US household debt since the turn of the twenty-first century.[9] As the liability to students and parents continued to climb, nearly everyone wondered whether undergraduates were getting their money's worth. Anxiety over return on educational investment gripped individual parents and students, but it also presented a national problem. College could not fulfill its ideologically necessary role if it seemed likely to reward those who could afford it regardless of the choices they made, excluding those who were not well-off or who found themselves deep underwater at graduation.[10] This divide exposed anew the core contradiction of the American university system: higher education has been built both to ameliorate and to reproduce social hierarchies.

Collecting and disseminating more and more data about university outcomes emerged as the de facto response to the uncertain future of merit. Sharply divided on the question of whether declining public funding or individual irresponsibility should be blamed for the student debt problem, partisans seemed able to agree that information about economic return on tuition investment would help.[11] Addressed to anxious students and parents, news stories and ratings services informing microeconomic guesstimates of how particular schools and majors might pay off overwhelmed macroeconomic considerations of rising social inequality and workforce composition, which were mostly written by and for policy wonks. Conservatives pivoted away from the defense of "culture" that characterized their 1980s and 1990s approach. The new strategy instead emphasized that the humanities had little public value because they would not "get someone a job."[12] Consenting (again) to this framing, humanities defenders responded by declaring that a rejection of such narrowly instrumental thinking was precisely why they mattered—and also that they did get people jobs, by the way, often good ones.[13]

Lists and databases comparing institutions proliferated. While attempts to assess the likely return on tuition investment tended to be a common denominator, different lists offered different measures to different audiences. In 1983, US News focused student attention on the puzzle of finding the "best" college that matched one's qualifications and interests. By 2017, it had competition from magazines like Money and the Economist as well as from the social media company LinkedIn and websites like Thebestcolleges.org. Other lists were more precisely tailored for specific niches, like the eco-friendly readers of Sierra's "Cool School" rankings. Meanwhile, the New York Times' "College Access Index" pointedly responded to its own editorial proclamation about the American Dream in peril by listing schools based on the number of lower- and middle-income students they enrolled and the price they charged.[14] Most significantly, the federal government joined the rankings game. In his 2013 State of the Union address, President Barack Obama introduced "a new college scorecard that parents and students can use to compare schools based on a simple criteria: where you can get the most bang for your educational buck."[15] This unprecedented federal effort notwithstanding, the choice of which rankings to consult itself became part of the decision-making process for many college applicants. For aspiring undergraduates, rankings constituted a complex and portentous field of choices.

National political conversation assumed that student selection rather than institutional discrimination would set vocational trajectories. At midcentury, *General Education in a Free Society* dreamed of a national educational system coordinated to provision common knowledge and certify merit. The Harvard professors who wrote it felt confident that the nation's instructional staff could determine which students should exit the system after high school and which students should go on to trade school, college, or a graduate degree. Their confidence was misplaced: the American system evolved in no such fashion. Its contrasting reality was disclosed in 2014 when President Obama observed that "folks can make a lot more, potentially, with skilled manufacturing or the trades than they might with an art history degree."[16] When a lecturer from the University of Texas promptly emailed the White House to protest this slander against art history, Obama took the opportunity to reinforce the notion that students' judgments, not his, and not those of professors, determined educational pathways. "I was making a point about the jobs market, not the value of art history," he wrote in response, "and understand that I was trying to encourage young people who may not be predisposed to a four year college experience to be open to technical training that can lead them to an honorable career."[17] Betsy DeVos, secretary of education for the new Trump administration, echoed this point at her Senate confirmation hearing: "For too long a college degree has been pushed as the only avenue for a better life. The old and expensive brick-mortar-and-ivy model is not the only one that will lead to a prosperous future."[18] Notably, all parties imagined an educational system in which art history baccalaureates and technical training were equally available to everyone. Management of merit was less a matter of certification and selection than of "pushing" options to students.

A tool for its time, the Scorecard informed a stratified public familiar with database media. It took an approach intuitive to Netflix audiences and Amazon customers, each of whom experience a different version of those shared platforms based on their search inputs and algorithms that take their past preferences into account. In this, the Scorecard was unlike Great Books, movies, network television, and other point-to-mass communications efforts. While search results emphasized return on investment, search criteria included degree, program of study, location, size, public/private/for-profit, and religious affiliation. A "special mission" drop-down menu allowed students to select single-sex schools, "Historically Black Colleges and Universities," "Tribal Colleges and Universities," and kindred markers of demographic distinction. Thus the Scorecard imagined a national whole while also addressing the manifold nature of the undergraduate population, whose choices it aimed to empower. To the extent that the Trump administration's approach to the Scorecard differed from that of the Obama administration, it promoted the manifold at the expense of the national. DeVos promised to give students more choices by encouraging "locally driven innovation and customization" at every educational level and rolling back the Obama-era regulation of for-profit colleges.[19] As of our writing, however, she had not yet deleted the Scorecard.

The Scorecard grasped its media moment but arguably failed to seize it. High-school students were expected to thrill at the news, in the summer of 2015, that collegescorecard.ed.gov had been rebuilt as "a customizable, consumer-oriented website" with "more data than ever before."[20] Setting aside their video-game controllers, eager youths would presumably employ the streamlined search tool to visualize the cost, graduation rate, and salary "at 10 years after entering" any school, as compared to the national average. Refusing all Snapchat distractions, they would then select specific degree programs, pull up multiple schools in a given state or region, and drill down to get more detailed information on costs, financial aid and debt loads, retention, and SAT results. Obama's Department of Education had made it that easy for conscientious students to make informed decisions.

A 2016 study by two researchers at the College Board put privileged faces on these data-driven teenagers. It confirmed that some high-schoolers were using the scorecard and that the earnings metric appeared to be swaying them the most.[21] The Scorecard was not, however, democratizing data usage. The students most responsive to it tended to be from "the subgroups of students expected to enter the college search process with the most information and most cultural capital."[22] This finding would seem to suggest that the inclination and ability to access and make use of ratings data was a form of class privilege. Avoiding that conclusion, the College Board study reasserts the presumption that the collective results of individual economic calculations could be improved (or made worse) by tweaking the environment in which such choices occurred.[23] Provide more carefully targeted information via more effective channels, and the Scorecard could reach new audiences who might then behave in a more rational manner. To the exclusion of other factors shaping college choice, this reasoning imagined it could vouchsafe meritocracy by addressing students as investors making informed decisions.

Return-on-investment calculations allowed parents and students to imagine themselves masters of their own destinies; economists found good reason to challenge this notion.[24] The Wharton School management professor Peter Cappelli, for instance, pointed out that the existing data simply would not support comparative analysis of likely earnings potential among particular majors and particular schools.[25] Moreover, he argued, the volatility of the workforce's composition militated against granular applications of the "investment" approach. "To give you an illustration of this," he noted in June 2015, "the hottest job in the U.S. for the last three years or so—and which pays about 50% more than the second highest paid job—has been petroleum engineers. A generation ago, or even ten years ago, those folks were waiting tables." In the year after Cappelli made this observation, the oil market tanked. Massive job cuts followed. Students fled petroleum engineering in droves.[26]

Cappelli found it important to note that college would not in fact "pay off" for everyone, but he stopped short of rejecting outright the proposition that students should be treated as rational economic agents. Rather, he recommended better metrics to train their choices. Instead of encouraging students to choose majors based on their predicted returns, he proposed measures more clearly related to personal performance, like how much time students spend studying. Developing assessment media designed to encourage individual attributes like "motivation" would be a better use of everyone's energy than constructing a vehicle that misleadingly benchmarked schools and programs, he argued.[27]

Numerous observers expressed concern that pushing students to choose differently would do little to address whatever remained of higher education's equalizing objective. They urged macroeconomic as opposed to microeconomic interventions. The American Association of University Women (AAUWP) reported that gender better predicted salary than choice of undergraduate major.[28] The National College Access Network's executive director Kim Cook observed that, in addition, "your ZIP code can really determine what your future will look like."[29] In a widely cited 2015 white paper, the economists Anthony P. Carnevale and Stephen Rose relied on input-output analysis to show that increasing economic inequality resulted from the underproduction of more highly skilled workers combined with a decline in the percentage of jobs for which a high-school diploma sufficed.[30] This had produced a record-high "college wage premium," the average salary difference between those with higher-education credentials and those without. To redistribute wealth in accordance with its traditional predilections, Carnevale and Rose proposed, the nation should lower that premium by sending many more people to college.

The AAUWP, Cook, and Carnevale and Rose demonstrated the power of quantitative analysis to change understandings of the environment on which policy should act. Cappelli called attention to the pitfalls inherent in unreliable metrics and to the virtues of alternative measures. Both styles of argument demonstrated, again, that metrics are media. They are contestable measures that attempt to inform the conduct of those who share them.

Importantly, an argument over measuring educational attainment ran alongside debate about representing the economic value of specific credentials. The sociologists Richard Arum and Josipa Roksa stoked alarm about existing assessment models with their 2010 bestseller *Academically Adrift*, continued in 2014 by *Aspiring Adults Adrift*. They proposed an exam that would show just how much universities were failing to teach skills that would allow students to succeed upon graduation. Particularly in its "performance task" component, which asked students to synthesize and interpret a set of background documents in a mock workplace context, the Collegiate Learning Assessment (CLA) promised to test skills employers desired, like critical thinking, complex reasoning, and written communication.[31] Results from a sample population of students throughout their college careers led to the conclusion that "gains in student performance are disturbingly low" and that "individual learning in higher education is characterized by persistent and/or growing inequality."[32] Pairing the test results with surveys of students' perceptions, the authors revealed a striking contrast: although a significant proportion of graduates admitted to having neglected academic pursuits, they nonetheless expected college to have prepared them to be better-off than their parents.[33] Arum and Roksa adduced causes for the phenomenon ranging from parenting styles to professorial disengagement and an emphasis on campus social life rather than the classroom. Grade inflation and reliance on student evaluations of teaching conspired to conceal the problem. Arum and Roksa's media fix—the CLA—not only revealed a systemic crisis, then, but also promised to ameliorate it by providing a more accurate measure of student accomplishment.

Yet the century-old fundaments of the elective system persisted in the form of grades, student evaluations, and the Carnegie unit, thus underscoring the difficulty of instituting new assessment media. Nothing bespoke the university's industrial past like those course "units of time and volume" Veblen had denounced in the 1910s.[34] The credit hour seemed antithetical to the manifold audiences of contemporary higher education and the just-in-time pressures of bang-for-the-education-buck. Such was the reasoning behind the activities of the Lumina Foundation, whose own widely disseminated assessment device, the Degree Qualifications Profile (DQP), identified five "proficiencies," such as "Specialized Knowledge" (no matter the specialization) and "Applied and Collaborative Learning," that could be used to evaluate any number of field-specific "competencies" in all kinds of educational situations.[35] Where the Carnegie unit treated learning contexts as if they were divisible into credit hours, Lumina asked faculty to manage outcomes. Where Carnegie organized student masses through the eminently intelligible "count," Lumina proposed a database solution. Myriad outcomes defined and assessed at the level of course, credential, and institution were commensurable to the degree they could be compared and audited, aggregated, and disaggregated—tasks difficult to imagine at scale absent algorithmic mediation.

Lumina scrupulously avoided a top-down approach to defining student success. Rather, it delegated the task not only of deciding how learning happened but also of fine-tuning the process of measuring it. As we completed this book, Carnegie unit–based measures of attainment continued to arrange academic work lives, yet in our roles as program director and department chair we found ourselves increasingly called upon to administer learning outcomes for courses and degrees. Although not widely known by name on either of our campuses, DQP-like strategies were increasingly discernable in approaches to course and program assessment. These approaches eschewed hours and grades in favor of more granular appraisals of whether students failed to meet, met, or exceeded expectations with respect to specific outcomes faculty had identified as important in advance. This process set as its goal the continuous improvement of student learning, faculty instruction, and the assessment process itself.

Like Carnegie before it, Lumina aspired to order diversity by establishing equivalencies among the credentials awarded by different institutions. It discovered that "more than 4,000 personnel certification bodies are at work in the United States and fewer than 10 percent are accredited or reviewed by a third party."[36] Even when their degree goals were consistent, students moved around more than before: "nearly three-quarters of students who earn a degree attend more than one institution."[37] This played havoc with attempts to measure completion rates. And while the Carnegie unit enabled student transfers, the lack of common curricula frustrated them, perpetually posing the challenge of which credits could travel for which purposes. Students themselves were significantly different from one another as well as from prior norms: "students we once called nontraditional are no longer the exception in postsecondary education . . . they are the rule."[38] A new approach to assessment promised to organize this jumble by conceptually separating outcomes from both the specific courses that satisfied them and the degrees to which those courses contributed. It no longer sufficed to require a certain number of credits in an area like "Science." Schools needed to explain what the expected outcome of courses meeting that requirement would be. At UC Davis, for example:

The objective of the requirement in Scientific Literacy is to create educated individuals who understand the fundamental ways in which scientists approach problems, pose questions, gather data, make conclusions, and then generate new hypotheses for testing. A course certified as meeting this requirement must also show students how scientific findings relate to other disciplines and to public policy.[39]

At the University of South Carolina meanwhile, "Scientific Literacy" meant that "Students must be able to apply the principles and language of the natural sciences and associated technologies to historical and contemporary issues."[40] The gradual alignment of such outcomes, Lumina in effect proposed, would provide a better rationale for considering different schools' courses and degrees equivalent than credit-hour distributions supplied. The idea also scaled. Lumina hoped the DQP would let "stackable" certificates, badges, and nanodegrees flourish, along with the traditional degrees measured by the National Center for Education Statistics (NCES). This was the Swiss Army knife of assessment tools, capable of summing up learning regardless of credential or institutional setting. It worked incrementally within the familiar division of labor to replace the administrative techniques the Carnegie unit had enabled.

Campus life eluded assessment tools like Lumina's even as it featured prominently in new rankings like *Sierra*'s. For all the attention return on investment received, it was hardly the only factor to inform student choice. The transmedia undertaking of college sports continued to compel multitudes. For instance, fall 2017 enrollments at the University of South Carolina experienced an upward "basketball bounce" attributed to the national championship victory of its women's team, which also won historically high ratings for the cable network ESPN and its streaming service Watch-ESPN.[41] The content, conventional forms, and media channels expressing campus life had clearly evolved since the Bulldogs first packed the Yale Bowl, but their function in promoting college as an experience remained much the same.

THE MOOC FEVER BREAKS

Like the proliferation of assessment vehicles, early-twenty-first-century controversies over the misleadingly named massive open online course indicated changes in how the universities imagined their audiences. They also indicated a persistent inability to perceive what was and was not new about instructional media. Appeal to the "mass" notwithstanding, MOOCs by and large dealt with student variety not by attempting to standardize a lowest-common-denominator address but by targeting specific niches and offering the responsive and flexible experiences made familiar by other database media. MOOCs made clear that higher education increasingly addressed neither masses nor publics but communities, friends, and networks knowable through their accumulated data traces. In highly visible new applications, data analytics promised to support institutional planning, improve learning, better completion rates, and predict outcomes. By mistaking a new medium as a new problem, however, commentators repeated a common error. Yes, some of the technologies behind online higher education were new. No, the university's reliance on nonprint media to extend and multiply its audiences was not.

Among early-twenty-first-century disruptors, the religion professor Mark C. Taylor perhaps best exemplifies the habit of ignoring the history of educational media. In 2010, he promulgated an institutional history that skipped straight from Kant to digital networks with nary a stop in between. The sage of Königsberg established the university's prototype in 1798,

Taylor explained, when his "The Conflict of the Faculties" proposed that universities should "handle the entire content of learning (really the thinkers devoted to it) by *mass production*, so to speak—by a division of labor, so that for every branch of the sciences there would be a public teacher or *professor* appointed as its trustee."[42] This mass-industrial model had dominated higher education ever since but was now obsolete; a curriculum structured like a "web of courses" should replace it.[43] Advocating "problem-focused programs" as alternatives to departments, he did not pause to point out a century of precedents ranging from the Tuskegee Institute to Chicago's New Plan, midcentury centers for communication research, new interdisciplinary programs demanded by students in the 1960s and 1970s, and persistent efforts by researchers in the natural and human sciences to engage one another. Attention to these precedents would have revealed an institution that strove to be "postindustrial" long before Detroit did, precisely because it made audiences, not cars.

A history in which the internet faces down universities unchanged since Kant, it turns out, is useful mainly for labeling one's opposition as backward looking. Such rhetoric was everywhere in 2012, which the *New York Times* declared the "year of the MOOC."[44] By 2015, the *Chronicle of Higher Education* blogger Jeffrey Young observed, caricature of the university's obsolete communications strategies had become a topos. "You might have seen an image of a lecture from the 14th century that is used in slide presentations by many ed-tech disruptors" to provide an occasion for the observation "that college courses are still taught in the same way," he explained.[45] Many people in a position to know better found it expedient to posit a history in which the university's twentieth-century-spanning engagement with mass media simply had not occurred. In so doing, they sacrificed an ability to understand the institution they hoped to reform. The fantasy of a MOOC-led revolution in quality education for the masses depended on forgetting there had long been distance complements to traditional undergraduate education, none of which had been able to replace campus life.

For a time, the EdTech disruptors claimed that MOOCs might fix all of the university's broken bits. MOOCs would contain exploding costs, with their dire consequences for access and widening income disparity.[46] They would replace inefficient, inflexible mass-industrial holdovers like the lecture and the Carnegie unit.[47] They would reorient faculty away from

insular research and toward urgent social needs and problems.[48] A sufficiently clever software design might even allow student peer review to replace
laborious marking by professorial graders.[49] In these ways and more,
MOOCs promised universities a wider and more diverse population of
undergraduates, many of whom could not or would not sign on for a four-
year residential-college degree.

For many on the faculty, these "fixes" looked like more of the same
problems. Administrative endorsement of MOOCs confirmed the triumph
of top-down management structures over faculty governance.[50] MOOC
staffing models seemed certain to promote bad labor practices, such as
increasing reliance on contingent faculty, and also to undermine quality
by casting faculty as mere content providers who would provision syllabi
and video lecture nuggets while other experts would design and manage
instruction online.[51] The whole phenomenon bespoke an unreflective
technological fetishism, in which merely invoking Silicon Valley caused
university chancellors, regents, and boards of trustees to swoon. By 2016,
even early champions of the approach, like the adaptive-learning innova-
tor Candace Thille, were voicing this concern.[52]

The millenarian fervor had cooled. In the fall of 2016, the *Chronicle of
Higher Education* commentator Phil Hill summarized the MOOC's widely
acknowledged failure to disrupt higher education as usual or to meet inves-
tor expectations. He observed that MOOCs had nonetheless inspired significant changes in how universities approached education online.[53] The
pioneers found uneven success in their effort to develop economically viable models and, for the most part, gave up on mass audiences in favor of
addressing targeted demographics. As startups, the major players envisioned "a world where anyone, anywhere can transform their life by access-
ing the world's best learning experience" (Coursera), in which they would
"increase access to high-quality education for everyone, everywhere"
(edX), and "change the future of education by bridging the gap between
real-world skills, relevant education, and employment" (Udacity).[54] These
providers initially positioned themselves to replace traditional undergraduate degrees. As it became clear that MOOCs could expect single-digit
completion rates, however, the Mountain View, California–based for-
profits evolved their business plans.[55] Udacity's founder Sebastian Thrun
(who aspired to make his firm the "Uber of education") pivoted toward
nanodegrees aimed at tech workers in search of marketable skills. To teach

these courses, Udacity turned to freelance educators from around the world.[56] Coursera took a similar turn, locating corporate sponsors for professional-development offerings.[57] Meanwhile, the nonprofits repositioned online courses as a supplement to traditional on-campus offerings. When the Harvard/MIT nonprofit edX launched "Global Freshman Academy" with Arizona State University, none of the universities involved expressed any interest in giving up their campus operations even as they sought to acquire new enrollments from around the world.[58] To complement their traditional classroom offerings, an increasing number of schools put more and more courses online.[59] Universities like Purdue got into the game (acquiring the for-profit online provider Kaplan University) with the expressed goal of building on rather than undermining its longstanding investment in campus-based education.[60] In this, as well as in its capacity to enliven debate about the university's division of labor, MOOC fever resembled previous arguments over educational uses of movies, radio, television, and computing.[61] Online courses moved into the space long occupied by correspondence courses, university extension, and nondegree programs, in addition to offering the kinds of classroom supplements pioneered by earlier forms of new media.

Amid this change in emphasis, critics kept up their complaints, continuing to position online education as a threat visited upon college by a villainous corporate world. David Theo Goldberg, for instance, damned "certification autogenerated by the platform" by analogizing it to Uber—perceiving very differently the analogy also invoked by Udacity's Thrun. Both implicitly likened professors to unemployed taxicab drivers in the process.[62] This was not an immanent danger. Although online education was growing, the capital-markets researcher Jeffrey Silber forecast that by 2020 it would constitute but "6% of the estimated $547 billion expected to be spent on postsecondary education in that year."[63] Online degrees, meanwhile, continued to cluster largely in a limited band of subject areas, Silber reminded investors, including business administration, nursing, and computer science.[64] The division of labor was changing, but not as much as some claimed. The profession of "instructional designer" was born, for instance, yet did not replace professors in the way that Uber threatened to replace taxi drivers.

Some MOOC-fever survivors discovered an appreciation for historical contingency. Following an invigorating closed-door Obama White House bull session in 2015, the MOOC pioneer George Siemens confirmed that "the trends—competency-based learning, unbundling, startups & capital inflow, new pedagogical models, technology, etc.—will change higher education *dramatically.*" In this assessment, Siemens could sound like the coiner of "disruptive innovation," Clayton Christensen, who wavered on MOOCs but remained convinced that "a novel technology or business model" would shake the very foundation of the allegedly moribund university.[65] Siemens was wise enough to point out that it was impossible to know in advance what this change would look like: "No one knows what HE [Higher Education] is becoming" because the sector is a "complex system with many interacting elements," and "we can't yet see how these will connect and inter-relate going forward."[66] This is a lesson one can draw from any point in the history of the American university. Certainly, I. A. Richards could not have anticipated that his pioneering effort to teach poetry on WGBH would help distinguish public television and its audiences (for example, *Sesame Street* and generations of young viewers) from distance education and its audiences (for example, Harvard courses and their Polaris submarine crewmember students). Nor could Allan Bloom and E. D. Hirsch have anticipated that their criticisms of canon-busting colleagues would find fertile ground outside the academy in a revival of the 1920s and 1930s paraeducational Great Books program, this time pitched mainly to parents of K–12 students. As with prior challenges, MOOC fever did not burn up the university's core programming model—a baccalaureate degree comprising a largely student-selected distribution of around 120 Carnegie units—but it did seem poised to produce some unanticipated programming alternatives.

Far from burying their heads in the sand, scholars in diverse fields strove to understand the media changes that implicated their work.[67] In 2013, such research informed Alan Liu's reasoned appraisal of what actually might be novel in the discussion surrounding the massive open online course. Rattling off a list of "dominant Web 2.0 memes"—collective intelligence, the long tail, the hive mind, folksonomy—Liu notes that they update a knowledge problem current "since at least the French Revolution," namely, that of the "mind, or mindlessness," of the crowd.[68] To conceive the crowd as a problem of big data shifted emphasis away from the dangerous, unreflective impulses once studied by figures like Gustave Le Bon. In contrast, MOOC planners, Google ad buyers, and DH data miners conceived the digital masses as continual sources of ever-more-detailed information. EdX placed particular emphasis on learning analytics, conceiving its platform not only as a means to deliver courses but also as a "powerful platform to conduct experiments, exploring how students learn and how faculty can best teach using a variety of novel tools and techniques."[69] Digital-media audiences provided a limitless array of data points and could be disaggregated and reaggregated in infinite combinations, while the masses addressed by movies, radio, and television "talked back" mainly in information-poor forms like ticket sales and Nielsen surveys. Accordingly, digital crowds seemed collectively smarter. Their capacity to prove disruptive was hardly limited to the classroom.

The degree to which the smart crowds of database media might be self-determining—might act like publics in the most ambitious sense of that term—emerged as an academic focus among those capable of learning from Palo Alto without behaving as if it ran the world. The FemTechNet collective developed the Distributed Open Online Course (DOOC), a MOOC alternative "built on the understanding that expertise is distributed throughout networks, among participants situated in diverse institutional contexts, within diverse material, geographic, and national settings, and who embody and perform diverse identities (as teachers, as students, as media-makers, as activists, as trainers, as members of various public groups, for example)."[70] From different positions, Cathy Davidson, Anne Balsamo, and Tara McPherson all emerged as leaders who equipped the university to engage digital-media audiences and industries. Davidson launched high-profile pedagogical experiments, cofounded with David Theo Goldberg the Humanities, Arts, Science, and Technology Alliance and Collaboratory (hastac.org), and directed the Futures Initiative at CUNY, which advocated "greater equity and innovation in higher education at every level of the university" in part by promoting "greater understanding of the complexities of the higher education landscape by spearheading data-driven research in areas critical to institutional change."[71] Balsamo's career bridged academy and industry. As a media-studies scholar she had held the position of principal scientist at Xerox Palo Alto Research Center (PARC). As the first dean for a new School of Arts, Technology, and Emerging Communication at the University of Texas, Dallas, she guided its mission of fostering "intentional future-making through the creation of new cultural forms, the design of new technological experiences, the production of new knowledge, and the transformation of the culture industries."[72] Meanwhile, McPherson's team launched a new publishing platform called Scalar at the University of Southern California and inaugurated two new journals dedicated to publishing work that pushed the boundaries of digital scholarship.[73] In repositioning the university as a means of empowering smart crowds, these leaders and others demonstrated the impotence of EdTech disruption. Their work revealed supposed alternatives as confirmations of existing systems of power and proved that universities could be remade without being ruptured.

OF ANCIENT MATING HABITS AND ADJUNCTS

Although a post–World War II trend, universities' reliance on term-contract employees for instruction began to attract something like the attention it deserved in the popular press in the early twenty-first century. The edge-surfing website *Gawker* published a series on "The Educated Underclass" in 2016.[74] The series began: "Before you go into great debt to send your kid to college, you should hear from the low-paid, ill-treated workers who will actually be educating them: adjunct professors."[75] That same year, the *New York Times* noted that the temporary-labor trend affected even mighty STEM, where recent PhDs could spend years in research labs "as poorly paid foot soldiers in a system that can afford to exploit them."[76] Unionization drives designed to answer labor inequity "sharpened debate," according to the *Wall Street Journal*, about the economics of academe and the politics of PhD education.[77] In such coverage, the plight of recent PhDs indicted the university as a whole and cast its tenure-line professors as elites more concerned to preserve their own privilege than to improve the lives of their students.

Faculty and administrators attempted to intervene in this narrative by updating venerable arguments about academic freedom that had, a hundred years before, helped promote the research endeavors of the American university. Those arguments did, indeed, require updating, because the professor's role had changed along with the division of labor. Who should participate in the management of academic institutions, what "shared governance" should look like, and why anyone off campus should care all emerged as open questions.

Early in the twentieth century, universities had instituted an administrative division of financial from scholarly matters. As Christopher Newfield explains, faculty members secured "freedom of intellectual inquiry, but preserved it by separating from management rather than by making management their own."[78] Administrative control of the purse strings placed de facto limits on what free intellectual inquiry might mean, even as the faculty maintained nominal control of curricula and played an advisory role in other policy areas. This faculty administrative labor was sometimes called "shared governance" and more typically called "service," by far the least heralded component of a position description that also included teaching and research. If they did not have an explicitly defined middle-management role such as department chair or center director, tenure-line faculty received a nominal service assignment with the expectation that they would spend most of their time on other work. This habit, cultivated in circumstances in which most instructors were tenure-line faculty, presented challenges in conditions where term-contract instructors and student-services professionals did much of the work. The updated subdivision of labor seemed to require that tenure-line faculty do more work planning and coordinating—that is, administrating—than the foundational early-twentieth-century arguments on behalf of academic freedom had imagined.

In nineteenth-century American parlance, the phrase "academic freedom" had referred to student choice.[79] In the twentieth, it came to mean faculty autonomy and was justified by the contention that teaching and research might have profound social implications. Protecting this capability required that faculty be shielded from dismissal for political or arbitrary reasons. Although this "freedom" was not "won" in any systemic institutional sense until much later, its raison d'etre was secured in the opening decades of the twentieth century through public contests around such issues as race, labor, and war. A core assumption was that faculty expertise would command attention in matters of public import. That is, the argument for academic freedom assumed not merely that faculty specialists might know truth to speak to power but also that they would command attention when they spoke it. Universities had a stake in that authority and that attention, even when administrators disagreed with faculty opinions.[80]

The 1894 case of the University of Wisconsin professor Richard T. Ely demonstrates better than any other the public relations potential of this defense of academic freedom.[81] In a column for the *Nation*, Wisconsin's superintendent of public instruction Oliver Wells alleged that Ely, director of the School of Economics, "believes in strikes and boycotts, justifying and encouraging the one while practicing the other."[82] Wells concluded that such propagation of "utopian, impractical, or pernicious doctrines" made Ely unfit for employment as a Wisconsin professor. The regents appointed a committee to investigate and serve judgment. That committee not only found Ely innocent of the charges leveled against him but also took the opportunity to question whether such allegations should have mattered to the university in the first place.[83] Professors should be free, the regents' committee declared, "to follow the indications of truth wherever they may lead." This pronouncement, aka the "Wisconsin Magna Carta," relied on the implication that such freedom would distinguish the state's leading university from other workplaces. "Whatever may be the limitations which trammel inquiry elsewhere," the committee wrote, "we believe the great State University of Wisconsin should ever encourage that continual and fearless sifting and winnowing by which alone truth can be found." This verdict was summarized in the *State Journal*, which noted, "Incidentally if not inadvertently the report contains a résumé of the good work done at the university ever since the civil war. . . . This handsome advertisement has been telegraphed all over the country."[84] Ever since, the Ely case has been treated as a landmark both in the history of academic freedom and, equally, the branding of the University of Wisconsin.

The twenty-first century brought signs, however, that "continual and fearless sifting and winnowing" had lost its appeal—as a slogan if not as a project. In June 2015, UW-Madison's Chancellor Blank enlisted this chestnut to sum up her article "Why State Lawmakers Must Support Tenure at Public Universities."[85] Preached to a choir of *Chronicle of Higher Education* readers, Blank's rhetoric proved unable to roll back changes to the state's tenure system advocated by Governor Scott Walker and his conservative backers, which included the powerful Lynde and Harry Bradley Foundation.

Some University of Wisconsin professors responded more creatively than Chancellor Blank to the assault on the Wisconsin Magna Carta. They sexed up "sifting and winnowing" as a Facebook page devoted to "ancient mating habits of whatever"—an appropriation of Assembly Speaker Robin Vos's remark that "Of course I want research, but I want to have research done in a way that focuses on growing our economy, not on ancient mating habits of whatever."[86] Wisconsin's President Van Hise had pioneered this style of rebuttal in his 1905 inaugural address, which famously declared, "It cannot be predicted at what distant nook of knowledge, apparently remote from any practical service, a brilliantly useful stream may spring."[87] Ancient mating habits had an allure comparable to Van Hise's distant nook, and studying them certainly sounded more interesting than relentless sifting and winnowing.

When the advocates of ancient mating habits turned Vos's antiintellectual remark against him, they demonstrated the need for tenure to protect faculty from the electorate. In proposing that academic research might attract interest and hold value beyond narrow calculations of economic growth, they updated an essentially elitist argument for an era when professorial elitism had gone out of fashion. The 1915 Declaration of Principles on Academic Freedom and Academic Tenure, which announced the American Association of University Professors (AAUP) as academic freedom's advocate-in-chief, argued that faculty appointments must be different from the relation of a "private employer to his employees" in order to avoid the "tyranny of public opinion":

An inviolable refuge from such tyranny should be found in the university. It should be an intellectual experiment station, where new ideas may germinate and where their fruit, though still distasteful to the community as a whole, may be allowed to ripen until finally, perchance, it may become a part of the accepted intellectual food of the nation or of the world.[88]

To exempt faculty from the usual American work rules, the AAUP defined the university as a redoubt shielded against groupthink, a bunker to protect the professors who would convince the nation to eat its fruits and vegetables. Selling the university was thus made congruent with selling initially unpleasant (but good for you!) ideas. The sex appeal of ancient mating habits cannily reversed the defensive posture, while advancing its logic.

The position that faculty differed fundamentally in kind from other employees was reaffirmed over the course of the twentieth century by august bodies including the US Supreme Court—but remains uncertain in application.[89] As Marjorie Heins points out on the AAUP's blog, however, this principle has met difficulty in practice, and the AAUP counsel's guidance on "The Current Legal Landscape" asserts that "the scope of the First Amendment right of academic freedom for professors remains unclear."[90] If, as classical liberalism imagines, law indexes the public's will, the public has not spoken clearly about tenure.

Competition among universities, not legal judgment or moral suasion, arguably explains the institutionalization of tenure. Despite AAUP successes in the 1910s and 1920s, tenure protections remained mostly informal and dependant on the will of senior administration for much of the century. That is, they were more PR than policy. When Rice University surveyed policies at seventy-eight universities in 1935, it found that under half had formal rules about tenure protection. Tenure was not a standard and ubiquitous feature of American higher education before the 1970s, Caitlin Rosenthal recounts. Lost in the usual history of professorial advocacy, she argues, is the development of an administrative consensus that the possibility of tenure would be necessary to recruit and maintain "excellent faculties," once it became clear that universities competed for top talent.[91] This practical commitment, we would argue, did not run counter to the idea that academic freedom ultimately served the public good. Rather, it underscored the elitism of Progressive Era professionalism: if some experts were more expert than others, administrators would do well by their institutions and the commonweal by securing their services.

Over a century of deployment, the argument for the faculty's academic freedom as a public good had not settled that case with the public as a matter of law, but it had worked within institutions to specify the professor's role in an increasingly complex division of labor. As academic labor subdivided further, the tenure system not only distinguished faculty from nonfaculty professionals but also stratified faculty into haves and have-nots.[92] Particularly at the large public universities, the AAUP's "refuge" of 1915 looked, a hundred years on, like a small-scale society comprising, in addition to various ranks of teachers, researchers, and administrators, a campus police force, medical services, commercial auxiliary enterprises, groundskeeping and maintenance personnel, and a communications staff to handle public relations. The tenure-line researcher's academic freedom distinguished her not only from term-contract instructors but also from grant-funded coworkers in the lab and myriad student-services professionals called upon to supplement their classroom work. Tenure also divided researchers along departmental lines, protecting sociology professors not only from administrative or public tyranny but also from the interference of physics professors.[93]

Some professors presented this kind of critique as a challenge to their peers. For decades, scholars including Michael Bérubé, Cary Nelson, and Marc Bousquet had urged colleagues across the nation to oppose more forcefully the trend to staff instruction with low-wage graduate student and temporary workers, to little effect.[94] Where they advocated unionization, professional associations took the less controversial path of defending tenure and failed to alter the trend.[95]

Amid this increasingly complex division of labor, some scholars reinvigorated the case for tenure by seeking to extend it to adjuncts. In 2015, Professor Jennifer Ruth joined Bérubé in urging faculty to fess up. They observed that departments filled with faculty poised to defend tenure often had no problem hiring adjuncts. "The result is that the profession of teaching in colleges and universities has been eroded by unprofessional hiring practices," they argued, "and none of us has been eager to admit that all of us engage in those practices, not just overpaid central administrators. Deans do it, department heads do it, even educated PhDs do it."[96] As an alternative, Bérubé and Ruth enjoined the tenured faculty to help professionalize the teaching track and thereby promote job security for colleagues currently hired as adjuncts. Making clear the value of expertise in teaching as well as research might, Bérubé and Ruth proposed, update the old academic-freedom argument and simultaneously confirm the university's status as an engine of upward mobility.

Arizona State University's President Michael Crow and his collaborator, ASU Director of Research William Dabars, also tried to redefine the role of faculty. In *Designing the New American University* (2015), they claimed Clark Kerr's visionary mantle. If Kerr's 1960s sloganeering allowed the problem of the "multi" to displace that of the "uni," Crow and Dabars's intervention had everything to do with reaffirming a public service mission for the university despite limited resources. In their view, "design thinking" that would overcome institutional inertia and revise the division of labor that left faculty looking like obstructionist elites.

For the New American University as for its twentieth-century predecessors, informing a public required explaining how the university worked.

Crow and Dabars usefully presented leadership as a complex organizational problem. On the one hand, they told a story in which bold administrative articulation of goals yielded dramatic increases in degree production, student diversity, faculty diversity, major faculty awards, and so on—all while containing costs. (The model for "a New American University was initially conceptualized by Michael M. Crow," the coauthors proclaim, "and it has been successfully operationalized there over the course of the past decade through the efforts of its faculty, staff, and students.")[97] On the other hand, Crow and Dabars presented academic institutions as impossible to lead effectively in a top-down fashion, a fact they learned, in part, by reading twentieth-century sociology of organizations. Their book offers paeans to the Marxist sociologist Immanuel Wallerstein, from whom they borrow a theory of the university as "complex and adaptive knowledge enterprise"; the midcentury open-systems approach of the social psychologists Daniel Katz and Robert L. Kahn; and the sociologists of institutions Paul DiMaggio and Walter Powell, who provide an awareness of the perils of "institutional isomorphism."[98] Each of these theories presents institutions as dynamic social systems in which aims cannot determine ends. Disciplines, for Wallerstein, are also "cultures"; Katz and Kahn treat organizations as organisms that survive by adapting to their changing environments; DiMaggio and Powell present institutional fields as bedeviled by the tendency to overconform to standards at the expense of their goals. No account informed by such sources could accept the premise that leadership dictated organizational change.

Indeed, Crow and Dabars imagined a substantial role for faculty in charting the university's future and in reframing the way taxpayers might talk about it. For the faculty to take on such a role required a behavioral shift on all sides, for which the term "design" suggested a model and provided a slogan. ASU reorganized numerous departments across four campuses into dozens of new transdisciplinary schools, the authors reported, and this decade-long makeover had required faculty to do much of the envisioning: "Each stage of the process has in practice been negotiated largely through exhaustive trial and error—often construed in terms of a 'design-build' metaphor."[99] Their appropriation of this architectural term redescribed an activity familiar to faculty—committee work devoted to planning—by adding urgency and a more experimental ethos.

In essence, Crow and Dabars sought to reinvigorate their faculty's sense of academic experiment and innovation by glorifying faculty service. Committee meetings acquired superpowers when they had a design vibe. "In some cases the relative autonomy of design teams arguably assumed the tenor of a 'skunkworks,'" Crow and Dabars explained, "an industry term that in broad usages specifies a 'small, frequently informal group within an engineering, computing, or other company, working, often in isolation from the rest of the company, on a radical and innovative project.'" In addition to urgency and experiment, "design" connoted a softening of role distinctions between faculty and administrative staff as well as among departments and disciplines.[100] Design teams were decidedly not the faculty senate, where faculty represented colleagues by department, due process could take years, and separation from financial administration often set up an adversarial dynamic with respect to budget setting. Precisely because the ASU charrettes tended to lump faculty with administration as design managers, they worked against models that addressed the faculty as a relatively autonomous body with which administration shared power.[101]

At the same time, design also sharply distinguished faculty who might participate in the process from those who did not. The *Inside Higher Ed* columnist John Warner implicated tenured professors in maintaining highly stratified instructional staff through the design revolution. He described Crow's New American University as a "terrifying" workplace whose reliance on adjunct labor made it "indistinguishable from Amazon."[102] Adjuncts were expected to implement, not design. He bemoaned the tepid professorial response to a proposed increase in the adjunct teaching load and concluded that "the tenured faculty in Arizona State's English department [which employed a large number of temporary instructors] are content to maintain the privilege of their personal gravy trains as long as possible, and they don't particularly care if it comes at the cost of others." Although Warner was right to call out the faculty, he was wrong to imply that ASU's English professors, administrators, and design philosophy were culpable. Adjunct exploitation was a sector-wide issue, exacerbated, perhaps, by ASU's drive to do more within financial constraints.

In an interesting exchange, Newfield credited Crow and Dabars's antielitism, their desire to offer a different model than that of Ivy League exclusivity, and their bid to refresh the land-grant university ideal.[103] For their part, Crow and Dabars endorsed Newfield's critique of the assumption that "mass scale and top quality" are antithetical properties of higher education. They parted company on the question of the correct funding pitch, with Crow and Dabars describing Newfield's hope for dramatically increased taxpayer support as "utopian."[104] Whether utopian or not, Newfield's vision was, like Crow and Dabars's, contingent on establishing a durable and substantial role for faculty in charting the university's future and in reframing the way taxpayers might talk about it. For faculty to play this role, Newfield agreed, would require a behavioral shift on the part of his colleagues. Eschewing design, he urged faculty to embrace the challenge of understanding the university's business operations, show up to meetings where they were discussed, and learn how to tailor their message for audiences that did not already agree with them.[105]

Newfield also recommended abandoning the rhetoric of exception that defined tenure as the freedom to "sift and winnow." Rather, he proposed linking the faculty's plight to the future of work in general. "Faculty members have gone as far as they can by pleading an academic exemption from the financial control and autocratic management that typify the U.S. workplace, crystallized in the power of summary dismissal."[106] He argued that tenure, reframed not as "academic freedom" but as "protection from the at-will employment practice of firing any employee without cause," should be promoted not as a special privilege but as a protection to which all American workers should feel themselves entitled. We like this idea and have observed that Newfield's framing nicely lumps tenure-line faculty with a range of university employees given stronger and weaker versions of protection from "at-will" termination by union representation and human-resources policies.[107]

That said, no such public relations strategy could hope to succeed without acknowledging that there is no longer a general or singular public to win over, if indeed there ever had been. Where the AAUP in 1915 could invoke "the tyranny of public opinion" as a shared danger, Facebook followers of the Ancient Mating Habits of Whatever inhabited a hotly polarized mediasphere. An argument likely to sway the 72 percent of Democrats who held a positive view of universities was unlikely to succeed with the 58 percent of Republicans who saw them as detrimental to national well-being. Student protesters also confronted such polarization. They had some success in transcending it.

STUDENT PROTEST, AGAIN

Students in the 1960s, left and right, established campus protest as potentially valuable resource. It could brand films and books as well as the schools themselves, and it could be coopted in ways that changed campuses for the better. In the 2010s, students continued to do this work, but they faced several generations of college graduates who had *also* learned to do it. Some of these graduates now worked for think tanks like the conservative Goldwater Institute, part of whose mission was intervening in campus politics to further their goals. They were not alone: the college politics game had many powerful off-campus players. This, more than the difference between underground newspapers and social media, distinguished student protest 2017-style from its precursors a half-century earlier. True, twenty-first-century students mastered the affordances of Twitter and Instagram, just as their forebears had learned to work with Portapak video. Far more than differences of format, however, the partisan mediasphere defined and challenged the organizing capacities of so-called digital natives.

Many student protests seemed to confirm that the university had become a battlefield for struggles funded and orchestrated by outsiders. The 2016–17 school year saw demonstrations by students appalled at a seeming uptick in white-supremacist activities as well as fierce skirmishes in response to right-wing speakers, many sponsored by the conservative Young America's Foundation, which shipped the pundit Ann Coulter to Berkeley and Robert Spencer (cofounder of Stop Islamization of America) to the University of Buffalo.[108] The Goldwater Institute wrote up "model legislation designed to ensure free expression at America's public university systems" that was subsequently taken up with uneven success by various statehouses.[109] The tone had been set in the fall of 2016, when University of Chicago's dean of students John Ellison informed the world that his school's support for free inquiry demanded rejection of "trigger warnings" and "safe spaces"—a contention rebutted by Student College Council President Eric Holmberg as an "effort to control the conversation on campus . . . and a false narrative of coddled millennials."[110] The fall of 2017 began where the spring left off. UC Berkeley's new chancellor, Carol Christ, announced a year of free-speech activities on campus that included speaking invitations to the Breitbart News editor Ben Shapiro and the alt-right provocateur Milo Yiannopoulos. Recalling the "racism, bigotry, violence and mayhem" of the far-right protesters who had caused late-summer bloodshed in the Virginia university town of Charlottesville, she found "the issue of free speech even more tense" and even more important to defend on her campus. "It is who we are," Christ proclaimed. She spoke for a "statelike" campus (replete with the policing functions that had been created in the wake of the 1960s demonstrations), a university that "has the responsibility to provide safety and security for its community and guests." "If you choose to protest, do so peacefully," she cautioned students, faculty, and staff. "That is your right, and we will defend it with vigor."[111] The editors of the *Daily Californian* demurred: "The campus is obligated to uphold the right of a student group to invite controversial speakers," they wrote in September, "but instead, it is serving the malicious interests of trolls." Instead of undergraduates debating the issues, the student paper saw the operations of a "vast PR and media machine."[112]

The university that made headlines in these episodes was not the special kind of institutional space the "Port Huron Statement" had envisioned as a "community of controversy"—a kind of community that students would first reform, the better to reform society. As both Holmberg and the editors of the *Daily Californian* suggest, students often struggled to influence the pre-scripted narratives circulated by the press and managed by university leaders. These narratives, it was widely acknowledged, divided audiences along partisan lines and reverberated in social-media echo chambers.

There were eruptions of creativity, as when students at the University of Texas, Austin, illegally brandished dildos to protest a recent law allowing concealed handguns on campus in the attention-grabbing "Cocks Not Glocks" campaign.[113] Campaigners used campus in a familiar way as a relatively safe platform for a media stunt that aimed to intervene in a major partisan issue: Second Amendment rights, or the need for gun control, depending on one's point of view. They cannily urged people to think again by articulating the issue with the equally politicized spheres of privacy and sexual expression, where no clear line had yet been drawn. Public sex-toy display may have offended as many as it amused, but (so far as we have been able to determine) there is no national lobbying organization devoted to open dildo carry and certainly none equivalent in influence to the NRA.[114] "Cocks Not Glocks" did not change state law, but it did show how students could reframe an issue.

In contrast, student protest over gender-inclusive bathrooms demonstrated how difficult reframing could be, particularly at the national level. In March 2016, North Carolina passed House Bill 2, the Public Facilities Privacy & Security Act, which required persons to use the bathroom designated for the sex indicated on their birth certificates and prohibited municipalities from enacting antidiscrimination laws. Hailed as a triumph of common sense on the right and denounced as discrimination against LGBTQ communities on the left, the law prompted vigorous resistance and was one of the issues that led North Carolinians to replace their governor in the fall.[115] Meanwhile, Obama administration officials advised in May 2016 that Title IX protected transgender students' selections of gender-appropriate bathrooms, which predictably mobilized conservative ire.[116] As participants in this high-stakes dispute, students protested against H.B. 2 at UNC Pembroke when the state university system's chancellor, Margaret Spellings, showed up there for meetings. They held a bathroom sit-in at UNC Wilmington. They petitioned their local chancellor at UNC Charlotte. They occupied the administration building at Appalachian State.[117] During a protest outside a Board of Governors meeting, a UNC Chapel Hill senior told the *Daily Tar Heel*, "I'm tired of the board refusing to acknowledge student voices . . . with H.B. 2, not only is the board denying the voices of students but denying the existence of some students—of trans students, and putting their bodies even more at risk in an environment where they should be safe."[118] The senior sought to reshape the argument by foregrounding concern with student safety and by raising the issue of democratic process, of listening to those students affected by the law. Students' insistence that they should be able to participate in decisions about bathrooms on their campuses failed to move the state or national debate. In February 2017, the Trump administration rescinded Obama's order.[119] In March 2017, North Carolina repealed and replaced H.B. 2 with House Bill 142, which eliminated the divisive birth-certificate requirement but also prohibited state agencies, including UNC and the North Carolina Community College System, from regulating multiple-occupancy restrooms.

The students faced an uphill fight because the conservative press had a bigger megaphone and used it to tell a very different story: gender-inclusive bathrooms were an academic imposition. The *National Review* columnist Heather Mac Donald explained that "a pipeline now channels left-wing academic theorizing into the highest reaches of government and the media."

Thanks to a conspiracy of eggheads and elites, "gender theory has leapt from the academy to the real world" in a frightening demonstration that "the public ignores arcane academic theory at its peril."[120] Mac Donald and the Chapel Hill senior were probably not talking to or about the same public. They likely held different views about gender identity and certainly disagreed about bathroom infrastructure. One hyperbolized the influence of "academic theorizing"; the other probably underestimated the power of student voices that had been "denied." Each assumed the university was a place where fairly fundamental changes to social organization might be tested—not only theoretically described, that is, but also enacted, debated, and modeled for broader audiences. Each had a stake in controlling a narrative about university politics. Mac Donald was paid to do this. The senior was not.

Successful student protest used the full array of available media to engage audiences not already positioned on opposite sides by the commercial news outlets. The exemplary case begins with a November 2015 tweet featuring a photo of some thirty black University of Missouri football players, a quote from Dr. Martin Luther King Jr., and the declaration: "We will no longer participate in any football related activities until President Tim Wolfe resigns or is removed due to his negligence towards marginalized students' experiences."[121] Wolfe did indeed resign two days after the tweet, leading the *Chicago Tribune* to marvel at "The Power of a Football Strike," *Time* to proclaim "Missouri President Toppled by the Power of the Student Athlete," and ESPN to make the team a 2016 winner of the Stuart Scott ENSPIRE Award.[122] These headlines overlooked the newer medium of Twitter for the message of football's commanding presence as an established media power. Nonetheless, the effectiveness of the protest clearly stemmed from the alliance of these two forms. When Missouri's football coach Gary Pinkel decided to support his players, he did so with a tweet of his own. It too featured a picture of the team, including white coaches and players, the declaration "The Mizzou Family stands as one. We are united. We are behind our players," and the hashtag #ConcernedStudent1950.[123] "Concerned Student 1950" named a movement led by the graduate student Jonathan Butler, then on hunger strike to protest the university's inability to deal with racism on campus. In addition to (and after) Wolfe's resignation, the group demanded that the university take a series of steps to foster racial awareness and inclusion.[124] In supporting Butler's movement, the football players' boycott focused more narrowly on Wolfe.

Because the protest took many media forms, it encourages reflection on the fact that, like much recent activism, it became identified with its hashtag. Crisis managers especially were inclined to assign Twitter awesome power. The public relations news aggregator *The Holmes Report* cautioned PR professionals in mid-2016 that the "overwhelming majority (94%) of crises either start or spread on Twitter."[125] The Mizzou incident did demonstrate that the right students with the right cause at the right time could use Twitter to precipitate dramatic change, but it also depended on the massive audience-binding powers of college football, which had long circulated in multiple media formats.

At the other end of the spectrum, a fourteen-page letter written by Oberlin College students in December 2015 offers perhaps the most salient counterexample to Mizzou's successful Twitter campaign. It sharply distinguished the specific university audience to which it was addressed from the national readership of mainstream journalism, which used the letter to cultivate a building consensus about what was wrong on campus. The letter inspired the *New York Times* columnist David Brooks to depict twenty-first-century campuses as sites of contradiction: "the admiration for achievement clashing against the moral superiority of the victim; the desire to let students run free, clashing against the desire to protect the oppressed from psychologically unsafe experiences."[126] Nathan Heller was less judicious in the *New Yorker*. He told a story of student activism as solipsism, of politics as whine. Although students confronted serious issues—racial violence and cultural appropriation chief among them—they made them small with complaints that "cafeteria dishes such as sushi and bánh mì were prepared with the wrong ingredients, making a mockery of cultural cuisine."[127] The call for "safe spaces" to prevent the airing of views seemed to threaten the notion of college as a place where certainties were "perpetually questioned." Heller described a college populated by "coddled youths and the self-defined, untested truths that they held dear." Where the Free Speech Movement mounted self-guided classes on the Constitution and screened daring experimental films, these kids demanded trigger warnings for *Antigone* and fresh paint to cover up the image of a snake charmer in a campus cafe mural.[128] They seemed prepared to reject the very idea that college would improve them. Heller quotes Jasmine Adams, an African American undergraduate, as wanting no part of the "middle-class values" of meritocracy. "I'm going *home*, back to the 'hood of Chicago, to be exactly who I was before I came to Oberlin." Such sentiments seemed to indict what Heller called the "inclusive-élite model" of higher education that Oberlin represents.

In their letter to the institution's president, Oberlin students present themselves differently. Signed by seven hundred individuals (at a school enrolling fewer than three thousand undergraduates), the document revealed a keen understanding of Oberlin's brand and its contradictions. "Oberlin College and Conservatory uses the limited number of Black and Brown students to color in its brochures," the letter writers maintain, "but then erases us from student life on this campus. You profit off of our accomplishments and invisible labor, yet You expect us to produce personal solutions to institutional incompetencies."[129] The students marry attention to reputation with a dissection of the college in all of its parts. Were it not for the repeated use of DEMAND in all caps, the letter might be mistaken for the work of a highly critical external review committee. The demands begin with three pages devoted to "Admissions, Recruitment, and Retention" and wind up with matters related to the college's relation to "Community: Oberlin & Beyond." No issue is too small: "We DEMAND that the AV system in Lord Lounge be maintained regularly—it is in desperate need of repairs and system upgrades."[130] Innovations abound. A demand that "Black student leaders be provided a $8.20/hr stipend for their continuous organizing efforts" speaks to a complaint from one of Heller's interviewees that "students felt really unsupported in their endeavors to engage with the world outside Oberlin"—engagements for which the college very much wished to be known. Pay for time away from a part-time job or a work-study appointment would in fact complement grade forgiveness for students devoted to community organizing and demonstrate that the school's famed embrace of social activism was not limited to students whose parents could foot the bill.

Like Mizzou's students, Oberlin's emphasized the struggle for racial justice. Differences of message as well as medium determined what that struggle could mean and whom it would be likely to engage. Where Mizzou's tweet singled out the president as a bad apple and demanded his ouster, Oberlin's letter provided a holistic review. Thus, a demand to increase grants

over loans for Black students speaks to "one of the core founding principles of Oberlin College & Conservatory, which is to promote the successful prosperity of Black people within the academic sphere and beyond."[131]
This was a sophisticated and specifically targeted communication that
pressed Oberlin administrators to make good on institutional rhetoric.[132]
Although this student protest was tweetable, the breadth and depth of its
appeal to administration was not.[133] That appeal could not hope for the reach
of the Missouri football players' viral tweet. It could hope to be co-opted
by the institution.

Then Oberlin college president Marvin Krislov understood cooptation
and worked it. He treated the petition as a teachable moment. In a statement
issued by the college, he agreed that "racism and all forms of injustice hinder
us from achieving . . . our goals for academic, artistic and musical excellence."[134] That said, he maintained, many of the student "demands contra-
vene principles of shared governance" and contain "personal attacks on a
number of faculty and staff members who are dedicated and valued members of this community." (Students had demanded moving some visiting
instructors onto the tenure track and the dismissal of particular professors
and administrators.) Recognizing that the kerfuffle had a broader audience,
Krislov also wrote a letter to the *New York Times* in response to Brooks's
column. He explained a need to "listen and respond to the real concerns,
while educating our students and maintaining our academic standards."[135]
"This process may at times be messy," he cautioned, and the stakes were
high. "By engaging in this dialogue, we not only strengthen our educational
institutions, but also create a model that may strengthen our democracy, our
civic discourse and our country." Readers could take both the protest and
his response as evidence that college would continue to level social differences and maintain them. Brooks's privileged snots were rebadged as the
nation's future leaders. The students focused their demands on a few key
priorities including, the *Chronicle of Higher Education* reported, "a website
of resources for low-income students and better data collection on minority
students' academic success," which became a bullet on the college's revised
strategic plan.[136]

Oberlin students did not overturn their institutions' hierarchy by challenging it, but they did win a seat at the table. They kept at it in the spring
of 2017, nosing their way into administrative matters like the question of
which company was contracted to provide food services.[137] Krislov knew

the script and sold his performance of it, flipping one presidential job into another. He left Oberlin in the fall of 2016 and was named president of Pace University in New York the following February. Oberlin changed incrementally, probably for the better, as a result.

As much as the ouster of Missouri's Wolfe testifies to the success of the students' protest, it also testifies to Wolfe's failure to have mastered the process of cooptation that, we have argued, makes student politics an engine of change and a source of valuable immaterial labor. Decision making panned as "autocratic," failure to recognize "stakeholders," and other signs of poor or entirely absent attention to cooptation were the sorry hallmarks of the Wolfe regime.[138] These bad habits made good news copy and appeared to indicate the pitfalls of choosing business executives to helm universities. Wolfe had been hired away from an executive position at the software maker Novell, and the *Atlantic*, for one, attributed his ouster to his misunderstanding of the university, which the magazine portrayed as a uniquely complex workplace in part because it included unruly students.[139] Wolfe's case thus joined a running argument over whether CEOs were prepared to manage universities at all.[140]

Missouri's student athletes precipitated leadership change and furthered a national conversation about the dangers of selecting CEOs as university presidents, but they did not win an ongoing role in making policies to address racism on campus.[141] Oberlin's student protesters did win such a role, but they also contributed to a "coddled millennials" narrative that probably served no one but the pundits who promoted it. Each of these protests used the array of media available to them, which mattered both to the complexity and to the reach of the messages they sent. We cannot understand the political effects of student (or any other) media work, however, by reducing the message to the medium. The message also matters, and so does the audience.

At the end of 2017, higher education, like every other American institution, was caught in the crossfire of opposing ideologies managed by think tanks, lobbyists, political parties, and increasingly various news outlets. The students of the 1960s had helped create this terrain. They incubated conservative think tanks, elaborated the conventions of campus protest, and sparked collaborations of academy and industry that produced powerful new tech companies. The students of the 2010s attracted the attention of outsiders who hoped to see the pattern repeated. As college students tested new media platforms and enacted national political dramas, professional intervention by those familiar with the process complicated what student protest could do. The scope of student action was similarly constrained by debt financing and the means-ends calculations urged by increasingly (if unreliably) granular ratings services, which underscored the expectation that college students would make their own choices while managing the scope of those choices. At most schools, students saw tenure-line faculty less often than members of their parents' generation had, and they were likely to be familiar with an argument that blamed this on professors themselves. They were also likely to perceive that twenty-first-century audiences mainly wished to have their opinions confirmed. Nonetheless, the university's students, faculty, and administrators could still challenge received opinion, generating effects even when they did not create consensus. The American research university had changed considerably since gathering masses for its gridiron spectacles. Its capacity to level the field of opportunity and simultaneously certify hierarchy had never seemed more in doubt. Yet the university continued to thrive as an information platform for which, it seemed, exciting and dangerous days lay ahead.

Epilogue

The American university thrives by informing audiences. By this we mean that the university shapes and patterns group interactions. Across campus and across the country, it forges connections among diverse groups, enabling collaboration and engendering debate. In 1945 at Harvard, the Redbook authors set "unity conditioned by difference" as a goal and imagined remaking the nation's entire educational system as a meritocratic sorting machine. In 1962, the Students for a Democratic Society envisioned campus as a "community of controversy" capable of interrupting what they saw as the university's prevailing tendency to extend mainstream mass media. In the 1970s, a loose constellation of activists, federal bureaucrats, and campus administrators agreed that universities could provide a means to redress systemic inequalities of race and gender. None of these visionaries got the changes they wanted, but all made change. Each confirmed that the US academy is a vehicle for managing demographic differences. They also, in different ways, informed new distinctions based on educational attainment, disciplinary specialization, and political affiliation. As the examples assembled by this book attest, to inform groups does not mean to create a consensus. It means, rather, to act or be acted upon despite disagreement. We hope to have established that some disagreements are better than others.

First, there is no point in engaging any argument that pits the university's "true" or "core" academic mission against football, movies, television, the internet, mobile phones, or any other commercially successful, widely adopted media form. For well over a century, such rhetoric of opposition has belied a far different dynamic, one in which the university learns to collaborate with and appropriate commercial media rather than defend against their supposedly pernicious influence. Examples from this history include John Erskine's Great Books roadshow, the National Educational Television distribution network, the personal computing industry, and the Distributed Open Online Course. No one armed with our book should find themselves sucked into an argument about whether mobile phones have destroyed students' will to read the classics. The devices may or may not be culpable (there are plenty of reasons to lose interest in the classics), but there is never a point in rising to this bait, since the solution is always the same. Complainers crediting mobile phones with the power to dictate reading habits should be counseled to follow the example set by I. A. Richards. Faced with a new medium that challenged the classics, he took to the television airwaves and produced a sexy abridgment of *The Iliad* for 1950s students, who (he thought) would be interested in the battles but not the lists. The message is not *only* the medium. For all the power of his insights, Marshall McLuhan was wrong to propose that new media render old media obsolete. The past century of adding new media to college classrooms has changed those classrooms without sweeping aside either lecture or seminar modes. To inform audiences connected by means of a medium, it only makes sense to work in that medium. We would be happy to play a videogame version of *The Iliad* on our phones. We would hope, however, for a version more playable than Richards's television was watchable. For all his admirable willingness to experiment, Richard's rejection of TV's affordances in favor of crumpled notes and a well-worn lecture style bespoke a love-hate relationship with the medium, and this relationship did not serve his larger purpose. The array of more and less strongly feminist approaches to new technologies described in chapter 10 better indicates how to engage new media critically, but not phobically, through collaboration with people who understand new formats and can make the most of them.

Second, avoid at all cost revivals of the stereotypical "two cultures" conflict, including calls to defend "the humanities." These appeals misrecognize the academic enterprise and undermine it. The American research university may have its own kind of institutional culture. It might also be said to have myriad and competing disciplinary cultures—for which "silos" provides one term of art. Academic culture may be singular or plural, but it has never been divisible by two. This was clear after World War I, when schools tried to implement general-education curricula and found them tending to fracture into (usually three) different parts that worked differently at different schools. It was clear at midcentury, when exciting work in communications, information theory, cybernetics, and design violated disciplinary boundaries with abandon and thereby created new fields. It was true in the early twenty-first century, when federal planners popularized the acronym "STEM" to yoke together otherwise distinct "cultures" of science, technology, engineering, and math. Lest anyone miss the point that such aggregation was more culture than nature, moreover, the Rhode Island School of Design took the lead in adding an "A" for "Art," to make it "STEAM." Among such successful initiatives, "science" versus "humanities" is a poisonous loser, a deadening schema that ahistorically forecloses collaboration and sometimes preposterously casts "science" against the "liberal arts" (of which science was historically a core component). Do not defend the humanities or the sciences, we urge you. Please defend instead specific initiatives that feature participants from across the disciplines engaged in projects that require collaboration. Follow Steve Fuller's advice in keeping an eye on the difference between those "who wish to protect the academy from the rest of society" and "those who wish to use the academy as a vehicle for reforming society."[1] In their *Designing the New American University*, Michael Crow and William Dabars up the ante on that distinction when they declare that in the Anthropocene universities "represent the best hope for the survival of our species."[2] Ecological initiatives are far from the only ones needed to secure the future. There is plenty of work to go around. The scope of the intervention, we suggest, matters less than the type of audience it creates.

Third, avoid easy slogans for abiding contradictions. Student debt, for example, is a much, much better problem to argue about than "the corporate university." When hurled as an epithet, "the corporate university" typically equates the university's bureaucratic form with an economic imperative. It thereby flattens the contradiction at the core of American higher education's mission to democratize access and promote meritocracy while also reproducing existing social relations. Concern with student debt, in contrast, strikes at the question of access while inviting debate about the value and cost of college, who should pay for whom, and who benefits from higher education. The difference in framing matters. "The corporate university" reduces what is wrong with higher education to a question of what is wrong with American capitalism—primarily for readers already predisposed to see capitalism as the root problem. In contrast, student debt reminds us that American capitalism takes the shape it does in part because the university has been so good at simultaneously reproducing both inequality and accessibility. For this very reason, audiences unprepared to blame capitalism can also perceive a student debt crisis.

In addition to economic relations, moreover, student debt also foregrounds the overburdening of student judgment. Students have been adults in the eyes of universities for decades, but they are not well positioned to assess, before they even begin college, which school and degree program will give the best return on their investment. The College Scorecard really should come with the warning, customary for grown-up investors, that past performance does not necessarily predict future results. Undergraduates may be even less well positioned to judge what kind of education will best serve their state or nation. That said, despite the limitations of youthful perspective, college students have had an uncanny ability to shape priorities for higher education. The Oberlin College activists we discussed in chapter 10 proposed paying a stipend to student protesters. Given their impact on higher education over the decades, it seems like they deserve it.

Fourth, there is little point in defending the Carnegie unit; the argument should be over what will replace it. When the Carnegie unit allows, say, a physics course at one university to be functionally equivalent to a chemistry course at another (because it satisfies a scientific-literacy requirement), it demonstrates the power of mediation by erasing variables like tuition costs, coursework requirements, grading standards, and class size that might distinguish the two courses and the educational value students realize through them. The Carnegie unit is, in this sense, perhaps the best example of how seemingly small media interventions can ramify through the entire apparatus of higher education. To satisfy themselves that any courses really are equivalent, universities typically create a set of bureaucratic procedures for reviewing syllabi and course descriptions, establish a schedule of fees for transfer credits, and rely on the judgments of accrediting bodies about other institutions—all indirect measures of what a student might be expected to have learned. For faculty and students alike, moreover, the Carnegie unit makes time-on-task the most important measure of instructional effort. Replacing the Carnegie unit might be expected to alter all of these habits. Depending on the implementation, the tendency to appraise outcomes as opposed to time spent could make establishing course equivalencies faster and more accurate. It might also facilitate experiments in co-teaching, experiential learning, and undergraduate research, activities that present technical challenges for everyone involved when they need to be rendered in Carnegie units. To replace the Carnegie unit is to broach an argument about who gets credit, for what, and at what price. These are good arguments to have, and foundations like Lumina are expending significant resources to stimulate them. Rather than resist this trend and the risks it poses for existing models of course delivery and curricular development, we recommend more faculty involvement in framing questions and answers.

Fifth, no share without reach. This is two injunctions in one. First, it is a reminder that although debate about higher education has long featured evocative rhetoric and often rewards historical reading, it is also a numbers game. Second, it underlines the conclusions of several chapters, each of which suggests that widely circulated aggregations of degree share into areas like "the humanities" or "STEM" misrepresent the defining features of the US system of postsecondary education as it has evolved over the century and especially after the mid-1960s. Good data is better than fast and loose stereotyping. Reach reminds us that there are ever more degree options, that these are not evenly distributed across schools, and that, as a corollary, there is more variety in the higher-education menu than is often supposed. As the number of degrees increases, so does institutional variety, while the share of completions falling to each degree is likely to decrease. The academic department has not well accommodated this dynamic of field proliferation. Its responsibility to marry transinstitutional disciplines to the local organization chart makes it a clunky mechanism for curricular experimentation, especially if such experiments appear to violate disciplinary norms. Reach, considered along with a disaggregated share number, makes each of these overall trends visible and reveals how particular degrees fit within them. Any argument about the prospects for disciplines and departments will be improved by consideration of this metric.

Sixth, do not rise to defend "academic freedom." Instead, change the narrative by leaping to defend job security for everyone. We have repeatedly observed that the university's division of labor evolves in tandem with descriptions of what the university does and whom it is for. The early-twentieth-century defense of academic freedom promoted the entire academic enterprise as a public service when it explained the research professor's role, but it could never entirely thwart the implication that tenure primarily benefited professors. (Upton Sinclair, we noted in chapter 2, zealously exploited that implication.) In the early twenty-first century, the professor's freedom often appeared to come at the expense of term-contract instructors. A new division of labor had resulted from research specialization, the academic star system, the rise of student services, and increased reliance on adjuncts to contain costs and preserve administrative flexibility. When the mainstream press looked at this university, it was inclined to see tenure less as a public benefit than as a professorial privilege. By clinging to tenure as the answer even as their departments hired more and more adjuncts, faculty only strengthened the impression that "academic freedom" was self-serving. We have argued, with Michael Bérubé and Jennifer Ruth as well as with Christopher Newfield, that the path forward lies in passionate advocacy for the job security of others.

We would go further by observing that the important protection from arbitrary dismissal is not the only reason tenured professors have decent jobs, the kinds of jobs worth saving and extending to many more people. Although we work long hours, confront increasing bureaucratic pressures, and, at most public schools, face static compensation, ours can be remarkably unalienated work. We mean this in an old-fashioned way. In *The German Ideology*, Karl Marx called attention to the limitations a division of labor imposes by imagining a society in which he might "hunt in the morning, fish in the afternoon, rear cattle in the evening, criticise after dinner, just as I have a mind, without ever becoming hunter, fisherman, herdsman or critic."[3] For all the ways it identifies persons with their occupational roles, the academic division of labor remains relatively unusual in the flexibility it affords many who participate in it. A professor might review grant proposals with peers across disciplines in the morning, address campus WiFi problems with IT staff in the afternoon, teach a class in her specialty during the evening, and write a book on something entirely different after dinner. It is possible to have too much of a good thing. Certainly, not everyone at the university moves easily across roles, or wants to. Nonetheless, precisely because connecting audiences by means of knowledge is inherently collaborative and creative work, universities must have teams that transcend specialty. If we better understood audience making as part of the job description for pretty much everyone who works at a university, we might all enjoy it a bit more.

Seventh, and finally, forget about a master plan. For every Booker T. Washington who seeks to broaden access through university extension, there has always been a W. E. B. DuBois who hopes to cultivate merit where it has been denied. The idea of mass quality education condenses the proposition that we should not have to choose between these two approaches. Yet insofar as quality entails determinations of merit, it will invariably make hierarchies that undo the leveling effects of access. Washington and DuBois each clearly perceived and sought to manage this contradiction by understanding that students were not the only people higher education was for. Tuskegee self-help was built to go viral, while the Talented Tenth were meant to rework racist ideology from the inside out. In other words, each educational leader engaged the core mediation problem, albeit with an emphasis on different audiences. If empowerment is to be more than a sales pitch, the audience problem cannot be avoided. The problem of whom the university benefits cannot be sundered from the problem of whom it addresses and how. The classroom is hardly academia's only means of address. Washington and Du Bois jostled for the attention of the same readers. Their early-twenty-first-century counterparts engaged a fractured and hotly polarized mediasphere, in which a wide array of gatekeepers managed which pitches reached which audiences. Such diversification has made it more difficult to imagine that the university could accomplish something so grand as managing the national welfare. We should face that difficulty without nostalgia. Universities have always informed widely various, often discontinuous audiences of different shapes and sizes. They do not produce shared ideas or maintain national culture so much as mediate more and less broadly shared experiences, habits, and arguments. In the United States, for good and ill, no master plan guides this effort, whose trends and tendencies can anticipate the future only after the fact.

NOTES

INTRODUCTION

1. The literature is extensive. On the sort of organization that has obtained absent federal coordination, see, for instance, John R. Thelin, *A History of American Higher Education* (Baltimore, MD: Johns Hopkins University Press, 2011). Our views have been shaped by the following foundational arguments about higher education and social hierarchy: Burton J. Bledstein, *The Culture of Professionalism: The Middle Class and the Development of Higher Education in America* (New York: Norton, 1976); Barbara Ehrenreich and John Ehrenreich, "The Professional-Managerial Class," in *Between Labor and Capital*, ed. Pat Walker (Boston: South End Press, 1979), 5–45; Richard M. Ohmann, *English in America: A Radical View of the Profession* (New York: Oxford University Press, 1976). For a more recent effort to bring awareness of these contradictions into policy discussions, see Anthony P. Carnevale and Stephen J. Rose, "Economy Goes to College: The Hidden Promise of Higher Education in the Post-Industrial Service Economy," Center on Education and the Workforce, Georgetown University, April 13, 2015, https://cew .georgetown.edu/cew-reports/the-economy-goes-to-college/.

2. Quoted in Carol S. Gruber, *Mars and Minerva: World War I and the Uses of the Higher Learning in America* (Baton Rouge: Louisiana State University Press, 1975), 244.

3. On the historical relation between the two corporate forms, see Christopher Newfield, *Ivy and Industry: Business and the Making of the American University, 1880–1980* (Durham, NC: Duke University Press, 2003). Also see Thorstein Veblen, *The Higher Learning in America: A Memorandum on the Conduct of Universities by Business Men* (New York: B.W. Huebsch, 1918), 85, v–vi.

4. Electric light "is a medium without a message" like all media, according to his definition. Marshall McLuhan, *Understanding Media: The Extensions of Man*, ed. W. Terrence Gordon (Corte Madera, CA: Gingko Press, 2003), 19.

5. Christopher Newfield, *Unmaking the Public University: The Forty-Year Assault on the Middle Class* (Cambridge, MA: Harvard University Press, 2008), 191.

6. Harvard Committee on the Objectives of General Education in a Free Society, *General Education in a Free Society; Report of the Harvard Committee* (Cambridge, MA: Harvard University, 1945), 213–14, https://archive.org/details/generaleducatiooo3244ombp.

7. Veblen, *The Higher Learning in America*, 106.

8. "The most powerful of the culture agencies, who work harmoniously with others of their kind as only managers do, whether they come from the ready-to-wear trade or college, have long since reorganized and rationalized the objective mind. It is as if some omnipresent agency had reviewed the material and issued an authoritative catalog tersely listing the products available." Max Horkheimer and Theodor W. Adorno, "The Culture Industry: Enlightenment as Mass Deception," in *Dialectic of Enlightenment: Philosophical Fragments*, ed. Gunzelin Schmitt-Noerr (Stanford, CA: Stanford University Press, 2002), 107.

9. Paul DiMaggio, "Market Structure, the Creative Process, and Popular Culture: Toward an Organizational Reinterpretation of Mass Culture Theory," *Journal of Popular Culture* 11, no. 2 (1977): 433–51.

10. Clifford reports being "naively shocked" at a dean's mention of "five" university divisions. "When I entered graduate school, we were members of an arts and sciences university, worrying about C. P. Snow's 'two cultures.' I assumed that I belonged to half the landscape. Now, at the airport, my world was a thin and shrinking slice of the pie." James Clifford, "The Greater Humanities," *Occasion: Interdisciplinary Studies in the Humanities* 6 (October 1, 2013): 1.

11. Clifford, "Greater Humanities," 2–4.

12. Clifford, "Greater Humanities," 1.

13. The strongest precursor focuses almost entirely on the European case and overleaps twentieth-century mass media entirely but nonetheless rightly perceives that the university names a mediation problem: Friedrich Kittler, "Universities: Wet, Hard, Soft, and Harder," *Critical Inquiry* 31, no. 1 (2004): 244–55. Another relevant set of inquiries, emphasizing the problem of "Enlightenment" and pulling academic knowledge into that orbit may be found in Clifford Siskin and William Warner, eds., *This Is Enlightenment* (Chicago: University of Chicago Press, 2010).

14. Readers in literary studies will likely be familiar with one example of this type of history, namely, Gerald Graff, *Professing Literature: An Institutional History*, 20th anniversary ed. (Chicago: University of Chicago Press, 2007). For even more self-reflexive reworkings of such a disciplinary tale devoted to women's studies and African American studies, see Robyn Wiegman, *Object Lessons* (Durham, NC: Duke University Press, 2012); and Roderick A. Ferguson, *The Reorder of Things: The University and Its Pedagogies of Minority Difference* (Minneapolis: University of Minnesota Press, 2012). Dana B. Polan, *Scenes of Instruction: The Beginnings of the US Study of Film* (Berkeley: University of California Press, 2007), is notable for trying to stretch the bounds of this form through an emphasis on curricula as opposed to disciplinary mission statements, but the basic narrative pattern remains the same.

15. On its status as just such a scenario, see the elaborate array of "philological annotations" on the prehistory of media in John Guillory, "Genesis of the Media Concept," *Critical Inquiry* 36, no. 2 (January 1, 2010): 326.

16. Michel Foucault and Raymond Bellours, "The Order of Things," in *Aesthetics, Method, and Epistemology*, ed. James D. Faubion, vol. 2 of *The Essential Works of Foucault, 1954–1984* (New York: The New Press, 1998), 263.

17. "The epistemological field traversed by the human sciences was not laid down in advance," Foucault argues: "no philosophy, no political or moral option, no empirical science of any kind . . . had ever encountered . . . anything like man; for man did not exist (any more than life, or language, or labour)." Michel Foucault, *The Order of Things: An Archeology of the Human Sciences* (New York: Vintage, 1973), 344.

18. Foucault, *The Order of Things*, 387.

19. To the reader attempting a natural history of the university: We support your efforts and would like to buy you a round of drinks.

20. With his genealogical turn, Foucault construes his own practice as both transient and instrumental, immanent to the institutions that enable it and capable of generating alternate forms. The lectures collected in *Society Must Be Defended*, for instance, begin with the reminder that genealogies are "antisciences" in that they conduct an "insurrection against the centralizing power-effects that are bound up with the institutionalization and workings of any scientific discourse organized in a society such as ours." Disciplines that in *The Order of Things* appear among "the human sciences" and that illustrate a shift in the relationship between signs and empirical order reappear in the lectures as part of a millennia-long story about institutionally situated knowledges that enable and contest the management of populations. Michel Foucault, *Society Must Be Defended: Lectures at the Collège de France, 1975–76* (New York: Picador, 2003), 9.

21. Michel Foucault, "Nietzsche, Genealogy, History," in *Aesthetics, Method, and Epistemology*, ed. James D. Faubion (New York: The New Press, 1998), 380.

1. CAMPUS LIFE

1. Historians of this tendency describe a trajectory that runs from early-twentieth-century efforts to control the "chaos" of the elective system, through more energetic efforts to design transdisciplinary courses and curricula after the Great War, diminished enthusiasm in the Great Depression, renewed energy after the Second World War, implosion under political and disciplinary pressure in the late 1960s, and finally to the reintroduction of general-education schemes, often favoring distributions of courses rather than specific requirements, in the 1970s and 80s. For one rehearsal of this broader history, see Kenneth Boning, "Coherence in General Education: A Historical Look," *Journal of General Education* 56, no. 1 (n.d.): 1–16.

2. Laurence R. Veysey, *The Emergence of the American University* (Chicago: University of Chicago Press, 1965); Frederick Rudolph, *The American College and University, a History* (New York: Knopf, 1962).

3. Daniel A. Clark, *Creating the College Man: American Mass Magazines and Middle-Class Manhood, 1890–1915* (Madison: University of Wisconsin Press, 2010); Andrew

Jewett, *Science, Democracy, and the American University: From the Civil War to the Cold War* (Cambridge: Cambridge University Press, 2012); Christopher Newfield, *Ivy and Industry: Business and the Making of the American University, 1880–1980* (Durham, NC: Duke University Press, 2003); Julie A. Reuben, *The Making of the Modern University: Intellectual Transformation and the Marginalization of Morality* (Chicago: University of Chicago Press, 1996); John R. Thelin, *A History of American Higher Education* (Baltimore, MD: Johns Hopkins University Press, 2011).

4. Charles Clotfelter et al., *Economic Challenges in Higher Education* (Chicago: University of Chicago Press, 1991), 31.

5. To bracket the shift: John Dewey, an early adopter, earned his PhD from Johns Hopkins University in 1884, while Robert Ezra Park, after earning an MA from Harvard, went to Heidelberg to earn his PhD in 1903—it still made sense at the time, particularly in Park's discipline of sociology. By 1930, they had trained decades of PhDs at Chicago (Dewey and Park) and Columbia (Dewey).

6. Thelin, *A History of American Higher Education*, 114. On this point see also Clark, *Creating the College Man*; and Richard Ohmann, *Selling Culture: Magazines, Markets and Class at the Turn of the Century* (New York: Verso, 1998).

7. Thelin, *A History of American Higher Education*, 156.

8. Thelin, *A History of American Higher Education*, 163.

9. Wisconsin laid out an elective system as early as the 1860s. See Merle Curti and Vernon Carstensen, *The University of Wisconsin: A History: 1848–1925* (Madison: University of Wisconsin, 1949), 1:79. Harvard's president Charles William Eliot moved that school toward such a system in the following decade. See Rudolph, *The American College and University*, 294.

10. Rudolph, *The American College and University*, 294.

11. See Jewett, *Science, Democracy, and the American University*, 198; and Edwin Emery Slosson, *Great American Universities* (New York, 1910), 29–31.

12. "Elective System Decried by Frank," *Harvard Crimson*, March 22, 1926, http://www.thecrimson.com/article/1926/3/22/elective-system-decried-by-frank-pmethods/.

13. That game was "the symbolic event that bound together all students, past and present." Helen Lefkowitz Horowitz, *Campus Life* (Chicago: University of Chicago Press, 1987), 131–32.

14. Horowitz, *Campus Life*, 111.

15. Quoted in Paula S. Fass, *The Damned and the Beautiful: American Youth in the 1920s* (Oxford: Oxford University Press, 1979), 182. Similarly: "When we all decide to put a shoulder to these activities," the Duke *Chronicle* averred in 1919, "we, as students, have done our share for our college" (quoted on 426n25).

16. George W. Pierson, *A Yale Book of Numbers: Historical Statistics of the College and University, 1701–1976* (New Haven, CT: Yale University Press, 1983), 8.

17. Raymond Schmidt, *Shaping College Football: The Transformation of an American Sport, 1919–1930* (Syracuse, NY: Syracuse University Press, 2007), 39–47. Schmidt notes (52–53) that not all the football powers managed to build such large facilities: both Chicago and Notre Dame failed in this regard. Other schools rued their construction almost immediately: the stock market collapsed before Iowa, Nebraska, Michigan, and Missouri had repaid their stadium-related obligations.

18. Rudolph, *The American College and University*, 389. US Bureau of Labor Statistics, "CPI Inflation Calculator," https://www.bls.gov/data/inflation_calculator.htm.

19. This point descends from Siegfried Kracauer's observation that stadium crowds "arranged by the stands in tier upon ordered tier" had something in common with the ornamental patterns displayed beneath them. Kracauer had been inspired not by gridiron contests (which have winning as an aim) but by the massed chorines, in which the point was patterning itself. We think the point borrowable, mutatis mutandis. Sigfried Kracauer, "Mass Ornament," in *The Mass Ornament: Weimar Essays*, trans. Thomas Y. Levin (Cambridge, MA: Harvard University Press, 1995), 75–76.

20. "Sports coverage increased by 50 percent over the first two decades of the new century, then more than doubled in the 1920s as it became a major reason for men to buy newspapers." Tabloids, especially the New York *Daily News*, relied on their sports coverage to entice readers, and the "sports section that we know today" became uniform in the broadsheets during the 1920s and 1930s. Michael Oriard, *King Football: Sport and Spectacle in the Golden Age of Radio and Newsreels, Movies and Magazines, the Weekly and the Daily Press* (Chapel Hill: University of North Carolina Press, 2001), 25–27.

21. Oriard, *King Football*, 23–25.

22. Quoted in Oriard, *King Football*, 164.

23. *The Freshman*, dir. Fred C. Newmeyer (1925; Pathé Exchange).

24. *The Wild Party*, dir. Dorothy Arzner (1929; Paramount Pictures).

25. For a case study describing how turn-of-the-century print fiction popularized college attendance as a pathway to middle-class manhood, see Christian K. Anderson and Daniel A. Clark, "Imagining Harvard: Changing Visions of Harvard in Fiction, 1890–1940," *American Educational History Journal* 39, no. 1 (2012): 181–99.

26. Quoted in Robin Lester, *Stagg's University: The Rise, Decline, and Fall of Big-Time Football at Chicago* (Urbana: University of Illinois Press, 1999), 19.

27. Ronald A. Smith, *Sports and Freedom: The Rise of Big-Time College Athletics* (New York: Oxford University Press, 1988), 131.

28. Irving Babbitt, *Literature and the American College: Essays in Defense of the Humanities* (Boston: Houghton Mifflin, 1908), 77–78.

29. Harvard University, *Report of the President of Harvard College and Reports of Departments 1920–21* (Cambridge, MA: Harvard University, 1922), 13–14.

30. Eleven deaths were reported in 1909 alone. Stories about paying students and dirty recruiting practices appeared in *McClure's*, *Harper's*, and the *Saturday Evening Post*, among other periodicals. John R. Thelin, *Games Colleges Play: Scandal and Reform in Intercollegiate Athletics* (Baltimore, MD: Johns Hopkins University Press, 2011), 15. See also John Sayle Watterson, *College Football: History, Spectacle, Controversy* (Baltimore, MD: Johns Hopkins University Press, 2000), 161.

31. Glenn E. Hoover, "College Football," *New Republic* (April 14, 1926): 256–58.

32. Howard J. Savage, *American College Athletics* (New York: Carnegie Foundation for the Advancement of Teaching, 1929), 141, 158, 310.

33. Quoted in Thelin, *Games Colleges Play*, 13.

34. Lester, *Stagg's University*, 17.

35. "The athletic work of the students is a vital part of the student life," Harper explained at the spring convocation in 1899, "a real and essential part of college education." Quoted in Lester, *Stagg's University*, 19.

36. Stagg thrived in the "enterprising environment" Harper sought to engender. Thelin, *A History of American Higher Education*, 179. Establishing football as a way of connecting with new alumni was a key part of this program: "Sitting in the stadium with a view of some of the campus buildings . . . will stir sentiment for the Alma Mater." Quoted in Schmidt, *Shaping College Football*, 48.

37. Oriard, *King Football*, 41.

38. John W. Boyer, "The Organization of the College and the Divisions," *Occasional Papers on Higher Education*, University of Chicago (October 30, 2001), https://col lege.uchicago.edu/sites/college.uchicago.edu/files/attachments/Boyer_Occasion alPapers_V8.pdf. See also William H. McNeill, *Hutchins' University: A Memoir of the University of Chicago, 1929–1950* (Chicago: University of Chicago Press, 2007), 29.

39. Quoted in Boyer, "The Organization of the College and the Divisions," 46.

40. Quoted in Watterson, *College Football*, 194.

41. Alums lost interest as well. Reporting to a fellow graduate via telegraph in 1939, the influential Chicago fundraiser John Nuveen recounted, "They [the alumni board] feel we should either play better football or discontinue playing." Quoted in Watterson, *College Football*, 194.

42. But not forever. Football returned as a club team in 1963 and as a varsity sport in 1969. It never returned to the champion status of Maroons football in the early decades of the century, however.

43. A commonly cited precursor is Amherst's two-part freshman survey, introduced in 1915, which President Alexander Meiklejohn called a "sane, searching, revealing of the facts of the human situation and a showing of the intellectual method by which these situations may be understood." Quoted in Adam R. Nelson, *Education and Democracy: The Meaning of Alexander Meiklejohn, 1872–1964* (Madison: University of Wisconsin Press, 2009), 73.

44. Quoted in Gilbert Allardyce, "The Rise and Fall of the Western Civilization Course," *American Historical Review* 87, no. 3 (June 1, 1982): 706–7.

45. See Jewett, *Science, Democracy, and the American University*, 203; and Allardyce, "The Rise and Fall of the Western Civilization Course," 707.

46. "Beyond its appeal to professors as an outlet for their patriotism, the War Issues Course was praised for having demonstrated the desirability and feasibility of educational reform to breach the walls separating the disciplines, to introduce some order in the chaos of the elective system, and to make room in the curriculum for the problems of the contemporary world." Carol S. Gruber, *Mars and Minerva: World War I and the Uses of the Higher Learning in America* (Baton Rouge: Louisiana State University Press, 1975), 243.

47. Herbert E. Hawkes, "A College Course on Peace Issues," *Educational Review* 58 (September 1919): 144, 150.

48. See Allardyce, "The Rise and Fall of the Western Civilization Course," 722; and Harry J. Carman, "Reminiscences of Thirty Years," *Journal of Higher Education* 22, no. 3 (March 1, 1951): 115–69.

49. Quoted in Gruber, *Mars and Minerva*, 244.

50. John Erskine, *My Life as a Teacher* (Philadelphia: Lippincott, 1948), 161.

51. Erskine, *My Life as a Teacher*, 169.

52. See Allardyce, "The Rise and Fall of the Western Civilization Course," 721; and Jewett, *Science, Democracy, and the American University*.

53. The course form has been summarized by its historian Gilbert Allardyce as "European history with American relevance—liberal, 'progressive,' concentrated on modern history and based on the premise of a common history that bound together the North Atlantic nations, connected the United States to the European past, and established Western preponderance in the world." Allardyce, "The Rise and Fall of the Western Civilization Course," 708.

54. See Julie Thompson Klein, *Interdisciplinarity: History, Theory, and Practice* (Detroit: Wayne State University Press, 1990); and for particular emphasis on the liberal arts and humanities, see Julie Thompson Klein, *Humanities, Culture, and Interdisciplinarity: The Changing American Academy* (Albany: State University of New York Press, 2005).

55. Carman, "Reminiscences of Thirty Years," 121.

56. "The word 'humanities' saw relatively infrequent use in America either by . . . classicists or by members of the younger humanistic disciplines until the end of the 1930s. It surfaces in print on scattered occasions, but far less often than the phrases 'culture' or 'liberal education.' More than these alternatives, one suspects, it was handicapped by musty connotations in an era when most men were anxious to appear up-to-date." Laurence R. Veysey, "The Plural Organized Worlds of the Humanities," in *The Organization of Knowledge in Modern America, 1860–1920*, ed. Alexandra Oleson and John Voss (Baltimore, MD: Johns Hopkins University Press, 1979), 51–106. Also see Bruce Kuklick, "The Emergence of the Humanities," *South Atlantic Quarterly* 81, no.1 (1990): 195–206.

57. Harold Innis, for one, made this connection, describing cinema and textbooks equally figuring the "monopolies of knowledge" encouraged by mechanization. H. A. Innis, *Empire and Communication* (Oxford: Clarendon, 1950), Project Gutenberg ed., 205–6, http://www.gutenberg.ca/ebooks/innis-empire/innis-empire-00-h.html. See Daniel A. Segal, "'Western Civ' and the Staging of History in American Higher Education," *American Historical Review* 105, no. 3 (2000): 770–805. See also Allardyce, "The Rise and Fall of the Western Civilization Course."

58. Carolyn C. Lougee, Morris Rossabi, and William F. Woehrlin, "[The Rise and Fall of the Western Civilization Course]: Comments," *American Historical Review* 87, no. 3 (June 1, 1982): 734.

59. Marshall McLuhan, *Understanding Media: The Extensions of Man*, ed. W. Terrence Gordon (Corte Madera, CA: Gingko Press, 2003), 19.

60. Mark Dowie, *American Foundations: An Investigative History* (Cambridge, MA: MIT Press, 2002), 27–28.

61. Carnegie Endowment for the Advancement of Teaching, *Second Annual Report of the President and Treasurer* (New York: Carnegie Foundation for the Advancement of Teaching, 1907), 20–26.

62. Carnegie Endowment for the Advancement of Teaching, *A Comprehensive Plan of Insurance and Annuities for College Teachers* (New York: Carnegie Foundation for the Advancement of Teaching, 1916), 52.

63. Carnegie Endowment for the Advancement of Teaching, *Second Annual Report of the President and Treasurer*, 63.

64. Quoted in Elena Silva, Taylor White, and Thomas Toch, *The Carnegie Unit: A Century-Old Standard in a Changing Educational Landscape* (New York: Carnegie Foundation for the Advancement of Learning, 2015), 6.

65. Carnegie Endowment for the Advancement of Teaching, *First Annual Report of the Carnegie Endowment of the President and Treasurer* (New York: Carnegie Foundation for the Advancement of Teaching, 1906), 38.

66. Carnegie Endowment for the Advancement of Teaching, *First Annual Report of the Carnegie Endowment of the President and Treasurer* 38–39.

67. Quoted in Silva et al., *The Carnegie Unit*, 8.

68. Carnegie Endowment for the Advancement of Teaching, *Second Annual Report of the President and Treasurer*, 63.

69. That said, the standard, multiple-choice exam would not feature prominently in college admissions until after the Second World War. Nicholas Lemann, *The Big Test: The Secret History of the American Meritocracy* (New York: Macmillan, 2000).

70. Starting with the Carnegie list, the AAU added selected sectarian institutions, which Carnegie did not consider. AAU institutions would admit as graduate students only those with bachelor's degrees from these institutions. It also recommended that German states consider bachelor's degrees from these schools equivalent to the *Maturitatszeugnis*. Audrey N. Slate, *AGS: A History* (Washington, DC: Association of Graduate Schools in the Association of American Universities, 1994), 36–37.

71. Irving Babbitt, *Democracy and Leadership* (Boston: Houghton, Mifflin Company, 1924), 240.

72. Thorstein Veblen, *The Higher Learning in America: A Memorandum on the Conduct of Universities by Business Men* (New York: B. W. Huebsch, 1918), 25–26.

73. Veblen, *The Higher Learning in America*, 26.

74. Veblen, *The Higher Learning in America*, v–vi.

75. Veblen, *The Higher Learning in America*, 229, 222–24.

76. William James, "The PhD Octopus," *Harvard Monthly* (March 1903): 1–9.

77. Paul DiMaggio, "Market Structure, the Creative Process, and Popular Culture: Toward an Organizational Reinterpretation of Mass Culture Theory," *Journal of Popular Culture*, 11, no. 2 (1977): 433–51.

78. For a synoptic overview, see Thelin, *A History of American Higher Education*, 127–28; for a more detailed account, see Thomas L. Haskell, *The Emergence of Professional Social Science: The American Social Science Association and the Nineteenth-Century Crisis of Authority* (Urbana: University of Illinois Press, 1977).

79. See Newfield, *Ivy and Industry*.

80. Rudolph, *The American College and University*, 399.

81. Quoted in Rudolph, *The American College and University*, 401.

82. James Champion Stone and Don DeNevi, *Portraits of the American University, 1890–1910* (San Francisco: Jossey-Bass, 1971), 37.

83. On the emergence of this theme with variations, see Ellen Schrecker, *The Lost Soul of Higher Education: Corporatization, the Assault on Academic Freedom, and the End of the American University* (New York: The New Press, 2010), 15.

84. The American system "mandates that decisions about what counts as good work in sociology shall be made by sociologists. And, practically speaking, 'sociologists' means the department of sociology." Louis Menand, *The Future of Academic Freedom* (Chicago: University of Chicago Press, 1998), 17.

85. Richard Hofstadter and W. P. Metzger, *The Development of Academic Freedom in the United States* (New York: Columbia University Press, 1955), 457.

86. Erwin Panofsky, "Three Decades of Art History in the United States: Impressions of a Transplanted European," *College Art Journal* 14, no. 1 (1954): 10, 22–24.
87. Rudolph, *The American College and University*, 400.
88. Curti and Carstensen, *The University of Wisconsin: A History: 1848–1925*, 2: 342, 348.
89. A proposition that has been challenged. See "In Elite Schools' Vast Endowments, Malcolm Gladwell Sees 'Obscene' Inequity," *Weekend Edition Saturday*, NPR, August 22, 2015, http://www.npr.org/2015/08/22/433735934/in-elite-schools-vast-war-chests-malcolm-gladwell-sees-obscene-inequity.

2. PUBLIC RELATIONS

1. We take this to be a postrevisionist consensus as exemplified by Julie A. Reuben, *The Making of the Modern University: Intellectual Transformation and the Marginalization of Morality* (Chicago: University of Chicago Press, 1996); and Andrew Jewett, *Science, Democracy, and the American University: From the Civil War to the Cold War* (Cambridge: Cambridge University Press, 2012).
2. Gregory Waller, "Institutionalizing Educational Cinema in the United States During the Early 1920s," in *Institutionalization of Educational Cinema*, ed. Marina Dahlquist and Joel Frykholm (forthcoming).
3. Graham Wallas, *The Great Society: A Psychological Analysis* (New York: Macmillan, 1914).
4. Shawn Shimpach, " 'Only in This Way Is Social Progress Possible': Early Cinema, Gender, and the Social Survey Movement." *Feminist Media Histories* 3, no. 3 (2017): 82–102.
5. John Erskine, *My Life as a Teacher* (Philadelphia: Lippincott, 1948), 144.
6. Dana B. Polan, *Scenes of Instruction: The Beginnings of the US Study of Film* (Berkeley: University of California Press, 2007), 357.
7. Erskine, *My Life as a Teacher*, 207.
8. See Ray on the history of the lyceum and its "deep roots in the particularities of British American Protestantism." "Although the relative value of the education and entertainment functions" of the Lyceum "changed through time," she explains, "both strands were ever present." In particular, "debates provided both serious training in argumentation and recreation for leisure hours in a clublike setting." Angela G. Ray, *The Lyceum and Public Culture in the Nineteenth-Century United States* (East Lansing: Michigan State University Press, 2005), 7, 174.
9. Erskine, *My Life as a Teacher*, 208.
10. Erwin Panofsky, "Three Decades of Art History in the United States: Impressions of a Transplanted European," *College Art Journal* 14 (1954): 12.
11. "The personalities, rather than the intellects, of the men who took part in the big Humanism debate in Carnegie Hall last week, won the interest of the young lady who accompanied us there," wrote the *New Yorker*'s correspondent. "Her attention kept drifting from what Mr. Irving Babbitt, the great Humanist leader, was saying to the way he wore his evening clothes," while of Van Doren, she remarked, "He's been playing tennis. . . . See how ruddy and healthy he looks." The reporter is little better, trying "to concentrate" on Canby's arguments and ruffling at Van

Doren's attack on Babbitt "in a most indecorous and unfair manner." "Humanists and Others," *New Yorker*, May 17, 1930. See Jewett, *Science, Democracy, and the American University*, 219.

12. Jewett, *Science, Democracy, and the American University*, 16.

13. Babbitt framed a struggle to reject the "humanitarianism" of the Progressive research university in favor of a new "humanism" that would provide standards of "discipline and selection." "At this crisis," he wrote, "when our crying need is a humane principle of restraint, the best that our sentimental and scientific humanitarians can evolve between them is a scheme for training for service and training for power." Irving Babbitt, *Literature and the American College: Essays in Defense of the Humanities* (Boston: Houghton Mifflin, 1908), 67.

14. A. A. Roback, "Review," *Philosophical Review* 36, no. 2 (March 1, 1927): 191, 194.

15. Moselio Schaechter, "The *Microbe Hunters* by Paul DeKruif—a Major Force in Microbiological History," *Small Things Considered Blog*, April 3, 2014, http://schaechter.asmblog.org/schaechter/2014/04/the-microbe-hunters-by-paul-dekruif-a-major-force-in-microbiological-history.html.

16. William C. Summers, "*Microbe Hunters* Revisited," *International Microbiology* 1, no. 1 (1998): 65.

17. Thurs and LaFollette are more ambivalent on this question. Daniel Patrick Thurs, *Science Talk: Changing Notions of Science in American Popular Culture* (New Brunswick, NJ: Rutgers University Press, 2007); Marcel C. LaFollette, *Making Science Our Own: Public Images of Science, 1910–1955* (Chicago: University of Chicago Press, 1990). Burnham thinks it was very bad for science, amounting to the triumph of a new form of superstition. John C. Burnham, *How Superstition Won and Science Lost: Popularizing Science and Health in the United States* (New Brunswick, NJ: Rutgers University Press, 1987).

18. Thurs, *Science Talk*, 2.

19. Jewett, *Science, Democracy, and the American University*, 211.

20. Milton Sanford Mayer and John Harland Hicks, *Robert Maynard Hutchins: A Memoir* (Berkeley: University of California Press, 1993), 293.

21. Mayer and Hicks, *Robert Maynard Hutchins*, 295–96; Mary Ann Dzuback, *Robert M. Hutchins: Portrait of an Educator* (Chicago: University of Chicago Press, 1991), 221. To generate the list that would be Great Books of the Western World (443 works by seventy-four authors in a fifty-four book set) took two years of deliberation among the members of an advisory board that included Erskine, Van Doren, and Alexander Meiklejohn (a veteran whose work designing and promoting a short-lived Experimental College at the University of Wisconsin had landed him on the cover of *Time* in 1928). Adam R. Nelson, *Education and Democracy: The Meaning of Alexander Meiklejohn, 1872–1964* (Madison: University of Wisconsin Press, 2009).

22. Erskine, *My Life as a Teacher*, 173–74.

23. In addition to continuing the legacy of Adler-style humanism, the Aspen Institute and the co-located International Design Conference synthesized and extended the midcentury approaches to communications and design we discuss in chapter 4. Both were projects of cultural administration. See Justus Nieland, *Happiness by Design: Modernism, Film, and Media in the Eames Era* (Minneapolis: University of Minnesota Press, in press), chap. 3.

24. William H. McNeil, *Hutchins' University: A Memoir of the University of Chicago, 1929–1950* (Chicago: University of Chicago Press, 2007), 122.

25. Polan, *Scenes of Instruction.*

26. Lee Grieveson and Haidee Wasson, *Inventing Film Studies* (Durham, NC: Duke University Press, 2008).

27. Antonia Lant and Ingrid Periz, eds., *The Red Velvet Seat: Women's Writings on the First Fifty Years of Cinema* (New York: Verso, 2006).

28. Lee Grieveson, "Cinema Studies and the Conduct of Conduct," in Lee Grieveson and Haidee Wasson, *Inventing Film Studies* (Durham, NC: Duke University Press, 2008), 3–37.

29. Joseph P. Kennedy, *The Story of the Films, as Told by Leaders of the Industry to the Students of the Graduate School of Business Administration, George F. Baker Foundation, Harvard University* (Chicago: A. W. Shaw Co., 1927).

30. "The Motion Picture in Its Economic and Social Aspects": special issue, ed. Clyde L. King and Frank A. Tichenor, *Annals of the American Academy of Political and Social Science* 128, no. 217 (November 1926).

31. Jennifer Horne, "A History Long Overdue: The Public Library and Motion Pictures," in *Useful Cinema*, ed. Charles R. Acland and Haidee Wasson (Durham, NC: Duke University Press, 2011), 149–77.

32. See John Nichols, "Countering Censorship: Edgar Dale and the Film Appreciation Movement," *Cinema Journal* 46, no. 1 (October 1, 2006): 3–22. See also Eric Smoodin, "'What a Power for Education!': The Cinema and Sites of Learning in the 1930s," in *Useful Cinema*, ed. Charles R. Acland and Haidee Wasson (Durham, NC: Duke University Press, 2011), 17–33.

33. Shimpach, "'Only in This Way.'"

34. Haidee Wasson, *Museum Movies: The Museum of Modern Art and the Birth of Art Cinema* (Berkeley: University of California Press, 2005).

35. Quoted in Lant and Periz, *The Red Velvet Seat*, 230.

36. Devin Orgeron, Marsha Orgeron, and Dan Streible, *Learning with the Lights Off: Educational Film in the United States* (New York: Oxford University Press, 2012).

37. Waller, "Institutionalizing Educational Cinema."

38. Hugo Münsterberg, *The Photoplay: A Psychological Study* (New York: D. Appleton and Co., 1916), 228–29.

39. Quoted in Gilbert Allardyce, "The Rise and Fall of the Western Civilization Course," *American Historical Review* 87, no. 3 (June 1, 1982): 701.

40. Quoted in Laurence R. Veysey, *The Emergence of the American University* (Chicago: University of Chicago Press, 1965), 231.

41. Münsterberg held a three-year appointment at Harvard from 1892 to 1895. After failing to secure a permanent position in Germany, he returned to a permanent post at Harvard in 1897. "Münsterberg, Hugo," American National Biography Online, http://www.anb.org/articles/14/14-00431.html.

42. Mark Lynn Anderson, "Taking Liberties: The Payne Fund Studies and the Creation of the Media Expert," in *Inventing Film Studies*, ed. Lee Grieveson and Haidee Wasson (Durham, NC: Duke University Press, 2008), 38–65.

43. Chicago's President Hutchins explained this in the foreword to Frederick Devereux, *The Educational Talking Picture* (Chicago: University of Chicago Press, 1933). On pages 142–44, that same volume noted how NYU's School of Commerce

and Accounts used film in an orientation course and predicted further applications in professional schools of all sorts (court scenes might be screened in law school, surgery films in medical school).

44. Quoted in Virginia Lantz Denton, *Booker T. Washington and the Adult Education Movement* (Gainesville: University Press of Florida, 1993), 106.

45. Denton, *Booker T. Washington*, 107.

46. Quoted in Denton, *Booker T. Washington*, 153.

47. University of the State of New York, *Regents' Bulletin* (Albany: University of the State of New York, 1891), 133.

48. Jewett, *Science, Democracy, and the American University*, 214–15.

49. Evening law schools in particular thrived until the lawyers' field began to professionalize more intensely and the American Bar Association tightened standards by requiring two years of undergraduate education before admission to an accredited program. Business schools like the NYU School of Commerce, Accounts, and Finance fought to fend off proprietary-school competition. NYU's secret weapon was that it served as the administrator for the New York State accountancy accreditation exam. Joseph F. Kett, *The Pursuit of Knowledge Under Difficulties: From Self-Improvement to Adult Education in America, 1750–1990* (Stanford, CA: Stanford University Press, 1994), 264–65, 272.

50. Michael Shinagel, *"The Gates Unbarred": A History of University Extension at Harvard, 1910–2009* (Cambridge, MA: Harvard University Press, 2009).

51. Charles T. Copeland's class on English literature invariably had the largest enrollments. See Shinagel, *"The Gates Unbarred"*, 43–44.

52. John R. Thelin, *A History of American Higher Education* (Baltimore, MD: Johns Hopkins University Press, 2011), 136.

53. Eduard Lindeman, *The Meaning of Adult Education* (New York: New Republic, 1926), 177.

54. Lindeman, *The Meaning of Adult Education*, 187–88.

55. Lindeman, *The Meaning of Adult Education*, 141.

56. Lindeman, *The Meaning of Adult Education*, 178.

57. Kett, *The Pursuit of Knowledge Under Difficulties*, 236–40.

58. New York, *Regents' Bulletin*, 1429.

59. Merle Curti and Vernon Carstensen, *The University of Wisconsin: A History, 1848–1925* (Madison: University of Wisconsin Press, 1949), 2:572.

60. Alfred Charles True, *A History of Agricultural Extension Work in the United States, 1785–1923* (Washington, DC: US Government Printing Office, 1928), 44.

61. Kett, *The Pursuit of Knowledge Under Difficulties*, 235.

62. Kett, *The Pursuit of Knowledge Under Difficulties*, 238.

63. Kett, *The Pursuit of Knowledge Under Difficulties*, 238. US Bureau of Labor Statistics, CPI Inflation Calculator, https://data.bls.gov/cgi-bin/cpicalc.pl.

64. Quoted in Curti and Carstensen, *The University of Wisconsin*, 2:563–64.

65. Curti and Carstensen, *The University of Wisconsin*, 2:573.

66. Eric Anthony Moyen, *Frank L. McVey and the University of Kentucky: A Progressive President and the Modernization of a Southern University* (Lexington: University Press of Kentucky, 2011), 81.

67. Polan, *Scenes of Instruction*, 26.

68. Picture study was "a synthetic method wherein all media and genres of spatial arts (representational or not) are subsumed under the concept of composition—its three main elements being line, shade and colour." Kaveh Askari, *Making Movies Into Art: Picture Craft from the Magic Lantern to Early Hollywood* (London: British Film Institute, 2015), 73.

69. Askari, *Making Movies Into Art*, 78.

70. Anne Walker Cook, "A History of the Indiana University Audio-Visual Center: 1913 to 1975," Ph.D. dissertation (Indiana University, 1980), 22. Waller, "Institutionalizing Educational Cinema."

71. Cook, "A History of the Indiana University Audio-Visual Center," 28–29.

72. L. Paul Saettler, *The Evolution of American Educational Technology* (Englewood, CO: Libraries Unlimited, 1990), 111.

73. "Extension Department Has Accomplished Great Service in South Carolina Education," *Gamecock*, January 15, 1926.

74. Devin Orgeron, Marsha Orgeron, and Dan Streible, "A History of Learning with the Lights Off," in *Learning with the Lights Off: Educational Film in the United States*, ed. Devin Orgeron, Marsha Orgeron, and Dan Streible (New York: Oxford University Press, 2012).

75. Quoted in Gregory A. Waller, "Cornering *The Wheat Farmer* (1938)," in *Learning with the Lights Off: Educational Film in the United States*, ed. Devin Orgeron, Marsha Orgeron, and Dan Streible (New York: Oxford University Press, 2012), 261.

76. Waller, "Cornering *The Wheat Farmer*," 241.

77. See Saettler, *The Evolution of American Educational Technology*; Michele Hilmes, *Network Nations: A Transnational History of British and American Broadcasting* (New York: Routledge, 2012).

78. Hugh Richard Slotten, *Radio's Hidden Voice: The Origins of Public Broadcasting in the United States* (Urbana: University of Illinois Press, 2009), 31.

79. Hilmes, *Network Nations*, 111. See also Slotten, *Radio's Hidden Voice*, 9.

80. To pick one recent and one classic example form the literature: James Livingston, *Pragmatism, Feminism, and Democracy: Rethinking the Politics of American History* (New York: Routledge, 2001); Robert H. Wiebe, *The Search for Order, 1877–1920* (Princeton, NJ: Hill and Wang, 1966).

81. James Livingston, *Origins of the Federal Reserve System: Money, Class, and Corporate Capitalism, 1890–1913* (Ithaca, NY: Cornell University Press, 1986).

82. The debate was reanimated after World War II, for instance, by C. Wright Mills, who, in updating its terms for the Cold War, also misconstrued some key positions. On Lippmann's often mischaracterized contribution to mass-communications scholarship, see Sue Curry Jansen, *Walter Lippmann: A Critical Introduction to Media and Communication Theory* (New York: Peter Lang, 2012).

83. John Dewey, *The Public and Its Problems* (1927), in *The Later Works, 1925–1953*, ed. Jo Ann Boydston (Carbondale: Southern Illinois University Press, 1981), 2:323–24.

84. "Systematic and continuous inquiry into all the conditions which affect association and their dissemination in print is a precondition of the creation of a true public," he wrote. "But it and its results are but tools after all. Their final actuality is accomplished in face-to-face relationships by means of direct give and take. . . . Publication is partial and the public which results is partially informed and

formed until the meanings it purveys pass from mouth to mouth." Dewey, *The Public and Its Problems*, 371.

85. Mary Parker Follett, *The New State: Group Organization, the Solution of Popular Government* (New York: Longmans, Green and Co., 1920).

86. See Jewett, *Science, Democracy, and the American University*, 173–74, for a discussion of Follett in relation to Dewey.

87. Curti and Carstensen, *The University of Wisconsin*, 2:90. Such public relations efforts at Wisconsin began even earlier as part of the extension system. By 1895–96, some 1,200 editors regularly received the *Bulletin for Editors* published by the university news service housed within the extension division. See Curti and Carstensen, *The University of Wisconsin*, 1:727.

88. Scott M. Cutlip, *Public Relations History: From the 17th to the 20th Century: The Antecedents* (New York: Routledge, 2013), 243, 247.

89. Moyen, *Frank L. McVey and the University of Kentucky*, 81.

90. Edward L. Bernays, *Propaganda* (New York: Horace Liveright, 1928), 140–42.

91. Edward L. Bernays, *Crystallizing Public Opinion, 1923* (New York: Boni and Liveright, 1934), 14, 53.

92. Bernays, *Propaganda*, 129.

93. Curti and Carstensen, *The University of Wisconsin*, 2:88.

94. Quoted in Frederick Rudolph, *The American College and University, a History* (New York: Knopf, 1962), 402–3.

3. COMMUNICATIONS COMPLEX

1. Quoted in Brett Gary, "Communication Research, the Rockefeller Foundation, and Mobilization for the War on Words, 1938–44," *Journal of Communication* 46, no. 3 (1996): 125.

2. Alex Roland, "Science and War," *Osiris* 1 (January 1, 1985): 247–72. Daniel J. Kevles, "George Ellery Hale, the First World War, and the Advancement of Science in America," *Isis* 59, no. 4 (December 1, 1968): 427–37.

3. For a more detailed account of how military desire to control scientific research combined with the lobbying efforts of the privately funded National Research Council to discourage academic/government collaboration once peace had been won, see Daniel J. Kevles, *The Physicists: The History of a Scientific Community in Modern America* (Cambridge, MA: Harvard University Press, 1995), 131–45.

4. Wisconsin English PhD Lenora Hanson presented early research on WARF's ongoing activities at the 2016 MLA convention. Lenora Hanson, "Tech Transfer After Academic Capitalism," presentation, Modern Language Association Convention, Austin, TX, January 10, 2016.

5. "History," Wisconsin Alumni Research Foundation, http://www.warf.org/about -us/history/history-of-warf.cmsx.

6. "Karl Paul Link," Wisconsin Alumni Research Foundation, http://www.warf.org /about-us/success-stories/karl-paul-link/karl-paul-link.cmsx.

7. Geiger observes that in the crucial four-year period after the war, the AEC, ONR, and NIH developed distinct but overlapping approaches to federal support for university research. "Instead of dominating the federal science matrix" as

Vannevar Bush and others had hoped, the NSF came late to the table and "would inherit the remaining unoccupied spaces." Roger L. Geiger, *Research and Relevant Knowledge American Research Universities Since World War II* (New York: Oxford University Press, 1993), 19.

8. US Bureau of Labor Statistics, "CPI calculator," http://www.bls.gov/data/infla tion_calculator.htm. US Department of Health and Human Services, "HHS FY1017 Budget in Brief—NIH," https://www.hhs.gov/about/budget/fy2017/budget-in-brief /nih/index.html.

9. A trend toward partnering with academic researchers outside government may be discerned as early as 1922. Donald C. Swain, "The Rise of a Research Empire: NIH, 1930 to 1950," *Science* 138, no. 3546 (December 14, 1962): 1233–34. See also Jennie J. Kronenfeld, *The Changing Federal Role in US Health Care Policy* (Santa Barbara, CA: ABC-CLIO, 1997), 72.

10. In 1979, the Department of Education was spun off from the Department of Health, Education, and Welfare, which had been established in 1953, with the Women's Army Corp veteran Oveta Culp Hobby as its first secretary. The NIH remained part of the renamed Department of Health and Human Services.

11. Wyndham D. Miles, "A History of the National Library of Medicine," US National Library of Medicine Digital Collections, https://collections.nlm.nih.gov/catalog /nlm:nlmuid-8218545-bk, 36.

12. Miles, "A History of the National Library of Medicine," 293–94.

13. Miles, "A History of the National Library of Medicine," 281, 300.

14. It handled more than six thousand requests in its first fiscal year (1941–42) and more than nine thousand orders in December 1944 alone. In 1945, it produced over two million pages of negative film and more than double that amount of positive film, "about 90 percent of which went to medical units overseas." Miles, "A History of the National Library of Medicine," 300–1.

15. V-mail provided a relatively secure wartime channel of communication between civilians at home and soldiers on the front. Messages written on special forms were censored, microfilmed, shipped abroad, and then printed for their recipients.

16. Miles, "A History of the National Library of Medicine," 331.

17. Miles, "A History of the National Library of Medicine," 355.

18. Colin Burke, *It Wasn't All Magic* (Washington, DC: Center for Cryptological History, National Security Agency, 2002), 15–18.

19. Harold D. Lasswell, "The Structure and Function of Communication in Society," in *The Communication of Ideas: A Series of Addresses*, ed. Lyman Bryson (New York: Cooper Square, 1948), 37.

20. Claude Shannon, "A Mathematical Theory of Communication," *Bell System Technical Journal* 27 (1948): 379–423, 623–56.

21. Claude E. Shannon and Warren Weaver, *The Mathematical Theory of Communication* (Urbana: University of Illinois Press, 1949), 8–9.

22. Because, Boltzmann writes, "it is related to the number of alternatives which remain possible to a physical system after all the macroscopically observable information concerning it has been recorded." This notion was subsequently developed by Leo Slizzard and John von Neumann. Shannon and Weaver, *The Mathematical Theory of Communication*, 3n1.

23. Shannon and Weaver, *The Mathematical Theory of Communication*, 9–10.
24. Shannon and Weaver, *The Mathematical Theory of Communication*, 7.
25. Shannon and Weaver, *The Mathematical Theory of Communication*, 33.
26. See Jonathan Sterne, *MP3: The Meaning of a Format* (Durham, NC: Duke University Press, 2012).
27. Homer, *The Wrath of Achilles: The Iliad of Homer*, trans. I. A. Richards (New York: Norton, 1950), 24–25.
28. I. A. Richards, *Practical Criticism* (London: Kegan Paul, 1930). New Criticism enshrined a wider modernist investment in communication evidenced in the literary and essayistic writing of poets like T. S. Eliot and novelists such as F. Scott Fitzgerald. In so doing, however, it executed its own reduction, excluding much of the period's literature from an approved New Critical canon. Mark Goble, *Beautiful Circuits: Modernism and the Mediated Life* (New York: Columbia University Press, 2013); Mark Wollaeger, *Modernism, Media, and Propaganda: British Narrative from 1900 to 1945* (Princeton, NJ: Princeton University Press, 2008). See also John Guillory, "Genesis of the Media Concept," *Critical Inquiry* 36, no. 2 (January 1, 2010): 321–62.
29. According to Gary, Richards worked against the grain in the seminar, submitting papers on "semantics" that none of the other members terribly wanted to read. Gary, "Communication Research," 136–37.
30. Cleanth Brooks and Robert Penn Warren, *Understanding Poetry*, rev ed. (New York: Holt, 1950), xxxvii.
31. John Crowe Ransom, "Criticism, Inc," *VQR: A National Journal of Literature & Discussion* 13, no. 4 (1937), http://www.vqronline.org/essay/criticism-inc-0.
32. Gary, "Communication Research," 144. Cf. Jefferson Pooley, "The New History of Mass Communication Research," in *The History of Media and Communication Research: Contested Memories*, ed. David W. Park and Jefferson Pooley (New York: Peter Lang, 2008), 54.
33. See Brett Gary, *The Nervous Liberals* (New York: Columbia University Press, 1999), and J. Michael Sproule, *Propaganda and Democracy: The American Experience of Media and Mass Persuasion* (New York: Cambridge University Press, 2005).
34. On the seminar as self-conscious precursor to propaganda efforts, see Pooley, "The New History of Mass Communication Research." Gary argues that the seminar "took up the slack," for a Roosevelt administration "hamstrung politically" by isolationism and "bad memories from World War I." Gary, "Communication Research," 125.
35. Gary, "Communication Research," 125.
36. Gary, "Communication Research," 130.
37. Gabriel A. Almond, "Harold Dwight Lasswell 1902–1978 A Biographical Memoir" (Washington DC: National Academy of Sciences, 1987).
38. Lerner's *The Passing of Traditional Society: Modernizing the Middle East* (1958) influenced use of mass media in US Cold War policy. Hemant Shah, *The Production of Modernization: Daniel Lerner, Mass Media, and The Passing of Traditional Society* (Philadelphia: Temple University Press, 2011).
39. For a convenient list of scholars and the wartime agencies that employed them, see table 12.1 in Christopher Simpson, "US Mass Communication Research, Counterinsurgency, and Scientific 'Reality,'" in *Communication Researchers*

and Policy-Making, ed. Sandra Braman (Cambridge, MA: MIT Press, 2003), 253–92.

40. Pooley, "The New History of Mass Communication Research," 55–56.

41. Wilbur Schramm, *The Beginnings of Communication Study in America: A Personal Memoir* (Thousand Oaks, CA: Sage, 1997), 92, 95.

42. See Christopher Simpson, *Science of Coercion: Communication Research and Psychological Warfare, 1945–1960* (New York: Oxford University Press, 1994), 63, 108–9.

43. Simpson, *Science of Coercion*, 52.

44. John W. Riley, *The Reds Take a City: The Communist Occupation of Seoul, with Eyewitness Accounts* (New Brunswick, NJ: Rutgers University Press, 1951), 32.

45. That it was designed as a USIA training manual is reported as positive by Katz in his 1956 *American Journal of Sociology* review because it lent an emphasis on international communication, an important and undeveloped research area, to the selections. Elihu Katz, "Review of Process and Effects of Mass Communication by Wilbur Schramm," *American Journal of Sociology* 61, no. 6 (May 1, 1956): 638–39. A revised edition of the influential volume appeared in 1971. Schramm and his coeditor Donald Roberts reported in their foreword that the 1954 version "did not sell enough to make the University of Illinois Press rich, but it sold steadily." Wilbur Schramm, *The Process and Effects of Mass Communication*, rev. ed. (Urbana: University of Illinois Press, 1971).

46. According to Simpson, "Several of the more important academics engaged in mass communication studies became activist supporters of US psychological warfare projects and derived part of their income from participation in such efforts over a period of at least two decades." He believes some State Department contracts (with the National Opinion Research Center) were illegal holdovers of OWI contracts during the war. Simpson, *Science of Coercion*, 54–55.

47. Allen H. Barton, "Paul Lazarsfeld and Applied Social Research," *Social Science History* 3, no. 3 (1979): 4–44.

48. Barton, "Paul Lazarsfeld," 6.

49. Jefferson Pooley, "Fifteen Pages That Shook the Field: 'Personal Influence,' Edward Shils, and the Remembered History of Mass Communication Research," *Annals of the American Academy of Political and Social Science* 608 (November 1, 2006): 130–56, 144.

50. Peter Simonson and Lauren Archer, "Women in Media Research," *Out of the Question*, http://outofthequestion.org/Women-in-Media-Research/Office-of-Radio-Research-Bureau-of-Applied-Social-Research.aspx.

51. See, e.g., Paul Felix Lazarsfeld, "Remarks on Administrative and Critical Communications Research," *Studies in Philosophy and Social Science* 9, no. 1 (1941): 2–16.

52. See Martin Jay, *The Dialectical Imagination: A History of the Frankfurt School and the Institute of Social Research, 1923–1950* (Berkeley: University of California Press, 1996), 168. According to the PsyOps veterans Herbert Friedman and Franklin Prosser, the Psychological Warfare Branch (est. 1942) and the Psychological Warfare Division (est. 1943) were separate, parallel operations, both under Allied command. Herbert Friedman and Franklin Prosser, "The United States PSYOP Organization in Europe During World War II," November 19, 2003, http://www.psywarrior.com/PSYOPOrgWW2.html.

53. Allison L. Rowland and Peter Simonson, "The Founding Mothers of Communication Research: Toward a History of a Gendered Assemblage," *Critical Studies in Media Communication* 31, no. 1 (March 2014): 3–26.
54. Richard Taruskin, *Music in the Late Twentieth Century* (New York: Oxford University Press, 2010), 17. On Adorno's work in the United States, see Jay, *The Dialectical Imagination.*
55. Alex Ross, *The Rest Is Noise: Listening to the Twentieth Century,* reprint ed. (New York: Farrar, Straus and Giroux, 2007).
56. Taruskin, *Music in the Late Twentieth Century,* 36–37, 158–59.
57. The historian Arthur Schlesinger provides this rationale in *The Vital Center* (1949), and Frances Saunders describes it as the cornerstone of CIA strategy for two decades. Frances Stonor Saunders, *The Cultural Cold War: The CIA and the World of Arts and Letters* (New York: The New Press, 2013), 53.
58. See Saunders, *The Cultural Cold War.*

4. NOT TWO CULTURES

1. Christopher Newfield, *Unmaking the Public University: The Forty-Year Assault on the Middle Class* (Cambridge, MA: Harvard University Press, 2008), 191.
2. Curtis Fletcher, "The Socio-Technical Humanities: Reimagining the Liberal Arts in the Age of New Media, 1952–1969: University of Southern California Dissertations and Theses," PhD diss., University of Southern California, 2014, 41–43. John R. Thelin, *A History of American Higher Education* (Baltimore, MD: Johns Hopkins University Press, 2011), 266.
3. Vannevar Bush, *Pieces of the Action* (New York: Morrow, 1970), 63. Bush is hardly alone in making this point. For instance, Lippit observes: "the atomic bombings produced symbols—as opposed to images of war—which drove the representation of atomic warfare from fact to figure, toward the threshold of art. The so-called mushroom cloud, which has come to embody the perverse organicity of atomic war, functions as a displaced referent for the obliterating force of atomic weaponry." Akira Mizuta Lippit, *Atomic Light (Shadow Optics)* (Minneapolis: University of Minnesota Press, 2005), 92.
4. As Kevles recounts, there was broad consensus that the bomb was a message-sending device, but there was also considerable divergence of opinion on exactly what that message was. For many, it indicated the need to fund physics: "In the atomic age," as Kevles sums up this lesson learned, "the United States could not do without a national policy of scientific, especially nuclear, research." For others, it entailed a forecast of geopolitical challenges to come, and even the dawn of a Cold War with the Soviets. According to a White House press release, the bomb represented nothing short of "a harnessing of the basic power of the universe." Daniel J. Kevles, *The Physicists: The History of a Scientific Community in Modern America* (Cambridge, MA: Harvard University Press, 1995), 333–34.
5. C. P. Snow, *The Two Cultures and the Scientific Revolution* (New York: Cambridge University Press, 1961), 53.
6. Snow, *The Two Cultures,* 10.
7. Snow, *The Two Cultures,* 9, 14.

289

4. NOT TWO CULTURES

8. Snow, *The Two Cultures*, 4.

9. F. R. Leavis, *Two Cultures?* (New York: Pantheon, 1963), 49.

10. Geoffrey Galt Harpham, *The Humanities and the Dream of America* (Chicago: University of Chicago Press, 2011), 165.

11. Harpham, *The Humanities*, 189.

12. Lionel Trilling, "The Leavis-Snow Controversy," in *Beyond Culture: Essays on Literature and Learning* (New York: Harcourt, Brace, Jovanovich, 1965), 143, 151.

13. Frances Stonor Saunders, *The Cultural Cold War: The CIA and the World of Arts and Letters* (New York: The New Press, 2013), 131, 138–58, 179.

14. Trilling, "The Leavis-Snow Controversy," 176.

15. The EDVAC report is "the first written description of the stored-program concept." After the war, von Neumann continued this work at Princeton's Institute for Advanced Study with the engineer Arthur Banks and the EDVAC veteran mathematician Herman Goldstein. Their design, described in a 1947 report, included shared memory for both machine instructions and data, as well as units for arithmetic, control, input, and output. See Steve J. Heims, *The Cybernetics Group* (Cambridge, MA: MIT Press, 1991), 19. Also see William Aspray, *John von Neumann and the Origins of Modern Computing* (Cambridge, MA: MIT Press, 1990), 39.

16. Heims, *The Cybernetics Group*, 15–16.

17. Norbert Wiener, *Cybernetics, or Control and Communication in the Animal and the Machine* (Cambridge, MA: MIT Press, 1965), 24–25.

18. Wiener, *Cybernetics*, 164.

19. Orit Halpern, *Beautiful Data: A History of Vision and Reason Since 1945* (Durham, NC: Duke University Press, 2015), 106, 105.

20. These efforts extended internationally as well. See Justus Nieland, *Happiness by Design: Modernism, Film, and Media in the Eames Era* (Minneapolis: University of Minnesota Press, in press), chap. 2.

21. Fred Turner, *The Democratic Surround: Multimedia and American Liberalism from World War II to the Psychedelic Sixties* (Chicago: University of Chicago Press, 2013), intro. During the war, Turner recounts, Mead and Bateson participated in efforts to counter Nazi propaganda through the nongovernmental Committee for National Morale (among other operations). The committee's effort ran parallel to the Rockefeller initiatives that moved into government bureaus, but it developed distinct psychological and anthropological premises. "Morale" named a more diffuse problem than "democratic propaganda." It concerned the "whole individual" and her ability to adjust creatively to her social situation. Both approaches emphasized communication, however.

22. Turner, *The Democratic Surround*, chap. 2.

23. Turner, *The Democratic Surround*, chap. 6, intro.

24. See also Halpern, *Beautiful Data*, chap. 4.

25. Harvard Committee on the Objectives of General Education in a Free Society, *General Education in a Free Society; Report of the Harvard Committee* (Cambridge, MA: Harvard University Press, 1945), ix.

26. Harpham, *The Humanities*, 153. In a somewhat more critical vein, Graff opines that the volume's endorsement of New Critical close reading practice supported the powerful fantasy that "if only literature itself could be allowed to work its potential

magic, all would be well." Gerald Graff, *Professing Literature: An Institutional History*, 20th anniversary ed. (Chicago: University of Chicago Press, 2007), 171.

27. Harvard Committee, *General Education in a Free Society*, v.
28. Harvard Committee, *General Education in a Free Society*, vii; CPI Inflation Calculator, https://www.bls.gov/data/inflation_calculator.htm.
29. Harvard Committee, *General Education in a Free Society*, xiv.
30. Bush, *Pieces of the Action*, 37.
31. Kevles, *The Physicists*, 300.
32. "This uranium business is a headache!" Bush wrote to a colleague in 1941. When the British Military Application of Uranium Committee concluded that "it will be possible to make an effective uranium bomb" and shared that finding with its American allies, Bush ignored the report. For details of this back and forth, see Richard Rhodes, *The Making of the Atomic Bomb*, 25th anniversary ed. (New York: Simon & Schuster, 2012), 366–74.
33. Rhodes, *The Making of the Atomic Bomb*, 377.
34. Aspray, *John von Neumann*, 27–30.
35. See Kevles, *The Physicists*; and Rhodes, *The Making of the Atomic Bomb*, for more detailed accounts of this research structure.
36. Harvard Committee, *General Education in a Free Society*, 206.
37. Harvard Committee, *General Education in a Free Society*, 213–14.
38. Harvard Committee, *General Education in a Free Society*, 221.
39. Harvard Committee, *General Education in a Free Society*, 207, 216.
40. James Bryant Conant, *Education in a Divided World: The Function of the Public Schools in Our Unique Society* (Cambridge, MA: Harvard University Press, 1948), 5.
41. Conant, *Education in a Divided World*, 108.
42. Conant, *Education in a Divided World*, 5.
43. Graff, *Professing Literature*, 167.
44. Harvard Committee, *General Education in a Free Society*, 112.
45. Harvard Committee, *General Education in a Free Society*, 110.
46. Harvard Committee, *General Education in a Free Society*, 108. For Guillory, this double move is part of literary criticism's disciplinary foundation: "Yet literature seems to be less conspicuously marked by medial identity than other media, such as film, and that fact has tacitly supported the disciplinary division between literary and media studies (and by extension between cultural studies and communication studies). The repression of the medial identity of literature and other 'fine arts' is rightly being questioned today. The aim of this questioning should be to give a better account of the relation between literature and later technical media without granting to literature the privilege of cultural seniority or to later media the palm of victorious successor." John Guillory, "Genesis of the Media Concept," *Critical Inquiry* 36, no. 2 (2010): 322n3.
47. Harvard Committee, *General Education in a Free Society*, 118.
48. Harvard Committee, *General Education in a Free Society*, 249.
49. Harvard Committee, *General Education in a Free Society*, 266.
50. Harvard Committee, *General Education in a Free Society*, 266–67.
51. Max Horkheimer and Theodor W. Adorno, "The Culture Industry: Enlightenment as Mass Deception," in *Dialectic of Enlightenment: Philosophical Fragments*, ed. Gunzelin Schmitt-Noerr (Stanford, CA: Stanford University Press, 2002), 100–1.

52. Horkheimer and Adorno, "The Culture Industry," 107.

53. Harpham, *The Humanities*, 162. See also President's Commission on Higher Education, *Higher Education for American Democracy, a Report* (Washington, DC: US Government Printing Office, 1947), 49.

54. Some decades after the Redbook, in fact, in 2013, Harvard's faculty revisited the terms of the 1945 report with a new document in the same vein: David Armitage et al., "The Teaching of the Arts and Humanities at Harvard College: Mapping the Future," http://artsandhumanities.fas.harvard.edu/files/humanities/files/mapping _the_future_31_may_2013.pdf. Although admittedly "less ambitious" than the Redbook, the new report retained its emphasis on the way "a liberal arts education encourages students to oscillate between the demands of specialization and a general education" (33). This is also a theme of the American Academy of Arts and Sciences report issued the same year, as part of a veritable summer season of the humanities report. Commission on the Humanities and Social Sciences, American Academy of Arts and Sciences, "The Heart of the Matter: The Humanities and Social Sciences for a Vibrant, Competitive, and Secure Nation," 2013, http://www.humanitiescomm ission.org/_pdf/hss_report.pdf.

55. Harvard Committee, *General Education in a Free Society*, 35.

56. Harvard Committee, *General Education in a Free Society*, 32.

57. Harvard Committee, *General Education in a Free Society*, 263–64.

58. Harvard Committee, *General Education in a Free Society*, 264.

59. It is clear that they have done some homework on this score. They indirectly reference Rockefeller radio research as well as a series of wartime government studies. See Harvard Committee, *General Education in a Free Society*, 265. They credit the "Commission on Motion Pictures in Education of the American Council on Education," but the psychologist Carl Hovland pioneered research in this area, which was further developed by the sociologist Samuel Stouffer and the social psychologist Leonard Cottrell after the war. See Wilbur Schramm, *The Beginnings of Communication Study in America: A Personal Memoir* (Thousand Oaks, CA: Sage, 1997), 92–93.

5. TELEVISION, OR NEW MEDIA

1. Curtis Fletcher, "The Socio-Technical Humanities: Reimagining the Liberal Arts in the Age of New Media, 1952–1969," PhD diss., University of Southern California, 2014, chap. 1.

2. In 1970, as PBS was spinning up, a major report found fifty-nine university-owned ETV stations in the United States, with annual operating budgets totaling $31.6 million. Anna L. Hyer and Council for Educational Media International, *The Audio Visual Services in Canada and the United States*, 2nd ed. (The Hague: ICEM Comparative Study of the Administration of Audio-Visual Services in Advanced and Developing Countries, 1974), 35.

3. NET started in 1952 as the Ann Arbor–based Educational Television and Radio Center (ETRC), which later morphed into the National Educational Television and Radio Center. Michele Hilmes, *Network Nations: A Transnational History of British and American Broadcasting* (New York: Routledge, 2012), 195–96.

4. See Anne Walker Cook, "A History of the Indiana University Audio-Visual Center: 1913 to 1975," PhD diss., Indiana University, 1980, 173.

5. Quoted in Anna McCarthy, *The Citizen Machine: Governing by Television in 1950s America* (New York: The New Press, 2010), 162.

6. McCarthy, *The Citizen Machine*, 158. For an account of how Ford's efforts fit into evolving concern with media literacy, see also Zoë Druick, "The Myth of Media Literacy," *International Journal of Communication* 10 (2016): 1129–31.

7. McCarthy, *The Citizen Machine*, 164.

8. As Chicago's chancellor, Hutchins had overseen the wartime Commission on Freedom of the Press (the Hutchins Commission), a body that drew on Rockefeller-seminar talent including Harold Lasswell and Archibald MacLeish and that helped pave the way for the Chicago Committee on Communication (1947–1960)—an early effort to organize training in mass communication at the school. The committee disbanded in 1960 because of a loss of core professors through retirements and recruitment, competition with the more permanently constituted sociology department, and the fact that institutional longevity was not necessarily its goal. "Like all other Chicago committees, [the Committee on Communication] was meant to explore, conquer, and die: It was designed to tag onto particular research problems, linked to individuals' interests or urgent questions of social import. . . . Members of the committee did not believe in the disciplinarity of communication." Thus, the Chicago Committees made key contributions to the emerging field without establishing institutional forms that would reproduce it. Karin Wahl-Jorgensen, "How Not to Found a Field: New Evidence on the Origins of Mass Communication," *Journal of Communication* 54, no. 3 (2004): 561.

9. Hilmes, *Network Nations*.

10. Philip Marchand, *Marshall McLuhan: The Medium and the Messenger: A Biography* (Cambridge, MA: MIT Press, 1998), 117, 125.

11. "Global Village, 1977," and "Global Village, 1967," Marshall McLuhan Speaks Collection, http://www.marshallmcluhanspeaks.com/.

12. Aniko Bodroghkozy, *Groove Tube: Sixties Television and the Youth Rebellion* (Durham, NC: Duke University Press, 2001), 38–43.

13. Charles R. Acland, "Never Too Cool for School," *Journal of Visual Culture* 13, no. 1 (April 2014): 14.

14. In the 1950s, GE decided that instead of sending promising executives back to college, it would bring the professors to its corporate school in Croton-on-Hudson, just north of New York City. "Corporate 'communications' in those days was very much considered to be a matter of writing letters and memos," remembers Ralph Baldwin, the organizer of the school. "I thought that, from top management on down, the Croton-on-Hudson students should be exposed to the latest thinking on the subject." Marchand, *Marshall McLuhan*, 137, 151.

15. "The Future of the Future Is the Present, 1967," and "My Statements as Probes, 1977," Marshall McLuhan Speaks Collection, http://www.marshallmcluhanspeaks.com/.

16. Alvin Toffler, comp., *The Futurists* (New York: Random House, 1972); Noah Shachtman, "Honoring *Wired*'s Patron Saint," *Wired*, May 2002, https://www.wired.com/2002/05/honoring-wireds-patron-saint/; Gary Wolf, "Channeling McLuhan," *Wired*, January 1996, https://www.wired.com/1996/01/channeling/.

17. Quoted in John Paul Russo, *I. A. Richards: His Life and Work* (Baltimore, MD: Johns Hopkins University Press, 1989), 516.

18. "Post-Literate Generation, 1977," Marshall McLuhan Speaks Collection, http://www.marshallmcluhanspeaks.com/.

19. Chief among those purposes for Richards was introductory language instruction. On Richards's program of teaching what he termed BASIC English worldwide, see David Simpson, "Prospects for Global English," *Yale Journal of Criticism* 11, no. 1 (1998): 299–305. See also John Paul Russo, *The Future Without a Past: The Humanities in a Technological Society* (Columbia: University of Missouri, 2005), 37.

20. I. A. Richards, *Design for Escape: World Education Through Modern Media* (New York: Harcourt, 1968), 3.

21. Richards, *Design for Escape*, 20.

22. Edwin Leonard Glick, "WGBH-TV: The First Ten Years (1955–65)," PhD diss., University of Michigan, 1970, 56.

23. Formed in 1946 to support educational broadcasting on radio and television, the council's members included, in addition to WGBH and Harvard, the Boston Symphony Orchestra, the Museum of Fine Arts, the New England Conservatory of Music, MIT, Boston University, Tufts University, Northeastern University, and Boston College. See "Lowell Institute Has Fifth Birthday; Niemans Discuss 'American Ideas,'" *Harvard Crimson*, February 4, 1952, http://www.thecrimson.com/article/1952/2/4/lowell-institute-has-fifth-birthday-niemans/.

24. "About the Lowell Institute," http://www.lowellinstitute.org/about/.

25. "I. A. Richards Terms 'Radar of Perception' Key to Understanding," *Harvard Crimson*, May 11, 1964, http://www.thecrimson.com/article/1964/5/11/ia-richards-terms-radar-of-perception/.

26. The information NET provided its distribution centers touts Richards's "background and insight" as well as his "dramatic flair." It remains, unclear, however to what extent Richards's programs were seen outside Boston. See "Individual Program Data: The Sense of Poetry," Educational Television and Radio Center, February 20, 1958, Indiana University Libraries Film Archive.

27. Glick, "WGBH-TV," 188.

28. David M. Davis, "Letter from David M. Davis to David W. Bailey," December 22, 1958, WGBH Archive, F.349421.

29. Reginald H. Phelps, "Letter from Reginald H. Phelps, Director of University Extension, Harvard University, to David W. Bailey, Secretary of the Corporation," December 1, 1959, WGBH Archive, F.287823.

30. Robert L. Larsen, "Memorandum on Harvard Lecturerships," March 9, 1962, WGBH Archive, F.349420.

31. Here, WGBH proved highly responsive to emphatic audience feedback. Fan mail flooded the station after the pilot aired in 1962, and WGBH responded by promoting the show "in a big way," running recipes from each episode in the *Boston Globe* along with a column by Child called "From the Pen of the French Chef." Dana B. Polan, *Julia Child's* The French Chef (Durham, NC: Duke University Press, 2011), 131.

32. Glick, "WGBH-TV," 162.

33. Michael Shinagel, *"The Gates Unbarred": A History of University Extension at Harvard, 1910–2009* (Cambridge, MA: Harvard University Press, 2009), 91. See also

Glick, "WGBH-TV," 103. And see "Enrollment in Extension Program, TV Courses Now at High of 7000," *Harvard Crimson*, May 25, 1962, http://www.thecrimson .com/article/1962/5/25/enrollment-in-extension-program-tv-courses/.

34. Hartford N. Gunn, "Letter from Hartford N. Gunn, Jr. to Reginald H. Phelps," 1968, WGBH Archive, F.349421.

35. See Shinagel, *"The Gates Unbarred."*

36. "McLuhanism, 1967," Marshall McLuhan Speaks Collection, http://www .marshallmcluhanspeaks.com/understanding-me/1967-mcluhanism/.

37. Video of McLuhan's performances in each of these modes is available from the Marshall McLuhan Speaks Collection.

38. "The content of a movie is a novel or a play or an opera," he writes. "The 'content' of writing or print is speech, but the reader is almost entirely unaware either of print or of speech." Marshall McLuhan, *Understanding Media: The Extensions of Man* (Corte Madera, CA: Gingko, 2003), 31. See also "Laws of Media, 1970," Marshall McLuhan Speaks Collection, http://www.marshallmcluhanspeaks.com/say ings/1970-laws-of-the-media/.

39. Anthony Grafton describes McLuhan as providing a "quirkily speculative" precedent for a 1970s and 1980s boom among historians investigating the epochal significance of print. Anthony Grafton, "AHR Forum Introduction: How Revolutionary Was the Print Revolution?" *American Historical Review* 107, no. 1 (2002): 85. *The Gutenberg Galaxy* (1962) describes an "initial shock" that leads to a "prolonged phase of 'adjustment' of all personal and social life to the new model of perception set up by the new technology." Marshall McLuhan, *The Gutenberg Galaxy: The Making of Typographic Man* (Toronto: University of Toronto Press, 1962), 23. Eisenstein's book sought to encompass what she described in a 2002 reflection as a "communications shift that occurred in Western Europe in the late fifteenth century encompass[ing] images and charts, advertisements and maps, official edicts and indulgences." Elizabeth L. Eisenstein, "AHR Forum: A Reply," *American Historical Review* 107, no. 1 (2002): 126. Although Eisenstein is one of the sources Benedict Anderson credits in his *Imagined Communities* (1983), he worries that she comes "close to theomorphizing 'print' qua print as the genius of modern history." Not that Anderson finds the emergence of print capitalism insignificant: he famously argues that "unified fields of exchange and communication," "fixity of language," and new "languages-of-power" afforded by print made national consciousness and, thus, national administration thinkable. Benedict R. Anderson, *Imagined Communities: Reflections on the Origin and Spread of Nationalism*, rev. and extended ed. (London: Verso, 1991), 44n21, 44–45.

40. Sometimes they reach McLuhan without touching the midcentury communications complex. See, for instance, Adrian Johns, *The Nature of the Book: Print and Knowledge in the Making* (Chicago: University of Chicago Press, 1998).

41. Barnow's 1976 *Tube of Plenty* saw broad use as an introductory text. On the vexed relationship between studies of television and broadcasting studies and film studies, see Michele Hilmes, "Nailing Mercury: The Problem of Media Industry Historiography," in *Media Industries: History, Theory, and Method*, ed. Jennifer Holt and Alisa Perren (Malden, MA: Wiley-Blackwell, 2009); and Derek Kompare, "Filling the Box: Television in Higher Education," *Cinema Journal* 50, no. 4 (2011): 161–66.

42. Fletcher, "The Socio-Technical Humanities," 122–23.

6. COOPTATION

1. Thomas Frank, *The Conquest of Cool: Business Culture, Counterculture, and the Rise of Hip Consumerism* (Chicago: University of Chicago Press, 1997); Orit Halpern, *Beautiful Data: A History of Vision and Reason Since 1945* (Durham, NC: Duke University Press, 2015); Andrew B. Lewis, *The Shadows of Youth: The Remarkable Journey of the Civil Rights Generation* (New York: Hill and Wang, 2009); Fred Turner, *The Democratic Surround: Multimedia and American Liberalism from World War II to the Psychedelic Sixties* (Chicago: University of Chicago Press, 2013).

2. Robert Cohen, *Freedom's Orator: Mario Savio and the Radical Legacy of the 1960s*, reprint ed. (New York: Oxford University Press, 2014).

3. "Berkeley FSM | Free Speech Movement 50th Anniversary," University of California, Berkeley, http://fsm.berkeley.edu/.

4. See Sylvia Tiersten, "What's In a Name? The Long Saga of Third College," *At UCSD*, May 2010, http://ucsdmag.ucsd.edu/magazine/vol7no2/features/feat4 .htm; "Department History," Ethnic Studies, University of Colorado Boulder, https:// www.colorado.edu/ethnicstudies/department-history; "History of Africana Studies at Cornell," Africana Studies & Research Center, Cornell University, http:// africana.cornell.edu/history; "History," African American & African Studies, University of Minnesota, https://cla.umn.edu/aaas/about/history.

5. Philip Selznick, *TVA and the Grass Roots* (New York: Harper & Row, 1966), 13.

6. Selznick, *TVA and the Grass Roots*, 15.

7. Selznick, *TVA and the Grass Roots*, 261.

8. Midcentury systems thinking informs Selznick's model. "The internal life of any organization tends to become, but never achieves, a closed system." Selznick, *TVA and the Grass Roots*, 10. Bureaucracies are driven to create formal rules and hierarchies that can anticipate the public on which, and in whose interest, they aim to act. "Coöptation reflects a state of tension between formal authority and social power. This authority is always embodied in a particular structure and leadership, but social power itself has to do with subjective and objective factors which control the loyalties and potential manipulability of the community. Where the formal authority or leadership reflects real social power, its stability is assured. . . . Where a leadership has been accustomed to the assumption that its constituents respond to it as individuals, there may be a rude awakening when organization of those constituents creates nucleuses of strength which are able to effectively demand a sharing of power." Selznick, *TVA and the Grass Roots*, 15.

9. Kurt Edward Kemper, *College Football and American Culture in the Cold War Era* (Champaign-Urbana: University of Illinois Press, 2009), 14.

10. Jeffrey Montez de Oca, *Discipline and Indulgence: College Football, Media, and the American Way of Life During the Cold War* (New Brunswick, NJ: Rutgers University Press, 2013), 73.

11. Montez de Oca, *Discipline and Indulgence*, 82.

12. Kemper, *College Football*, 40.

13. William Frank Buckley, *God and Man at Yale: The Superstitions of "Academic Freedom"* (Washington, DC: Regnery, 2013), 165.

14. Buckley, *God and Man at Yale*, lxvi.

15. Cohen, *Freedom's Orator*, 188.

16. Cohen, *Freedom's Orator*, 190.

17. Jean Genet's homoerotic *Un Chant d'Amour* (1950) had been prohibited, but the filmmaker Saul Landau would provide some others, Savio promised.

18. Cohen, *Freedom's Orator*, 192.

19. Clark Kerr, *The Uses of the University* (Cambridge, Mass.: Harvard University Press, 2001), 31.

20. Kerr, *The Uses of the University*, 68.

21. Kerr, *The Uses of the University*, 14–15.

22. Cohen, *Freedom's Orator*, 206.

23. Kerr, *The Uses of the University*, 14, 31–32.

24. Andrew Jewett, "The Politics of Knowledge in 1960s America," *Social Science History* 36, no. 4 (2012): 552.

25. Cohen, *Freedom's Orator*, 95, 104.

26. Cohen, *Freedom's Orator*, 183.

27. Students for a Democratic Society, "The Port Huron Statement of the Students for a Democratic Society," 1962, https://en.wikisource.org/wiki/Port_Huron_Statement.

28. While SDS chapters became more radical during the course of the 1960s, institutional takeover remained a project for some. At San Francisco State, the SDS ran "strike support" for the Black Student Union and Third World Liberation Front struggle to establish a Third World College and a degree-granting Department of Black Studies. See Martin Nicolaus, "SF State: History Takes a Leap," *New Left Review* 54 (April 1969): 17–31.

29. C. Wright Mills, *The Power Elite* (New York: Oxford University Press, 1956), 304.

30. Mills, *The Power Elite*, 317, 320.

31. Blair Davis, *The Battle for the Bs: 1950s Hollywood and the Rebirth of Low-Budget Cinema* (New Brunswick, NJ: Rutgers University Press, 2012).

32. Aniko Bodroghkozy, *Groove Tube: Sixties Television and the Youth Rebellion* (Durham, NC: Duke University Press, 2001), 5.

33. Aniko Bodroghkozy, "Reel Revolutionaries: An Examination of Hollywood's Cycle of 1960s Youth Rebellion Films," *Cinema Journal* 41, no. 3 (2002): 38–58.

34. Cohen, *Freedom's Orator*, 192.

35. Cohen, *Freedom's Orator*, 262.

36. "About Film and Media at Berkeley," Department of Film and Media UC Berkeley, 2015, http://filmmedia.berkeley.edu/about.

37. Television was added in 1974. See Michael Zryd, "Experimental Film and the Development of Film Study in America," in *Inventing Film Studies*, ed. Lee Grieveson (Durham, NC: Duke University Press, 2008), 190.

38. Zryd, "Experimental Film," 193.

39. Zryd, "Experimental Film," 190.

40. Ray Guest, "Film Society Elects Heads for Next Year," *Gamecock*, March 17, 1950.

41. "Speakers Are Feature of Film Society," *Gamecock*, September 30, 1955.

42. "Film Society Discontinued," *Gamecock*, September 20, 1957. The society declared that it had accomplished its mission of introducing better films to Columbia.

43. When the *Gamecock* published a lament that foreign films were not reaching Columbia, CFFS member Donald O. Bushman penned a defensive reply in which

he explained that "Unless advertising announces that a particular film is 'adult entertainment' students don't seem to be too interested in attending." Donald Bushman, "Letters to Editor," *Gamecock*, March 29, 1963, 2.

44. Lawrence E. Mintz, "On the Screen Scene," *Gamecock*, February 12, 1965, 6.

45. "New Group to Present Film Study," *Gamecock*, November 10, 1967, 3. The first on-campus screening included a set of hand-colored Méliès films, *Loony-Tom, the Happy Lover* (Broughton, 1951), *Ballet Mecanique* (Léger and Murphy, 1924), *Treadle and Bobbin* (Galentine, 1954), and *N.Y. N.Y* (Thompson, 1957).

46. "Coke Campus Activities Calendar," *Gamecock*, October 27, 1967, 9.

47. "Carolina YAF to Discuss Chinese Admission to UN," *Gamecock*, December 1, 1967, 2.

48. William W. Byler, "Film Audience Dissatisfied," *Gamecock*, October 20, 1969, 2.

49. See also Bryce H. Smith, "Who Picks Your Flicks? (letter to Editor)," *Gamecock*, September 17, 1969, 2.

50. "More Balanced Scheduling (Letter to the Editor)," *Gamecock*, May 17, 1971, 3.

51. Mario Berguistain, "Foreign Films in Columbia," *Gamecock*, February 14, 1969, 6.

52. "Flicks Featured," *Gamecock*, April 15, 1969, 4.

53. Marshall Swanson, "Dunlap, Film Course Incites Fervor," *Gamecock*, November 5, 1973, 3.

54. Steve Valk, "Media Arts," *Gamecock*, November 4, 1974, 4, 8.

55. "Report of Committee on Curricula and New Courses, University of South Carolina Faculty Senate," May 5, 1975, 27.

56. University of South Carolina, ed., *University of South Carolina Columbia Campus . . . Mini Factbook* (Columbia, SC: Office of Institutional Planning & Analysis, 2004).

57. "The U.S. has bred a generation zonked on films," observed *Life* in 1969. "More and more young Americans are getting behind the camera and expressing themselves as never before." Quoted in Zryd, "Experimental Film," 195.

58. Thomas Fensch, *Films on the Campus* (South Brunswick, NJ: A. S. Barnes, 1970), 29, 197–198, 199, 265, 14.

59. Aviva Dove-Viebahn, "The State of the Field of Film and Media Studies," Society for Cinema and Media Studies, December 2015, http://c.ymcdn.com/sites/www .cmstudies.org/resource/resmgr/SCMS_StateoftheField2015.pdf.

60. Roderick A. Ferguson, *The Reorder of Things: The University and Its Pedagogies of Minority Difference* (Minneapolis: University of Minnesota Press, 2012), 5.

61. Ferguson, *The Reorder of Things*, 6.

62. Ferguson, *The Reorder of Things*, 37.

63. Lisa Lowe, *Immigrant Acts: On Asian American Cultural Politics* (Durham, NC: Duke University Press, 1996), 41.

64. She notes further that women's studies would dispense with the idea that disciplines could be wholly defined by their objects but at the price of "persistent theory wars, race wars, and sex wars . . . in the 1980s." Wendy Brown, "The Impossibility of Women's Studies," *differences: A Journal of Feminist Cultural Studies* 9, no. 3 (1997): 83. In the 1990s, Robyn Wiegman argues, use of the term "gender" came to represent one way "Women's Studies" might transgress its limits while retaining a certain coherence. "Gender's now characteristic proliferations stand as evidence of the field's ability to transcend the compromise of its founding paradigm" and to

organize teaching and research on masculinity, sexuality, and all manner of differences within the category "women." Robyn Wiegman, *Object Lessons* (Durham, NC: Duke University Press, 2012), 52.

65. Barbara Christian, *New Black Feminist Criticism, 1985–2000*, ed. Gloria Bowles, M. Giulia Fabi, and Arlene Keizer (Urbana: University of Illinois Press, 2007), 15.

66. Evelyn Hu-DeHart, "The History, Development, and Future of Ethnic Studies," *Phi Delta Kappan* 75, no. 1 (1993): 54. Compare, on women's studies, Lauren Berlant, "'68, or Something," *Critical Inquiry* 21, no. 1 (October 1, 1994): 129.

67. Wiegman, *Object Lessons*, 83.

68. Ferguson, *The Reorder of Things*, 18. Compare on the interdisciplines' "potentially volatile mixture of liberalism and radicalism," Christopher Newfield, *Unmaking the Public University: The Forty-Year Assault on the Middle Class* (Cambridge, MA: Harvard University Press, 2008), 47.

69. And further: "The minority" was the "stimulus for unforeseen positivities in the midst of newly evolving regulations and exclusions." Ferguson, *The Reorder of Things*, 39–40.

70. Ferguson, *The Reorder of Things*, 75.

71. Angela Yvonne Davis, *Angela Davis—an Autobiography* (New York: International Publishers, 1974), 156, 157.

72. "UJIMA Network, a UCSD Association," http://blink.ucsd.edu/sponsor/ujima/.

73. Bettina Aptheker, *The Morning Breaks: The Trial of Angela Davis* (Ithaca, NY: Cornell University Press, 2014).

74. Roderick A. Ferguson, *We Demand: The University and Student Protests* (Oakland: University of California Press, 2017), 31.

75. Thomas Snyder, "120 Years of American Education: A Statistical Portrait," Washington DC: US Department of Education, January 19, 1993, http://nces.ed.gov/pub search/pubsinfo.asp?pubid=93442.

76. See Nikolas Rose and Peter Miller, *Governing the Present: Administering Economic, Social, and Personal Life* (Cambridge: Polity, 2008). On the possibilities for framing politics in terms of population-driven governmentality, see Partha Chatterjee, *The Politics of the Governed: Reflections on Popular Politics in Most of the World* (New York: Columbia University Press, 2004).

77. Civil Rights Act of 1964, Pub. L. No. 88-352, §601; Higher Education Act of 1965, Pub. L. No. 89-329, §301a.

78. The new laws envisioned a society "in which there is an optimization of systems of difference . . . in which minority individuals and practices are tolerated . . . in which there is an environmental type of intervention." Michel Foucault, *The Birth of Biopolitics: Lectures at the Collège de France, 1978–79* (New York: Palgrave Macmillan, 2008), 259–60.

79. As early as the 1930s, he argues, ordoliberal theorists from Germany's Freiburg School were generating an account of government emphasizing "the multiplicity and differentiation of enterprises," a theme that would dominate in later American neoliberal thought. This emphasis, however, did not entirely dispense with the more totalizing form of disciplinary state administration Foucault thinks of as emblematic of nineteenth-century European government. Instead, he argues, such "different ways of calculating, rationalizing, and regulating" tend to appear as if "overlapping each other." "What is politics," he asks, "if not both the interplay

of these different arts of government . . . and the debate to which these different arts of government give rise?" Foucault, *The Birth of Biopolitics*, 149, 313.

80. And in Department of Defense schools outside the United States.

81. National Center for Education Statistics, "Higher Education General Information Survey (HEGIS), 1976–1977: Earned Degrees: Version 2," May 3, 1984, http://www .icpsr.umich.edu/ICPSR/studies/07651/version/2.

82. Diane Ravitch, *The Troubled Crusade: American Education, 1945–1980* (New York: Basic Books, 1983), 283.

83. Nicholas Lemann, *The Big Test: The Secret History of the American Meritocracy* (New York: Macmillan, 2000), 65.

84. Lemann, *The Big Test*, 85.

85. US Department of Labor, CPI Inflation Calculator, https://www.bls.gov/data/ inflation_calculator.htm.

86. The 1964 Economic Opportunity Act funded college work study; the 1965 Higher Education Act created the Educational Opportunity Grant for low-income students; and the 1968 Trio programs were also addressed to lower-income students.

87. Mr. B, "The Back Bench: Tuition at the University of California (1970)," *Back Bench*, August 16, 2007, http://thebackbench.blogspot.com/2007/08/tuition-at-university-of -california.html. "College, Radcliffe Tuition Raised to $1250; Increase Permits Higher Faculty Salaries," *Harvard Crimson*, January 8, 1958, http://www.thecrim son.com/article/1958/1/8/college-radcliffe-tuition-raised-to-1250/.

88. Rupert Wilkinson, *Aiding Students, Buying Students: Financial Aid in America* (Nashville, TN: Vanderbilt University Press, 2005), 55.

89. See Wilkinson, *Aiding Students*, 57; and John Thelin, *A History of American Higher Education* (Baltimore, MD: Johns Hopkins University Press, 2011), 324.

90. Which amounted to 2.4 percent of total current fund revenue at all reporting institutions. "Digest of Education Statistics, 1996," National Center for Education Statistics, December 12, 1996, table 319, https://nces.ed.gov/pubsearch/pubsinfo.asp ?pubid=96133.

91. US Department of Labor, CPI Inflation Calculator, https://www.bls.gov/data/ inflation_calculator.htm.

92. Thelin, *A History of American Higher Education*, 326–28.

93. See Leah Gordon, "The Coleman Report and Its Critics: The Contested Meanings of Educational Equality in the 1960s and 1970s," *Process: A Blog for American History*, March 22, 2017, http://www.processhistory.org/gordon-coleman-report/.

94. Kerr, *The Uses of the University*, 91.

95. Kerr, *The Uses of the University*, 91.

96. Thelin, *A History of American Higher Education*, 347.

97. Title IX of the Education Amendments of 1972, 20 U.S.C. §1681 et seq., https:// www.justice.gov/crt/title-ix-education-amendments-1972.

98. Susan Ware, *Title IX: A Brief History with Documents* (Long Grove, IL: Waveland, 2014), 5.

99. Ware, *Title IX*, 5.

100. Football powers became increasingly frustrated with the NCAA for limiting the number of games to be shown on television. To seek their own deals, they formed the renegade College Football Association in 1978. This schism ultimately led to a Supreme Court battle in which the NCAA was found guilty of antitrust violations.

Keith Dunnavant, *The Fifty-Year Seduction: How Television Manipulated College Football, from the Birth of the Modern NCAA to the Creation of the BCS* (New York: Macmillan, 2004).

101. Office for Civil Rights, "Title IX 1979 Policy Interpretation on Intercollegiate Athletics," Policy Guidance, Federal Register Notices, October 16, 2015, http://www2 .ed.gov/about/offices/list/ocr/docs/t9interp.html.

102. As defined by the *Princeton Review* beginning in 1993.

7. STUDENT IMMATERIAL LABOR

1. Maurizio Lazzarato, "Immaterial Labor," in *Radical Thought in Italy: A Potential Politics*, ed. Paolo Virno and Michael Hardt, trans. Paul Colilli and Ed Emory (Minneapolis: University of Minnesota Press, 1996), 133.

2. Lazzarato, "Immaterial Labor," 137.

3. This is a widely noted point in a number of creative domains. For a media history of the general tendency, see Fred Turner, *The Democratic Surround: Multimedia and American Liberalism from World War II to the Psychedelic Sixties* (Chicago: University of Chicago Press, 2013).

4. Apple's "Think Different" campaign dates from the mid-1990s, but it has strong precursors in a 1979 ad that announced an essay contest to find the most "original" use of the Apple and in the well-known "1984" Super Bowl ad, in which a colorful runner smashed through a grey Orwellian mise-en-scène to reveal how Macintosh would ensure that 1984 wouldn't be like *1984*. Mindy Parkhurst, "A Visual History of Apple Ads: 4 Decades in the Making," http://blog.hubspot .com/marketing/visual-history-of-apple-ads.

5. We feel Lazzarato's suggestive periodization wants testing in the US context. Lazzarato, "Immaterial Labor," 132–33.

6. Theodore Roszak, *The Making of a Counter Culture: Reflections on the Technocratic Society and Its Youthful Opposition* (Berkeley: University of California Press, 1995), 36–37.

7. Roszak, *The Making of a Counter Culture*, xxvi. In his classic first-wave account of the movement, the SDS veteran Gitlin gave "the media" an even more sinister complexion as a "spotlight turned to a magnifying glass" that "brought the incandescent light of social attention and then converted it to the heat of reification and judgment." Todd Gitlin, *The Whole World Is Watching: Mass Media in the Making and Unmaking of the New Left* (Berkeley: University of California Press, 1980), 256. This analysis continues one Gitlin was making as early as 1972. See Todd Gitlin, "Sixteen Notes on Television and the Movement," in *Literature in Revolution*, ed. George Abbott White and Charles Newman, (New York: Holt, Rinehart and Winston, 1972), 335–36.

8. See also John Markoff, *What the Dormouse Said: How the Sixties Counterculture Shaped the Personal Computer Industry* (New York: Penguin, 2005); and, on why it is a bad idea to strongly separate a mainframe era emblematized by IBM from the age of the iPhone, Hannah Higgins and Douglas Kahn, eds., *Mainframe Experimentalism: Early Computing and the Foundations of the Digital Arts* (Berkeley: University of California Press, 2012).

9. Fred Turner, *From Counterculture to Cyberculture: Stewart Brand, the Whole Earth Network, and the Rise of Digital Utopianism* (Chicago: University of Chicago Press, 2006).

10. Turner, *The Democratic Surround*.

11. At a 2005 Stanford commencement address, Jobs appropriated the *Whole Earth* motto, "Stay hungry. Stay foolish." "I have always wished that for myself," he told the students. "And now, as you graduate to begin anew, I wish that for you." Steve Jobs, "Text of Steve Jobs' Commencement Address (2005)," *Stanford News*, June 14, 2005, http://news.stanford.edu/2005/06/14/jobs-061505/.

12. Jerry Garcia summarized the Trips Festival as "Thousands of people, man, all helplessly stoned, all finding themselves in a room of thousands of people, none of whom any of them were afraid of. It was magic, far-out beautiful magic." Quoted in Turner, *From Counterculture to Cyberculture*, 66.

13. See, for example, Steven Levy, *Hackers: Heroes of the Computer Revolution*, 25th anniversary ed. (Sebastopol, CA: O'Reilly Media, 2010). And also see Tristan Donovan, *Replay: The History of Video Games* (East Sussex: Yellow Ant Media Limited, 2010); as well as Markoff, *What the Dormouse Said*.

14. For a scholarly treatment, see Steven L. Kent, "Super Mario Nation," in *The Medium of the Video Game*, ed. Mark J. P. Wolf (Austin: University of Texas Press, 2010), 35–48.

15. David Horowitz, *Student* (New York: Ballantine, 1962).

16. Lynn Conway, "VLSI Reminiscences," *IEEE Solid-State Circuits Magazine* 4, no. 1 (2012): 15.

17. Conway, "VLSI Reminiscences," 22.

18. Conway, "VLSI Reminiscences," 28.

19. Business leaders not only perceived the student counterculture as a market but also "approved of the new values and anti-establishment sensibility being developed by youthful revolutionaries." Thomas Frank, *The Conquest of Cool: Business Culture, Counterculture, and the Rise of Hip Consumerism* (Chicago: University of Chicago Press, 1997), 26.

20. Turner, *From Counterculture to Cyberculture*, 210.

21. Heather Hendershot, "Firing Line and the Black Revolution," *Moving Image* 14, no. 2 (Fall 2014): 4.

22. See "*Firing Line* Broadcasts," Hoover Institution Library and Archives, https://digitalcollections.hoover.org/advancedsearch/Objects/archiveType%253AItem%253BcollectionId%253A21/list.

23. "A Dialogue with Young Americans for Freedom," December 8, 1970; "The Concerns of Young Conservatives," August 15, 1975; and "Young Americans for Freedom," August 29, 1977, Hoover Institution Library and Archives, https://digitalcollections.hoover.org/search/%2522Young%2520Americans%2520for%2520Freedom%2522/objects/list?filter=collectionTitle%3AFiring%20Line%20broadcast%20records&page=1#filters.

24. The historian Gregory Schneider opines that if campus leftists, "upset at how unbending some institutions were to change, disappeared into the smoky pall of exploded buildings or into the purple haze of personal politics," conservative activists "worked at grass roots to construct an alternative political culture based on their ideas, captured the Republican Party, and wound up profoundly reshaping

American politics in the process." Gregory L. Schneider, *Cadres for Conservatism: Young Americans for Freedom and the Rise of the Contemporary Right* (New York: New York University Press, 1999), 1. On the comparison between the SDS and YAF, see John A. Andrew, *The Other Side of the Sixties: Young Americans for Freedom and the Rise of Conservative Politics* (New Brunswick, NJ: Rutgers University Press, 1997). And see Rebecca E. Klatch, *A Generation Divided: The New Left, the New Right, and the 1960s* (Berkeley: University of California Press, 1999). On think tanks, see David Callahan and National Committee for Responsive Philanthropy (US), *$1 Billion for Ideas: Conservative Think Tanks in the 1990s* (Washington, DC: National Committee for Responsive Philanthropy, 1999). Callahan argues that conservatives changed the game in the 1970s and 1980s from pragmatic and technocratic to ideological and political and from "knowledge-based" action to "moral precepts." Sixties liberals were about saying they wanted to solve problems and work toward agreed-upon common goals, conservatives all about changing the goals. For a journalistic account, see Sidney Blumenthal, *The Rise of the Counter-Establishment: The Conservative Ascent to Political Power* (New York: Union Square Press, 2008); and Timothy Shenk, "Where Conservative Ideas Come From," *Chronicle of Higher Education*, June 26, 2016, http://www.chronicle.com /article/Where-Conservative-Ideas-Come/236922.

25. Deirdre Boyle, *Subject to Change: Guerrilla Television Revisited* (New York: Oxford University Press, 1997), 71.

26. Boyle, *Subject to Change*, 68.

27. Boyle, *Subject to Change*, 170.

28. "Intermedia Arts Programs," https://www.intermediaarts.org/programs.php.

29. Michael Zryd, "The Academy and the Avant-Garde: A Relationship of Dependence and Resistance," *Cinema Journal* 45, no. 2 (2006): 23.

30. For example, academic rentals accounted for 60 percent of the total at Film-Makers' Cooperative in 1967, when Michael Snow's *Wavelength* provided a start point for the "structural film" tendency. Zryd, "The Academy and the Avant-Garde," 19.

31. The university satisfied unique patronage requirements of the avant-garde in that it proved capable of endorsing "experimentation and artistic risk for its own sake (or for some other purpose or interest, such as the educational value of art making). Sally Banes, "Institutionalizing Avant-Garde Performance: A Hidden History of University Patronage in the United States," in *Contours of the Theatrical Avant-Garde: Performance and Textuality*, ed. James Harding (Ann Arbor: University of Michigan Press, 2000), 219.

32. Timothy Hagood, *A History of Dance in American Higher Education: Dance and the American University* (Lewiston, NY: E. Mellen Press, 2000), 190.

33. Quoted in Hagood, *A History of Dance in American Higher Education*, 195.

34. Hagood, *A History of Dance in American Higher Education*, 216.

35. In addition to attributing the growth of film study to student agitation, Zryd corrects the received narrative that depicts underground, avant-garde, and experimental cinemas as anti-institutional movements that thrived before academization absorbed them in the 1970s. Probing the records of the Film-Makers Cooperative (the major, New York–based distributor), he points out that academic rentals sustained underground cinema at its apogee, accounting for some 60 percent of bookings by 1967. Zryd, "The Academy and the Avant-Garde," 18.

36. Mark McGurl, *The Program Era: Postwar Fiction and the Rise of Creative Writing* (Cambridge, MA: Harvard University Press, 2009), 196.

37. McGurl, *The Program Era*, 196.

38. McGurl, *The Program Era*, 190.

39. Loren Glass, *Counterculture Colophon: Grove Press, the* Evergreen Review, *and the Incorporation of the Avant-Garde* (Stanford, CA: Stanford University Press, 2013), 8.

40. Glass, *Counterculture Colophon*, 32.

41. *New York Times* ad quoted in Glass, *Counterculture Colophon*, 130.

42. From *Advertising Age*, quoted in Glass, *Counterculture Colophon*, 131.

43. Glass, *Counterculture Colophon*, 130–31.

44. Quoted in Glass, *Counterculture Colophon*, 195.

45. "The story of Grove's rise and fall reveals how the moral discourse of good and evil that proliferated around pornography in the 1960s generated the conditions of possibility for a political discourse of power and powerlessness in the 1970s." Glass, *Counterculture Colophon*, 196–97.

46. Before the Grove occupation, Morgan led a takeover of the counterculture magazine *Rat* and used the first issue of the reclaimed magazine to declare: "goodbye forever, counterfeit Left, counterleft, male-dominated cracked-glass mirror reflection of the Amerikan Nightmare.... Power to all the people or to none." "Fair Use Blog : 'Goodbye to All That,' by Robin Morgan (1970)," http://blog.fair-use .org/2007/09/29/goodbye-to-all-that-by-robin-morgan-1970/.

47. Ruth Rosen, *The World Split Open: How the Modern Women's Movement Changed America* (New York: Viking, 2000), 206–7.

48. "Dougherty, Ariel. Papers of Ariel Dougherty, 1946–1993: A Finding Aid," http:// oasis.lib.harvard.edu/oasis/deliver/~sch01216. "Bargowski, Dolores," http://socialar chive.iath.virginia.edu/ark:/99166/w62832wt. Kristen Fallica, "More Than 'Just Talk': The Chelsea Picture Station in the 1970s," *Camera Obscura* 28, no. 82 (January 2013): 124–33.

49. Katy Gray, "Interview with Debra Zimmerman," *Films for the Feminist Classroom*, no. 5.2 (2014), http://ffc.twu.edu/issue_5-2/feat_Zimmerman_5-2.html.

50. Fallica, "More Than 'Just Talk,'" 129.

51. Women Make Movies, Film Catalog, http://www.wmm.com/filmcatalog/subjects /sub1.shtml.

8. BY THE NUMBERS

1. "Ncsesdata.nsf.gov—WebCASPAR|Home—US National Science Foundation (NSF)," https://ncsesdata.nsf.gov/webcaspar/index.jsp?subHeader=WebCASPAR Home. See also "Note on the Data Used to Calculate Humanities Degree Counts and Shares," http://www.humanitiesindicators.org/content/document.aspx?i=187.

2. See, e.g., National Center for Education Statistics, *Digest of Education Statistics, 2014*, table 318.50, 'Degrees conferred by postsecondary institutions, by control of institution, level of degree, and field of study: 2012–13," https://nces.ed.gov/pro grams/digest/d14/.

3. Jennifer Levitz and Douglas Belkin, "Humanities Fall from Favor," *Wall Street Journal*, June 6, 2013.

4. "Media Definitions," *Nielson Media*, http://www.nielsenmedia.co.nz/en/pdf/mri/28/mediaterms.pdf.

5. "Media Definitions."

6. Ben Schmidt, "A Crisis in the Humanities?—The Edge of the American West," *Chronicle of Higher Education*, http://www.chronicle.com/blognetwork/edgeofthewest/2013/06/10/the-humanities-crisis/.

7. National Center for Education Statistics, "Higher Education General Information Survey (HEGIS) II: Degrees and Other Formal Awards Conferred Between July 1, 1966, and June 30, 1967: Version 1," July 26, 2004, http://www.icpsr.umich.edu/ICPSR/studies/02082/version/1.There were 988 programs at PhD-granting institutions in the academic year ending 2015. National Center for Education Statistics, Integrated Postsecondary Education Data System (IPEDS), "Institutional Characteristics" and "Completions" (preliminary release data), 2015, https://nces.ed.gov/ipeds/datacenter.

8. Although official crosswalks are available, and we have used them, these do not resolve all cases. The data requires some cleaning for purposes of longitudinal comparison. We have generally avoided detailed discussion of examples where taxonomic changes may introduce ambiguities.

9. The American Dental Hygienists Association's website, for example, lists associate programs as entry level. http://www.adha.org/dental-hygiene-programs.

10. This list also shows why it would be a bad idea to compute reach in terms of the proportion of total institutions where specific programs are offered. Such a measure would require us to overlook the fact that some institutions only graduate a handful of students while others graduate many thousands.

11. Although these numbers may be derived easily from publicly available data, NCES does not typically publish them. Rather, its annual *Digest of Educational Statistics* reports all completions in the family (23) as English Language and Literature/Letters. Differences within English are registered, then erased.

12. As mentioned in the preceding chapter, reliable sources like the American Film Institute (AFI) survey reveal that CIP's inclusion of the field followed a couple decades of particularly rapid growth.

13. The directorate asked: "How can a scientific education prepare us to meet the challenges of adult life, work, and citizenship? What does scientific literacy mean today and how can we measure it? What must NSF do to support the changes in education that will be needed to prepare all students, whatever their career goals, to be scientifically literate? How must NSF itself change to demonstrate the qualities of mind and practice that will support the development of the people, the ideas, and the tools needed to improve science education for all students?" Judith A. Ramaley, Barbara M. Olds, and Janice Earle, "Becoming a Learning Organization: New Directions in Science Education Research at the National Science Foundation," *Journal of Science Education & Technology* 14, no. 2 (June 2005): 173–89.

14. Clark Kerr, *The Uses of the University* (Cambridge, MA: Harvard University Press, 2001), 31–32.

15. Paul Anson Bloland, Louis C. Stamatakos, and Russell R. Rogers, *Reform in Student Affairs: A Critique of Student Development* (School of Education, University of North Carolina at Greensboro, 1994), 4, http://files.eric.ed.gov/fulltext/ED366862.pdf. Colleges and universities were required to alter their working

relationship to students in the wake of the 1961 federal court ruling *Dixon v. Alabama*. That case rewrote 1913's *Gott v. Berea College*, which stipulated that "college authorities stand in loco parentis concerning the physical and moral welfare, and mental training of the pupils, and we are unable to see why to that end they may not make any rule or regulation for the government, or betterment of their pupils that a parent could for the same purpose." The later *Dixon*, which turned on Alabama State College's decision to expel African American students who participated in a civil rights demonstration, curtailed this authority. The court ruled "that due process requires notice and some opportunity for hearing before a student at a tax-supported college is expelled for misconduct." On these rulings, see Philip Lee, "The Curious Life of In Loco Parentis at American Universities," *Higher Education in Review* 8 (2011): 69–71. A parade of demonstration and free-speech cases followed, the result being a new idea of the undergraduate as legally responsible adult. The 1972 Higher Education Amendments to the Civil Rights Act further eroded in loco parentis because Title IX barred schools from discriminating in educational programs or activities receiving federal financial assistance and Title VII barred employee discrimination.

16. Gordon B. Stein and H. A. Spille, "Academic Advising Reaches Out," *Personnel & Guidance Journal* 53 (September 1974): 61–64.

17. "University 101 Programs—Welcome," http://www.sc.edu/univ101/, accessed July 1, 2016.

18. John H. Schuh, Susan R. Jones, and Shaun R. Harper, *Student Services: A Handbook for the Profession* (San Francisco: Jossey-Bass, 2010), 75–76.

19. Michael Roth, blog posts tagged "diversity," *Roth on Wesleyan*, http://roth.blogs .wesleyan.edu/tag/diversity/.

20. "Just from 1975–85," Rhoades observes, "the numbers of administrative, managerial, and executive positions grew at three times the pace of faculty. But the number of support professionals increased more than three times that of administrators." By 2000, these support professionals "accounted for nearly 30 percent of the professional positions on campus and more than three times the number of administrative positions." Gary Rhoades, "The Study of the Academic Profession," in *Sociology of Higher Education: Contributions and Their Contexts*, ed. Patricia J. Gumport (Baltimore, MD: Johns Hopkins University Press, 2008), 128–29.

21. Larry L. Leslie and Gary Rhoades, "Rising Administrative Costs: Seeking Explanations," *Journal of Higher Education* 66, no. 2 (March 1995): 188. See also Kenneth E. Andersen, "Anatomizing Bloat," *Academe* 77, no. 6 (November 1, 1991): 20–24. Looking back from the perspective of 2014, the researchers at the Delta Cost Project describe the difficulty in delimiting the expanding and rapidly changing field "because student services is a broad category that includes a variety of activities." Donna Desrochers and Rita Kirshstein, "Labor Intensive or Labor Expensive? Changing Staffing and Compensation Patterns in Higher Education," Delta Cost Project, February 2014, http://www.deltacostproject.org/sites/default/files /products/DeltaCostAIR_Staffing_Brief_2_3_14.pdf.

22. For student/staff ratios, see the 1992 *Digest*, page 168, figure 16; page 221, table 208. For enrollments, see page 172, table 160. National Center for Education Statistics, *Digest of Education Statistics, 1992*, https://nces.ed.gov/pubsearch/pubsinfo.asp ?pubid=92097.

23. According to NCES, at public four-year institutions, nonfaculty professionals rose from 10 percent of all employees in 1976 to 24.1 percent in 2011, while at privates their numbers increased from 8.6 percent to 21.6 percent. 1992 *Digest*, table 207; 2012 *Digest*, table 286. National Center for Education Statistics, *Digest of Education Statistics, 2012*, https://nces.ed.gov/pubsearch/pubsinfo.asp?pubid=2014015. The highest percentage, 23.6 percent, was at private for-profit schools. The economist Caroline Hoxby observes that by the early 2000s the "highest selectivity schools" were spending about $92,000 per student, where "low-selectivity schools" spent around $12,000. Caroline M. Hoxby, "The Changing Selectivity of American Colleges," *Journal of Economic Perspectives* 23, no. 4 (December 2009): 109.

24. Instructional spending at publics plunged from 35.1 percent of expenditures in 1980 to 26.48 percent in 2011–12. In contrast, academic support and student service were essentially unchanged, with the former dropping slightly (from 7.2 percent to 6.64 percent) and the latter rising slightly (4.6 percent to 4.63 percent). 1992 *Digest*, table 323; 2013 *Digest*, table 334.10. National Center for Education Statistics, *Digest of Education Statistics, 2013*, https://nces.ed.gov/pubsearch/pubsinfo.asp?pubid=2015011. Money in public institutions appeared to move out of instruction and into a variety of growth areas that included scholarships (as a higher-tuition, higher-scholarship model took hold), hospitals, and "other," which is 3.84 percent in 2011–12.

25. Instruction increased from 27 percent of expenditures in 1980 to 32.66 percent in 2011–12, while academic support rose from 5.7 percent to 8.87 percent, and student services nearly doubled from 4.4 percent to 8.06 percent. These numbers were different for alternate types of private institution, whether nonprofit or for-profit, four-year or two-year. 1992 *Digest*, table 324; 2013 *Digest*, table 334.30.

26. Thomas Joseph Grites, "Academic Advising: Getting Us Through the Eighties," American Association for Higher Education, 1979, http://files.eric.ed.gov/fulltext/ED178023.pdf.

27. Donna M. Bourassa and Kevin Kruger, "The National Dialogue on Academic and Student Affairs Collaboration," *New Directions for Higher Education* 2001, no. 116 (2001): 9, 11–12.

28. Delta Cost Project researchers summed up the trend in which "student-related activities (ranging from course and career guidance to disciplinary actions) that were previously under the purview of faculty have been centralized." Desrochers and Kirshstein, "Labor Intensive or Labor Extensive?" 18.

29. Robert Dubin and Fredric Beisse, "The Assistant: Academic Subaltern," *Administrative Science Quarterly* 11, no. 4 (March 1, 1967): 545.

30. At four-year publics, faculty represented only 31.9 percent of the professional workforce in 2013, but 66.7 percent of them were full time. 2014 *Digest*, table 314.30. In private nonprofit four-years, by contrast, faculty were 38.7 percent of all employed professionals, but only 56.5 percent were full time. In private for-profit four-year schools, faculty were 62.3 percent of employees, with merely 15.5 percent full time. At publics, graduate assistants increased from 10 percent of total staff in 1976 to 15.3 percent in 2013. 1992 *Digest*, table 208; 2014 *Digest*, table 314.30. While at privates, the growth rate was negligible: graduate assistants were 6 percent of the academic workforce in 1976 and 6.5 percent at nonprofit four-year schools in 2013.

31. Sue Doe and Mike Palmquist, "An Evolving Discourse: The Shifting Uses of Position Statements on the Contingent Faculty," *ADE Bulletin* 153 (2013): 23–34.

32. Michael Bérubé and Cary Nelson, *Higher Education Under Fire: Politics, Economics, and the Crisis of the Humanities* (New York: Routledge, 1995), 20.

33. Bérubé and Nelson, *Higher Education Under Fire*, 25.

34. In the language and literature fields served by the MLA, a 2014 report compiled by a special task force precipitated substantial debate, hand-wringing, and reform. MLA Task Force, "Report of the MLA Task Force on Doctoral Study in Modern Language and Literature," Modern Language Association, May 2014, https://www.mla.org/content/download/25437/1164354/taskforcedocstudy2014.pdf. The American Historical Association was just as active in the second decade of the twenty-first century, producing a bevy of reports and sponsoring a host of initiatives. The society's executive directors looked back: See James Grossman and Emily Swafford, "Graduate Education Reconsidered," *Perspectives on History*, April 2016, https://www.historians.org/publications-and-directories/perspectives-on-history/april-2016/graduate-education-reconsidered.

35. Peter Uwe Hohendahl, "Humboldt Revisited: Liberal Education, University Reform, and the Opposition to the Neoliberal University," *New German Critique* 38, no. 2 (2011): 189.

9. BAD ENGLISH: THE CULTURE WARS RECONSIDERED

1. By focusing on conservative policy and public relations initiatives, Ira Shor usefully provides an alternative periodization: Ira Shor, *Culture Wars: School and Society in the Conservative Restoration, 1969–1984* (Chicago: University of Chicago Press, 1992).

2. Alan Sokal, "A Physicist Experiments with Cultural Studies," *Lingua Franca Archive*, May/June 1996, http://linguafranca.mirror.theinfo.org/9605/sokal.html.

3. David R. Shumway, "The Star System in Literary Studies," *PMLA* no. 112 (1997): 86.

4. Allan Bloom, *The Closing of the American Mind: How Higher Education Has Failed Democracy and Impoverished the Souls of Today's Students* (New York: Simon and Schuster, 1987), 379.

5. Janny Scott, "Scholars Fear 'Star' System May Undercut Their Mission," *New York Times*, December 20, 1997, http://www.nytimes.com/1997/12/20/arts/scholars-fear-star-system-may-undercut-their-mission.html.

6. Shumway, "The Star System in Literary Studies," 91–92.

7. Shumway, "The Star System in Literary Studies," 94. The argument was extended by numerous attacks and amendments. Bruce Robbins alleged nostalgia as well as ignorance about precedents for today's conference circuit. Bruce Robbins, "Celeb-Reliance: Intellectuals, Celebrity, and Upward Mobility," *Postmodern Culture* 9, no. 2 (1999). Ann Pellegrini observed that star status was as much about culture-war style animosity (and even sexism or racism) as it was idealization: "if a Judith Butler has become a household name, it is in no small part due to the way she has been attacked, what has been said about her and not for what she has herself said or written." Ann Pellegrini, "Star Gazing," *Minnesota Review* 52, no. 1 (2001): 213.

8. Akbar Ahmed, "Whitney Looks Back on 30 Years," *Yale Daily News*, February 29, 2012, http://yaledailynews.com/blog/2012/02/29/whitney-looks-back-on-30-years/.

9. Bernd Magnus, "How Does Collaborative Research Work in the Humanities?" Report of the Fall 1988 Resident Research Group, UC Humanities Research Institute, 1988.

10. George Levine, Peter Brooks, Marjorie Garber, E. Ann Kaplan, and Catherine R. Stimpson, "Speaking for the Humanities," American Council of Learned Societies, 1989, http://archives.acls.org/op/7_Speaking_for_Humanities.htm.

11. Julie Thompson Klein, *Humanities, Culture, and Interdisciplinarity* (Albany: State University of New York Press, 2005), 77.

12. Russell Jacoby, *The Last Intellectuals: American Culture in the Age of Academe* (New York: Basic Books, 1987), 6.

13. Russell Jacoby, *The Last Intellectuals: American Culture in the Age of Academe*, rev. ed. (New York: Basic Books, 2000), xv.

14. Jacoby, *The Last Intellectuals*, rev. ed., xvi.

15. "Report of the MLA Task Force on Evaluating Scholarship for Tenure and Promotion," Modern Language Association, 2006, 22, https://apps.mla.org/pdf/task forcereport0608.pdf.

16. "Report of the MLA Task Force," 32.

17. Barbara R. Bergmann, "Bloated Administration, Blighted Campuses," *Academe* 77, no. 6 (November 1, 1991): 15.

18. Jeffrey J. Williams, "Name Recognition," *Minnesota Review* 52, no. 1 (2001): 198.

19. Williams, "Name Recognition," 198.

20. Ewen Callaway, "Beat It, Impact Factor! Publishing Elite Turns Against Controversial Metric," *Nature News* 535, no. 7611 (July 14, 2016): 210.

21. Bill Readings, *The University in Ruins* (Cambridge, MA: Harvard University Press, 1996), chap. 2.

22. Edward B. Fisk, "Report Assails College Failures in Humanities," *New York Times*, November 26, 1984, http://www.nytimes.com/1984/11/26/us/report-assails-college-failures-in-humanities.html?pagewanted=all.

23. William J. Bennett, *To Reclaim a Legacy: A Report on the Humanities in Higher Education*, National Endowment for the Humanities (1984), 2, https://catalog .hathitrust.org/Record/001548265.

24. Bennett, "To Reclaim a Legacy," 4.

25. Bennett, "To Reclaim a Legacy," 6.

26. David Callahan, "$1 Billion for Ideas: Conservative Think Tanks in the 1990s," National Committee for Responsive Philanthropy, 1999, https://www.ncrp.org /publication/1-billion-ideas.

27. Jonathan Yardley, "Higher Education: A Privilege, Not a Right," *Washington Post*, February 18, 1985, https://www.washingtonpost.com/archive/lifestyle/1985 /02/18/higher-education-a-privilege-not-a-right/f9486285-61f5-405d-be227c89 69f87b80/.

28. Shor, *Culture Wars*, 19.

29. Allan Bloom, *The Closing of the American Mind: How Higher Education Has Failed Democracy and Impoverished the Souls of Today's Students* (New York: Simon and Schuster, 1987), 338, 340–41.

30. Bloom, *The Closing of the American Mind*, 340–41.

31. Bloom, *The Closing of the American Mind*, 372.

32. E. D. Hirsch, *Cultural Literacy: What Every American Needs to Know* (Boston: Houghton Mifflin, 1987), 177.

33. Gerald Graff, *Beyond the Culture Wars: How Teaching the Conflicts Can Revitalize American Education* (New York: Norton, 1992), 22.

34. Graff, *Beyond the Culture Wars*, 37–38.

35. Bennett Lovett-Graff, "Culture Wars II," *Modern Language Studies* 25, no. 3 (1995): 102.

36. Lovett-Graff also makes this point about Jacoby, noting also that some on the left write well (he names Stanley Fish, Michael Bérubé, and Terry Eagleton). Lovett-Graff, "Culture Wars II," 116.

37. Hazel V. Carby, "The Multicultural Wars," *Radical History Review* 54 (1992): 17.

38. Richard M. Ohmann, "English in America, Ten Years Later," *ADE Bulletin* 82 (1985): 15.

39. Richard M. Ohmann, *English in America: A Radical View of the Profession* (New York: Oxford University Press, 1976).

40. Ohmann, "English in America," 16.

41. John Guillory, "Canonical and Non-Canonical: A Critique of the Current Debate," *ELH* 54, no. 3 (1987): 496.

42. Guillory, "Canonical and Non-Canonical," 519.

43. The "project of critique," he writes, "indissolubly linked to the question of the 'non-canonical,' is better served by discarding the problematic of representation for a problematic whose object is the constitution and distribution of cultural capital." Guillory, "Canonical and Non-Canonical," 520–21.

44. Nancy Armstrong, "Who's Afraid of the Cultural Turn?," *differences: A Journal of Feminist Cultural Studies* 12 (Spring 2001): 17–49.

45. "This might have been an advance," Klein writes, "if everyone agreed cultural studies was the work of the future; if faculty in other disciplines leapt at opportunities for collaboration; and if administrators, trustees, journalists and voters saw the change as an exciting revolution. None of this happened to an appreciable degree, however. Internal strife and resentment followed, along with mockery from the media and political Right. The curriculum lost whatever coherence it had, importing material and methods from outside and spilling into interdisciplinary and multicultural studies." Klein, *Humanities, Culture, and Interdisciplinarity*, 101.

46. Peter Novick, *That Noble Dream: The "Objectivity Question" and the American Historical Profession* (Cambridge: Cambridge University Press, 1988), 573.

47. Each could, of course, be characterized in different disciplinary ways and located in different "home" departments. This is the point.

48. Committee on Prospering in the Global Economy of the 21st Century (US), and Committee on Science, Engineering, and Public Policy (US), *Rising Above the Gathering Storm: Energizing and Employing America for a Brighter Economic Future* (Washington, DC: National Academies Press, 2007), 3.

49. Paul R. Gross and Norman Levitt, *Higher Superstition: The Academic Left and Its Quarrels with Science* (Baltimore, MD: Johns Hopkins University Press, 1997). For

context, see Steve Fuller, "Science Studies Through the Looking Glass: An Intellectual History," in *Beyond the Science Wars: The Missing Discourse About Science and Society*, ed. Ullica Segerstrale (Albany: State University of New York Press, 2003), 185–217.

50. That he was right in this particular, and not the fact that *Social Text* failed to recognize bad science, accounts for the force of the scandal, John Guillory convincingly shows. John Guillory, "The Sokal Affair and the History of Criticism," *Critical Inquiry* 28, no. 2 (2002): 470–508.

51. *Social Text* editor Andrew Ross was far from alone in blaming the press in general and *Lingua Franca* in particular for what he called a "yellow media exposé," which reduced difficult concepts and challenging intellectual debates "to the status of gibberish." Andrew Ross, "Reflections on the Sokal Affair," *Social Text* 50 (1997): 149.

52. Fuller, "Science Studies Through the Looking Glass," 203.

53. As Ullica Segerstrale recounts, Sokal followed the inclination of activist scholars who tended to treat "social constructivists and postmodern humanists" as the "original aggressors" in a war begun in the 1960s over scientific facticity. Ullica Segerstrale, "Science and Science Studies: Enemies or Allies?" in *Beyond the Science Wars: The Missing Discourse About Science and Society*, ed. Ullica Segerstrale (Albany: State University of New York Press, 2000), 2.

54. Fuller, "Science Studies Through the Looking Glass," 209.

55. In the humanities, a comparable feat could be claimed for African Americanists including Cornel West. West's "radical traditionalist" combination of teaching Matthew Arnold at Princeton, speaking to standing-room-only crowds at the New-York Historical Society, and writing columns in the *Nation* was given star treatment in 1991 by the *New York Times Magazine*. Robert S. Boynton, "Princeton's Public Intellectual," *New York Times Magazine*, September 15, 1991, http://www.nytimes.com/1991/09/15/magazine/princeton-s-public-intellectual.html.

56. Readings, *The University in Ruins*, 67.

57. Readings, *The University in Ruins*, 87.

58. One prominent player was the philosopher Martha Nussbaum, who made the case for liberal education through reference to the long history of Western philosophy in a number of books. Her rhetorical themes could be found in diverse reports by, among others, the American Academy of Arts and Sciences. See, for an example, Martha Craven Nussbaum, *Cultivating Humanity: A Classical Defense of Reform in Liberal Education* (Cambridge, MA: Harvard University Press, 1997).

59. Geoffrey Galt Harpham, *The Humanities and the Dream of America* (Chicago: University of Chicago Press, 2011), 156–57.

60. This is where Christopher Newfield puts a spin on the usual story of decline, arguing that "just as the American middle class was starting to become multiracial," the old humanist "vision . . . of a full political, economic, and cultural capability that would be in reach of more or less everyone through higher education" came under assault. Christopher Newfield, *Unmaking the Public University: The Forty-Year Assault on the Middle Class* (Cambridge, MA: Harvard University Press, 2008), 3.

61. Eric Gould, *The University in a Corporate Culture* (New Haven, CT: Yale University Press, 2003), 20.

10. THE LONG TWENTIETH CENTURY

1. For a recap, see National Association of Student Financial Aid Administrators, "2016 Presidential Candidates' Higher Education Proposals," October 14, 2016, https://www.nasfaa.org/2016_presidential_candidates.
2. On climate change, see "Climate Leadership," *Second Nature*, http://secondnature.org/what-we-do/climate-leadership/. And for one example of the response to the travel ban, see Susan Svrluga, "Nearly 600 Colleges Object to Trump's Travel Ban," *Washington Post*, February 3, 2017, https://www.washingtonpost.com/news/grade-point/wp/2017/02/03/nearly-600-colleges-object-to-trumps-travel-ban/.
3. Bill Nye, the "Science Guy," among others led a public relations campaign resulting in worldwide marches notable for their meme-ready signs and chants of "What do we want? Science! When do we want it? After peer review!" Nicholas St. Fleur, "Scientists, Feeling Under Siege, March Against Trump Policies," *New York Times*, April 22, 2017, https://www.nytimes.com/2017/04/22/science/march-for-science.html.
4. "Thanks to Trump, Scientists Are Going to Run for Office," *Atlantic*, January 25, 2017, https://www.theatlantic.com/science/archive/2017/01/thanks-to-trump-scientists-are-planning-to-run-for-office/514229/.
5. "Sharp Partisan Divisions in Views of National Institutions," *Pew Research Center for the People and the Press*, July 10, 2017, http://www.people-press.org/2017/07/10/sharp-partisan-divisions-in-views-of-national-institutions/.
6. David Leonhardt, "The Assault on Colleges—and the American Dream," *New York Times*, May 25, 2017, https://www.nytimes.com/2017/05/25/opinion/sunday/the-assault-on-colleges-and-the-american-dream.html.
7. On the challenges and perils of this approach, see Christopher Newfield, *The Great Mistake: How We Wrecked Public Universities and How We Can Fix Them* (Baltimore, MD: Johns Hopkins University Press, 2016).
8. Ben Miller, "The Student Debt Review," New America Education Policy Program, 2014, 2–6, http://na-production.s3.amazonaws.com/documents/the-student-debt-review.pdf.
9. Shahien Nasiripour, "Student Debt Is Eating Your Household Budget," *Bloomberg.com*, May 18, 2017, https://www.bloomberg.com/news/articles/2017-05-18/student-debt-is-eating-your-household-budget.
10. Debt-funded higher education "not only results in higher loan balances for low-income, Black and Latino students," according to Department of Education and 2013 Federal Reserve data analyzed by the think tank Demos, "but also results in high numbers of low-income students and students of color dropping out without receiving a credential." Mark Huelsman, "The Debt Divide," *Demos*, May 15, 2015, http://www.demos.org/publication/debt-divide-racial-and-class-bias-behind-new-normal-student-borrowing.

11. A parade of well-promoted studies encouraged students to look for the value proposition when comparing colleges and majors. Oft-cited and recent studies include those from Pew ("Is College Worth It?" *Pew Research Center's Social & Demographic Trends Project*, May 15, 2011, http://www.pewsocialtrends.org/2011/05/15/is-college-worth-it/), PayScale ("Is College Worth It?" *Economist*, April 5, 2014, http://www.economist.com/news/united-states/21600131-too-many-degrees-are-waste-money-return-higher-education-would-be-much-better), and the Hamilton Project of the Brookings Institution (Michael Greenstone and Adam Looney, "Is Starting College and Not Finishing Really That Bad?" Hamilton Project, June 6, 2013, http://www.hamiltonproject.org/papers/what_happens_to_students_who_fail_to_complete_a_college_degree_is_some/).

12. Attacks from governors in North Carolina and Wisconsin received considerable attention. See Valerie Strauss, "N.C. Governor Attacks Higher Ed, Proposes Funding Colleges by Graduates' Jobs," *Washington Post*, February 7, 2013, https://www.washingtonpost.com/news/answer-sheet/wp/2013/02/07/n-c-governor-attacks-higher-ed-proposes-funding-colleges-by-graduates-jobs. And on Wisconsin's Governor Walker's efforts to shift the emphasis of his state's university system toward "the jobs and opportunities that are available in the state," see Dan Simmons, "Scott Walker Backtracks from Striking 'Truth,' 'Human Condition' from Wisconsin Idea," *Wisconsin State Journal*, February 5, 2015, http://host.madison.com/wsj/news/local/govt-and-politics/scott-walker-backtracks-from-striking-truth-human-condition-from-wisconsin/article_a4ca4220-7211-5fc8-b2b9-0ab5313c6937.html.

13. To prove career viability, for example, Beckie Supiano contextualized data from the Association of American Colleges and Universities. Beckie Supiano, "How Liberal-Arts Majors Fare Over the Long Haul," *Chronicle of Higher Education*, January 22, 2014, http://www.chronicle.com/article/How-Liberal-Arts-Majors-Fare/144133. Recent influential books rejecting instrumental thinking on behalf of humanities professors include Maggie Berg and Barbara Seeber, *The Slow Professor: Challenging the Culture of Speed in the Academy* (Toronto: University of Toronto Press, 2016); Martha C. Nussbaum, *Not for Profit: Why Democracy Needs the Humanities* (Princeton, NJ: Princeton University Press, 2016); and Benjamin Ginsberg, *The Fall of the Faculty* (New York: Oxford University Press, 2013).

14. "Top Colleges Doing the Most for the American Dream," *New York Times*, May 25, 2017, https://www.nytimes.com/interactive/2017/05/25/sunday-review/opinion-pell-table.html.

15. "Barack Obama's Fifth State of the Union Address," *Wikisource*, February 12, 2013, https://en.wikisource.org/wiki/Barack_Obama%27s_Fifth_State_of_the_Union_Address.

16. "Remarks by the President on Opportunity for All and Skills for America's Workers," January 30, 2014, https://obamawhitehouse.archives.gov/the-press-office/2014/01/30/remarks-president-opportunity-all-and-skills-americas-workers.

17. Jennifer Schuessler, "President Obama Writes Apology to Art Historian," *New York Times*, February 18, 2004, https://artsbeat.blogs.nytimes.com/2014/02/18/president-obama-writes-apology-to-art-historian/.

18. "Opening Statement of Betsy DeVos," January 17, 2017, https://www.help.senate.gov/imo/media/doc/DeVos.pdf.

19. "US Secretary of Education Betsy DeVos' Prepared Remarks to the Brookings Institution," March 29, 2017, https://www.ed.gov/news/speeches/us-secretary -education-betsy-devos-prepared-remarks-brookings-institution. Adam Harris, "For Student Advocates, a Worrying Week of Departures from Obama-Era Policy," *Chronicle of Higher Education*, June 15, 2017, http://www.chronicle.com .pallas2.tcl.sc.edu/article/For-Student-Advocates-a/240362.

20. Goldie Blumenstyk, "Education Department Now Plans a College-Rating System Minus the Ratings," *Chronicle of Higher Education*, June 25, 2015, http://www .chronicle.com/article/Education-Department-Now-Plans/231137.

21. Michael Hurwitz and Jonathan Smith, "Student Responsiveness to Earnings Data in the College Scorecard," Social Science Research Network, May 1, 2016, https:// papers.ssrn.com/sol3/papers.cfm?abstract_id=2768157. In September, however, the *Chronicle* reported that the tool had proved more useful for adult college advisors than it had for students themselves: Sarah Brown, "Where the College Scorecard Has Gained Traction So Far—and Where It Hasn't," *Chronicle of Higher Education*, September 28, 2016, http://www.chronicle.com/article/Where-the-College -Scorecard/237919.

22. The researchers could not determine whether "differential responsiveness to the Scorecard earnings data" resulted from the fact that "overrepresented groups" were simply more aware of the data "or whether lower-income students feel less empowered to adapt their college lists based on the information." They observed that "confusion about financial aid processes, particularly at the nation's most competitive colleges, may unnecessarily prevent low-income students from adjusting their initial college list in response to Scorecard-like data." Hurwitz and Smith, "Student Responsiveness to Earnings Data," 22–23.

23. See, on that presumption, Michel Foucault, *The Birth of Biopolitics* (New York: Palgrave, 2008), 239–65.

24. As Mark's economist colleague points out, such reasoning derives from human-capital theory, which assumes that "just as corporations want to earn a particular rate of return on their capital investments, people invest in their human capital by going to college, acquiring new skills, and so forth." There are two challenges facing this approach: "First, to hold constant all other factors that determine the rate of return on college education, and second, the assumption about future interest rates. The latter is important because the costs are incurred today but the benefits occur in the future." Drucilla Barker, email message to author, August 14, 2015.

25. "Colleges are not required to report that information," he noted. "When they report it, they report it in different ways." Peter Cappelli, "'Will College Pay Off?' A Surprising Cost-Benefit Analysis," interview by *Knowledge@Wharton*, June 2015, http://knowledge.wharton.upenn.edu/article/will-college-pay-off-a-surprising -cost-benefit-analysisision-youll-ever-make/.

26. Tom DiChristopher and John Schoen, "Petroleum Engineer Degrees Going from Boom to Bust," *CNBC.com*, December 4, 2015, http://www.cnbc.com/2015/12/04 /petroleum-engineering-degrees-seen-going-from-boom-to-bust.html. Denver Nicks, "Why Students Are Dumping This Major That Once Guaranteed a Fat Paycheck," *Time*, March 18, 2016, https://finance.yahoo.com/news/why-students -dumping-major-once-163758247.html. Jeff Forward, "Low Price of Oil Affecting

College Programs, Students," *Community Impact Newspaper,* July 27, 2016, https://communityimpact.com/houston/education/2016/07/13/low-price-oil-affecting-college-programs-students/.

27. Quoted in Bourree Lam, "The Danger of Picking a Major Based on Where the Jobs Are," *Atlantic,* June 12, 2015, https://www.theatlantic.com/business/archive/2015/06/college-major-job-hottest-industry/395570/.

28. "The Simple Truth About the Gender Pay Gap," AAUW, 2018, http://www.aauw.org/research/the-simple-truth-about-the-gender-pay-gap/.

29. Erin Einhorn, "Rich School, Poor School," *NPR.org,* February 9, 2015, http://www.npr.org/sections/ed/2015/02/09/382122276/rich-school-poor-school.

30. Anthony P. Carnevale and Stephen J. Rose, "Economy Goes to College: The Hidden Promise of Higher Education in the Post-Industrial Service Economy," Center on Education and the Workforce, Georgetown University, 2015, https://cew.georgetown.edu/wp-content/uploads/EconomyGoesToCollege.pdf.

31. The CLA had been developed by the nonprofit Council for Aid to Education, which Arum and Roksa acknowledged for supporting their research. This council had been around: Alfred P. Sloan orchestrated its establishment in 1952, and for a time it was a subsidiary of the RAND Corporation. "History," Council for Aid to Education, http://cae.org/about-cae/history/.

32. Richard Arum and Josipa Roksa, *Academically Adrift* (Chicago: University of Chicago Press, 2010), 30.

33. "While almost one-quarter of the college graduates we studied were living back at home with their families two years after finishing college, a stunning 95 percent reported that their lives would be the same or better than those of their parents." Richard Arum and Josipa Roksa, *Aspiring Adults Adrift: Tentative Transitions of College Graduates* (Chicago: University of Chicago Press, 2014), 3.

34. Thorstein Veblen, *The Higher Learning in America: A Memorandum on the Conduct of Universities by Business Men* (New York: B. W. Huebsch, 1918), 25–26.

35. The five proficiencies are: Specialized Knowledge (no matter the specialization—any field of study will do), Broad and Integrative Knowledge (the capacity to bridge concepts from across, say, the humanities or the social sciences), Intellectual Skills (analytic inquiry, use of information resources, communication fluency, etc.), Applied and Collaborative Learning, and Civic and Global Learning. Cliff Adelman, et al., "The Degree Qualifications Profile," Lumina Foundation, October 2014, https://www.luminafoundation.org/files/resources/dqp.pdf. Lumina was established in 2000 as a public charity with seed money derived from a selloff of operating assets to Sallie Mae by the USA Group (then the nation's largest private guarantor and administrator of education loans, as per Lumina's website).

36. Evelyn Ganzglass and Larry Good, "Rethinking Credentialing, American Council on Education," Lumina Foundation, July 27, 2015, http://www.luminafoundation.org/resources/rethinking-credentialing.

37. Jamie Merisotis, "Toward Learner-Centered Higher Education: Why Faculty-Led Assessment Is the Key," Lumina Foundation, http://www.luminafoundation.org/news-and-events/toward-learner-centered-higher-education-why-faculty-led-assessment-is-the-key.

38. "Goal 2025—Increasing Degree Attainment," Lumina Foundation, http://www.luminafoundation.org/goal_2025.

39. "GE Scientific Literacy—Course Approval Description," University of California, Davis, February 19, 2007, http://ge.ucdavis.edu/local_resources/docs/Scientific -Literacy-final.pdf.

40. "Carolina Core Requirements," University of South Carolina, http://www.sc.edu /about/offices_and_divisions/provost/academicpriorities/undergradstudies/car olinacore/requirements/index.php. These became policy in December 2010.

41. Steve Ruiz, For the Win: USA Today Sports, blog, http://ftw.usatoday.com/2017/04 /mississippi-states-upset-connecitcut-tv-ratings-viewers-national-championship -south-carolina-espn

42. Quoted in Mark C. Taylor, Crisis on Campus: A Bold Plan for Reforming Our Colleges and Universities (New York: Knopf, 2010), 35.

43. Taylor, Crisis on Campus, 79. Taylor's thinking had been shaped by personal experience leading (with the New York investment banker Herbert Allen Jr.) the failed 1998 startup Global Education Network, a MOOC platform avant la lettre (41).

44. Laura Pappano, "Massive Open Online Courses Are Multiplying at a Rapid Pace," New York Times, November 2, 2012, http://www.nytimes.com/2012/11/04/educa tion/edlife/massive-open-online-courses-are-multiplying-at-a-rapid-pace.html.

45. Jeffrey R. Young, "Pioneer of Ed-Tech Innovation Says He's Frustrated by Disruptors' Narrative," Chronicle of Higher Education Blogs: Wired Campus, August 6, 2015, http://www.chronicle.com/blogs/wiredcampus/pioneer-of-ed -tech-innovation-says-hes-frustrated-by-disruptors-narrative/57159.

46. "The Attack of the MOOCs," Economist, July 20, 2013, https://www.economist .com/news/business/21582001-army-new-online-courses-scaring-wits-out -traditional-universities-can-they.

47. Jonathan Haber, "When MOOCs Are Better Than College Classes," Inside Higher Ed, August 13, 2014, https://www.insidehighered.com/blogs/higher-ed-beta/when -moocs-are-better-college-classes.

48. Steve Kolowich, "The Professors Behind the MOOC Hype," Chronicle of Higher Education, March 18, 2013, http://www.chronicle.com/article/The-Professors -Behind-the-MOOC/137905.

49. Barry Peddycord III, "Why It Makes Sense for Students to Grade One Another's Papers," Chronicle of Higher Education Blogs: #FutureEd (blog), February 12, 2014, http://www.chronicle.com/blogs/future/2014/02/12/why-it-makes-sense-for -students-to-grade-one-anothers-papers/.

50. Ry Rivard, "San Jose State University Faculty Pushes Back Against EdX," Inside Higher Ed, May 3, 2013, https://www.insidehighered.com/quicktakes/2013/05/03 /san-jose-state-university-faculty-pushes-back-against-edx.

51. Jonathan Rees, "More Than MOOCs," Academe, May/June 2014, https://www .aaup.org/article/more-moocs.

52. Thille told the Chronicle of Higher Education that colleges and universities had reason to be wary of Silicon Valley firms and their proprietary algorithms. "Just trust the black box," is what such firms are saying, Thille observed. "That's alchemy, that's not science." See Goldie Blumenstyk, "As Big-Data Companies Come to Teaching, a Pioneer Issues a Warning," Chronicle of Higher Education, February 23, 2016, http:// www.chronicle.com/article/As-Big-Data-Companies-Come-to/235400.

53. Phil Hill, "MOOCs Are Dead: Long Live Online Higher Education," Chronicle of Higher Education, August 26, 2016, http://www.chronicle.com/article/MOOCs

-Are-Dead-Long-Live/237569. Similarly, "Godfather of Silicon Valley" John Hennessey told *Times Higher Education* that the MOOC was "not the kind of revolutionary thing I think people were hoping for. It's not a disrupter." Ellie Bothwell and Chris Havergal, "Moocs Can Transform Education—But Not Yet," *Times Higher Education*, July 21, 2016, https://www.timeshighereducation.com/features /massive-open-online-courses-moocs-can-transform-education-but-not-yet.

54. "About," https://www.coursera.org/about/; "About Us," https://www.edx.org /about-us; "About Us," https://www.udacity.com/us.

55. Study after study brought the bad news on completions. See Jarrett Carter, "Study: MOOC Learning Outcomes Unchanged by Customized Instruction," *Education Dive*, http://www.educationdive.com/news/study-mooc-learning-outcomes -unchanged-by-customized-instruction/421926/. The *New York Times* effectively took back its year-of-the-MOOC rhetoric in light of such completion data. See Tamar Lewin, "After Setbacks, Online Courses Are Rethought," *New York Times*, December 10, 2013, http://www.nytimes.com/2013/12/11/us/after-setbacks-online -courses-are-rethought.html.

56. "We have a guy in South Africa who makes $11,000 a month," Thrun told the *Financial Times* in 2015. "We want to be the Uber of education." Jonathan Moules, "Udacity Founder Takes on Virtual Study Revolution," *Financial Times*, July 26, 2015, https://www.ft.com/content/3a3af70a-1a74-11e5-a130-2e7db721f996?mhq5j=e1.

57. The *Wall Street Journal* reported Coursera's shift as its latest attempt to find a successful business model—a recurring problem among EdTech startups—while *Fortune* confirmed the move had secured new streams of venture capital. Douglas Belkin, "Coursera Partners with Tech, Financial Firms for Online Classes," *Wall Street Journal*, August 4, 2015, https://www.wsj.com/articles/coursera-partners -with-tech-financial-firms-for-online-classes-1438696601. And see Kia Kokalitcheva, "Coursera's Latest Funding Shows That (Online) Classes Are Still in Session," *Fortune*, August 25, 2015, http://fortune.com/2015/08/25/coursera-funding -online-education/.

58. John A. Byrne, "Arizona State, edX to Offer Entire Freshman Year of College Online," *Fortune*, April 22, 2015, http://fortune.com/2015/04/22/arizona-state-edx -moocs-online-education/.

59. Laura Pappano, "Massive Open Online Courses Are Multiplying at a Rapid Pace," *New York Times*, November 2, 2012, http://www.nytimes.com/2012/11/04/educa tion/edlife/massive-open-online-courses-are-multiplying-at-a-rapid-pace.html. A widely cited 2017 report issued by the Babson Survey Research Group found that public and private nonprofit institutions of higher learning dominated online distance learning, with private nonprofits growing faster than any other sort of institution. The for-profit University of Phoenix remained the largest player, but it was losing market share. The fastest-growing school was Southern New Hampshire University, followed closely by Western Governors University and Brigham Young, all private nonprofits. I. Elaine Allen and Jeff Seaman, "Digital Learning Compass: Distance Education Enrollment Report 2017," Babson Survey Research Group, May 2017, https://onlinelearningconsortium.org/read/digital-learning -compass-distance-education-enrollment-report-2017/.

60. Paul Fain and Rick Seltzer, "Purdue Acquires Kaplan University to Create a New Public, Online University Under Purdue Brand," *Inside Higher Ed*, April 28, 2017,

https://www.insidehighered.com/news/2017/04/28/purdue-acquires-kaplan
-university-create-new-public-online-university-under-purdue.

61. In particularly, they reanimated 1960s and 1970s arguments over the value of "programmed instruction" that we did not pause to consider. Programmed instruction is now called "adaptive learning." See Wilbur Schramm, *The Research on Programmed Instruction: An Annotated Bibliography* (Washington, DC: US Department of Health, Education, and Welfare, Office of Education), 1964. See also Audrey Waters, "The History of the Future of Education," *Hack Education*, February 19, 2015, http://hackeducation.com/2015/02/19/the-history-of-the-future -of-education. On the interrelation of programmed instruction and other educational media technologies of the 1960s, see Curtis Fletcher, "The Socio-Technical Humanities: Reimagining the Liberal Arts in the Age of New Media, 1952–1969: University of Southern California Dissertations and Theses," PhD diss., University of Southern California, 2014, chap. 2.

62. David Theo Goldberg, "The Dangers of the Uberization of Higher Education," *Inside Higher Ed*, August 12, 2016, https://www.insidehighered.com/views/2016/08 /12/dangers-uberization-higher-education-essay.

63. Jeffrey Silber, "Education and Training," Montreal: BMO Capital Markets, September 2015, 325.

64. Silber, "Education and Training," 328.

65. Clayton M. Christensen, Michael E. Raynor, and Rory McDonald, "What Is Disruptive Innovation?" *Harvard Business Review*, December 2015, https://hbr.org /2015/12/what-is-disruptive-innovation?

66. George Siemens, "White House: Innovation in Higher Education," *Elearnspace*, http://www.elearnspace.org/blog/2015/08/03/white-house-innovation-in-higher -education/.

67. As we wrote this book, scholars in media studies, post-poststructuralism, cognitive science, sociology, and anthropology were working energetically to explain how changes to information, to social control involving information, and to the public addressed and responsive to information had changed. See, for example Steve F. Anderson, *Technologies of Vision: The War Between Data and Images* (Cambridge, MA: MIT Press, 2017); Anne Balsamo, *Designing Culture: The Technological Imagination at Work* (Durham, NC: Duke University Press, 2011); Luc Boltanski and Eve Chiapello, *The New Spirit of Capitalism*, trans. Gregory Elliott (London: Verso, 2007); Wendy Hui Kyong Chun, *Updating to Remain the Same: Habitual New Media* (Cambridge, MA: MIT Press, 2016); Heidi Rae Cooley, *Finding Augusta: Habits of Mobility and Governance in the Digital Era* (Hanover, NH: Dartmouth College Press, 2014); Michael Curtin, Jennifer Holt, and Kevin Sanson, eds., *Distribution Revolution: Conversations About the Digital Future of Film and Television* (Berkeley: University of California Press, 2014); Cathy N. Davidson, *The New Education: How to Revolutionize the University to Prepare Students for a World in Flux* (New York: Basic Books, 2017); Pierre Dardot and Christian Laval, *The New Way of the World: On Neoliberal Society* (New York: Verso, 2013); Paul Dourish and Genevieve Bell, *Divining a Digital Future: Mess and Mythology in Ubiquitous Computing* (Cambridge, MA: MIT Press, 2011); Johanna Drucker, *Graphesis: Visual Forms of Knowledge Production* (Cambridge, MA: Harvard University Press, 2014); Keller Easterling, *Extrastatecraft: The Power of Infrastructure Space* (New York:

Verso, 2014); Alexander R. Galloway, *The Interface Effect* (Malden, MA: Polity, 2012); Lisa Gitelman, *"Raw Data" Is an Oxymoron* (Cambridge, MA: MIT Press, 2013); Orit Halpern, *Beautiful Data: A History of Vision and Reason Since 1945* (Durham, NC: Duke University Press, 2015); Sarah Kember and Joanna Zylinska, *Life After New Media: Mediation as a Vital Process* (Cambridge, MA: MIT Press, 2012); Rob Kitchin and Martin Dodge, *Code/Space: Software and Everyday Life* (Cambridge, MA: MIT Press, 2014); Shannon Mattern, *Code and Clay, Data and Dirt: Five Thousand Years of Urban Media* (Minneapolis: University of Minnesota Press, 2017); Malcolm McCullough, *Ambient Commons: Attention in the Age of Embodied Information* (Cambridge, MA: MIT Press, 2015); Tara McPherson, *Feminist in a Software Lab: Difference + Design* (Cambridge, MA: Harvard University Press, 2018); Scott McQuire, *Geomedia: Networked Cities and the Future of Public Space* (Cambridge, MA: Polity, 2016); Zizi Papacharissi, *Affective Publics: Sentiment, Technology, and Politics* (New York: Oxford University Press, 2014); Adriana de Souza e Silva and Jordan Frith, *Mobile Interfaces in Public Spaces: Locational Privacy, Control, and Urban Sociability* (New York: Routledge, 2012); Jonathan Sterne, *MP3: The Meaning of a Format* (Durham, NC: Duke University Press, 2012); Tiziana Terranova, *Network Culture: Politics for the Information Age* (Ann Arbor, MI: Pluto, 2004); Pasi Väliaho, *Biopolitical Screens: Image, Power, and the Neoliberal Brain* (Cambridge, MA: MIT Press, 2014).

68. Alan Liu, "The Meaning of the Digital Humanities," *PMLA* 128 (2013): 412.

69. "Research & Pedagogy," *edX*, November 12, 2013, https://www.edx.org/about/research-pedagogy.

70. "What is a DOOC?," femtechnet.org, https://femtechnet.org/docc/.

71. "The Futures Initiative," https://www.gc.cuny.edu/Page-Elements/Academics-Research-Centers-Initiatives/Initiatives-and-Committees/The-Futures-Initiative.

72. "ATEC Mission and Vision—The University of Texas at Dallas," https://www.utdallas.edu/atec/about/.

73. McPherson's co-pis at the Alliance for Networking Visual Culture are Steve Anderson, Craig Dietrich, Phil Ethington, and Erik Loyer, and Phil Ethington. "People," Alliance for Networking Visual Culture, https://scalar.usc.edu/people/ .

74. Matt Drange, "Peter Thiel's War on Gawker: A Timeline," *Forbes*, June 21, 2016, http://www.forbes.com/sites/mattdrange/2016/06/21/peter-thiels-war-on-gawker-a-timeline/; "The Educated Underclass News, Video and Gossip," *Gawker*, http://gawker.com/tag/the-educated-underclass. This link no longer functions: see the Wayback Machine, https://web.archive.org/web/20160627142525/gawker.com/tag/the-educated-underclass.

75. Hamilton Nolan, "'Academic Apartheid' in Higher Education," June 26, 2016, https://web.archive.org/web/20160626052253/http://gawker.com:80/academic-apartheid-in-higher-education-1781357648.

76. Gina Kolata, "So Many Research Scientists, So Few Openings as Professors," *New York Times*, July 14, 2016, https://www.nytimes.com/2016/07/14/upshot/so-many-research-scientists-so-few-openings-as-professors.html. See also Rachel L. Swarns, "Crowded Out of Ivory Tower, Adjuncts See a Life Less Lofty," *New York Times*,

January 19, 2014, https://www.nytimes.com/2014/01/20/nyregion/crowded-out-of-ivory-tower-adjuncts-see-a-life-less-lofty.html.

77. Douglas Belkin, "As Adjunct Professors Unionize, Debate Sharpens Over Cost to Schools," *Wall Street Journal*, March 20, 2016, https://www.wsj.com/articles/as-adjunct-professors-unionize-debate-sharpens-over-cost-to-schools-1458466208.

78. Christopher Newfield, *Ivy and Industry: Business and the Making of the American University, 1880–1980* (Durham, NC: Duke University Press, 2003), 88.

79. Richard Hofstadter and W. P. Metzger, *The Development of Academic Freedom in the United States* (New York: Columbia University Press, 1955), 397.

80. "Universities have," Louis Menand writes, "a compact with the rest of society on this matter: society agrees that research which doesn't have to answer to some standard of political correctness, economic utility, or religious orthodoxy is a desirable good, and agrees to allow professors to decide among themselves the work that it is important for them to undertake." Louis Menand, *The Future of Academic Freedom* (Chicago: University of Chicago Press, 1998), 8.

81. The occasion for this observation by Bowen and Tobin was the 2015 move by Governor Scott Walker to undo key features of academic freedom in Wisconsin's higher-education system. William Bowen and Eugene Tobin, "Scott Walker's Test of Academic Freedom," *Chicago Tribune*, June 22, 2015, http://www.chicagotribune.com/news/opinion/commentary/ct-scott-walker-tenure-university-wisconsin-perspec-0623-20150622-story.html.

82. Merle Curti and Vernon Carstensen, *The University of Wisconsin: A History* (Madison: University of Wisconsin Press, 1949), 1:509.

83. Partly their charge involved figuring out what among Ely's various activities while in the university's employ was relevant to the case. They decided that their purview only extended to his teaching. Everything else, "anything that Prof. Ely may have stated in recent lectures before the public here or elsewhere," the committee considered "outside of his school work," although they did leave open the possibility that his books could come into play if they said anything pertinent. Quoted in Curti and Carstensen, *The University of Wisconsin*, 1:515, 521.

84. Quoted in Curti and Carstensen, *The University of Wisconsin*, 1:526.

85. Rebecca M. Blank, "Why State Lawmakers Must Support Tenure at Public Universities," *Chronicle of Higher Education*, June 24, 2015, http://www.chronicle.com/article/Why-State-Lawmakers-Must/231093.

86. Pat Schneider, "UW-Madison Researchers React to Robin Vos' 'Ancient Mating Habits of Whatever' Remark," *Madison.com*, November 4, 2014, http://host.madison.com/news/local/writers/pat_schneider/uw-madison-researchers-react-to-robin-vos-ancient-mating-habits/article_3144b1da-66a7-11e4-93fc-e3c72cb3062d.html.

87. Quoted in Curti and Carstensen, *The University of Wisconsin*, 2:88.

88. AAUP, "Declaration of Principles on Academic Freedom and Academic Tenure," American Association of University Professors, 1915, https://www.aaup.org/NR/rdonlyres/A6520A9D-0A9A-47B3-B550-C006B5B224E7/0/1915Declaration.pdf.

89. In 1966, Justice Brennan declared that "our Nation is deeply committed to safeguarding academic freedom, which is of transcendent value to all of us and not merely to the teachers concerned." "*Keyishian v. Board of Regents* 385 U.S. 589 (1967)," *Justia Law*, https://supreme.justia.com/cases/federal/us/385/589/case.html.

90. Marjorie Heins, "The Keyishian Ruling, 45 Years Later," *Academeblog*, January 23, 2012, https://academeblog.org/2012/01/23/the-keyishian-ruling-45-years -later/. Donna R. Euben, "Academic Freedom of Professors and Institutions," May 2002, https://www.aaup.org/issues/academic-freedom/professors-and-insti tutions.

91. Caitlin Rosenthal, "Fundamental Freedom or Fringe Benefit? Rice University and the Administrative History of Tenure 1935–1963," *AAUP Journal of Academic Freedom* 2 (2011): 16.

92. A point made most effectively by Jennifer Ruth, "A University Without Shared Governance Is Not a University," *Remaking the University*, July 16, 2015, https:// utotherescue.blogspot.com/2015/07/a-university-without-shared-governance .html.

93. Menand, *The Future of Academic Freedom*, 10. The canonical account remains Hofstadter and Metzger, *The Development of Academic Freedom in the United States*.

94. For decades, scholars including Michael Bérubé, Cary Nelson, and Marc Bousquet had urged colleagues across the nation to oppose more forcefully the trend to staff instruction with low-wage graduate student and temporary workers, to little effect. See Michael Bérubé and Cary Nelson, *Higher Education Under Fire: Politics, Economics, and the Crisis of the Humanities* (New York: Routledge, 1995). Cary Nelson, ed., *Will Teach for Food: Academic Labor in Crisis* (Minneapolis: University of Minnesota Press, 1997). Marc Bousquet, *How the University Works: Higher Education and the Low-Wage Nation* (New York: New York University Press, 2008).

95. Colleen Flaherty, "Rosemary Feal, Executive Director of the MLA, Announces Her Departure, Effective Summer 2017," *Inside Higher Ed*, February 25, 2016, https: //www.insidehighered.com/news/2016/02/25/rosemary-feal-executive-director -mla-announces-her-departure-effective-summer-2017.

96. Michael Bérubé and Jennifer Ruth, *The Humanities, Higher Education, and Academic Freedom: Three Necessary Arguments* (New York: Palgrave Macmillan, 2015), 20.

97. Michael M. Crow and William B. Dabars, *Designing the New American University* (Baltimore, MD: Johns Hopkins University Press, 2015), 18.

98. Daniel Katz and Robert L. Kahn, *The Social Psychology of Organizations* (New York: Wiley, 1978), 63. P. J. DiMaggio and W. W. Powell, "The Iron Cage Revisited," *American Sociological Review* 48, no. 2 (1983).

99. Crow and Dabars, *Designing the New American University*, 247.

100. Former provost Elizabeth Capaldi described the interaction of administrative staff and faculty at every level of design-build and indicated that "staff" included "administrative help, a business office, and possibly a publications function and/or a personnel office." Elizabeth Capaldi, "Intellectual Transformation and Budgetary Savings Through Academic Reorganization," *Change: The Magazine of Higher Learning* 41, no. 4 (2009): 21–26.

101. This lack of autonomy also differentiated them from the design industries that inspired Crow and Dabars, as Newfield pointed out: design "groups need to be nonhierarchical, a term Tom Kelley used to describe 'hot teams' at his legendary IDEO design lab in Silicon Valley." Christopher Newfield, "What Is New About

the New American University," *Los Angeles Review of Books*, April 5, 2015, https://lareviewofbooks.org/article/new-new-american-university/.

102. John Warner, "ASU Is the 'New American University'—It's Terrifying," *Inside Higher Ed*, January 25, 2015, https://www.insidehighered.com/blogs/just-visiting/asu-new-american-university-its-terrifying.

103. Christopher Newfield, "What Is New About the New American University?" *Los Angeles Review of Books*, April 5, 2015, https://lareviewofbooks.org/review/new-new-american-university/.

104. Crow and Dabars, *Designing the New American University*, 37.

105. Christopher Newfield, "Time for a New Strategy," *Inside Higher Ed*, July 20, 2015, https://www.insidehighered.com/views/2015/07/20/essay-calls-new-strategy-protect-faculty-rights.

106. Newfield, "Time for a New Strategy."

107. Mark Cooper and John Marx, "From Academic Freedom to Organizational Democracy," *Humanities After Hollywood*, July 31, 2015, http://humanitiesafterhollywood.org/2015/07/31/academic-freedom/.

108. Sarah Larimer, "American University Is Dealing with a Racist Incident on Its Campus. It Is Not Alone," *Washington Post*, May 6, 2017, https://www.washingtonpost.com/local/education/american-is-dealing-with-a-racist-incident-on-its-campus-it-is-not-alone/2017/05/06/b748bd72-3192-11e7-8674-437ddb6e813e_story.html. Stephanie Saul, "The Conservative Force Behind Speeches Roiling College Campuses," *New York Times*, May 20, 2017, https://www.nytimes.com/2017/05/20/us/college-conservative-speeches.html.

109. Stanley Kurtz et al., "Campus Free Speech: A Legislative Proposal," Phoenix: Goldwater Institute, 2017, http://goldwaterinstitute.org/en/work/topics/constitutional-rights/free-speech/campus-free-speech-a-legislative-proposal/.

110. Beth McMurtrie, "U. of Chicago's Free-Expression Letter Exposes Fault Lines on Campus," *Chronicle of Higher Education*, September 2, 2016, http://www.chronicle.com/article/U-of-Chicago-s/237672.

111. "Chancellor Christ: Free Speech Is Who We Are," *Berkeley News*, August 23, 2017, http://news.berkeley.edu/2017/08/23/chancellor-christ-free-speech-is-who-we-are/. On the rise of a statelike campus and its mix of educational and policing functions, see Roderick A. Ferguson, *We Demand: The University and Student Protests* (Oakland: University of California Press, 2017).

112. "Right-wing student groups invite bigoted trolls to invade campus under guise of free speech," *Daily Californian*, September 27, 2017, http://www.dailycal.org/2017/09/22/right-wing-student-groups-invite-bigoted-trolls-invade-campus-guise-free-speech/.

113. Tom Dart, "Cocks Not Glocks: Texas Students Carry Dildos on Campus to Protest Gun Law," *Guardian*, August 25, 2016, https://www.theguardian.com/us-news/2016/aug/25/cocks-not-glocks-texas-campus-carry-gun-law-protest.

114. The stunt did have precedents, however: http://www.couriermail.com.au/news/world/evolve-video-playthings-with-dildo-sex-toy-puts-gun-control-at-new-level/news-story/09b7166ca2231938f2fb9318b0189763.

115. Mark Joseph Stern, "It Looks Like Pat McCrory, North Carolina's Anti-LGBTQ Republican Governor, Is Out of a Job," *Slate*, November 9, 2016, http://www.slate

.com/blogs/outward/2016/11/09/north_carolina_gov_pat_mccrory_lost_thanks_to_hb2.html. There is a backstory here, too. See Kevin Drum, "A Very Brief Timeline of the Bathroom Wars," *Mother Jones*, May 14, 2016, http://www.motherjones.com/kevin-drum/2016/05/timeline-bathroom-wars.

116. "Dear Colleague Letter on Transgender Students," US Department of Justice, May 13, 2016, http://www2.ed.gov/about/offices/list/ocr/letters/colleague-201605-title-ix-transgender.pdf. This letter was subsequently rescinded and has been removed from the federal website.

117. For a summary of these activities, see Zack Ford, "UNC President's Compliance with Anti-LGBT Law Enrages Students Across North Carolina," *ThinkProgress*, April 8, 2016, http://thinkprogress.org/lgbt/2016/04/08/3767923/unc-hb2-protests/.

118. Danielle Chemtob and Grant Masini, "Protesters Disrupt Board of Governors, Demand Action on HB2," *Daily Tar Heel*, April 15, 2016, http://www.dailytarheel.com/article/2016/04/protesters-disrupt-board-of-governors-demand-action-on-hb2.

119. Jeremy W. Peters, Jo Becker, and Julie Hirschfeld Davis, "Trump Rescinds Rules on Bathrooms for Transgender Students," *New York Times*, February 22, 2017, https://www.nytimes.com/2017/02/22/us/politics/devos-sessions-transgender-students-rights.html.

120. Heather Mac Donald, "From 1970s-Era Academic 'High Theory' to Transgender Bathrooms on Campus," *National Review*, May 16, 2016, http://www.nationalreview.com/article/435419/transgender-bathrooms-college-campuses-fall-prey-academic-high-theory.

121. LBC, "We Are No Longer Taking It. It's Time to Fight. #ConcernedStudent1950 #MizzouHungerStrikepic.twitter.com/mnPZBviqJF," Microblog, *@MizzouLBC*, November 8, 2015, https://twitter.com/MizzouLBC/status/663177684428566532?ref_src=twsrc%5Etfw.

122. Editors, "The Power of a Football Strike," *Chicago Tribune*, November 9, 2015, http://www.chicagotribune.com/news/opinion/editorials/ct-missouri-football-tim-wolfe-racism-edit-20151109-story.html. Sean Gregory, "Missouri President Toppled by the Power of the Student Athlete," *Time*, November 9, 2015, http://time.com/4104973/university-of-missouri-timothy-wolfe-athlete/. Belen Michelis, "Second Annual Sports Humanitarian of the Year Awards Presented by ESPN to Take Place July 12," *ESPN MediaZone*, June 16, 2016, http://espnmediazone.com/us/press-releases/2016/06/second-annual-sports-humanitarian-year-awards-presented-espn-take-place-july-12/.

123. Coach Gary Pinkel Verified Account, "The Mizzou Family Stands as One. We Are United. We Are behind Our Players. #ConcernedStudent1950 GPpic.twitter.com/fMHbPPTTKl," Microblog, *@GaryPinkel*, November 8, 2015, https://twitter.com/GaryPinkel/status/663410502370856960.

124. Bill Pollock, "Concerned Student 1950 Re-Issues Demands to the University of Missouri," *Missourinet*, February 24, 2016, http://www.missourinet.com/2016/02/24/concerned-student-1950-re-issues-demands-to-the-university-of-missouri/.

125. "Studies Examine Twitter's Growing Importance in Crisis Communications," *Holmes Report*, August 1, 2017, https://www.holmesreport.com/research/article/studies-examine-twitter's-growing-importance-in-crisis-communications.

126. David Brooks, "Inside Student Radicalism," *New York Times*, May 27, 2016, http://www.nytimes.com/2016/05/27/opinion/inside-student-radicalism.html.

127. Nathan Heller, "The Big Uneasy: The New Activism of Campus Life," *New Yorker*, May 30, 2016, http://www.newyorker.com/magazine/2016/05/30/the-new-activism-of-liberal-arts-colleges.

128. Rod Dreher, "Oberlin Is an Insane Asylum," *American Conservative*, May 25, 2016, http://www.theamericanconservative.com/dreher/oberlin-is-an-insane-asylum/.

129. Anonymous Petition Authors, "Oberlin College," petition, Oberlin College, December 2015, http://new.oberlin.edu/petition-jan2016.pdf.

130. Anonymous Petition, 10.

131. Anonymous Petition, 9.

132. The Oberlin students were not alone in refusing to keep their managerial critiques to themselves. In September 2016, the editorial board of the *Harvard Crimson* felt empowered to weigh in on a question that might certainly appear above their pay grade, namely, the care and feeding of the university's endowment, which had posted a $2 billion loss for the recently concluded fiscal year. Crimson Editorial Board, "The Urgency of the Present," *Harvard Crimson*, September 28, 2016, http://www.thecrimson.com/article/2016/9/28/endowment-loss-2016/.

133. Precisely because they worked within the branding they tested, these students and their protests could be, and were, misconstrued as business as usual, "Oberlin being Oberlin." John Warner, "What's the Matter with Oberlin?" *Inside Higher Ed*, May 31, 2016, https://www.insidehighered.com/blogs/just-visiting/whats-matter-oberlin.

134. Marvin Krislov, "Response to Student Demands," *The Source* (Oberlin College), January 20, 2016, https://oncampus.oberlin.edu/source/articles/2016/01/20/response-student-demands.

135. Marvin Krislov, "Student Radicalism and Identity Politics on Campus," *New York Times*, June 3, 2016, http://www.nytimes.com/2016/06/04/opinion/student-radicalism-and-identity-politics-on-campus.html.

136. Sarah Brown, "How 3 College Presidents Are Trying to Move Their Campuses Past Racial Tensions," *Chronicle of Higher Education*, August 17, 2016, http://www.chronicle.com/article/How-3-College-Presidents-Are/237479.

137. Melissa Harris, "Students, CDS Workers Protest *Bon Appétit*," *Oberlin Review*, May 5, 2017, http://oberlinreview.org/13742/news/students-cds-workers-protest-bon-appetit/.

138. Arthur G. Jago, "How Three Bad Decisions Signaled Doom at Mizzou," *Chronicle of Higher Education*, November 19, 2015, http://www.chronicle.com/article/How-Three-Bad-Decisions/234278.

139. "A student protest about racism isn't a pesky union grievance that can be managed behind closed doors or an inappropriate email that is outsourced to the Human Resources department." Laura McKenna, "Why Are College Presidents Going Corporate?" *Atlantic*, December 3, 2015, https://www.theatlantic.com/education/archive/2015/12/college-president-mizzou-tim-wolfe/418599/.

140. Vauhini Vara, "Do Businesspeople Make Good University Presidents?" *New Yorker*, September 10, 2015, http://www.newyorker.com/business/currency/do-businesspeople-make-good-university-presidents. The spectacular 2016 failure of private equity bigwig–turned–Mount Saint Mary's University president Simon

Newman fueled this argument. See Rebecca Schisler and Ryan Golden, "Mount President's Attempt to Improve Retention Rate Included Seeking Dismissal of 20–25 First-Year Students," *Mountain Echo*, January 19, 2016, http://msmecho.com/2016 /01/19/mount-presidents-attempt-to-improve-retention-rate-included-seeking -dismissal-of-20-25-first-year-students/. See also the *Chronicle of Higher Education*'s summary of the "showdown" over leadership at the University of Virginia in 2012: Sara Hebel, Jack Stripling, and Robin Wilson, "U. of Virginia Board Votes to Reinstate Sullivan," *Chronicle of Higher Education*, June 26, 2012, http://www .chronicle.com/article/U-of-Virginia-Board-Votes-to/132603.

141. Although there were indications that the demands of Concerned Student 1950 influenced the administration's agenda. "One year after protest rocked Missouri, the effects on the football team and university remain tangible," *Sports Illustrated*, November 8, 2016, https://www.si.com/college-football/2016/11/08/how-missouri -football-has-changed-1-year-after-boycott#.

EPILOGUE

1. Steve Fuller, "Science Studies Through the Looking Glass: An Intellectual History," in *Beyond the Science Wars: The Missing Discourse About Science and Society*, ed. Ullica Segerstrale (Albany: State University of New York Press, 2003), 209. We discuss Fuller in chapter 9.
2. Michael M. Crow and William B. Dabars, *Designing the New American University* (Baltimore, MD: Johns Hopkins University Press, 2015), preface.
3. Karl Marx, *The German Ideology* (1845), Marxists Internet Archive, https://www .marxists.org/archive/marx/works/1845/german-ideology/ch01a.htm.

INDEX